The Truth About the Music Business

A Grassroots Business and Legal Guide

The Truth About the Music Business

A Grassroots Business and Legal Guide

By Steve Moore, B.A., J.D.

Foreword by Mike Lawson

THOMSON
™
COURSE TECHNOLOGY
Professional ■ Trade ■ Reference

The Truth About the Music Business: A Grassroots Business and Legal Guide

SVP, Thomson Course Technology PTR: Andy Shafran
Publisher: Stacy L. Hiquet
Executive Editor: Mike Lawson
Senior Marketing Manager: Sarah O'Donnell
Marketing Manager: Heather Hurley
Manager of Editorial Services: Heather Talbot
Senior Editor: Mark Garvey
Associate Marketing Manager: Kristin Eisenzopf
Marketing Coordinator: Jordan Casey
Project Editor: Dan Foster, Scribe Tribe
PTR Editorial Services Coordinator: Elizabeth Furbish
Copy Editor: Sean Medlock
Cover Designer & Interior Layout Tech: Stephen Ramirez
Indexer: Katherine Stimson
Proofreader: Andy Saff

ISBN: 1-59200-763-5
Library of Congress Catalog Card Number: 2005921043

Printed in the United States of America
05 06 07 08 09 BH 10 9 8 7 6 5 4 3 2 1

Thomson Course Technology PTR, a division of Thomson Course Technology
25 Thomson Place
Boston, MA 02210
http://www.courseptr.com

Dedicated to the memory of:

Col. Jake & Maj. Billy
The two best friends anyone could have ever had!

Foreword

"The music business is a cruel and shallow money trench, a long plastic hallway where thieves and pimps run free, and good men die like dogs. There's also a negative side."

The above quote, often misattributed to *gonzo journalist* Hunter S. Thompson, sets the stage for the world that soon awaits the often naïve yet fiercely dedicated musicians seeking to navigate their journey through the minefield of the music industry. The quote points out the perils of working in this industry, holding them up as perhaps the best most can hope for, while warning that things can also be worse. In a humorous way, this quote, sometimes used with the words "music business" replaced by any number of entertainment-related professions, illustrates that these travelers will be accompanied by shady characters, and the good-intentioned spirits will often find their muse crushed along the way.

For most musicians, this journey begins with a love of music as a child, with the inspiration to perform brought on by another musician or group popular during their childhood or youth, and inevitably at some point the ability to seek riches, fame, and the adoration of fans (often of the opposite sex). It also seems to many a suitable replacement for the daily doldrums of a "real job" with the perceived leisurely lifestyle of a musician.

"That ain't workin'. That's the way you do it. You play the guitar on the MTV. No that ain't workin'. That's the way you do it. Get your money for nothing and your chicks for free."—Dire Straits

Unfortunately, the music business is work. While the guy installing microwave ovens, refrigerators, and custom kitchens might not understand that it really is work, he also is not likely to make the sub-par hourly rate most musicians end up making when wages are all broken down at the end of the gig. Making the way from playing in a five-piece band earning $250 a night at a bar using the band members' expensive equipment (usually including investment in a PA system), the business-side return on investment of this career path often is a fast way to make a slow buck. (With setup, sound check, four 1-hour set performances, and breaking down time, a band like this would earn about $8 an hour before taxes, with no benefits.) Those who choose this life full-time while seeking the larger stardom their music deserves face the life of an independent contractor with no benefits, no 401k plan, no company-provided insurance, or anything else found in the corporate world.

Making the leap from this beginning level to the big-time usually involves talent, luck, and intensive business planning. Unfortunately, while excelling in their performance abilities, many musicians never progress in their business savvy, and those are the musicians most vulnerable to exploitation, financial ruin, and downward-spiraling career choices that lead to either a change in profession or a future playing hotel lounges and the free stage at the local area casino.

One embarks on a career in the music business for different reasons than one might become a plumber, a landscaper, a sales clerk, and so on, and the underlying artistic motivation tends to passionately overrule one's intelligence at times when dealing with business, financial, and legal issues. The child-like innocence of an artist first stepping out on this journey is quickly eroded when faced with the real-world experiences of dealing with their art and craft as a functional legal entity—that is, a *business*. This intimidating new revelation finds an artist suddenly dealing with issues of law, taxation, intellectual property, partnerships, entity structures, capital requirements, hiring of management for personal, business, and financial issues, and the hiring of lawyers for a multitude of tasks from the most basic formation of a corporate structure to negotiation of contracts that affect the life and livelihood of their art—all of which allows the artist to come full circle and finally enjoy the riches, fame, and adoration he sought in his youth.

Beyond understanding the basic legal and business issues surrounding the life of a working musician who makes a living solely from performing, the much more involved knowledge required to create an intellectual-property-based revenue stream from songwriting, recording, and other professional areas of a music career requires a great deal of study. This career requires much more than the ability to count double-four time, how to augment a seventh-chord, or sing high-harmony without doubling the lead vocal line.

Clearly, having a destination and a road map are the best ways to set about on any journey. Knowing where one can re-fuel, eat, rest, and get services on a trip typically results in making the journey end successfully with the destination reached and the least amount of expected and unexpected challenges met along the way.

Foreword

These analogous references to travel are appropriate to the career of a musician, as a large proportion of one's time in that career is spent traveling on the road. The typical career path travels to roadside bars to nightclubs, college fraternities to theaters, concert halls to stadiums, and, unfortunately for many musicians, the frequent full-circle right back to roadside bars and nightclubs. Having a plan for the business and legal needs and fully understanding who the players are in those areas, what the objectives are, and how best to protect your art along the way serves only to shorten the time between playing at roadside bars to reaching the concert halls and stadiums, while also hopefully increasing the time between those larger venues and the full-circle back to where you started.

This book will help you plan your journey. You'll understand where to stop along the way, where you can re-fuel, eat, and rest, and how far you will need to go to reach your final destination. Having followed this path myself from childhood to roadside bars, to frat houses, and on to concert halls, record releases, publishing contracts, songwriting partnerships, producer relationships, and all the rest, having this book in my hands early on would have certainly made things easier. While there is a lot to take in given the scope of the author's work in providing this atlas, it is a long road to travel. Have a nice trip!

Mike Lawson

Special thanks to:
Dr. Ben Fisher
Mike Lawson
Clay Barnes
Ralph Murphy
W. G. (Pan) Doss
Stephen E. McCord
Keith & Jerene Sykes
My Family and Friends

About the Author

Steve Moore launched his music career in 1977 when he began playing music professionally. Later, he embarked on a solo career as a singer/songwriter in addition to fronting several of his own bands. He has worked in live sound and lighting production, as a studio owner, recording engineer, record producer, publisher, and as independent label head for New South Records. For over ten years, he worked as an entertainment attorney in Nashville, TN, where he represented a number of music clients including national and international acts. Moore has been a contributing writer to national magazines and has lectured on the music industry throughout the Southeast United States. In 2002, he formed High Cotton Records, signing independent alt country and rock artists from the Southeast. He is also the founder of Music Square One, a new venture that focuses on new marketing and delivery systems for unreleased music. He is currently still writing music, making records, and taking time out when he can for his first love—playing live.

Contents

Introduction

If you want to be in the music business, or you are already, and you would like more information about how to protect yourself in your professional life and business ventures, this is the book for you. You may or may not have already decided on a particular area of the music business. However, whether you are an artist or writer, sideman or front man, engineer or producer (live or recorded), booking agent or promoter, studio manager or owner of your own independent studio, major label executive or independent record label, etc., learning more about the business and legal end of what you are trying to pursue will be extremely useful on your path to success.

To that end, if you're really serious about the music business, you'd better arm yourself with some knowledge that will protect you! Didn't Warren Zevon say, "If I had it to do all over again, I'd arm myself with a law degree and submachine gun"? Well, this book is designed to arm you with the basic concepts of law and business that may affect you. It will also lay a foundation so that you will know when you need to hire a good lawyer and forego the machine gun.

You may find that a good deal of information in this book is plain old common sense, and for the most part it is. Still, there is a lot of stuff that I have had to deal with through the years, either personally or for my entertainment clients, and when you've seen what I've seen, you tend to learn from it. This book is intended to answer some simple questions and to shed some light on some basic issues so that you'll get a general idea as to what you can do to further your music career and avoid some costly mistakes. Regardless, my sincere hope is that you will be able to find some valuable information that may help you at some point in your career.

So now it's time to start collecting all those big checks, riding in limousines, and dating supermodels, right? Better guess again. Don't forget about the *business* part of the music business. There are many pitfalls along the way, and the road is long and extremely rocky. Get ready to start treading water while the sharks are circling; the water is wide and extremely deep, and the current is strong.

Stop to consider how you plan to handle your business affairs before you set out on your road to success. Have you thought about a business plan, a business structure, business licenses and tax considerations, the costs of doing business, getting all of your contracts in order so that you won't get burned, and making sure that you always get paid? Mistakes can be costly, so you should do everything you can to "Get it right… the first time!"

You will learn about entertainment lawyers, what they can do for you, how much they charge and how they charge, and a lot of other useful information about attorneys. You will learn how to cover yourself without hiring a lawyer as well as when you have to hire one!

This book provides detailed information about selecting a business structure, and some simple ideas about setting goals and incorporating them into a simple business plan. It will also cover some basic information on how to promote and market your business, as well as some very useful tips to help you or your business to be more memorable and therefore more successful.

Since copyrights and related intellectual property are the cornerstone of the music industry, I will cover the basics of intellectual property, such as copyright to protect your work and trademark to protect your name, so that choosing a name will not come back to bite you. I will also talk about other areas of intellectual property, such as patents, trade secrets, publicity, and privacy rights.

I'll cover the basics of music publishing and digital music rights, and how important digital rights are to the future of the music business. I will discuss the differences between demos and master recordings, as well as what to expect when you go into the studio. I will discuss the basic elements of a record deal, and whether you should sign with a major label or try to do it yourself by taking a proactive approach to your career.

This book will also cover all of the people who you may need to hire throughout your career, such as business managers, personal managers, road managers, booking agents, publishers, accountants, attorneys, personal assistants, public relations people, and other ancillary services that you may need. It will give you an idea of when you may need these people, as well as a breakdown of how much of your money will be going out the door when you hire them.

This book will also briefly discuss the general principles of contracts so that you can at least familiarize yourself with them. I will discuss what makes up a contract and whether or not a contract has to be in writing. Does a contract need a bunch of terms such as "whereas" and "heretofore," or can it be in plain old English so that anyone can understand it? I will also discuss the basics of negotiating and how you can try to stay on top of your business dealings.

I'll describe some of the questionable practices that you may encounter from some rather unsavory characters in the music industry. Of course, there is also a chapter on collecting your money, which will discuss how you can make sure that you are collecting all of your royalties from publishing or music deals.

I will discuss what you can do if you need to sue someone to protect your rights, or what could happen if you were to get sued. The more you know about a lawsuit, the more likely you will want to avoid one; however, if you have no choice but to sue, you will know the anatomy of a lawsuit: best evidence rules, hearsay, witnesses, etc. This book includes many tips about what you can expect, what you should file, where to file, what to say, and so on.

For reference, I've included a chapter on organizations that you may consider joining to further your goals and increase your networking prospects. There is also a chapter on music conferences, festivals, seminars, and the like, explaining what you will need to do to prepare for these events and make the most out of the time and money you spend there.

Since insurance is such a big part of your business and personal life, there is a chapter on what type of insurance you may need, how to find the right agent, what to do if you need to file a claim, how to deal with adjusters, and what rights you have if you feel that you are not getting what you paid for when you bought your insurance.

Finally, in the last chapter I discuss wills and estates. No matter what happens, nobody gets out of here alive. Therefore, we will discuss making plans for what will happen to you and your property, such as your copyrights and the rest of your personal property, once you have shuffled off this mortal coil.

You may find a good deal of information that you already know, or you may wonder why certain topics were included in the first place. This book is not intended to be condescending in any way. Rather, it's designed to be a primer of sorts, covering the basic concepts that you could face in the music business so that you can be prepared for just about any situation.

Caveat: This book contains *no legal advice* and is not intended to be a replacement for a qualified attorney!

CHAPTER 1

Entertainment Attorneys

"Life is a board game…and the lawyers have read the rules on the top of the box.…" —*Durphey Doucette*

The Pocket Guide to Entertainment Lawyers

We've all heard our share of lawyer jokes, and some are actually warranted. Perhaps you've heard what some say is the first lawyer joke:

"The first thing we do, let's kill all the lawyers." —*King Henry VI, Part II*

Even though this line by William Shakespeare may sound funny, it is actually quite serious. Although we can't possibly know what Mr. Shakespeare meant by this statement without asking him, many argue that he was not saying that we should *actually* kill all the lawyers. Rather, he meant that if there were no lawyers, there would be nobody to be the advocate for the common man.

1

In our society, with all its rules and regulations, lawyers are a necessity whether you like it or not. Unless you want to read all the rules and learn all the laws that govern our everyday lives, you are better off having a lawyer to protect your rights than trying to do it yourself. So, for those of us in the entertainment industry, this brings us to our first question.

What Is an Entertainment Lawyer?

The term "entertainment lawyer" covers a wide spectrum of legal practitioners. I have often heard that an entertainment lawyer is usually a general practitioner who happens to do entertainment law, or who just represents people or companies in the entertainment industry.

Although that generalization applies to many entertainment lawyers, they come in all shapes, sizes, and areas of expertise. Some may be strictly negotiators and never set foot in a courtroom. Others may be strictly litigation attorneys who focus on entertainment-related issues, or only represent music companies for their litigation needs. (This type of lawyer does not negotiate contracts, but only defends or prosecutes cases on behalf of the labels. In-house counsel negotiates contracts.) Some entertainment attorneys work for big companies as in-house counsel and never represent individuals and never go to court on behalf of the record label.

More often that not, an entertainment lawyer has a combination of different types of legal knowledge and can handle a wide spectrum of issues in the music industry. Some entertainment lawyers are even musicians, songwriters, or artists, or used to be. However, the law is a jealous mistress, and to master the ins and outs of entertainment law requires a great deal of time and effort. That doesn't leave much time for creative pursuits on much more than a part-time basis, if at all.

What Does an Entertainment Lawyer Do?

Your entertainment lawyer can offer a number of different services, and can be there (and most times *should* be there) to help you negotiate the maze of contracts that you will encounter during your entertainment career. But in some cases, an entertainment lawyer may be required to handle certain personal matters for his entertainment clients, such as divorce(s), wills, trusts, and even criminal matters. Many of these matters may have certain types of entertainment-related issues.

For instance, a divorce in which one or (not always both) both parties are artists or songwriters will have any number of different entertainment-related issues, such as the evaluation of a song catalogue, artist royalties, assignment of copyright(s), etc. Of course, if you are going through a nasty divorce, you may want to hire a divorce specialist, but he probably won't be very well versed in entertainment issues. Thus, he will have to consult with an entertainment attorney to make sure that he has covered these important issues completely.

Wills and trusts may have the same types of entertainment-related issues. Copyright laws protect the creator of a copyright for his entire life plus 70 years, so the client must have the foresight to protect his intellectual property rights long after he is gone. Also, copyright infringement can be a criminal matter because the copyright code specifies penalties .

Finally, a client may run afoul of the law by shooting off a gun from his tour bus, or getting a traffic ticket or a drunk driving charge. He may be arrested for playing a gig under what the venue or promoter deems to be a trademark infringement, which also carries criminal penalties. Or it could be any number of criminal matters that can arise during the course of an entertainer's life. (All of these are actual cases that were handled either by myself, my firm, or another attorney I know.) When an entertainment client finds a lawyer that he trusts, he likes to deal with that lawyer, even when he has to hire another lawyer.

Your attorney may also be able to handle a number of different business issues, such as setting up your business or helping out with tax issues, or he may work closely with your accountant in regard to business or tax issues. Regardless, it's most important that your entertainment lawyer have an extremely good understanding of contract law and be well versed in all types of entertainment contracts. He must also be completely familiar with intellectual property rights, which are the cornerstone of the music industry: copyright, trademarks, trade secrets, and sometimes patents. However, we will save the in-depth discussion of contracts and intellectual property rights for later in this book. These issues are critical to anyone's future in the entertainment industry and are worthy of a much more detailed discussion.

Sometimes lawyers who purely negotiate are called *solicitors*, while those who go to court are called *barristers*. This is especially true in Canada and the United

Kingdom, and in legal systems that model themselves after those countries. However, that distinction is not normally used in the United States. Whatever your legal representative may be called—attorney, lawyer, barrister, solicitor, counselor, or any number of other colorful names—he can play an invaluable role in your affairs. When you need the help, all of the lawyer jokes you've heard will seem a lot less funny.

A good entertainment lawyer can make a huge difference in your career. He can steer you away from trouble, if you have the good sense to see him before trouble happens. Or he can get you out of trouble once you're in it, which can, unfortunately, happen in the blink of an eye. Unless you are extremely lucky, at some time or another you will encounter problems where you will be glad to have a good attorney on your side.

Unfortunately, more often than not, people either can't afford to see an entertainment lawyer for every issue that comes up, or they just don't think they'll need one until it's too late. It's very much like going to a car mechanic. If you see your mechanic regularly and keep your car in good shape, you are less likely to have major problems. But bad things happen and cars break down, and eventually you'll end up paying for major repairs. In the same way, if you retain an experienced lawyer to assist you along the path of your career, you are much less likely to have to pay him to fix major problems later.

We all go into our business ventures with the anticipation that we're going to be successful and that things are going to work out for the best. And why shouldn't we? Nobody would go into any business venture without some degree of optimism. Often, however, the people that you do business with don't live up to their promises, or some other unanticipated situation arises, and you wish that you had sought the advice of competent legal counsel. This is especially true when you sign an agreement that comes back to bite you or enter into a businesses deal that may go awry at some point in the future, or some unanticipated event arises that exposes you to some legal liability. I can't tell you how many of my clients completely trusted the people they were working with, only to find out later that they were being taken advantage of, in more ways than one.

Unfortunately, I've seen a good deal of this type of trust with creative or artistic types. They're just glad to be offered any type of deal, and they prefer to live their day-to-day lives without having to deal with the pressures of business issues. In the case of songwriters, they've got enough to deal with just trying to write hit songs and constantly crank out good material, day after day and year after year. In the case of recording artists, they have enough to do: touring, making appearances, recording in the studio, and trying to keep from getting dropped from their label and fading into obscurity. This is why many songwriters sign publishing deals so that their publisher will handle their copyrights, and why they hire business managers to handle their money so all they have to focus on is writing songs. This is also why most artists hire personal managers and/or business managers, and sign record deals where all they are expected to do is be an artist.

But whether you're a songwriter, artist, musician, or anything else, if you don't know what is going on with your business matters and how to "mind the store," you could be setting yourself up for a hard fall, or at least an eye-opening wake-up call. Experience can cost money, and you don't want to have to buy more than you can afford.

Again, many artists, songwriters, musicians, and entertainers get themselves into some type of non-advantageous business deal because they're just starting out. They're not very well established in the entertainment industry and don't have a very strong negotiating position. If you are about to sign some type of major deal and you have been discussing it with your publisher, label, manager, or whomever, don't think for one second that everything is what it appears to be. You should not try to handle matters on your own unless you know exactly what you are doing and exactly what your contract says.

I can't tell you how many times I've had clients who were told that a deal said one thing, only to find out that the written contracts actually were very different from what was promised verbally. A good entertainment attorney will be able to negotiate many points or issues on your behalf, explain exactly what a deal entails, and advise and guide you through the maze of problems that may occur during the term of your contract, or even in the event of its termination.

What Can an Entertainment Lawyer Do for You?

Consulting an attorney and keeping him on retainer can be a good way to make sure that someone is always in your corner to represent your concerns. If you pay your lawyer today, you'll probably save money, headaches, and a whole host of other problems tomorrow. It's amazing how just a letter from a lawyer can make people own up and do what they are supposed to be doing. Even though lawyers get a bad rap in our society today, you will be pretty darned glad that you have one on your side when the proverbial stuff hits the fan.

A really good entertainment lawyer will also be beneficial in furthering your career. He will have many connections in the music industry and can shop a deal for you, get you in to meet the right people, or assist your career in any number of other ways.

If you submit your material to a major publisher or record label without them requesting you to do so, you'll probably receive your material back with a huge stamp on it that says "RETURN UNSOLICITED." The reasons for these companies not accepting material from unknown outside sources are many. I will discuss three of the main ones here.

First, these companies are already bombarded with material from legitimate and trusted sources. If they accepted material from just anyone who walked in off the street or sent it through the mail, they would never be able to get through it all. There are thousands and thousands of people out there trying to get a deal of any kind, and these companies just don't have the manpower to handle all the material they receive. By having enter-tainment lawyers act as gateways and cull through the crop, these companies are much more likely to receive viable or commercially exploitable material. No enter-tainment lawyer that is worth his salt will want to put his name behind something that could jeopardize his hard-earned reputation among his contacts at successful entertainment companies.

Second, if these companies opened your letters with your songs or recordings enclosed, they could be proven to have had "access" to your material for the purposes of a copyright infringement suit. There are thousands of people out there writing songs every day, and chances are fairly good that some of those songs are similar to each other. Every song has a title, a story line, and a melody. The chances are extremely good that the title of one song is exactly the same as another, but song titles are *not* copyrightable. There's less of a chance that the lyrics are very similar, but they could be. (The lyrics often follow the title.) Finally, most popular songs are based on simple hooks or melodies. Even though there are millions of combinations of chords and melody lines, most songs usually follow some type of formula that makes them pleasing to the ear and fit in with the sound of the times. It's an extremely long shot that two songs written by two different parties, at two different times and at two different places, will be exactly alike, but it can happen. That's a chance that these companies can't afford to take. They don't want to have to defend themselves from less than appropriate or even legitimate claims.

To prove infringement, you must be able to prove substantial similarity and access. If these companies accepted unsolicited material, half the proof for an infringement action would be there. The only thing left to prove would be substantial similarity. Even though that is a tough burden of proof, these companies could end up spending a good deal of money defending numerous copyright infringement suits, whether they were warranted or not. Since they have a policy of not accepting unsolicited material, they have a pretty solid defense in regards to "access" and are much less likely to lose any infringement suits in this regard.

Over the years, I've had lots of people call my office wanting to file a copyright infringement action because a song on the radio is very similar to a song they have written. In some cases the songs were very similar, and I have even seen a song or two that was almost identical, but there was no way to prove that the writer or company that published the song, or the company that released the song, had "access" to the "similar" song that was allegedly infringed upon. Therefore, there was really no way to bring the lawsuit.

So, if you have an "established" entertainment lawyer submit your material, the company you're submitting to won't worry that it will be involved in some type of frivolous suit if it accepts that material.

Third, if you have a reputable manager or entertainment lawyer who is well connected, you are much more likely to get through the door. These companies know that your manager or attorney isn't working for free, and this serves as a natural weeding-out process. Furthermore, they know that your manager or attorney isn't going to waste time pitching a client that he doesn't believe in. In fact, you probably won't have a reputable manager unless you have some degree of commercial viability, nor will you be able to get an entertainment lawyer to pitch your material unless he believes that you have a very good chance of making it. If a manager or lawyer brings one of his contacts a fairly marginal act, or an act that really doesn't stand a chance of getting a deal, he won't be taken seriously the next time he comes knocking on that company's door. So, lawyers and managers are very, very careful about who they pitch to their contacts at major labels, publishers, and other companies.

Another thing to remember is that your lawyer or prospective manager has an opinion too, and it might not be what you want to hear. It might not even be correct. There is no accounting for taste, and your career isn't over just because one person doesn't care for your music. I have been in the business as an artist, a songwriter, and a musician long enough to know that what *I* like isn't necessarily what is going to be right for commercial radio. When trying to decide whether or not to pitch something, I've always used the measure of commercial exploitability. "Is the product of good enough quality that I won't end up being embarrassed if I pitch this to my contacts?" It is a purely subjective call, so don't get discouraged if the first people you meet don't believe in your product enough to work with you.

Keep trying to find a manager or lawyer who truly believes in your ability and your material. After all, your relationship with your attorney may not be on an informal or personal basis, but it should be based on mutual trust, respect, and belief in each other's abilities.

One thing that I *don't* recommend is hiring a local lawyer who says he does entertainment law, unless you live in a major city with many experienced entertainment lawyers to choose from. Anyone can say he is an entertainment lawyer, even if he represents only one or two local artists. Many of these lawyers have absolutely no chance of ever getting you a deal because they just don't have the necessary contacts. So ask any prospective lawyer about his experience in the entertainment field. He may not be able to reveal his client list without his clients' consent, because that is confidential, but you should find out the depth of his experience and how he'll handle whatever you're asking to him to handle.

No matter what your talents may be, one thing is for sure: *Don't expect your lawyer to spend his time on you without some type of compensation.* And lawyers don't come cheap. So, this brings us to the next question.

What Does a Lawyer Charge?

An attorney's time and talent are pretty much all that he has to offer. He has worked very hard and spent a great deal of money to be able to offer you his services. It takes four years of undergraduate school and really good grades to be a candidate for law school. You also have to get a pretty high score on the Law School Aptitude Test (LSAT) just to be considered for acceptance. Once you're accepted to law school, it takes three more years to get a degree, and the graduates with the highest grade point averages get the best jobs. Law school is extremely competitive, so much so that I thought many of my law school peers were blinded by their quest for success. In some schools, the attrition (dropout) rate is so incredibly high that just graduating can be a real accomplishment.

To make matters even more difficult, *then* the lawyer has to pass the bar exam, which is usually a three-day test that is not the easiest in the world to pass. In fact, I'm sure you've heard about people who have taken the bar exam several times before they passed, just so they could begin to work as an attorney.

Finally, once you become an attorney, it's trial by fire every day. Every new answer brings home 10 new questions. The law is incredibly complex, is always changing, and requires a great deal of constant research. A lawyer has to continue to learn every day and put in incredibly long hours. The work is extremely difficult and sometimes overwhelming. So treat your attorney with the respect he deserves. He's earned it.

After becoming licensed, some lawyers set out on their own from the outset, while others go to work for a law firm. Still others work for a firm and *then* set out on their own. Whatever the case may be, there are many expenses they must pay to keep the business afloat. There's rent, phones, advertising, malpractice insurance, Continuing Legal Education (CLE), volumes and volumes of books, updates, legal journals, staff, postage, copiers, computers, office furniture, files, paper (they burn through tons of trees a year), etc. All of these expenses for the cost of doing business, or *overhead*, continually increase the rates that lawyers charge. As in all businesses, eventually this overhead is passed on to the client.

Retainers

In some instances, you may want to consider hiring an attorney to be on call for you when you need him. You can pay your attorney a general *retainer* to be used when that time comes. This way, he should be much more willing to take your calls when you need him, before he takes the calls of those who have not paid him—if and when you need him, that is, but it is more likely than not that you will.

Of course, if you are just starting out, you may not need to retain an attorney in the very near future. But if you are ready to start taking your music to a higher level, you may want to consider it.

If you have a case or other legal matter that requires an attorney, most likely you'll need to pay an up-front retainer before he will begin working for you. This will ensure his services until the retainer is gone. Then, depending on the attorney, he may continue working on your case or legal matter and bill you for his services thereafter. Furthermore, if your legal issue is involved in court proceedings, he cannot withdraw as your legal representative without the court's permission. However, his retainer agreement may specify that if you don't pay him another fee within a certain time, or don't pay your bills on time, he can withdraw from your case and possibly put a lien against any earnings you get from it.

This is very important to note, so I will repeat myself: If you have retained a lawyer to represent you in a court matter, he cannot withdraw unless he has the permission of the court. Also, there may be matters that he must take care of even though your initial retainer has been depleted. If so, you may get a bill for services for which he is required by law or the court to perform. Thus, you'll incur further costs, including drafting, filing, and appearing in court on a motion to withdraw from your case. So, if you don't pay your lawyer, he won't be working for you very long, and you may end up spending more money just so that your attorney can be allowed to withdraw.

Be that as it may, there are several different ways that a lawyer can charge you: hourly rates, flat fees, value added billing, contingency fees, spec deals, double billing, and incidentals.

HOURLY RATES

The most common type of billing is the hourly rate. This can range from $75 an hour for the least experienced or junior associates to over $600 an hour for senior attorneys or partners with vast experience in their field. Most lawyers bill in fractions of an hour. Usually, they mark their time by .1, .2, .25, .3, and so on, which equals tenths of an hour. Most have a minimum of .2 hours, because usually they can't handle any certain task in less than that time.

For example, let's say your attorney is working on a matter other than your case (which is very likely, because most attorneys have many clients who demand their time), and you call him on the phone. The attorney has to drop what he is concentrating on and take your call. He may discuss your matter with you for just a couple of minutes, and yet he still charges for .2 hours. The reason is that after he hangs up the phone with you, he has to give some thought to the ramifications of your call, make note of your phone call for your file, place the note in the filing bin or in your file, give your file a review, mark his billing sheet, and then return to what he was doing before you called.

It may be hard to understand, but these little distractions can be very taxing. Your attorney wants to make absolutely sure that he has not made any mistakes or misquoted the law in some way. *So don't make any unnecessary calls to your attorney.* If he has something important to tell you, he will. If you absolutely have to call, make sure that you are prepared and *you* ask concise questions so you don't waste his valuable time or your valuable money.

Another scenario is having your attorney send out a letter. Many lawyers charge .3 hours for a letter because they don't type. They have to dictate the letter on tape, send the tape for typing, review the typed letter, perhaps send it back for errors or redactions, and then sign it. More often than not, when an attorney has a conversation with a client or an opposing attorney, he will document the conversation in a letter and then send a courtesy copy to the client to keep him informed. Of course, the file may have to be reviewed again, a copy of the letter must be placed in the file, etc. So in order to be thorough, it usually takes about .3 hours.

You should be aware that no lawyer can be expected to know all of the law all of the time. Even if your lawyer is very skilled and keeps up with as many of the changes in the law as he can, he still has to do research to make sure that the law has not changed recently on any particular issue. If he misses a certain change in the law and applies an old law to your case, he may cause you irreparable harm and be subject to a malpractice suit. For these reasons, a lawyer is always as thorough as he can be, and always strives to represent his client to the best of his ability.

So always be mindful that your attorney is ethically bound to do the best work that he can for you, but it's not always easy. There is a lot more going on behind the scenes than you may imagine.

FLAT FEES

Sometimes a lawyer charges a flat fee for a particular service. This is especially true if he knows in advance how long it will take for him to do the work. Some examples are contract drafting, contract negotiation, setting up a corporation, or any other matter that can be done in a specific amount of time.

An attorney will sometimes charge a flat fee for a service with the proviso that if the matter is closed as expected in a certain amount of time, no further charges will be incurred. However, nothing is ever cut and dried. Sometimes things change, negotiations may take longer, etc., and therefore the lawyer may have some contingencies drafted into his flat fee agreement. However, if you pay your attorney to do a certain task just for a flat fee and it takes him longer than he expected, you have a binding contract and the lawyer will have to do the extra work without charging you any extra money.

VALUE ADDED BILLING

Some lawyers may charge a *value added* fee for certain things. You may ask your lawyer to provide a contract that he has already written, or to perform some other task where he just has to push Print on his computer. Since he doesn't really have to do much work, he may bill you a flat rate based upon how much work he did to produce the original document. This fee is usually much less than what it would take for him to redo the work. This is helpful when you have a single-song publishing agreement or simple booking agreement. You don't have to pay full price, and yet you get the benefit of the work he did before, perhaps for another client.

CONTINGENCY FEES

In some cases, a plaintiff's lawyers (litigation attorneys who file suit against other parties as a means of getting their client compensation) may charge *contingency fees*. This means you will not have to pay the attorney unless he collects your money. These fees can range from 20% to even 50%, depending on what your state allows for contingency fees, as well as the amount of work that's required for the successful handling of your case. Furthermore, many of these lawyers will advance the costs of filing suit for you and all litigation expenses, which can be very expensive.

However, these lawyers won't take your case and pay your upfront costs unless your case is an absolute slam-dunk. They have to know that they will win, that the defendant can pay, and that they will make more money from the contingency fee than if they billed their hourly rate. If they think for even a minute that the case could end up costing them more than they could make by billing an hourly rate, they probably won't take it on a percentage basis.

Also, even if you don't win your case and the lawyer doesn't make any money, you will still be responsible for all court costs, costs of service of process, private investigator fees, court reporter fees, costs of transcripts, deposition costs, incidentals, and so on. In many cases, you may be able to get the attorney to advance those costs. This can be a great help, but be advised that the attorney is not in the business of paying for other people's problems. Be prepared to pay these costs, which can be hefty, out of your own pocket. In fact, even if your attorney wins your case, he's going to expect you to pay all of these ancillary costs out of your share of the percentage. In some cases, this could leave you with very little money even after you have gone through all of the headaches, hassles, and time expense of a trial.

So you should be very careful about the contingency fee agreement. Consider the amount of money that you are trying to collect, and balance that against how much the lawsuit will cost. Just keep in mind that a large lawsuit can be very expensive if you have to pay all costs, legal fees, and so on up front. Many people just can't afford that, so they go with a contingency fee.

Also, you may want to change attorneys during a lawsuit. Usually, your first attorney's retainer agreement will allow him to put a lien against any recovery that you get. This is to pay the attorney for the time that he put into the case before you retained another attorney. Also, in some cases, the attorney will expect to be paid his hourly rate for his time on the case before he was relieved. Therefore, you may end up owing that attorney a great deal of money and in some cases more than you recover from your lawsuit.

There are always two sides to every story, and in some cases the best defense is a good offense. The party you're suing may file a countersuit to muddy up the waters. Or they may feel that they can win their countersuit and that your original case has no merit. One thing is for sure: If you are countersued in your original case, your attorney will no longer wish to work on a contingency because he will have to do twice as much work. He'll have to prosecute your case successfully and at the same time successfully defend the countersuit. So he will either have to renegotiate with you or ask to be relieved from representing the countersuit or from representing you altogether. He may still feel that you will be successful and will continue to work on a contingency basis, but most likely he will have to charge you for his time spent defending the countersuit.

If you are a defendant in a case, you will never get an attorney to work on a contingency basis. Don't even ask. It just doesn't work that way. You will have to pay your attorney up front, and perhaps monthly after that, or he will not represent you for very long.

SPEC DEALS

These types of deals are also known as *speculation deals*, and to an experienced attorney, they usually mean "I 'spec' I won't ever get paid." However, there are some attorneys out there who will shop a deal for you for a percentage of the advance, or even a percentage of the entire deal. Since there are only so many record deals and publishing deals handed out by companies that are big enough to actually pay an advance, or that generate enough money to make it worth your attorney's time, you aren't likely to find anyone who will work on spec. After all, if every entertainment lawyer worked on spec for all of his clients, he'd go broke.

However, you may be able to find an attorney who thinks you are the hottest thing since sliced bread. He may be willing to put his time, money, expertise, and hard-earned contacts on the line just to pitch you on spec. If you can find one, go for it! What do you have to lose?

DOUBLE BILLING

This is something that every person in the entertainment field should definitely watch out for. As mentioned earlier, there are some entertainment lawyers who *never* go to court. They are purely transactional or negotiating lawyers with a solid knowledge of entertainment issues. If your attorney is one of these types, he will have to work with another attorney to handle the litigation aspects of your case. Each time these attorneys meet, correspond, or otherwise work on your case, you will have to pay them both their hourly rates (unless you were lucky enough to get them to work on a contingency basis on a plaintiff-type suit). This means that if each of them charges $200 an hour, you'll be paying $400 an hour when they are working together.

Furthermore, the litigation attorney may not be well versed in intellectual property issues or entertainment contract issues, and the entertainment lawyer will not have much litigation experience. Therefore, the litigation attorney *and* the entertainment lawyer will have to spend extra time getting up to snuff with the issues of your case, which costs you more time and money.

Another scenario where you can be charged almost double is when you hire a big firm and more than one attorney works on your case at one time. (This is not usually the case, but it's worth mentioning.) Sometimes a junior associate will do most of the work, and when a deposition comes up or there's some other matter that the junior associate can't handle, a senior associate or partner comes in to make sure everything is handled correctly. The junior associate is still present and working on your case too. So make sure you ask about this scenario, and try not to get billed for the senior partner's time as well as the junior associate's time. Just ask about who will be working on your case, and when.

INCIDENTALS

Some, if not most, attorneys and firms charge for incidental expenses incurred on behalf of the client, to help control overhead. They may charge $.25 to $.50 a page for copies made on their copy machine. They may bill for the charges incurred for long distance or overseas phone calls. They may bill for postage, file folders, file boxes, or other office supply charges. I have even seen bills from larger firms charging $5.00 a page for faxes. Beware of these incidentals, because they can add up quickly! Ask your attorney up front what he or his firm will bill for incidentals. Remember, you can always negotiate with your attorney or his firm. If they are not willing to concede about what you won't pay for, you don't have to hire them.

Overbilling

Most lawyers are not going to do this, but there are some unscrupulous attorneys out there who overbill their clients or pad their bills. The only way to protect yourself from this practice is to get a good referral for an attorney from someone you trust. If they have used that attorney before, they should know what that attorney's bills are like and how affordable he is.

Also, make sure that you keep records of the time you spend with your attorney, both when you meet with him and when you are on the phone with him. If your time and his time are different, he might be overbilling you. Make sure to read your entire bill and understand what you are being billed for in each instance. If you think you're being overbilled, you may want to check with another attorney or the bar association.

There are even some attorneys who have their secretaries or paralegals do a considerable amount of the work and then charge you as if the attorney did it all. Check your billing statement for what type of work was done. If the attorney is charging for stuff that you doubt he has the time or the inclination to do, such as general research, drafting pleadings, typing letters, filing, etc., he may be charging you *his* rate for his *staff's* time. In many instances, the firm's retainer agreement provides for billable rates for non-attorney time. So make sure that you ask about this issue up front.

If you have a good relationship with the person or company on the other side of your legal matter this may present antoher way to check for overbilling. For instance, if you are entering into a publishing agreement and you have a good relationship with your publisher, you may ask what his attorney has charged for certain services and compare that to the time spent by your attorney. If your publisher is billed .2 for a conversation between the two attorneys and you get billed .5, that should put up a serious red flag.

No matter how your lawyer bills you, he should advise you of all costs associated with handling your matter, and you should have a retainer agreement setting forth all the terms and conditions of his representation. Be sure to ask your lawyer all the questions you can during your first visit, so you won't be shocked when you get your bill. In some instances, he may not charge for the initial consultation. However, only personal injury lawyers advertise that there's no charge for the initial consultation, because they make their money from contingency fees after the case is over. So, ask the lawyer if there is an initial charge for your first visit *before* you visit him.

And remember, attorneys can't make a living by giving away their time, even if you only want to ask them a few questions. Attorneys are paid to have the answers, and most attorneys don't like to give them away. In fact, there have been many times when I told a client that the answers are available at the library—feel free to look them up. But I'm not going to "give" them away or, worse, incur any liability if my "free" answers are misinterpreted.

Saving Legal Costs

Remember that you can save a good deal of money by being prepared when you talk to or see your attorney about any matter. Have all of your documents ready and try to stick to the facts of your case (what happened or is happening) and don't go on about how it has made you feel, etc. Giving your lawyer a bunch of emotional embellishment may make you feel better but it won't have any effect on your legal matter but will end up costing you more money unless, of course, you are actually suing for some type of emotional distress.

Another way to save costs for an attorney is to always ask the other side to have their attorney draft an agreement or whatever is needed and just have your attorney review it. You can also find copies of other agreements and make them specific for your needs and then have your attorney review it to make sure that you haven't done something that could get you into trouble. However, I don't advise trying to draft some extremely important document or agreement that may have serious consequences without the assistance of an experienced attorney.

Attorney Referrals

If you don't know anyone who can refer you to an entertainment attorney or you can't find one in your area, you can go to a library, a local law office, or a local courthouse and find the books called Martindale & Hubble or go online to www.martindale.com. This company has attorneys pay to be listed in its books and on-line for this very purpose. The listings include where the attorneys went to school, what type of practice they specialize in, their qualifications or certifications, as well as other information. Also, larger cities usually have bar associations that have referral services that can refer you to an attorney who practices in the area that you need. And the best way to find an attorney is to rely upon your friends or associates who may have had the need for a lawyer in the past.

Getting Along with Your Attorney

You have to remember that in order for your attorney to make a living, he must be able to service many different clients with many different types of problems. This means that the better your attorney is, the busier he is going to be. He may have hundreds of open files (pending issues or cases) at any given time, and he must attend to them all as quickly, efficiently, and professionally as possible. Closing files is his absolute goal so that he can move on to other matters.

But sometimes there aren't enough hours in the day to get all of his work done. Furthermore, there may be other pressing matters that have to be filed with the court or that were in line before yours. Many attorneys work extremely long hours and weekends just to catch up with their workload. I and many of my attorney friends preferred to work on Sundays. It was one of the few times that we could focus on important tasks without being interrupted by clients stopping by, or the constant influx of phone calls that always took up our time.

The point is this: *Be patient*. The wheels of justice move slowly, and each task takes a good deal of time if the attorney is going to be thorough.

When you first meet with your attorney, sit down and discuss how long it will take to handle your issue or case. Make your expectations clear, and ask how he plans to meet those expectations. If they are not unreasonable and he can fulfill them, he'll tell you. If you reach an understanding about both of your roles, you will be much less likely to have a misunderstanding later.

Make sure that your attorney communicates with you, but he shouldn't have to call you every day. Also, don't call and bug him about your case unless it is warranted. Ask him to send you courtesy copies of all of his correspondence in regard to your file , as well as copies of everything in your file, if you don't already have copies. If you keep a well-organized file that basically mirrors your attorney's file, you can tell what is going on with your case at any given time. Again, this will prevent possible problems with your attorney.

Finally, remember that attorneys are people too. They have feelings, and usually they're trying to do the best they can. Being courteous and patient will make dealing with your attorney much more amicable. That way, you'll get the best representation that you can.

Summary

You might never know when you need an attorney until it's too late. So don't get taken advantage of just to save yourself a little money. It's better to be safe than sorry. Remember, if you don't understand what you are getting into, at least *consult* an attorney. In the end, he can save you a good deal of trouble and, more importantly, money.

CHAPTER 2

Choosing a Business Structure

"It's not as simple as you might think.…"

No matter what you plan to do in the music business, unless you plan to work for someone else, you have to think about what type of business structure you are going to operate under. Being self-employed is one of the big attractions of the music business, and choosing a business structure can play a huge role in your success. It also affects how the problems that often arise can and will affect your business, or even your personal life. There are lots of advantages and disadvantages for each type of business structure, so give this plenty of thought and be very careful before you make your next move. If you don't take the right steps now, you could end up losing everything you own later, even though you might not think you've done anything wrong.

There are only a few types of business structures to choose from: sole proprietorships, partnerships (general, limited partnership, and joint venture), corporations, Limited Liability Companies (LLC), and Limited

Liability Partnerships. There is also the Professional Corporation or Professional Limited Liability Company, as well as nonprofit or not-for-profit companies. Each type of business structure has its own advantages and disadvantages, and this brief description is *not* intended to explain every single one. There are many different scenarios that could have an effect on your choice. However, you should get enough information here to help you choose a business structure and how to go about it.

Your main concerns should be the limitation of liability, tax advantages, and the ability to obtain financing. The *limitation of liability* means limiting your exposure to being sued for just about anything, including bad debts, an act of negligence, breach of contract, or any other type of lawsuit that could be filed against you, whether it's for a good reason or not. We live in a very litigious society. When people or companies feel that they have been wronged in some way, they are quick to fire off a lawsuit to seek money or set things right. If you have limited liability, you have personal security and you don't risk losing your personal assets. This alone can let you rest a lot easier each night.

As for being able to obtain loans or financing, if your personal credit is not exactly the best, having another business structure could allow you to enter into agreements for loans or financing, depending on how well your business is doing.

Tax advantages are different for each type of business structure. They all stem from the state and federal tax codes, which can be a real pain to read, much less understand. Unless you study taxes for a living, it's almost impossible to learn everything you should know to file your taxes yourself and get all the deductions you can. This doesn't mean you can't file your taxes yourself. But to get the most out of your deductions and other benefits in the tax code, you need to seek professional advice. You don't want to miss something that could save you a good deal of money, or worse, end up owing money because of an incorrect filing.

Furthermore, the tax code is anything but static. Each time you learn the tax rules, they change. In some cases, keeping up with the changes in the tax codes can take up a lot of precious time that may be better spent taking care of your business. The good news is that if start off on the right foot and achieve some measure of success, you should be able to afford a team of people to help you with these tasks, such as accountants, attorneys, or others. And this brings us to the discussion of the different types of business structures to choose from.

Sole Proprietorship

A sole proprietorship is when you are "doing business as" (D.B.A.) a particular name, or under your own name. In other words, you, John Q. Artist, may be doing business as John Q. Artist, or you may have a company name, such as AB-CD Productions. If you choose this type of business structure, you and only you are on the hook for everything that you do. You are solely responsible for the running of that business, and you will be solely liable for all debts and possible lawsuits. If you are sued successfully and you don't have the appropriate insurance, you could lose your music equipment, your car, and/or your home. In fact, if you are found to be liable and the judgment is more than you can pay, you could end up having to file personal bankruptcy.

You also have to pay your taxes as an individual. Therefore, you have to pay quarterly taxes in advance based upon money that you haven't even earned yet, and you only get deductions as an individual. This can really cost you in the end, if you consider car insurance, car payments, and other things that could be written off if they were under a corporate or LLC name. However, as an individual, you can write off your expenses against any other income from another source, such as a day job. Finally, once you have shuffled off this mortal coil, the business ends. If you have any loved ones who are dependent on your business, this may not be the best way to go. Of course, if you are the only one who can run the business, that point is moot once you are gone.

The single best advantage to a sole proprietorship is that you are the boss and you don't have to answer to anybody. You also don't have to split any of the money you make with anyone after you pay your taxes and overhead—unless you are married, of course, which means you're not necessarily in business for yourself. You may share assets with your spouse, depending on the state you live in. This means you *and* your spouse could be on the hook if you incur any liability that your sole-proprietorship business can't pay out of your business account, or assets for any act of liability for which your sole-proprietorship business may have some type of exposure. Finally, with a sole proprietorship, you don't have a bunch of government red tape or paperwork to file with the state each year, as you may with a partnership, corporation, or limited-liability company. Because you are the only one responsible for paying the bills, it can be harder to get financing, get some type of loan, or find investors if you need to raise capital for any reason.

This type of business is the most common and user-friendly, but you may want to give some serious thought to limiting your liability. This is especially true if you have acquired quite a few assets. You can lose it all if you are not extremely careful. One simple mistake, such as a bad car wreck on the way home from a gig or some other act of negligence, can wipe you out or force you into bankruptcy if you don't have the proper amount of insurance!

The main problem is that most people don't plan on bad things happening, but you would be surprised at how many businesses have closed due to some unforeseen circumstance. If you are a sole proprietor, you should expect the best but always plan for the worst that could happen to you or your business.

General Partnerships

A partnership is when two or more people go into business together. This includes a duo act, a band, or any other type of musical association. Whether the partnership has any formal agreement or not, by virtue of the fact that two or more people are working together, a de facto partnership is formed. This means that an implied contract (not written or express) is created, whereby each partner is assumed to have consented to form the partnership.

Dealing with partners is a lot like being married. Everyone has to agree on everything that is done in the name of the partnership. Because everyone usually has an equal say, sometimes one or more members of the partnership won't agree with the decisions made by the group. From personal experience, I can say that being in a partnership can be really difficult. You had better choose your partners wisely, and make sure that each partner has a very clear understanding of what their rights, duties, and obligations are going to be. Otherwise, you are going to be at odds with one another over any number of issues, and doing business together could become difficult, if not impossible. Most likely, one of the partners is going to feel like he's doing most of the work and therefore should be entitled to more of the profits.

One upside to a partnership is that there's less paperwork to file with the state. In most cases, all you need are a business license and a joint checking account. You don't even need any sort of formal partnership agreement in writing, although this is where the problems can begin.

Each partner is responsible for the day-to-day decisions of running the partnership, each partner has authority to enter into contracts on behalf of the partnership, each partner shares in the profits of the partnership, and each partner is jointly and severally liable for all debts and liabilities of the partnership. *Joint* and *several liability* means that if someone sues the partnership, they can come after any of the partners individually or jointly. The suing party most likely will try to get a judgment against all of the partners, but may be more concerned with the partner who has the most assets. Also, if a partner screws up and incurs a debt that the partnership can't pay, or somehow opens up the partnership to be sued for liability, you can end up having to pay for your partner's mistake if that mistake is made in the normal course of business of the partnership.

Let's say that you are in a de facto partnership with your band, and the drummer goes out and buys a whole new monitor system under the partnership's name so he can hear himself play at your band's gigs. His credit is bad, so he talks the equipment vendor into selling him the gear under the company's name. The vendor knows that your band has a bunch of gigs coming up, and the drummer promises to pay for the gear from those gigs. Due to circumstances beyond anyone's control, most of those gigs are cancelled and the band breaks up. Each band member could be held liable for the debt incurred by the drummer. The vendor could sue each band member separately, or could just sue the lead singer because he has the best job and the most cash or other assets.

This is just one bad scenario—the situation could be a whole lot worse.

Let's say that the sound guy or some other member of the partnership is driving the van that the partnership bought to transport the band's equipment to and from gigs. The driver has been drinking and gets in a bad wreck, maiming or even killing the other driver. Since he's driving the van in the normal course of business, not only will he be liable for the car crash, the medical bills, and the pain and suffering of the other driver, but each member of the partnership may be held liable. They may have to pay for the damages that are not covered by any insurance, even though they had nothing to do with it.

So this can be a very dangerous way to do business. The last thing you need is to be responsible for the negligence of one or your partners. Be very careful about how you handle your business affairs in a partnership, especially with regard to liability, whether in the form of bad debts or negligence.

As for tax considerations, a partnership can obtain a Federal Employment Identification Number (FEIN) and a company/partnership checking account, but each partner is required to pay his individual taxes because the partnership is not required to file. Furthermore, partnerships do not allow for tax deductions for pension and profit sharing, or a host of other deductions that are allowed with corporations and limited liability companies, such as health insurance, car payments or car insurance for the company van, and so on.

Unlike a corporation or limited liability company, a partnership doesn't exist beyond the lifetime of the partners. Also, when a partnership is dissolved, the assets are either liquidated or distributed fairly to the partners, if there are no debts or liabilities at that time. Furthermore, if one partner wants to leave the partnership, it will be very hard to find another partner who is suited for the job, much less a new partner who is willing to step in and take over the liabilities and/or debts of the partnership.

However, if you want to raise capital, it is a lot easier and less costly to find another partner than to make stock transfers and so forth, as you would with a corporation. But you must be careful if the partnership agreement does not allow for adding new partners or losing a partner, because the partnership can be dissolved by operation of law. Therefore, you should draw up a really good partnership agreement.

Here is a scenario: Jean, Paulette, Jorge, and Ringlet decide to form a band. They name themselves The Beat-less and start to play gigs around Liverpuddle. They are now in a de facto partnership. This means that by operation of law, they are in a partnership automatically. It also means that even though the band gets paid under the name The Beat-less, each person is supposed to be paid out of the partnership account. If the band is paid by a check made out to The Beat-less, they had better have a joint checking account with its own Tax ID number, or they may not be able to cash the check. Again, each partner is responsible for his own taxes when he's paid from the account and must claim any deductions personally even if that means splitting up costs and making copies of receipts.

After a fairly long time together, the band has acquired a good deal of musical equipment with money from the partnership. Furthermore, they have recorded a number of records and have acquired a lot of money from both record royalties and publishing royalties. After several years and a lot of disagreements between the partners and their respective girlfriends, the members of The Beat-less decide they would like to pursue solo careers.

Of course, we all know that this is a bad idea, but it happens all the time. If the band breaks up, what happens? Who gets the band's assets, such as the P.A., the lighting equipment, and the van? Who gets to use the band's name? Or can each partner play under the name The Beat-less? (Probably not: If each partner has his own band called The Beat-less, there could be some confusion in the marketplace and somebody could get sued.) Unless the partnership has some type of formal agreement setting forth what happens when a member leaves or the partnership is dissolved, the band could end up in court to decide who is going to receive what from the partnership's assets.

As you can see, a partnership can be a very difficult thing to hold together, even among the best of friends. It is very wise to draft a partnership agreement so that each member understands his rights, duties, and obligations, as well as how the benefits and liabilities of the partnership will be shared. The partnership agreement also should cover what will happen if the partnership is dissolved.

Limited Partnership

A limited partnership can be useful if you have an investor who is willing to put up some money, but doesn't want to have any exposure to liability other than what he has invested. A limited partnership works pretty much like a regular partnership. It can be one person who is looking for an investor, or a partnership of two or more people who are looking for an investor. The individual or partnership has liability and tax advantages, but the limited partner is mainly just an investor. He has no duties or obligations regarding the day-to-day operation of the limited partnership. In fact, he is supposed to stay out of all management decisions if he wants to maintain his limited partner status. The limited partner puts up the cash (or part of the cash) for the business venture, and if anything goes wrong, he is liable only for that amount of cash. He cannot be sued for anything above that amount, which means that his liability is limited—thus the name "limited partnership."

A limited partnership can be set up for a particular venture, somewhat like a joint venture, but often it's formed so that the limited partner helps out the partners in return for a payout that is to be paid over time. Once the limited partner has been paid in full, the limited partnership is closed.

Let's say your band is trying to buy a new P.A. system and lighting for your gigs. You can't obtain financing to buy the equipment on your own, but you find someone to loan you the money. You agree to pay back the loan plus interest over time. However, the partner is not protected by anything other than your promise to pay. If he is somewhat sophisticated, he may file a security interest with the state so that he can take your equipment if you don't pay. But if he is *very* sophisticated, he will enter into a limited partnership to protect him totally from any unforeseen liability due to his business relationship with your band. The limited partner will not have any say in your day-to-day business decisions, and when he is paid back with interest, the limited partnership will be dissolved.

However, there is a catch. Paperwork for the limited partnership will need to be filed with the state. This paperwork will protect the limited partner from any liability that may stem from the equipment he's purchasing, such as if someone is electrocuted by faulty wiring at a gig. Depending on the situation, the amount of money involved, and the investor, you will find many different possibilities to offer, such as stock options for a corporation, personal loans, etc., if you need capital for a business venture. Therefore, a limited partnership may or may not be the best option.

Also, be advised that limited partnerships must comply with very stringent government regulations and are very difficult to set up. They are closely tied with securities regulations, so you should let an experienced attorney set up any type of limited partnership. Because of this, they can be quite costly. But you should at least be aware of this type of business structure. You never know when you'll run into an investor who's willing to put up a serious amount of cash so your partnership can realize its business goals. He probably won't just hand over the cash without as much protection as he can possibly get, so always keep the option of limited partnership in the back of your mind.

Joint Ventures

Joint ventures are formed to handle a certain task, to pursue a well-defined and temporary business venture or some other type of undertaking. Once that undertaking has been completed, the joint venture is dissolved and the involved parties have no further rights, duties, or responsibilities. Joint ventures can be formed between two people, a person and a company, two companies, a partnership and a person, a company and a partnership, etc. In essence, any type of business structure can do business with any other type of business structure.

A joint venture is very similar to a general partnership. All rights, duties, and responsibilities are divided up in some fashion or another, pursuant to the joint venture agreement. This also means that the profits, assets, liabilities, and debts are divided between the parties. A joint venture agreement can and should be very detailed. You should not enter into it lightly, especially if you are a sole proprietor or a member of a partnership with no limitation of liability, except maybe if you are a limited partner.

There are many different types of joint ventures in the music industry today. One common joint venture is between an independent record label and a major label. Sometimes an independent label will find an act that is very commercially exploitable, but the major labels have all passed on the band for some reason.

Let's say a band has self-recorded a CD and sent copies to every label it could, but the major labels and most of the larger independent labels returned most of the copies as unsolicited. However, there *was* an independent label that was interested in signing the band. When the band signed with that label, it included its first master recording in the deal and then recorded another CD on that label. Both CDs had two or three singles that stood a very good chance of getting radio play, but there just wasn't enough money to promote the CDs properly in the major markets. The band has also been playing regionally for a few years and has developed a very good following. During its tenure at the independent label, the band has sold over 40,000 CDs and a good deal of "swag," and has garnered a dedicated fan base of over 60,000 members. However, its independent label has not been able to break the band big and get any national or international exposure, even though the label has invested a good deal of time and money in the band. The label does not want to let the band go from its contract, so it decides to approach a major label and try a joint venture.

The CDs that the major label now wants to acquire have already been recorded, so the major label doesn't need to pay to record any more masters. This saves the major label the entire recording budget and a good deal of the development costs for the band. The major label decides to do a joint venture with the independent label to handle the marketing, promotion, distribution, tour support, and many other aspects of taking the act to the next level. The independent label wants to continue to have certain input as to the creative direction, promotion, and other facets of the band's career, but definitely needs help with marketing, promotion, and distribution. So the two labels enter into a joint venture and carefully set up a formal agreement delineating all of the rights, duties, and obligations for all of the parties. With both companies pooling their resources, the band stands a very good chance of breaking out in the national and international markets, which was the intention of the independent label in the first place.

This is a win-win situation for all involved. You can see how a joint venture can be very beneficial to all parties if the pieces of the puzzle fall into place at the right time.

Another example of a joint venture is when two or more bands pool their resources to put on a show, a festival, or even a full tour. This is a great way to expose your band to new people. You get the benefit of the other bands' fan bases, as well as your own. All of the bands can pool their resources, rent venues, and split the costs for the P.A., lights, security, insurance, and other costs.

Also, they can split the risks if there's a loss. If all of the bands combine their resources to promote the show and ensure a good turn out, and if they sell enough CDs and swag, it should be a profitable venture for all parties involved. Perhaps it might even become an annual event.

With the joint venture, the bands have an agreement for that show or group of shows, and all of the bands reap the benefits. On the other hand, if the shows are a complete failure, all of the bands share the loss as agreed upon in the joint venture agreement. Since these bands were smart enough to enter into a joint venture, they can either do another joint venture or cut their losses and move on to other opportunities.

Corporations

A corporation is nothing more than a fictitious entity that has the legal right to carry out business just like an individual or partnership. Corporations can sue or be sued, raise capital, enter into partnerships or joint ventures, enter into contracts, acquire debts, purchase assets, and a whole lot more. Individuals, partnerships, limited liability companies, other corporations, or any combination of the above can own a corporation. Since corporations can own other corporations, it can become very difficult to figure out who actually owns what, or who derives their income from these multilayered corporations. This also explains how multinational conglomerates can end up owning the vast majority of music and entertainment companies today.

In many states, filing a corporation is really quite simple. You will need a charter, which sets forth the name, corporate address, incorporators, and corporate agent of your new corporation and sometimes the stockholders. You have to file the charter and pay a fee, and then your corporation is up and running. Once you have your charter, you need to get your business license, FEIN, and a banking account. The bank may require a central banking resolution before you can get your account, but it will have forms for this because it wants your business.

Also, in some states you may have to file the articles of incorporation with the Register of Deeds in your county. You should ask the office of the Secretary of State about what is required and how much filing for incorporation will cost. Usually the Secretary of State's office has how-to manuals and other materials that you need and will answer most questions you have. You can also find do-it-yourself books or software on the subject. Doing it yourself can save a lot of time and money, but if you don't understand what you are doing, consult a lawyer. You don't have to let him do *all* of the work, but do as much as you can and then consult the lawyer. This will save a good deal in attorney's fees and give you a leg up in getting started. Also, the more you know about your corporation, the better prepared you'll be to deal with the day-to-day operations and all of the filings that are required to maintain your corporation in good standing with your state. Whether you hire an attorney or not, do your homework and try to learn as much as you can.

Corporations are required to keep regular minutes of their meetings of the board of directors, officers, or shareholders. All of these documents must be maintained carefully and kept at the parent offices of the company. These meetings and the records related thereto do not have to be incredibly formal, but without them you can lose your corporate status or, worse, your limited liability. So be very careful to keep up with everything you are required to do to maintain your corporate status. Keep a list of all of the filings that are required and when they are due so that you don't risk having your corporation dissolved by operation of law. If that happens, you will lose your corporate status and all of the benefits that come with it.

Corporations have many advantages and disadvantages. One of the most important advantages is limited liability. This means that the owners of the corporation are shielded from any personal liability if the corporation is sued for bad debts, acts of negligence by the corporation or its employees, or any other matter.

For example, a corporation can benefit from limited liability if one of its employees has a serious car wreck and someone is killed. A judgment for a wrongful death suit can be millions of dollars. If the employee was driving the company car within the scope and purpose of his job, the corporation can be sued for the employee's actions. If the insurance policy on the company car is for less than the total liability of the judgment against the company, *only* the corporation can be made to pay the remainder of that judgment. In all likelihood, the corporation will not have the money to pay this debt and will be faced with bankruptcy. If so, the corporation can just close its doors, and the owners will not have to pay this bad debt out of their own personal funds. The owners will lose their company, but they will not lose any of their personal assets, or worse, have to file personal bankruptcy. It's an unfortunate circumstance for all involved, but at least the owners of the corporation are not on the hook for the bad acts of their employees or other officers of the corporation.

Another scenario: A band has booked a gig and had set up its P.A. at a frat party. The stage is made of wood and is a little rickety. Also, the circuit breakers at the frat house are insufficient to handle the lights and P.A., so the main circuit has to be tapped. Sometime during the party, things get a little out of control. Perhaps some drunk spills a drink on the power cable going to the lights and P.A. and is electrocuted, or the crowd gets so out of hand that the P.A. speaker columns fall over and someone is hurt really badly or even killed. Let's say the band or sound company is *really* unlucky, and not only do the P.A. speaker columns take a dive into the crowd, but they sever the power cable to the lights and someone is electrocuted. (Stranger things have happened.)

The lawyer for the deceased or severely injured is most likely going to sue the fraternity *and* the band. If the judge or jury decides that the band is at fault, the band members are going to be on the hook to pay all of the damages. This could bankrupt everyone in the band. However, if the band is incorporated, it can pay the judgment out of corporate funds. If the corporation doesn't have the money, the band can just close the corporation, and none of the band members will be on the hook.

If you think that something like this could never happen to you, just remember what happened to Great White. In 2003, the band played a show in a bar in Rhode Island, and one of its pyrotechnics went awry. The whole bar burned down with a lot of people in it. It could happen to you. But some prior planning can prevent you, your band, or your business from having to pay out of pocket for some terrible tragedy. Of course, your business may have some type of liability insurance for such an occurrence, but you may not have enough insurance to cover the total liability, or it may not cover a particular contingency.

The main thing to remember is that bad things can and do happen, so you need to set things up so that you are not personally liable. If you own a corporation that goes belly up for any reason, your only risk is what you've invested in that company. That could be a lot to lose, but at least you won't have to give up your house, your car, your personal equipment, or other personal assets.

A corporation also protects you from bad debts. As long as the debts are incurred in the corporate name, there is no way that you can be sued for those debts unless you've signed to be personally liable. In some instances, a brand new corporation with very few assets may not be able to borrow money unless one of the principals in the corporation signs as personal guarantor for that debt. Banks and other lending institutions are very wary of startup corporations, because they don't have any track record of making money. These banks don't want to be left holding the bag if a corporation fails, so they require some personal guarantee. Once the corporation has sufficient assets and its profit and loss statement shows a considerable influx of cash, it should have no problem borrowing money. Then the owners are shielded from liability for that debt. Of course, your corporation will need a really good business plan to get any type of loan. (For more information, see Chapter 3, "Making a Business Plan.")

But be advised that sometimes a person may be held liable for corporate debt. This can occur if one or more of the owners does something called *ultra vires*. This means that they have done something outside the scope and purpose of the corporation, which makes them personally liable. This allows creditors or those who sue the corporation successfully to "pierce the corporate veil" and go after the personal assets of the owners.

Furthermore, if the corporation does not maintain its records properly and does not follow all of the laws that affect corporate status, a court can ignore its corporate status. Therefore, the owners of the corporation could be on the hook personally for any liability.

Finally, the corporation should not mix the personal records of the owners with the records of the corporation. This is further grounds for the corporation's veil to be pierced, leaving the owners personally liable.

A disadvantage of a corporation is that there are many administration costs, as well as paperwork that must be filed with the state. A corporation is required to have bylaws, organizational minutes, regular minutes from meetings of shareholders and/or directors, etc., etc. All of these documents must be kept on file, and some of them must be filed with the state each year (or more often, depending on your state's requirements). Fortunately, the Secretary of State usually has free handouts that instruct you exactly how to file for and maintain your corporation so that you can enjoy all of the benefits of corporate status.

Corporations are *share-driven*. This means that shares of the corporation are issued to the owners, whoever or whatever they may be. Each owner of a share is entitled to vote, and that vote carries the same power as any other share. The number of shares an individual or other company owns determines how much power it has in controlling the corporation. If the corporation is dissolved, the proceeds are divided up (after all bills and liabilities are paid, etc.) based upon who owns what percentage of shares.

There are several types of shares that a corporation can issue. There is *common stock*, which is at the low end in ownership priority. If the corporation is liquidated, common stock holders will not receive any money until after all bond holders, security holders, loans, debts, and preferred stock holders have been paid. Holders of *preferred stock* don't usually have a voting interest in the corporation, as do common stockholders, but they get paid first out of any proceeds. Preferred stockholders also have more claims to the assets of a corporation than common stockholders. They are paid dividends from corporate profits more frequently than common stock-holders. Sometimes the corporate officers and directors will decide that no money can be paid out of the corporate coffers. This can be for any number of reasons, but usually because the corporation didn't do well that year.

Another advantage of a corporation is that it can be easier to attract investors if they believe your company will be successful. But keep in mind that sometimes people invest money in a business venture in the hopes of getting a tax writeoff if their investment is lost, which could be beneficial to them. These investors are more likely to invest in a corporation if their liability is limited.

If an investor is looking for collateral and your company doesn't have much, you can issue shares in the company instead of pledging any of your corporate property or other assets. This means that the investor now owns a part of the corporation. Just remember that one share equals one vote. Never sell more shares in the corporation than you or your initial corporate founders own, or you will lose control of the corporation. You could become a mere employee of your own company, with very little say in how it's run.

There *is* a way to sell shares to raise capital and still retain 100% of your stock. If you think you can pay back the investor in a short amount of time, you can put a *call option* on the stock that you sell. This will allow you to pay back the investor his money plus an agreed-upon amount of interest, and therefore *call back* your stock. You get your stock back, and the investor makes a nice return on his investment but doesn't end up owning a piece of your growing company.

Be advised, though, that selling stock in a corporation involves security laws, which are extremely complicated. To raise capital without running afoul of security regulations, you may have to write a business prospectus and even a *private placement memorandum*. Private placement or private investment capital is money invested in your company by private investors in return for stock or even bonds. In some cases in the United States, private placement doesn't need to be registered with the Securities Exchange Commission, and it can be less expensive and much easier than trying to take your company public. Furthermore, private investors are much easier to deal with than investment capitalists or banks. Often they're more patient and expect lower returns.

However, you may be required to provide a solid business plan and a private placement memorandum. You shouldn't try to handle this type of investment by yourself, because you could run afoul of securities laws and wind up in a serious amount of trouble. Hire an experienced attorney.

Corporations also give you a number of tax advantages. Sometimes you can write off your car payments, if the corporation owns your car and you use it more for business than personal use. Most of us only drive our cars to and from work anyway, so why not take advantage of the tax breaks? You should check with your accountant to see what tax breaks are available for your particular type of business. You may also be able to write off your health insurance and other expenses. These deductions are very similar to a benefits package that you would get for working at someone else's company. Also, you can get other deductions for your corporation, such as pension and retirement breaks. Check with your state government and the IRS to take advantage of all of the deductions to which you are entitled.

A big tax *dis*advantage is that a corporation is taxed twice. It pays taxes on the money it makes, and then, when it pays its shareholders, they're taxed separately. But the law has provided protection from *double taxation* too. A corporation can avoid this by becoming a Subchapter S corporation, also known as a Small Business Corporation. The company is allowed to pay the shareholders out of the profits, so the company doesn't really have to make any money other than what it spends to avoid paying taxes at the corporate level. The shareholders pay taxes from their income. In other words, if there is any money left over at the end of the year after all debts and liabilities have been paid, the corporation pays out that money to the owners and/or shareholders in the form of bonuses or other payments, so that the corporation will not owe any taxes.

A Subchapter C corporation is usually a larger company with a larger number of shareholders, so it pays out corporate taxes, and then the owners or shareholders pay taxes on their income from the company.

There are a few other types of corporations that you should be familiar with, such as closely held corporations, holding companies, and public corporations. A *closely held corporation* is owned, managed, and wholly controlled by the principals in the corporation. There is only one class of stock and no public shares issued, and therefore there are no other owners. *Holding companies* are set up just to own stock in other companies. They have no management duties or any obligations to the companies that they own. Finally, *public corporations* are the big companies that go public by making an initial public offering. They solicit stockholders or buyers from the general public in the big common markets, and therefore are able to raise very large sums of capital to finance their corporate growth.

If you build a company big enough to warrant an initial public offering or IPO, pat yourself on the back and get ready to make some serious money. By making an initial public offering, you are offering to sell shares of your company to the general public and be listed on the public stock exchanges. Going public can infuse a great deal of capital into a company, thus allowing it to reach its full potential.

Of course, there are some pitfalls. Before you take any steps to go public, you should seek serious legal representation with a very reputable securities law firm. This can be a massive undertaking and incur some serious legal bills, but it can be extremely lucrative. Most owners of companies that go public make enough money to retire right off the bat. If they *don't* retire, though, they actually have to answer to all of their stockholders. Sometimes the stockholders take over the company and kick out the original founders.

One last thing you should consider when you're filing a corporation is the amount of excise taxes you will have to pay. *Excise taxes* are what a corporation must pay for the privilege of doing business. They're based upon the amount of money the corporation makes, but sometimes they're not calculated on the first few hundred thousand dollars. Each state is different, so check with your Secretary of State, the IRS, and your state's tax agency to make sure that you comply with all of the tax laws. The good news is that in many states, excise taxes can now be avoided and limited liability can still be achieved. This is one of the reasons that the LLC was created.

Limited Liability Company

The Limited Liability Company, or LLC, is the newest form of doing business and is a combination of a corporation and a partnership. It allows for limited liability for all members, just like a corporation, but has the tax advantages of a partnership. It is very similar to a Subchapter S Corporation, but instead of being share-driven, it is contractually driven. Each member of an LLC shares in the rights and duties of the company based upon the contractual rights, duties, and obligations set out in the operating agreement, and no member can be held personally liable for any debts or liabilities of the LLC.

Although some states don't require a written operating agreement, you would be ill-advised to do without one. A written agreement sets out the rules of the company. It dictates who will do what work, how the profits are to be split, and what happens if someone decides to quit. The operating agreement also serves as the record of your initial agreement with your partners or members, to avoid disputes over money and how it is managed. Finally, if there is any dispute over the liability protection issue, the more formal your LLC is, the more likely the courts are to uphold limited liability.

In most states, an LLC does not need to hold regular ownership and management meetings like a corporation, but you can hold meetings and keep minutes. It is best to have written minutes approved by all members so that there is less likelihood of confusion or dissent. People remember things differently, so it's best to have the specifics of meetings or agreements in writing and signed by all members. Furthermore, as the LLC moves forward, the members will need to deal with many issues and contingencies. If minutes are drawn up and signed by all of the members, nobody can say that they never agreed to a particular course of action.

In most states, an LLC is not required to pay excise taxes on income, and this can be a huge savings. An LLC can be more costly to form than a corporation, though, because the filing fees are usually higher. Since an LLC is contractually driven, you may want to have a lawyer review your most important contracts. This also drives up your costs. But, like sole proprietorships and partnerships, an LLC is not considered separate from its owners for tax purposes. This means that the LLC does not generally pay any income taxes itself. Rather, each LLC member pays taxes on his share of profits and deducts his share of business losses on his personal taxes. Each state is different, so check with your Secretary of State, the IRS, and your state tax office.

If you are looking for investors, you must apply with your state tax office or the IRS for an exemption from having to file with the Securities Exchange Commission. A *security* comes about when a person invests money in a company but does not work for, manage, or otherwise operate the company in any way. So the security laws can come into play even with an LLC, hence the need for an exemption. However, these exemptions are not that hard to qualify for if all of your investors live in your home state. But you must check with your state tax office and the IRS to make absolutely sure.

Of course, you may find people to loan you money without any paperwork, so why worry about it? Well, if you get caught or a lender gets upset about things such as late payments, you can be in some serious trouble.

One other thing to consider is that LLCs are very new compared to corporations and partnerships. The laws haven't been able to adapt to them and clearly define their place. In fact, some attorneys may advise against this form of doing business because there has not been enough litigation over certain issues. In other words, there's not enough legal precedent to predict what will happen in court. If you are concerned about these types of issues, check with a local attorney who is experienced in these matters. Better safe than sorry!

Limited Liability Partnerships

These companies are very similar to LLCs but with much less paperwork and restrictions, and consequently, less protection from liability. Generally, it's not necessary to file any articles of organization or comply with certain other formalities that are required with an LLC. But be careful to have a rock-solid operating agreement so there aren't any loopholes that could remove the veil of limited liability. Some states may even require a large liability insurance policy for negligence or other acts of the LLP or its members.

Also, in many states an LLP gets less liability protection than a corporation or an LLC, because the LLP only protects a member from the *other* members' bad acts or negligence. The LLP will not protect you from your *own* bad acts or negligence.

Finally, in some states, an LLP will not protect your personal assets if the LLP racks up bills that it can't pay. So make sure you really want this form of business before you go through all of the trouble of drafting any agreements.

Professional Associations, Professional Limited Liability Companies, and Professional Corporations

Sometimes associations of professionals, such as doctors, lawyers, or accountants, form partnerships or professional associations. They can also form Professional Limited Liability Companies (PLLC) or Professional Corporations for the purpose of conducting business. As a musician, you shouldn't worry about these too much. If you're also a doctor, lawyer, or accountant, you should know how this is done already. Come to think of it, if that's the case, you probably don't have much use for this book anyway!

Nonprofit, Non-Profit, Not for Profit, and Not-for-Profit Companies

Is there a difference between nonprofit, non-profit, not for profit, and not-for-profit companies? Some say yes, others say no. *Not-for-profit* refers to an activity by its members, such as a hobby like guitar collecting, while a *nonprofit* organization refers to an association that is established for purposes other than making a profit. For the purposes of this book, I will stick to using the term *nonprofit corporation* for any company that is set up as nonprofit, non-profit, not for profit, or not-for-profit.

A nonprofit corporation is run very much like a regular corporation, but there are extra rules that come with the territory. It's a corporation formed to carry out a charitable, educational, religious, literary, or scientific purpose. It doesn't have to pay federal or state income taxes on any profits it makes from activities that achieve its objectives. As far as the IRS and state tax agencies are concerned, the benefits the public gets from these organizations entitles them to a tax exemption.

A nonprofit corporation is permitted to raise funds by acquiring public and private grant money and donations from individuals and companies. The tax laws actually encourage people and companies to donate money and property, allowing them to deduct their contributions on their tax returns. Structuring an organization as a nonprofit corporation also shields its directors, officers, and members from personal liability for the corporation's debts and liabilities.

You must set up a nonprofit corporation just like any other corporation. You file with the Secretary of State in your home state, and you register to do business in any other state. You must also hold meetings of directors and members, and keep minutes of these meetings in a corporate records book. Check with your Secretary of State for instructions on forming a nonprofit company and keeping it in compliance with all local, state, and federal laws. You may also want to check with local, state, and federal tax agencies to make sure that your company complies with all applicable tax laws.

The IRS also has certain restrictions in regards to what a nonprofit can and cannot do. For instance, a nonprofit cannot make political lobbying (influencing legislation) a substantial part of its total activities, and it must make sure that its activities don't personally benefit its directors, officers, or members.

Additional benefits of organizing a nonprofit corporation are special postage rates, property tax benefits in the form of welfare exemptions, and a whole lot more.

You should seek competent legal representation and an accountant to make sure that you get the most out of any tax deductions.

So What's Next After Choosing Your Business Structure?

Each state is different, so always check with your Secretary of State to make sure that you fulfill all of the requirements for your chosen business structure. Check with your local government to see if you need a business license, name reservations, or any other filings. Each state has its own requirements, sometimes each county, so follow them to the letter and cover your bases.

You also want to check with your bank for the required documents or paperwork to start a checking account. Some banks may require a copy of your business license, your corporate charter, or even a central banking resolution.

Finally, no matter which business structure you choose, you need to contact your state and federal tax offices to comply with any tax laws or filing requirements. In most cases, you will need a tax identification number. But if you are careful and diligent, you can do a good deal of this work without needing any legal or accounting assistance.

Caveat: If you plan to run your business from your home or apartment, as many do, you should definitely make sure there are no restrictions. If you are in an apartment, read the apartment association's bylaws to see if you can run a business from home. If you own a house, check out the restrictive covenants for your neighborhood to make sure that you can have your band practice there or run a business. Go to the register of deeds in your county. The staff should be able to assist you. Some counties are still on the old "book" system, but many larger counties are on computers or micro-fiche. You can usually make copies of any restrictive covenants or apartment bylaws for your records.

If you're not allowed to a business from your home or apartment, you either have to move or be very careful not to let anyone find out. This can be a very difficult task. I'm not suggesting that you break the law, but I'm know people who are discretely running their businesses from home and they never have any problems at all. This doesn't mean that your band should rehearse or record in your apartment, or that you should have high-volume traffic coming in and out, but you can handle the day-to-day business, such as communications, paperwork, etc. Just be very careful not to disturb your neighbors. Use your head, be considerate of others, and you should have no problems.

Finally, it costs more for a business license if the business does not have a storefront. But since business licenses are not that expensive, it shouldn't be too much of a concern.

Why Worry About It?

If you're just a small local business, why do you need to worry about any of this? There are thousands of artists, writers, and bands out there who've never actually set up a business structure, so they're operating as either a sole proprietorship or a de facto partnership. They may have consulted a lawyer first and made sure that they did everything correctly, or maybe they were just very lucky.

In my experience as a lawyer, I was usually contacted after a problem occurred that could have been prevented. Unfortunately, it usually cost the client more to fix the situation than I would have charged he had asked me to advise him in the first place. Be that as it may, you never know what lies ahead, and the road is often rocky and fraught with danger. Most people would never go into any business venture if they didn't expect to be successful, but bad things can happen to good people. Sit down and ask yourself whether you can afford to do business without the limited liability and tax advantages of a corporation or a limited liability company, even if they require more work and more money. I'm not trying to make your mind up for you, but spending a little time and money on the front end can save tons of time, headaches, personal security, and money in the end.

You never know, the music business can be a very lucrative gig. You just might hit it big one day! If you do, you'll be glad that you got it right the first time.

CHAPTER 3

Making a Business Plan

"Save your duct tape…fix it *before* it breaks."

Now that you've set up your business, let's move on to what you can do to make your business more successful. Coming up with a plan, defining your goals, and learning more about your company and its potential markets are your keys to success. You don't necessarily need a full-blown business plan for everything you do, but it can be a really big help to have a good solid plan and define your objectives. It's a roadmap to where you are headed and how you plan to get there.

You should also try to anticipate any problems that could arise. If you just put down in writing what you're trying to achieve and everything you'll need to do, you'll make a huge step toward solving any possible problems.

A business plan is a tool that allows you and everyone you are working with to focus on the goals of your business, such as financial and marketing strategies. This way everyone is on the same page, instead of pursuing their individual ideas of what must be done to make the business successful. It also helps potential investors or business partners to understand exactly what you're trying to do. Furthermore, a good business plan makes allowances for all of the problems that could arise throughout the life of your business, and offers solutions. The more you plan for potential problems, the better prepared you'll be to solve them, and the more attractive your business will be to potential investors and bank loan officers.

This chapter discusses whether you need a business degree, how to define what you want to do, the elements of a business plan, the elements of a financial plan, and a lot of the day-to-day problems for which you will need to be prepared. There are also some resources so you can research your market and prepare for the future.

Do You Have a Business Degree? Do You Even Need One?

There are plenty of very successful businesspeople out there who never went to college. Some went to college but hardly ever went to class. Some never finished high school. College can be a great learning experience, but more often than not it's just a great time. After all, college really just teaches you how to learn. There are no hard and fast rules, but the more you educate yourself about your chosen business, the more likely you'll be successful. The most important thing that you can do is to read, read, and read some more. If you don't like to read or are unwilling to spend the time learning everything you can about your chosen field, reading about new trends, new technologies, and the like, you're much more likely to fall behind everyone else. Besides, your real learning experiences come from actual work in the field that you have chosen. No matter what theories you have learned, the real-life application of those theories will prove or disprove them.

I have found that the harder I work, the luckier I seem to get. So I strongly suggest that you never develop in you the notion that your education is complete, but always find the strength and zeal to enlarge your knowledge continually. The more you understand about your problems, the more likely you'll be able to solve them.

Furthermore, putting a problem in writing is the best way to grasp it fully, and will go a long way toward the final solution. For example, have you ever tried to solve a complicated math problem in your head? Trying to keep all of the variables in order and solve the problem without writing it down can be very hard to do. But if you write it down, it is easier to see the different possible solutions. and therefore to solve the problem.

Once you decide to really bear down and pursue a long-term career in the music business, you should seriously consider the actual day-to-day concerns. After all, business is business, and knowing as much as you can about your business is going to make life much easier in the years to come. Therefore, you should give some thought to a business plan.

What Is It That You Plan to Do?

A *business plan* is a way to set out your goals in writing, monitor your progress in achieving those goals, prepare for contingencies that may occur along the way, and ultimately attain your goals. To solve any problem, the best place to start is to write it down. This allows you to look at the problem in an objective way. You can look at the different angles and possible solutions without having to keep everything in your head.

Writing a business plan is the first step to obtaining your goals. It doesn't have to be some huge document with charts and graphs (although visual representations can be a plus), but it should be a clear and concise representation of what you know about your business and how you plan to make it a success. A business plan is a good tool to show others that you have given your business a great deal of thought. It can also be one of your only options for obtaining a loan, attracting investors, bringing in partners and managers, etc. Just make sure it's as perfect as you can make it before you show it to them, and also be aware that they're going to be looking at the people *behind* the business plan as well.

Your business plan doesn't need to be in any particular order or include all of the following sections, but the more thorough you are, the better prepared you will be. In certain instances, some of the following sections can be somewhat redundant. They are included so that you can choose which sections best define your business and help everyone whom you are working with understand your goals.

Be careful whom you pitch your business plan to, especially if they are outside of the company, such as potential investors. They might like your idea so much that they keep it *and* your business plan for themselves. You also don't want your business partners, employees, or associates to steal your business plan and open up a similar business across town. You can protect yourself from this with employee non-compete agreements or non-compete/non-disclosure agreements. This will prevent your associates from competing with you, and will keep potential investors and the like from using your business plan for their own benefit.

The cover page of your business plan should clearly state that photocopying or duplicating it is strictly prohibited. If your products and services involve an invention or a totally new concept, you need to protect against infringement or theft of intellectual property by filing the appropriate copyrights, trademarks, or patents. You may also want to protect your business plan by filing a copyright on the *expression* of your idea. (See Chapter 6, "Intellectual Property," for more information.)

The following are the elements of a business plan.

COVER PAGE

This is simply the page that tells all interested parties exactly what you do and where. Include the name of your business, the address, and a description of the products and services that you will be offering. You will also need a table of contents with page numbers, so that the reader can go directly to the sections that interest them.

SUMMARY

A business plan can include many different elements, but the place you should start is your *summary*, also referred to as the *executive summary*. This is a clear, concise statement about what you plan to do. Just write down everything that you want to include in your business plan. It is very similar to the opening paragraph of a term paper.

Writing the summary makes you really think about what your overall plan will include. It's sort of like a skeleton, so that you can "flesh out" the plan later on. The summary is the first place a potential investor or anyone else will look when considering doing business with you, because he will want to know exactly what the business and business plans are all about.

This summary will change as you work on each element of your business plan. Remember to keep it clear and concise. If you don't have a decent summary, nobody will be interested in reading more about your business.

MISSION STATEMENT

Write out a very thoughtful and clear *mission statement*. It should include what products and services your business is offering, your target market, and why you are taking on this business venture. Write down all of the advantages that you have, such as any newer technologies, and how you plan to exploit these advantages. In short, who are you and what are your business goals?

If you are a band or an artist who plans to sell records, tour to support your records, and collect as much money as you can from artist and/or writer royalties, you may want to include the steps to getting a record deal. Or you may want start your own label and build a very strong regional act. Then you can sell enough of your independent records to attract a major label for a record deal or perhaps a joint venture. So, your mission statement would start by setting the number of units you think you'll need to sell in order to do that. Remember, if you and your band put out a CD, you are in essence a record label.

If you own a recording studio, the mission statement may include how many clients you will need each year so that you can make a good living, buy new equipment and toys for the studio, etc. Your long-term goals may also include starting a record label, a publishing company, or any other related business. Sit down and make a whole plan based upon how much money you can make with your current client base. Include advertising, equipment repair, and other unforeseen expenses. Then figure out how much money it will take to make that business grow. Again, be clear, simple, and concise.

BUSINESS OBJECTIVE

You may have covered most of what you need to in your executive summary. But if you want to go into more detail, you should also consider setting out your *business objectives*. This can be as simple as stating your short-term, mid-term, and long-term goals, as well as what your business is offering to your target market.

Defining what your business is offering is quite simple. Just list all of your products and services. After that, you need to determine what your target market is going to be. Define who you want as your clients and how you plan to get them to do business with you.

Defining your goals can be a little more involved. You may look at your long-term goal and think it sounds pretty easy. After all, look how many people before you have been successful, and you are much better than they are. Right? Trust me, it's not that easy.

Or, you may think about how many talented people never make it and decide that long-term success is unattainable. Don't think like that for one second!

Whatever the case, you need to set long-term goals and then focus on the mid-term goals you must meet. Once you have written down your long-term and mid-term goals, set as many short-term goals as you need to achieve the mid-term goals. When you have the steps written down, you will get a good sense of accomplishment as you cross off each step on the list. You get to your ultimate destination one milestone at a time. But the road can be long, and on the way there are a lot of wrong turns, potholes, dead ends, dangerous curves, flat tires, engine trouble, bad gas mileage, and many other problems. Make sure your business is roadworthy, and give yourself a roadmap with alternative routes. Then you won't get detained or lost along the way, and if you need to take a detour or two, you won't lose too much time getting back on the right road.

If you are including specific figures in your business plan, you need to say exactly what you are doing and how it makes money. For instance, if you're a songwriter, you want to list how many songs you will need to write each year to build up enough quality material for a publishing deal. You also want to find out *how* songwriters get paid, and how long it takes to get paid. If you are lucky enough to get a cut (which means that you have gotten a "single" released by a major label on radio), you need to know how many companion cuts you will need to make a living. (A companion cut is a song placed on a major label record release but never released as a single.) If you are lucky enough to have an actual hit or two, you need some idea of how much money you will make over the life span of your copyrights. In short, if you want to be a songwriter, you should learn everything you can about songwriting, how songs get cut, how to publish your own material, how to get a publishing deal, how to exploit your copyrights, how money is made in the song-writing industry, etc.

If you are a band or an artist with your own independent label, your business objective should include the number of CDs you need to sell to pay for the manufacturing, marketing, and promotions of the CD. Figure out your cost per CD (including studio time) and how many you can buy from the start. Next, figure out how much you are going to sell your CDs for, both retail and whole-sale. Then figure out what type of marketing you plan to do. Will you leave your CDs on consignment at your local record store? Will you sell them only at your gigs? Will you look for some type of distribution deal in your region? If so, what will that cost? In short, you need to lay out every single avenue for making money and figure out the steps that you must implement.

If you own a studio, you will want to figure out how much to charge per hour or day. Then you will know approximately how many hours or days you will need to work to make your business run. You should plan on how to get clients and repeat business. Include any information about revenue streams, etc., etc.

Define Your Products and Services

Figure out which services and/or products you are going to offer. Be as thorough and creative as you can. Consider any product or service that will generate revenue, and determine whether you can make it profitable. The more you know about what you are going to offer, the better off you will be when you open your business.

Try doing some role playing with friends or family to see if you present your products and/or services in a clear and concise way. Be prepared to answer as many of your customers' questions as you can so you will not be caught off-guard and lose any sales. Remember, if you don't know as much as possible about your products and/or services, don't expect potential customers to have much confidence in what you are offering.

Business Structure

Your business plan should include the type of business structure you plan to use. This step is very important and will determine some of the costs of setting up your business. As stated in Chapter 2, there are only a few different types of business structures to choose from: sole proprietorships, partnerships (general, limited partnership, and joint venture), corporations, Limited Liability Companies (LLC), and Limited Liability Partnerships. Please refer to Chapter 2 for a very detailed analysis of each type of business structure.

Company Ownership/Management

This section defines who owns all of the interests in your company, what their particular rights, duties, and obligations will be, and the strengths or weaknesses that they bring to the company. Here is your chance to speak to any potential investor about the principals in your company, such as your bandmates, partners, associates, etc. You should include each person's higher education, if applicable, as well as his particular talents or skills. If you are not looking for investors, you should still write this information down, because it will be a great tool for deciding what each person's rights, duties, and obligations will be. If everyone knows exactly what role he is to play and what is expected of him, you will get the maximum benefit of his time and efforts.

If you don't put this in writing, people will say that they never agreed to do this or that. You will end up with a lot of unnecessary arguments over what should and should not be done, as well as what each person should get for his investment of time, energy, and money.

Marketing Strategy

You have to define every single aspect of what you are selling. You must also determine what benefits your customers are going to receive from your products and services. Remember, the best way to make a profit is to provide products and services that help people make money, save money, or feel good about your products and services.

You can try to keep your strategy very simple, but the more you know about marketing and sales, the better off your business is going to be. No matter what happens, you must be able to show that there are enough potential customers to keep your business afloat. Where are these customers going to come from? Will they just appear out of thin air? That's highly doubtful. So you must focus on how you are going to reach them.

You should also state whether your market is growing or shrinking. If the market is shrinking, explain why, and specify how you plan to gain market share. You may have a new process or method that will allow you to gain market share. Just because the market is declining doesn't mean you can't make a living from it. On the other hand, if the market is growing, you need to show how you are going to capitalize on that growth.

Do a Comparison with Your Competition

This is your chance to figure out what you should charge for your products and services, as well as what is going on with your competition in the marketplace. The best way to figure out what you should be charging is to learn as much as you can about your direct competition in your region or in the national marketplace. List your competitors' strengths and weaknesses. What makes them successful? What can you do to beat them at their own game? How can you exploit their weaknesses and draw business from them?

All of these points will give you a clear and well-defined set of goals. If you want to get sneaky, contact your competition directly and ask what they charge for certain products and services. The more you know about your competition, the more likely you are to succeed.

Promotions

Advertising and public relations are the key ways to promote your business actively. Determine what type of advertising will best suit your needs. Should you have an ad in the Yellow Pages? Should you do direct marketing through the mail? Can you gather a list of e-mail addresses for potential or existing clients, so that you can follow up with sales information, specials, new products and services, and the like?

There are a number of different ways to reach your target market. Some are more costly but reach a broader range of potential customers, while others are much less expensive but don't have as much reach. You must find a way to get the most bang for your buck. (For more information on this, see Chapter 4, "Advertising, Marketing, and Promotions.")

Sales Strategy

This is an extremely important element. If you are not making sales, you are not making money. Even if you are offering services, like a lawyer or doctor, you will not be very successful unless you can sell them to people. You have to find people with money, they have to want what you're selling, and they have to give you their money in exchange for it.

You should also think about how you are going to train your sales staff and other personnel. You will learn as you go, and if you keep a written document of the lessons you have learned, you can pass it along to your employees. An even better idea is to have your employees write their own manuals, describing what they do and how they do it. If an employee writes his own job description, it's more likely that he will be able to handle his job.

The employee manuals should also clearly set forth what is expected of all employees, and how they can get their work done efficiently and expeditiously. If an employee leaves, the next employee will know exactly how to do that same job with a minimum of mistakes.

At my law firm, I had a three-page document on how to answer the phone. That way, I didn't have to train a new person every time. Three pages may seem like a bit much, but every single contingency was covered. The memo was constantly updated to account for new contingencies. The main focus was that the clients who were calling had some sort of problem that needed to be dealt with. They needed to be assured that their problem was important to us and that we would handle it as soon as possible. My staff was trained to either make the call a priority for me to handle or delegate it to someone else who could handle the problem.

Here's an example:

Staff: "Thank you for calling [the name of my firm], may I help you?"

Caller: "I'd like to speak to [my name]."

Staff: "May I tell him who is calling?"

Caller: "Yes, this is [caller's name]."

Staff: "And what is this pertaining to?"

Stating the name of the firm told the caller immediately that he had the right number. Then the employee asked who was calling and wrote down the message in case I wasn't in the office. The message was logged in the computer system so that it could be passed along to me. If the call was about a new case or client, the staff knew to page me immediately so that the potential client didn't have time to call another lawyer.

Of course, there were many other contingencies and ways to respond to phone messages. Without that memo on how to answer the phone, I would have lost business or wasted valuable time on unproductive phone calls, costing me time and money.

Another element of sales is to always find ways to motivate your sales staff. Do you have employee incentives for high performance levels? Are they motivated to meet their quotas? Have you defined the sales pitch that they are supposed to follow? Role playing is a great way to see what works and what doesn't. You may enlist some of your friends to see if your sales pitch works on them. If they have questions that you can't answer, you need to refine the pitch. Again, you should write an employee manual that sets forth what you want your staff to do and how to do it. You will get more out of your current employees and be much better prepared to train the next salesperson.

Furthermore, you should consider having your existing sales personnel contribute to your sales manual. As they try different methods and strategies, they should make note of what works, what doesn't work, and the reasons why or why not. This will help you fine-tune your sales pitch to maximize sales and profits.

Distribution

How do you plan to get your products to the market? If there is a demand for your products and services, how will you ensure that people will actually be able to buy them?

One of the big concerns of any marketing and promotions plan is how much product you should ship. If you ship too much, you risk putting too much on the shelves and getting a whole bunch of returns. On the other hand, if you don't ship enough product, people will want to buy it and it won't be available. You will lose those sales. So make sure that you have the proper distribution, and coordinate it with advertising, marketing, and promotional strategies. This will insure a maximum of profits with the least amount of loss.

Outsourcing

In some cases, it may be much cheaper to pay others to do certain tasks or create certain products for you. You may not be able to manufacture certain items at your place of business. If you hire another company to manufacture your goods, you need to know what your cost per unit will be. Usually, this is based upon the size of your orders. Obviously, the more you buy, the cheaper the units will be. Furthermore, it may be cheaper to hire a bookkeeper and any number of other employees who work part-time. Then they will be there only when you need them, as opposed to sitting around drawing a paycheck even though there is nothing for them to do.

However, be very careful about sending manufacturing overseas or outside of the country. Those companies may start competing with you once your patents are up. If you are not protected by patent or even copyright, you could be inviting competition or even infringement, and you could lose substantial revenues because of it. Remember, if you have to travel outside of the country to protect your rights, you could end up losing a lot of money.

How Do You Plan to Use Newer Technologies?

Computers are indispensable for just about every single business. The Internet is an unbelievable resource with a wealth of information at your disposal. If you are willing to read a lot, sort through some bad information, and be persistent, you can find just about anything on just about any topic. Caution: Just because you read it doesn't mean it's true! Check as many resources as you can, and then decide on the quality, usefulness, and truthfulness of what you've read.

I don't think I could live without my computers. I use them to keep all of my song lyrics, letters, writings, e-mail addresses, and much, much more. I prefer e-mail to snail mail, so that's how I do most of my correspondence.

Computers allow you to communicate with everyone within your organization. You can keep track of all existing accounts and other client information, spreadsheets for the business, all bank accounts and credit accounts, and much, much more.

I also do all of my Web site design and graphics on the computer. In fact, there isn't much that I do on paper anymore. We even keep all of our recordings on computers. We do our basic tracks and overdubs and then mix them down to two tracks, all on computers. If I need a session player who's not in town, I just FTP him the two-track mix, he records his parts, and then he FTPs them back to me at the studio for mixdown. We even do most of our mastering work on computers, and then we burn our masters to CD and send them off to manufacturing.

You can even buy the equipment to duplicate, print, and shrinkwrap your products in-house, which is much cheaper than sending them out. In short, technology is making the little guy much more competitive with the big guys than ever before. So knowing as much as you can about computers will be extremely beneficial to your career.

As far as your startup business is concerned, you need to think about what type of information technology (IT) infrastructure you are going to use. Do you have more than one computer at your place of business? If you have more than one employee, most likely you will need more than one computer. If so, how are these computers going to be set up so that information can be shared between them? Do you know how to network your computers so that data entry can be retrieved from anywhere on the network? Do you plan to hire a full-time IT person or staff? If so, what will that cost?

Do you have a Web site? Do you even need one? It is my feeling that just about every business must have a Web site. Potential customers can come to your site to find out more about your products and services. The site also informs the general public about your business. It should have information about your entire organization, and more specifically, about what each person does in your organization.

Furthermore, if you are selling something, you need to use the currency of the Internet: credit cards. You will need to set up merchant accounts and an e-commerce section for your site. You may also want to consider something called cgi.bin, which allows your customers to use forms to interact with you. If you spend the time and effort to set up a good computer infrastructure, you will be amazed at how much more quick and efficient your business will be. Just take care of your computers by investing in the right virus protection and always remember to back up your data often, or you could end up losing a lot of very valuable information.

Financial Plan

This is where you actually get down to basic numbers and determine whether your business is going to be a success or a failure. If your financial plan is not met or you get sidetracked by unforeseen expenses or setbacks, you may not be in business for very long. So give this section of your business plan the attention that it deserves. If you are not sure how to do any part of the financial plan, there is a wealth of information on the Internet that can help. Or you can see the last section of this chapter, which points you to a lot of resources.

STARTUP COSTS

Take a good look at the financial side of your business. At this stage in your business plan, you should consider every single cost you'll need to incur to get your business going. Do you need computers? Do you need printers? What types of software do you need to purchase? How much will it be for business cards, rent, electricity, phone, gas, personnel, and whatever else you can think of? Include all filing fees for a corporation or a Limited Liability Company, business license fees, insurance, attorney's fees, trade magazines, business seminars, continuing education, and other expenditures that your business will incur.

Also, how much do you need to pay yourself, your partners, associates, members, or stockholders to make sure that everyone has enough money to live on? The more you know about your potential costs, the better prepared you'll be to pay off those costs and still have money left over to pay yourself and everyone else. Sounds like common sense, but you'd be surprised how many people just go blindly into it.

Include your month-to-month costs and expenses. Then look at what your quarter-to-quarter and year-to-year costs and expenses will be. Write down your total assets, such as equipment, car, etc. These can be used in your balance sheet, but will also serve as collateral or leverage if you need a loan. If you keep track of all this, you'll know whether you will still be in business after the first year.

Your financial plan should include most of the following elements:

► Income statement (P&L)

► Break-even analysis

► Projected cash flow

► Balance sheet

► Paying off debt

INCOME STATEMENT

Your income statement is a very simple report of your business's ability to generate cash. This is sometimes referred to as the *profit and loss statement* or *P&L*. It breaks down the difference between sales and expenses. It should include your revenue, expenses, capital assets minus depreciation, and your cost of goods. By factoring in all of these elements, you can see exactly what you are making or losing every single year. In fact, during the first year of your company, you should figure the P&L monthly and quarterly. Then do it every single year that you are in business. Looking at your P&L over time will give you valuable insight into how you are doing and what you should change, and you'll be able to make projections into the future.

To calculate your P&L, you should look at the following:

► All income generated by your business

► Your cost of goods and services

► Your gross profit margin, which is the difference between revenue and cost of goods and services

▶   Operating expenses, including all overhead and labor costs

▶   Net profit, or the difference between gross profits and total expenses, as well as your business debt and capital

▶   Depreciation, which shows the decrease in value of all your capital assets

▶   Net profit before interest, which is the difference between net profit and depreciation

▶   All interest for both short-term and long-term debts, and in some cases interest owed to the company

▶   The difference between net profit before taxes and interest

▶   All taxes that the business must pay

▶   Profit after taxes, which is the basic bottom line of your company

As you can see, this income statement analysis will show you exactly where your company stands at any given time.

BREAK-EVEN ANALYSIS

The break-even analysis simply tells you when you can expect to break even after all of the expenses, startup costs, etc., have been paid, and when you'll start to see any profits. This is pretty much the easiest part of your business plan to calculate, but it's not necessarily the easiest point for your business to reach. Once you reach your break-even point, you will start to see returns on your investment of time, energy, and money. If you never reach your break-even point, you won't be in business for long. If you can't break even, you will *never* see *any* profit.

PROJECTED CASH FLOW

Cash flow is different from profits. It is a record of the cash that is available at different points in time, as well as how much cash your company needs to meet all of its obligations, when the cash will be available, when it's required, and where you can get it. Your projected cash flow should show the money available when sales are made, when your bills are paid, and when cash is collected. Just because you have cash flow doesn't mean that your business will be successful. Without the appropriate *amount* of cash flow, your company may not be able to keep up with expenses, much less grow. Also, both profits and losses should be carried over to a new column on the cash-flow statement to show the cumulative amount. If you run a loss on your cash-flow statement, you will need additional cash to meet your outstanding expenses.

The cash-flow statement should be prepared on a monthly basis during the first year, on a quarterly basis during the second year, and annually after that. It should include the following:

▶ Cash sales: Income from cash paid for sales

▶ Merchant account sales: Income paid by credit card vendors for the services and products that you provide to your customers

▶ Other income: Income from accounts receivable, investments, interest on loans, and any liquidation of company assets

▶ Total income: The total of all income sources

▶ Materials or merchandise: Either the costs of raw materials for manufacturing, money paid out for inventory, or the equipment or supplies that are used for any services that you offer

▶ Labor costs: The cost of your labor to produce goods and provide services

▶ Overhead: All of your fixed costs and sometimes variable costs to operate your business

▶ Marketing or sales: All salaries, commissions, incentive costs, and any other costs that are attributed to your sales staff

▶ Administrative costs: What must be paid to managers, officers, etc., who actually run the company, including all fringe benefits

▶ Capital costs: All expenses paid out to buy assets for the company

▶ Taxes: All taxes, except withholding for your employees

▶ Total expenses: The sum of all money being paid out

► Cash flow: The difference between total income and total expenses

► Cumulative cash flow: The difference between the current cash flow and the cash flow from the previous period, either monthly, quarterly, or yearly

BALANCE SHEET

This is the benchmark of how your business is doing. It gives anyone who is interested a boiled-down version of the financial strength of the company at any given time, detailing the company's assets and liabilities. This can be done yearly, but in your first year, you should do it on a quarterly or even a monthly basis.

The balance sheet should include the sum of all the company's assets, which are valued at the time that they're acquired. If you start out a business by buying computers, equipment, etc., you need to write down the total cost of these assets. Next, you have to figure out the depreciation that is to be assigned to each asset. Then you can come up with the net assets of the company by calculating the cost of the assets minus their depreciation. The net is what the assets are actually worth to the company.

You may also want to include any capital that is being invested in new construction or other new installations, such as computers. They will be included as a capital work in progress and can be considered assets to the company. If your company has made any cash outlays from surplus cash, that will be considered an investment and should be recorded on the balance sheet. Include your inventory, or goods on hand for sale, as well as any accounts receivable, or money that is owed to the company for products and services.

Other current assets you should include are any assets that can be converted into cash, such as money in the bank. You should include your total debt for both long-term and short-term loans, and financing for any particular assets. Furthermore, you should include all other liabilities of the company, such as all the money that is owed.

If you include all of this, you should be able to ascertain the total net worth of the company at any given time. By looking at your balance sheet, you should be able to find any problem areas. For instance, are your accounts receivable too high? Do you have too much inventory? Are you falling behind on your payments to creditors? If you keep track of all this, you will always know exactly where you stand, and you can address any problem areas before it's too late.

In short, the balance sheet is a summary of your financial information that is broken down into assets, liabilities, and equity. Total assets are the sum of your cash on hand, accounts receivable, and inventory. You should also include long-term assets, such as your office building's equity if you own the building. If you work out of your home, include your office furnishings and equipment minus depreciation. Total liabilities are the sum of accounts payable, accrued liabilities, and taxes you owe. You should also include any long-term liabilities such as mortgages, notes, or long-term loans. To determine your equity, you take the difference between total assets and total liabilities. The more equity you have in your business, the more likely you can obtain a loan or financing for goods or services, such as new construction or other growth.

PAYING OFF DEBT

Debt equity can make or break a business. Most businesses cannot even start out without incurring some type of debt from bank loans, private investors, or worse, credit card debt at a very high interest rate. Furthermore, without loans of some sort, most businesses cannot grow. But the real test is whether you can stay ahead of your debt. If not, your business can't grow or even stay afloat. Make sure that your assets and accounts payable always stay ahead of your debt, or you will be having a Going Out of Business sale very soon.

Conclusion

Having a business plan is no guarantee of success. In fact, many companies with great business plans have failed. But your business plan is your roadmap to success. Remember that nothing lives in a vacuum. Things change constantly, so stay on top of what's going on. Being flexible, creative, persistent, and determined will give you the best advantage.

You don't need to create a complete business plan for everything you do, but you should at least write down the necessary steps to get everything done in a timely fashion. I've found that keeping "punch lists" tells me exactly what has to be done that day, that week, that month, or that year. If you write it down, you are less likely to forget an important task. It also gives you a sense of achievement as you move through all of the required tasks. You always know exactly where you are and what needs to be done next.

Also consider joining as many business associations as you can, to take advantage of decreased costs for insurance and the like. For example, the United States Small Business Administration (www.sba.gov) is an excellent federal resource to help small businesses obtain loans or grants. It also offers a host of educational materials and can assist with a number of problems that face the small businessperson today.

Another great source of information is www.bizstats. com. This site offers analysis of many different types of business throughout the United States. You can see how the business you are planning to enter will fare in today's marketplace.

You can also find a lot of good information at sites like www.entrepreneur.com. They allow you to calculate your cash flow, break-even analysis, monthly profits, investment required, and money at risk. They even have free templates for business plans.

Also, you can buy software applications on-line that can help with every single aspect of writing, implementing, and maintaining a good business plan. One example is Smithfam.com at http://www.smithfam.com/tutorials. html.

It is virtually impossible to list all the elements of every single type of business plan for every type of business. But the basics apply to just about any company.

CHAPTER 4

Advertising, Marketing, Promotion, and Distribution

"Hey, where are all our customers?"

Now that you've got your business set up and ready to go, how are you going to get your business identity out there to the buying public? How do you plan to get customers? How are you going to keep them? If you have produced a CD, how will you get it to the people who will buy it? I don't care what type of business you are in, it's all about marketing and sales. If you aren't selling, you aren't making money.

To get your products or services out there, you need to consider three main strategies: advertising, marketing, and promotion. Once you have these strategies in place, you should move on to distribution.

A lot of people confuse advertising with marketing. Advertising is the description or presentation of a product or service to entice people to buy, support, or approve of it, while marketing is used to introduce products or services to the marketplace. In short, advertising is about telling folks that your product or service is available, while marketing is a much more detailed analysis of how your product or service is perceived in the marketplace. Thus, marketing is a much more long-term endeavor.

Advertising

Figuring out what type of advertising to buy can be a daunting task. You want to get the most return for your advertising dollar, but in some cases you could just be throwing your money away. There are a number of advertising media that you can choose from:

► **Newsprint** is a relatively inexpensive way to reach a broad market in a particular geographic area. Often referred to as "dailies" because they are printed every day, they are good for promoting specials or sales on goods or services for a specific time period. If you want to make a quick announcement or "splash," consider advertising in the dailies. On the other hand, there are a lot of ads in every paper, and most people only read certain parts of the paper. Further, your ad will not have much effect after that day the paper is printed and distributed, as it is usually tossed into the trash.

► **Newsweeklies,** such as local entertainment guides, are another form of newsprint. They basically offer the same advertising capability as dailies, except your ad has a seven-day shelf life. Also, newsweeklies typically attract or even focus on a younger demographic, so they're much better suited to advertising entertainment-based goods and services.

▶ **Magazines** offer a broader reach and can target a more specific audience. Depending on the type of publication, magazines typically have a shelf life of one to six months. However, because magazines offer a broader reach, ad costs are higher than newsprint ad costs. Unless you have a great relationship with a particular magazine, or have pretty deep pockets, magazines may not be your first choice. However, you can target your audience by advertising in trade magazines that may be better suited to promoting your company's image or to giving you credibility in the short term. For example, you may want to advertise your record release with *Rolling Stone*, if you can afford it. Or if you are promoting your new recording studio, you may want to focus on a magazine that caters to people who use recording studios such as *Recording* magazine (www.recordingmag.com) .

▶ **Radio ads** can target a particular region and demographic based upon the station's listening audience, but people are often doing something else when they are listening to the radio. Therefore, they may not pay much attention to your ads. You may have to buy a lot of ads over a long period of time before your message sinks in. Also keep in mind that there are two types of radio advertising. The first type is generated by programmed airplay (such as when a song is added to a station's playlist). The other type is purchased airtime in the form of a commercial spot. Radio is arguably the number one medium for music sales. Buying advertising can be very expensive; it can also be the most effective way of generating sales.

▶ **Television ads** can get a lot of attention, but can be very expensive to make, and they cost a lot to run for a very long period of time. National television advertising is extremely costly, and even local advertising can be beyond the budgets of most businesses. However, you've probably seen a number of national, regional, or sometimes even local advertising campaigns for compilation CDs for certain artists, with an 1-800 number to call. "Have your credit card ready!" These types of campaigns must have some degree of success, or you would not see so many of them.

▶ **Billboards** are a good way to target an audience who's traveling through that particular area, but they can be quite costly and tend to work only for certain products or services. They are best used for nearby restaurants and hotels. Of course, in Los Angeles, Nashville, New York, and other major cities, is it not uncommon to see major artists being promoted on billboards.

▶ **Bus stop and bench advertising** can also be considered. Before you spend your money, you should think about how much traffic will be passing by the ad and how much attention anyone will actually pay to it. But it can work if you place such an ad in an area with a lot of venues where you'll be playing. In fact, I know of some bands that put their name and logo on sheets, backdrops, or even flags, and place them wherever they can to garner more attention. Every little bit of advertising can help, so don't be afraid to try.

▶ **Direct mail** can be a good way to advertise certain products or services, but the print cost and postage can be too costly if the ads don't bring in enough customers. Also, junk mail can sometimes offend people. They might even toss it in the trash without reading it.

▶ **E-mail advertising** can be a very cost-effective way to reach a particular group of people with similar interests. However, you have to be very careful not to spam people, or it could have a negative effect.

▶ **The Yellow Pages** may be the best type of advertising for local businesses. When someone is looking to buy a product, the Yellow Pages may be the first place they start. But these ads are very expensive, and must be purchased for a whole year and paid for by the month. A very small ad can end up costing thousands of dollars, and once it's in print, you can't make any changes.

▶ **Fliers** are tried and true and are always a great idea. They're also relatively inexpensive, but you'll need to do a good deal of work to get them out there. You can pass them out at your gigs to tell fans where your next show is, or paste them everywhere you can in high-traffic areas. You can also put them on the cars of people you know are likely to come to your gigs, such as at bars and fraternity and sorority houses. However, you may have to check with the local government to make sure you don't put up fliers in places you shouldn't.

▶ **Magnets** can be printed with your logo and you can place them on your cars, vans, trailers, rental trucks, etc. They can have the name of your business or band, as well as your Web site address. As you drive around, people will see your magnet ads and it will increase awareness of your brand.

▶ **Restroom advertising** can also be a good idea, if it's cost-efficient. Putting some type of advertising in public restrooms can guarantee a captive audience for a short while, so you can increase awareness of your business or band. You may be able to get away with just putting up fliers in the restrooms of local bars. However, there are some legitimate companies that offer this service, so you should at least check their pricing.

▶ **Remembrance advertising**, or "swag," is probably the most cost-effective and directly targeted advertising that you can buy. It is any item with your logo or other identifying information on it. This includes t-shirts, hats, coffee mugs, travel bags, coasters, beer cozies, and just about any other item that you can slap your logo on. The best thing is that in many cases, you can actually *sell* this type of advertising. The more products you sell, the more people will be exposed to your brand. That is definitely a win-win situation.

Before you advertise in any medium, make sure that it will actually reach the customers you need to reach.

Always remember that repetition is the key to effective advertising, so placing an ad here and there won't get you much business. Usually, consumers won't notice an ad until they have seen it several times. So be persistent.

Also, remember that advertising is only one small part of an overall marketing plan. Make sure to promote your business through public relations, direct mail, special events, promotions, trade shows, brochures, and as many other marketing strategies as you can implement with cost-effectiveness.

All of these methods are very effective ways to advertise, but if you are still a local band, the best way to sell your records and merchandise is to get gigs. And to get gigs, you need a great promotional package (see Chapter 5, "Useful Tips"), and you need to do a whole lot of *cold calling*. You have to get on the phone with various venues, bars, and clubs and be willing to listen to a lot of "no" before you hear a "yes." Pick places that will be receptive to what your band has to offer, and you may be surprised what could happen. Remember, if you persist, you will succeed. Don't get discouraged if you aren't playing the best gigs right away. Continue to hone your act, pick the right songs, and play as much as you can. Also keep in mind that you may be able to help your prospects by getting others to work with you, such as a manager, booking agent, road manager, etc. (See Chapter 11, "Management—Ancillary Services.")

Marketing

Advertising is just one small part of a much bigger picture: marketing. This includes market research, media relations and planning, product placement and pricing, sales strategies, distribution, public relations, and much more. Marketing is about influencing how the consumer feels about your company and its products and services. It's also how you are perceived in the marketplace, from the simple things, like what you wear and how you answer the phone, to broader issues, such as how your products and services affect your clients' lives.

Marketing research can be an excellent way to put your finger on the pulse of the public. It can tell you who is out there and what they are buying. When you gather data from a variety of sources, such as focus groups and the like, you can analyze your findings, define or quantify issues, address those issues, and come up with creative solutions. Then you can expand your marketing base in a scientific way, so that money is not wasted on markets that won't have any interest in your products and services. After all, can you really sell snow cones to Eskimos? Probably not, but you could sell them the syrup. So you probably shouldn't be trying to sell heavy metal records to traditional country music fans, and vice versa. Marketing research allows you to pinpoint your advertising and marketing strategies so that they reach the right people.

Something that you may want to consider when marketing your music is how to establish your identity in the marketplace. You must be able to define your music so that others will know exactly what to expect Of course, many artists don't want to be pigeonholed into a certain musical genre. They try to transcend the boundaries of established tastes. That is all fine and good, but if people don't have any idea what kind of music you play, don't expect them to buy your CD based upon the artwork on the cover or some other whim. You need to describe the basic format that your music fits into, such as rock, pop, hip-hop, or country, so that your CDs can be put in the correct place in the store.

Furthermore, if you are going to stand out from other acts in your genre, you need to figure out where you fit *within* that genre, such as: "An alternative country artist who leans more toward folk and rock styling, interlaced with a country flavoring on vocals, that is not really geared toward traditional country fans." Defining your music helps you focus on the people who are interested in that type of music.

You should also define your existing fan base, as well as the potential fans you want to target. You want to check out the people who come to your shows and figure out who they are, what they are interested in, and what they have in common. Learn what you can about their interests, likes, and dislikes. Learn about their musical tastes, what magazines they read, what Web sites they like to visit, and any other information you could use to create a market profile. When you compile this type of information, it will help you find similar people in your region and in other markets.

In short, try to color inside the lines. Remember, the whole idea is to sell as much as you possibly can. So focus on who is interested in buying your stuff, and don't waste time trying to sell your heavy metal CD at an old folks' home.

BUILD YOUR BRAND

Building your brand is a key aspect of your marketing and promotions. Your brand includes your company's name, logo, marketing concepts, and identity. The best example of a band that built their brand over a long period of time, and basically did it by themselves, was the Grateful Dead. They used what I call the *jam band model.* Since jam band music isn't played much on the radio, a jam band isn't going to sell a lot of CDs through normal retail channels in the beginning stages of its career. In fact, the Grateful Dead only had one charted hit. They put out a lot of albums (which did not sell very well, by the way) and toured constantly until they became one of the biggest live shows. More importantly, everyone has heard of the Grateful Dead. After all, when you hear that someone is a "deadhead," you know exactly what that means. What better example of being branded in the music industry can you think of? The Grateful Dead were a textbook example of how you can break all the rules of music industry and still be extremely successful.

And deadheads weren't all hippies and patchouli oil. Doctors, lawyers, accountants, and businesspeople went to shows and bought CDs and other related merchandise.

Using the jam band model, you can actually make a decent living by constantly touring and selling merchandise, building your fan base one fan at a time. As time goes by, your market share should increase as more and more people start to come to your shows. After all, even if you have a record deal, most of your money will come from touring.

PUBLICITY/MEDIA MARKETING

At some point, you may want to consider hiring a publicist or public relations company. A publicist promotes the public side of your career or business, getting you across to the audience so that you can sell records, merchandise, or whatever. A publicist should be very knowledgeable about the music industry, and should have a lot of solid contacts and relationships with all types of magazines, radio and television stations, newspapers, and other media sources. Good publicists are very personable, and usually will not take "no" for an answer! They will develop a plan with you to make sure that you are constantly in the public eye. They'll promote your music by getting interviews with targeted media outlets, from college newspapers all the way up to appearances on radio, television, and other public events.

Having a representative speak for you to a media outlet or other targeted contact can create a very professional perception. A publicist will be very good at writing effective copy (artist bios, press releases, etc.) for others to use. In short, they will be able to schmooze the right people in the music industry and the news media, saving you the embarrassment of trying to sell yourself to such a tough audience.

The best time to hire a publicist depends on two main criteria: when you have a story to tell, and when you can afford the service. An experienced publicist's fee can range from $500 to $5,000 a month. Until you can afford that, you can always enlist friends, family, or even your fans to help you with this work. But remember, you have to get out there and tell folks about yourself, and hiring a publicist can make that task a whole lot easier. People don't necessarily want to hear you talk about how good you are, but coming from a pro it can be more easily stomached.

Finally, before you hire a publicist, make sure that he is actually interested in what you are doing and believe in your talents. And make sure they have a good reputation in the music industry. Good publicists are worth their weight in gold, and the money you invest will reap serious returns.

PROMOTIONS

If you want to promote your business in the traditional sense, you can always turn to standard promotional practices such as having sales, clearances, onsite radio promotions, and a host of other activities that are designed to draw traffic to your business and create more sales. But a promotion in the music business doesn't necessarily mean that you are having a sales promotion on your CDs. You need to take a proactive approach to getting your music played on the radio so that you can generate record sales. Getting airplay is the best way to sell a whole lot of CDs, unless you find success through the Internet.

So how do you get radio stations to play your music? Well, before we answer that question, we should look at how things used to be and how they are now.

Before 1960, there was blatant *payola*, the paying of cash or gifts in exchange for radio airplay, often by managers, labels, or other interested parties. This was done under the table because it was illegal, but it was happening all the time and just about everywhere. The government finally got wind of it, and Alan Freed, one of the first rock and roll deejays who helped popularize the art form, became the fall guy and was arrested. After that, Congress made payola a crime and imposed some fairly hefty fines. However, the record labels or other parties that were doing it didn't get into trouble. Only the deejays did.

Shortly after that, the record labels figured out a way to get around the anti-payola statutes. They simply hired a third party called an *independent record promoter* to push records to the radio stations. An independent promoter sits behind a desk with a telephone and calls up both major-market and regional stations, pushing records put out by major labels that have large promotion budgets, sometimes in the millions of dollars. Therefore, the only way you are going to get any airplay in a major market is to hire an independent marketer to pay the radio stations for the privilege of playing your music. After all, radio play *is* advertising. It's not called payola, because the money is passed through a third party. To be honest, I'm not so sure that I understand the difference, but that is just the way that it is. Unless we can get Congress to change it, it's going to stay that way for a long time to come.

To make matters worse, there is Arbitron, a radio and Webcast rating service that keeps track of what's going on in particular markets. Program directors look at the Arbitron reports and decide on the best type of music or other content that should be played on certain stations. Unfortunately, Arbitron is solely based upon what is being independently promoted in the major markets. So, you're going to hear the same stuff on your local radio station that somebody else is hearing completely across the country. It's a real catch-22 for anyone who's trying to get their record played in just about any market, whether in larger cities or in Smalltown, U.S.A.

I'm sure you have wondered why you don't hear very much variety of music on the radio. You hear the same stuff over and over again. The radio term for this is *familiarity*. Through years of callout research, audience testing, and other focus group studies, radio stations have determined that people tend to stay tuned longer to stations that play familiar music. Furthermore, the longer a listener stays tuned to a particular station, the greater the *time spent listening* or *TSL*. Radio advertising rates are directly determined by a station's potential reach and its listeners' TSL. The higher the audience numbers, the higher the station's advertising rates.

Unfortunately, you will find that this is similar to booking your band at certain types of venues. It's very simple: People want to hear what they are familiar with, so most bands are forced to play cover songs if they expect to get rebooked at any of these venues. You may be able to squeeze in an original song or two throughout your set of covers, but that's it. Of course, if are getting some airplay for your original music, then you can play more of your own songs.

What really bothers me the most is that you hear the same song by the same band being played time and time again until you just get completely sick of it and the band. How is that any incentive to go out and buy the CD just so that you can hear that same song even more? This is really nuts when you consider that radio stations don't own the radio airwaves. We do. The licenses and frequencies are owned by citizens of the United States and controlled by the federal government, which is supposed to be "we the people." And yet "we the people" have no control over it. Big business does. And that doesn't bode well for the independent record company that is trying to bring something new and different to the market, or for John Q. Public, who's tired of being bombarded with the same homogenized corporate swill on the radio.

There is an organization that you should check out if you are interested in such matters. It's called the Future of Music (www.futureofmusic.org/news/radioissuesstatement.cfm).

In January 2000, the FCC approved low-power FM radio services. This means new stations can apply for licenses that will allow for more localized services that support the public interest. However, this merely strengthens the existing laws, which state that all television and radio stations are solely for furthering the public interest. Unfortunately, this is only a band-aid where major surgery is needed. The only interests that are actually being served are those of big business and the people behind the scenes counting their money. Furthermore, how can these low-power stations possibly compete with higher-power stations that have all of the money and commercial advantages?

To the federal government's credit, the FCC has held a number of meetings in various parts of the country, where consumers and others are getting a chance to voice their opinions about radio and television not serving the public interest as they are supposed to do under the current laws. People are concerned with profanity and violence on television, as well as homogenized music and information over the radio airwaves. Meanwhile, media conglomerates such as Clear Channel are making sweeping statements about how localism is the focus of their radio stations, and that if they don't cater to the public, listeners should just turn the dial. Unfortunately, the public doesn't have as much input as they should, and there aren't many stations that do cater to the public interest because they can't compete financially with these media conglomerates.

Despite this, you should not give up hope. Take a proactive approach and write your representatives and senators. The address for all representatives is:

United States House of Representatives
Washington, D.C. 20515

The address for all senators is:

United States Senate
Washington, D.C. 20510

Make sure the representative or senator is in your voting district, and keep your letter short and to the point. Longer letters will receive less attention. Make sure to sign your letter, so your representative will have permission to forward your concerns to the proper agency. If enough people with similar concerns get together and make enough waves, the law can be changed in time.

If you are concerned about specific legislative action, such as a particular bill, you can find out about your representative's position on the matter or see how he has voted on other bills. The Library of Congress has a service called THOMAS that allows you to do this. Unfortunately, the bureaucratic process is slow, and often things just won't go your way. I know from personal experience that trying to get things done in Washington can be very much like trying swim upstream in class five rapids.

Fortunately, if you can't wait for the laws to change in your favor and you're willing to take a proactive approach to building your market share, now you can reach the entire world without having to rely on radio airplay. Your new avenue is the Internet.

INTERNET MARKETING

I am a huge fan of the Internet and all of the ways it can help you in your day-to-day life. It's an incredible tool that can allow you to reach the entire world, right from your home.

Build a Web Site

The first thing you should do is build a Web site. Any business that is not on the Web is falling behind. Fortunately, building and posting a site has never been easier. There are a number of places where you can get a free templates. Simply add your information and you have a Web site. These companies also offer free Web hosting. In some cases, you may even be able to get your own personalized domain name. If not, it doesn't cost much to get one.

There are also a number of applications that allow you to build a site quickly and easily, such as Front Page and Dreamweaver. Most of these applications are WYSIWYG (What You See Is What You Get) editors, which allow you to build a site without having to read and write code. They work very much like word processing software, and the learning curve is not that steep. Then, you can find very affordable hosting for your site, and even set up e-commerce so that you can sell your products on line. There is no better time that now to start learning about this incredible opportunity.

Once you have your site up and running, you should think about how to point people to it. Unless somebody already has your specific URL (uniform resource locator), he's not just going to stumble on your site by accident. Your Internet marketing plan should start with getting the highest search engine placement you can. The main search engine that you should be concerned with is Google (google.com). There are other search engines out there, too, and you want to make sure that you are listed with them. But that can be a very daunting task because there are so many. A number of different companies will list your site with these search engines, and they don't cost that much.

But before you do any of this, you need to make your site search engine–friendly. The first step is to use meta tags, which are HTML (Hypertext Markup Language) tags embedded in your Web site. Since meta tags are embedded in the HTML code, browsers don't see them. They provide keywords and a description of your site's content so search engines can find it. The best keywords describe your business, your location, what you are selling, etc. So choose your keywords carefully. The better your keywords, the more traffic you will get.

The next step is to go through your entire site to make sure that you don't have any external or internal blind links. An *internal blind link* is a link to another page on your site that doesn't exist, and an *external blind link* goes to another site that doesn't exist.

There are a number of different tricks and techniques for getting the most out of search engines, and the rules are always changing as the Internet changes. If you need more information, do a Google search for "search engine optimization."

One of the easiest ways to promote your site is to include it in your e-mail signature. The signature line should include your name, company name, address, phone number, and URL. Then the people you e-mail can check out what you do, who you work for, and what you are selling.

Finally, you should take every opportunity to drive traffic to your site. Make sure to advertise it at every single performance. Take lots of pictures at your gigs and post them, because that will drive more traffic to your site. People like to show pictures of themselves to their friends, family, business associates, etc. A digital camera will more than pay for itself in hits to your site. And the more traffic you get, the more CDs and swag you'll sell. You might also hold drawings or giveaway specials for your visitors, or any other promotional schemes that can drive traffic and increase your exposure.

Start a Fan Club

If your band is playing lots of live shows, that's your best opportunity to interact with your fans. Ask folks to sign up for your mailing list. Have a sign-up sheet at every gig. That way you can stay in touch with your fan base and tell them about upcoming gigs, new releases, and all of the swag you're selling. You may be surprised when they start showing up at your shows.

You should also consider doing a newsletter to tell fans what's going on with your band. This will keep your name and brand out there.

Internet Promotions and Publicity

Finally, you should make the most of the Internet by doing a lot of promotions and publicity. There are a number of e-zines (Internet magazines) that will review your record or even interview you. It's a great way to promote your music to a specific fan base. You can place your music on a number of services that will give you direct feedback from listeners. There are services where you can sell MP3s and CDs. Look for e-mail newsletters that will expose you to a broader range of potential customers. If you spend some time researching what is out there, you will be surprised at what you find.

POSTCARDS

If you can't seem to get into the on line thing, or even if you do have a site, fan club, and newsletter, you can always take the low-tech approach. You can do some "old school" marketing and advertising by sending out postcards to your fans or clients. Tell them what's going with your band or business, and let them know that you appreciate their interest in your products or services.

Distribution

Now that you've recorded your CD and you are starting to build a fan base, what do you do next?

Let's assume that you are selling quite a few of your CDs at gigs, and you're getting some airplay at local radio stations and college stations. You've gotten some good reviews in local newspapers and college papers, and you've even gotten a write-up in a magazine or two. There's a good buzz going on about your band. But what happens if people go to their local music store and can't find your CD? You just lost a sale.

You don't ever want someone to go into a store to buy your CD and not be able to find it. Nor do you want to manufacture a bunch of CDs that just gather dust in your closet, or that are placed in retail outlets and don't sell, only to be returned for full credit. This costs you money and can devastate the best of promotional plans. You need to set up some sort of distribution system to get your products to the buying public.

There are a number of ways to distribute your products. One of the first things you should do is put your CDs on consignment at your local record store. This is quite simple, and you can do it yourself. If you have a good relationship with a store, you may be able to get them to display your CD in a prominent place. If you know the manager of the store, he might even sell your CDs and let you keep all of the profit. If not, you can at least sell them at wholesale prices just like the big boys, so that the store will make a little profit as well. Just make sure your CDs have a uniform product code (UPC) so that the store can log them for tax and inventory purposes.

Another way to increase sales is to market your CDs to as many non-music stores as you can. If you get your CDs placed as impulse items in point-of-purchase displays at local convenience stores, truck stops, and the like, you'll sell a lot more CDs.

You can also try to find some type of regional distribution deal through larger music store chains. However, these types of stores are much less likely to carry your CD unless you're going to be playing near that local outlet, or unless you have a regional following there. These stores don't want a bunch of CDs just gathering dust and taking up space, so make sure you have some type of marketing plan in place to get exposure in that region. The more exposure and reputation you build, the more traffic you'll drive to those stores for your CDs. If you build a good regional sales base, you can start looking for a national distribution deal.

Never forget that *you don't have to wait for a record deal to make this happen*. You can do it yourself if you make the effort and never, ever quit.

Summary

With a good advertising, marketing, and promotional plan, you can grow your business, your brand, and your market share. You'll be surprised at what you can do with a little creativity, know-how, and good old-fashioned hard work. If you can plan for growth and get the right people to help you out, you could find yourself with a host of new customers. You just have to get out there and find them!

Of course, it's difficult to stand out amongst the hordes of artists out there. But if you follow the ideas laid out in this chapter, you can do it. Get busy, though, because it won't just happen. There's no such thing as a magic wand that will make you a star, and nobody is going to come knocking at your door. You have to be proactive and do anything and everything you can to increase your chances of success.

CHAPTER 5

Useful Tips

"The harder you work, the luckier you'll get."

Now that you've honed your act, set up your business, done your business plan, and developed marketing, promotions, and distribution strategies, what other things can you do to get ahead of the competition? I've met tons of people who are trying to make it in the music industry, and the ones who have the best chance of making it are doing a whole lot more than just writing songs, doing the odd showcase, sending in demos, or whatever. Some of these simple, effective ideas will take very little capital investment, but can pay off in the long run.

Work Hard and Then Harder

There is no substitute for hard work. If you want to rise above your competition, you'll have to work harder than they do. The good news is that hard work doesn't cost anything. It just takes a lot of time, which we all should have plenty of. And if we don't, we had better *make* the time if we want to be successful. Furthermore, you will find that when you are working long hours, it's really hard to spend a whole lot of money, much less have the time to get yourself in trouble.

I've seen so many talented people who seemed to have everything come so easy to them. But you can bet that they have put their time in one way or another, because there really are no overnight successes. People who seem to make it overnight actually work tremendously hard for years. And then suddenly, like magic, they get noticed and everything just falls into place. Next thing you know, you are seeing them all over the place. Of course, there are some exceptions to the rule, especially some of the artists who break out at a very early age. They just happened to have the right level of natural talent and marketability, and were in the right place at the right time. But luck can be an elusive thing. I think you should always try to make your own luck. And it's my personal belief that the harder you work, the luckier you will get. So if you're going to lay your money and your time on the table, don't you want to improve your odds?

If you're a musician, practice, practice, and practice some more. If you're a songwriter, write, write, and write some more. If you're an artist, sing and entertain, sing and entertain, and then sing and entertain some more. Whatever your field, the more you work at it, the better you'll get. The more you learn, the more you will realize how much more there is to know. Each answer usually brings home 10 new questions. If you are averse to hard work, you may want to consider another field. Unless you are blessed with an extraordinary amount of natural talent, you won't stand much chance against the vast numbers of extraordinarily talented people who are willing to work harder than you.

You'll probably need some type of day job to pay the bills, which only leaves time after work to push your music career forward. So at the end of the day, psych yourself up for that extra push so you can get things done. If you are too tired to practice or to sit down and write a song, you will fall behind everybody else who is willing to put in the extra time or effort. Give yourself little milestones to achieve. Continue to work toward those goals, and in time you will find that they are much closer than you think. If you just say that you always *wanted* to do this or that, but don't do anything to achieve those goals, you can rest assured that you never will. Nobody is waiting on you to do anything.

You can bet that if you get any type of deal, you'll be working extremely long hours with no end in sight. To give you some idea of what it takes, let's say you get a major record deal. What will your typical day be like?

In some instances, just signing a deal doesn't mean that you go directly into the studio to record your first album and then hit the tour bus to promote it. Some artists go straight into development and pre-promotion. This means that their day is filled with writing appointments, or poring over thousands of songs to find the right material to record. They work on their music constantly. They make demo after demo, only to have them rejected by their record label. They may even go out across the United States and Europe to make radio appearances before their record is out, so that their songs will get airplay. They have appointments with the different department heads at the label to work on their marketing and promotional plans. They play as many engagements as they can to hone their act, along with lots of long rehearsals between gigs. They have lunch appointments and dinner engagements, attend showcases, make appearances on radio and television, and so on. In short, they are busy as they can possibly be and eighteen-hour days are very common.

After that, things *really* pick up. There isn't any downtime until they attain a good deal of success. They go directly into the studio and begin working on their record, which can take weeks and weeks of incredibly long days. When they finish their record, they immediately begin rehearsals for their tour. At the same time, they still have to go to lunch and dinner appointments, interviews, meetings with the label, and much, much more.

Then they start their tour. A typical day on tour can start very early in the morning with radio or television appearances, and that can go on all day. In fact, they are sometimes required to do so many interviews that their voices start to break up, and they still have to sing that night! They have to eat, but usually they have lunch appointments with some bigwig or radio personality in that town. They may have to stop and do an in-store or two at local record stores. They may have to make appearances at any number of events and make lots of phone calls to people they didn't have time to meet with, etc., etc.

Next they have sound check, and then maybe a "business" dinner with more VIPs, before the show. After the show they have a couple of hours of meet-and-greets with their fans and others. Then they get back on the bus, go to the next city, and the entire process starts all over. This is repeated for the next record, and the one after that, and so on, unless they somehow don't break the first record big and they get dropped by their label.

If you are a songwriter and you want to write the next big hit or even the next standard, you need to get a publishing deal. You will be required to turn in at least 12 songs a year as a minimum commitment, and every single song has to be acceptable to the publisher. They can't be some songs that you just throw together to meet the terms of your contract. After all, aren't you trying to write hits? Isn't that what your publisher is expecting from you? You will have to be writing all the time.

Furthermore, where are you going to get all those ideas? I know a number of songwriters who write over 100 songs a year just to meet their minimum writing commitment. They have extremely long days, making it to all of their writing appointments and demo sessions. After that, they go out and hit writers' nights, music business functions, and all the happening restaurants and bars. In short, when they're not writing, they're constantly networking to get their songs cut. I know a lot of writers who were able to get their own cuts for their number-one hits, even though they were in a publishing deal.

A publishing deal gives you a lot of financial help and other resources, but that doesn't mean these writers rely on their publisher to pitch all of their songs or to get them cuts. In fact, just because you are writing all the time to get that next cut and hopefully that next number-one hit, don't think you can rest on your laurels and your publisher will get you the next cut. You have to get out there and meet people, see the new up-and-coming artists who can record your songs, and establish relationships with artists, managers, and the like. To achieve any measure of success, you have to keep your name out there as long as you possibly can!

In order to keep getting ideas for so many songs and keep that well of creativity flowing, songwriters have to read constantly. They read books, magazines, newspapers, and just about anything else they can. Almost all of my most successful friends, no matter what field they are in, read several books a month. They make time for reading before going to bed, or when there is other downtime during travel. The good writers, the pro writers, are usually very well read. Reading will help you keep that creative well from drying up, and books are free and plentiful at the public library.

If you are an engineer, producer, studio owner, or all three, your day will start out with studio sessions very early in the morning that can often last long into the night. There are plenty of engineers out there, and the competition is stiff. If you are in demand, you will be extremely busy, moving from project to project. If you are lucky, you may be the house engineer and get to work on a bunch of different projects. However, if you are not busy, you have to keep your name out there and constantly look for that next project.

Also, you should keep in mind that even if you're popular now, someday you may not be in demand. Your gig may only last for a few weeks, so you had better keep working the phones and going out to meet the new bands and their management teams, who may be looking for an engineer for their next project.

If you are a producer, you have to keep your name out there and constantly look for the next act that will make your career. You have to spend an inordinate amount of time in pitch meetings and a host of other appointments, and you have to go out all the time to "check your traps." That is, you need to make sure that you are on the tip of everyone's tongues when they are looking for a producer for that next hit project.

As for studios, there are tons of them out there. To keep ahead of studio payments for the latest gear, a studio has to block out as much time as possible. This can often mean keeping the studio booked day and night. In fact, if a studio is going to keep up with all the latest and greatest expensive gear, it can't afford to be idle for any time at all.

Obviously, with so much to do and so little time, it helps to be extremely organized. Even that takes time! Getting and staying organized increases efficiency, but it takes planning and lots and lots of precious time.

Be Organized

There is no substitute for organization. In fact, if you are not organized you will never be able to keep up with all of the tasks you need to attend to on the road to success. The day is just not long enough, and days turn into weeks, weeks into months, and next thing you know the year is gone. If you can't maximize the use of your time and be able to keep up with everything you need to do, you will inevitably fall behind or, worse, end up sacrificing the quality of your work just to make your deadlines.

DAY TO DAY

Getting in the habit of being extremely organized will reap big benefits in the long run. Remember when I told you to write down all your information in Chapter 3, "Making a Business Plan"? This will help you get your day-to-day stuff accomplished in a much more efficient manner. Keep a *punch list* of all the things that you have to do each day. That way you can look at the tasks that need to be accomplished instead of keeping them all in your head. Take care of the most important things first, and then move on to other tasks. All the while, keep referring to your list to make sure that you are not wasting any time by forgetting something or getting sidetracked.

I usually carry around a pen and 3×5 note cards so I don't have to keep my dayplanner with me everywhere I go. When my next great idea comes to me, or some other task that may have slipped my mind, I write it down. Later I transfer it to my dayplanner, my song notes, my computer, or wherever they need to go.

Another really handy device is a small cassette recorder. I keep one in my car and one next to my bed, in case I have an epiphany while I'm driving down the road or just before I fall asleep. This way I don't let that great idea slip by, but I don't cause a wreck trying to write while driving. Also, I can't tell you how many times I've been able to see things more clearly right before I fall asleep. When it's dark and very quiet, that's when I come up with a solution to a problem or have some great idea just appear to me. If I don't get it down right then and there, in the morning I'll remember that I *had* a great idea, but I won't be able to remember what it was!

Each night I go through all of my notes and listen to my cassette recorder to make sure that I'm completely organized and everything is in its place. That way when I get up in the morning, all I have to do is get the coffee on, look at my schedule, and get to work. By figuring out my next move before I even go to bed, I am much more efficient in the morning and don't have to sit around thinking about what I need to do next.

WEEK TO WEEK

Once you start keeping track of what you need to do from day to day, it's easy to start keeping track of what's happening week to week. And you will be amazed at how quickly the time will pass, especially as you get older. By tracking what's going on from week to week, you can be much more efficient with your time. Plan out which activities or duties should come first and what can be left for later on. It's all about *economy of motion*. This was taught to me by a surgeon who seemed slow compared to all of the young doctors around him. But he was actually quicker than all of them put together, because he had planned out exactly what he was going to do and never wasted a single step. Furthermore, he never had to repeat any process due to sloppy work, because he did it right the first time! If you're going to do something, why not do it right and get it out of the way once and for all?

MONTH TO MONTH

This is not much different than day-to-day or week-to-week planning. The only difference is that you don't have to plan menial tasks and other simple things. By keeping a weekly/monthly calendar of the very important things you need to accomplish, you won't forget about that important meeting because it's booked a month or so in advance.

Furthermore, if you keep a monthly schedule, you can look back at the end of the year to see how you've progressed and how efficiently you've used your time. The more data you have written down, the more data you can analyze, and that is a good thing. You will get a feeling of accomplishment when you look at your monthly calendar to see all of the things that you managed to get done. Also, analyzing monthly data will make you much more prepared to look at quarterly data that may be required for your business plan or personal goals.

Finally, if you are in a sole proprietorship and work for yourself, you need to pay your taxes quarterly in advance, so it just makes good sense to keep up from month to month.

YEAR TO YEAR
You will be surprised at how quickly a year can pass when you are really busy working. So be prepared for each of your year-to-year business goals. You have to file taxes yearly, so make sure you plan for that. If you split up your tax work into quarters, you will have less work to do at year's end. You may have a lease that's up in a year that you don't want to lose, so speak with your landlord to see if you can renew it. You may have corporate papers that must be filed, annual dues for memberships, and any number of business tasks. If you know that these expenses are coming up, you can plan for them and come up with the cash. I realize that most of this is just plain old common sense, but you would be surprised how many people forget about these simple steps, only to have them come back to haunt them. If you write down these important things and keep that information organized, you are much less likely to forget about it. When you are very busy, it's easy to get distracted.

Furthermore, if you write things down but then forget where you put your notes, you are going to be in trouble. So get organized, and keep up with it every day. You will be very glad you did. No more last-minute scrambling just to take care of stuff that could have been done a year ago! Never put off until tomorrow what you can get done today.

Look to the Future to Keep Working

If you've been in the music business for very long, you know that many jobs are transient at best. In fact, most jobs as a musician only last for a day or a week. You may be lucky enough to work for a music company, or in some field where you are guaranteed to have a full-time job with lots of job security. But even then, the turnover at record labels and other jobs in the music business is incredible.

So I suggest that you continually book jobs or gigs as far into the future as you possibly can. If you have a permanent job, always be looking for that next best thing, and never assume that your job will last forever. Be prepared, and keep your options open. Otherwise, you may find yourself out of work and out of money.

As far as booking is concerned, most places book their calendars as far in advance as they can. That's one less thing they have to deal with, because finding a good band on short notice can be a daunting task. So always make sure to fill up your calendar with gigs. If you are turned down for a gig, don't burn that bridge. Let them know that they can always call you if someone cancels a show. If you're offered somebody else's cancelled gig but you're already booked, you can try to get one of your friends to cover it. Remember, the more you help out other people, the more likely that they will help you later on.

Go to Where the Action Is

When you're starting out in any business, you should move to where the business is happening. I once wrote an article for *Gibson Guitar* magazine about this very subject. If you want to make it in Nashville, you have to get in line behind everyone else who's moved there. If you want a record deal or a full-time job in the music business, nobody's going to come knocking on your door.

That means moving to a major metropolitan area with a lot of opportunities. Of course, if you are in a band, you may not be able to afford to move the whole band to a big city. But think about this: It's rare for a band to get discovered playing at a club in some small town, because record company executives tend to look for talent in big cities. Of course, there are talent scouts out there looking for acts all the time. But you never know if they are going to be in a town on the exact night that you are playing there or if you are having one of your best nights.

You have to pay to play and be present to win....

Do Your Homework

Let's say you've decided to really pursue a career in the music business, and you've moved to where the action is. Now you need to do your homework. This is so important, but so many people miss it. They think that someone is just going to realize how great they are, come knock on their door, and give them a deal, but that's not going to happen. Once you decide you're going to be a songwriter, musician, or whatever, you have to seek out your own opportunities.

If you are looking to get some kind of recording or writing deal, make a list of every record label and publishing company you are interested in. Find out the key players at those companies, as well as all of the acts and writers they've signed. If your act is similar to another act on that label, it's doubtful that they will sign you, so focus your energy somewhere else. If you're looking for a publishing deal, seek out the other writers at the company and get to know them. Remember, they will *not* knock on your door.

Be persistent, but be patient. Don't expect anybody to just offer you a deal out of the gate. Take your time and get to know the right people. Remember, they already have a gig, and they see folks every day who are trying to get a deal. Don't expect too much too quick. Success takes time.

Join as many organizations as you possibly can, and get to know people in those organizations. (For a list of organizations you might wish to join, refer to Chapter 17.) Attend a lot of functions, and you will find out who is doing what. Again, I can't stress enough the importance of doing your homework. Find out who works at which label and what their jobs are. This information is readily available and free *if you do your homework*. It can really help break the ice when you meet these folks. You can compliment them on their recent accomplishments, ask questions about their jobs, and make them feel like it's not about *you* but about *them*. Find out if they have families or hobbies, and ask about them. The more you can get people to talk about themselves, the more they'll like you. Everybody likes to be complimented and made to feel important. It's a win-win situation that's the cornerstone to good business practices. Truly successful people are great at this.

Finally, if you are no good at remembering names, you had better practice and *get* good at it. For instance, when you meet someone, always repeat his name back to him. "It's nice to meet you, Mr. Big." Use word association or other mnemonic devices to remember his name and where he works. I've seen people who are exceptionally good at this, and one of them is Garth Brooks. He can walk into a room and remember everyone's name, which goes a long way to ingratiating himself with people. I'm sure that this played a strong role in his success.

Make Yourself Memorable

If you keep in mind how valuable other people's time is, you will ingratiate yourself with them and make yourself more memorable. There are a number of things that you can do to achieve this.

BE GRATEFUL

Get a box of plain and simple "Thank You" cards, and handwrite notes on the inside to thank people for their time. After you have a meeting with someone important or they do anything at all for you, send a simple thank you note. It only takes a little time to write a few words like, "I appreciate you meeting with me, because I know how important your time is. I look forward to seeing you again!" No matter how high up the food chain people are, they still like to feel appreciated.

When you send a thank you note, try to stay away from mentioning any business, because it's supposed to be personal. It's about showing your appreciation when someone has done you a favor.

You should also think about buying some cheap blank notes to send to people. If you meet somebody and he gives you his card, write a little note like, "Nice to meet you. I look forward to speaking with you again soon." This shows that you are willing to take time out of your day to do something nice for someone else.

I can't tell you how many times I have had people in my office who were only concerned about getting what they could out of me. They didn't even realize that I was giving them some of my time, and that they didn't have to break out the old checkbook and actually pay me. The few hopefuls who thanked me for my time were the ones who stood out. What harm does a "thank you" do? People remember that stuff, and a thoughtful note never looks contrite or calculated. Nor is it ever unwanted amongst the pile of bills and such that comes through the mail every single day. If you spend 50 cents on a card and a postage stamp, you will make yourself memorable to those who are in a position to help you out.

Another good idea is to send out Christmas cards to people you have a fairly good relationship with. This simple gesture is a good way to keep yourself in the minds of the people who are important to you, and it's usually appreciated. Also remember that the people who make decisions about record deals often get started at the first of the year.

Finally, if somebody goes out of his way to help you out, send him a simple present. It doesn't have to be expensive, but you can bet that it will be appreciated. It can be a local trinket such as a coffee mug from your state or anything that is somewhat personal such as a handmade item or a t-shirt. A subscription to a magazine is also a great idea. That person will be reminded of your gift 12 times a year, and it'll cost you less than $20.00. This will make you a lot more memorable than the rest of the folks who think they actually *deserve* an important person's time.

BE PROFESSIONAL

Be a business professional by being on time, courteous, and grateful, and by using all of these tools and more. People in the recording industry act like they're in it for the love of music, but it's all about making a buck. Sure, they *do* love music, but love doesn't pay the bills. Look for the win-win situation in all your business dealings, so that both parties walk away happy. Always remember that anyone who is in a position to pay you money wants all he can get for his buck. If you know how he makes money, you're going to have an advantage over everyone else who's trying to get a deal.

Of course, there are lots of artists and writers who don't do any of this and still are very successful. But I've met thousands of people in this business, and most of the ones who make it use every possible angle to realize their dreams of success.

CHECK YOUR EGO AT THE DOOR

I've seen all types of people come and go, and musicians are my favorite type of people to be around. They're creative and funny, and we have something very much in common: music. But musicians are notorious for their egos. I guess it's kind or hard not to have a huge yet fragile ego if you lay your heart out in front of lots of people. When you're trying to get a deal, check that ego at the door. I've had quite a few clients who had a good shot at getting a deal, but ended up blowing it by putting out too much attitude.

Here's a story: A really talented artist had managed to get a meeting with the head of a major label for the final negotiations of a contract. The label head asked if the artist was willing to wear a hat, and the artist said he was *not* going to be a hat act. The label head promptly thanked the artist for coming and ushered him out the door. The artist never heard back from the label again. He's probably selling guitar strings at some music store or playing gigs at a local bar.

What the artist didn't get was that the label wasn't going to *force* him wear a hat. In fact, it wasn't about the hat at all. It was about the artist being open to suggestions and easy to work with. Most companies don't want to deal with people who aren't willing to listen to advice.

BE A TEAM PLAYER

Be open to criticism, be ready for direction, be completely honest about your willingness to change, be open to new and different ideas… in other words, be a team player. If you are going to work with a major publisher or label, a whole lot of people are going to have a great deal to say about which direction you should take. That doesn't mean you have to become a puppet, but you need to be willing to compromise. Major companies want to mold talent into what will be the most marketable, and therefore the most profitable. So keep in mind that it's not just about you, it's about you *and* the company using your talent and your music in the best possible way.

Get Business Cards

As soon as possible, you need to get some business cards. This is just one small tool that tells people you are serious about your business. Whether it's simple and clean or very graphically oriented and cool-looking, be ready at all times to pop it out. It's your calling card. Napkins are best used for writing songs or other ideas, not your contact information. Even though many people will just lose your card or throw it away, that shouldn't stop you from giving it to them.

Make sure to include all of your contact information. If you are just starting out in the business, the more ways you give people to contact you, the better. Pager numbers, cell phones, Web site addresses, and e-mail addresses are all really good ideas. The last thing you want is to hear about missing an opportunity just because someone couldn't get in touch with you.

Of course, if you don't want to be bothered at certain numbers or places, you can get social cards printed. They can contain just your name and an e-mail address you have set up so that people won't be able to contact you in any other way. You're filtering who can contact you, and you can choose whether or not to get back to them. You don't want to give out your address to someone you don't know anything about. There are a lot of people in the music business who are trying to take advantage of the unsuspecting.

Put Together a Professional Promo Kit

Your promo kit is critical when you are trying to get a deal, so make sure you spend enough time and money on it. In many cases, your promotional package will be your first impression to someone in the music industry, so it has to be as professional as possible. Take into account that whoever is viewing your package has seen hundreds, if not thousands, of promo kits. So don't expect to wow them with a huge package that proves you're the greatest thing since sliced bread. Keep it simple, lean, and clean. You really only need a short biography, a good picture, an example of your music, and maybe some sort of press information.

Put all of that in a nice binder that can be kept together easily, and make sure that your name, address, phone, and other contact information are printed on everything that will be removed from the package, including the cassette case *and* the cassette, or the CD case *and* the CD. I've received lots of packages, and sometimes I've lost the CD cover but had the CD, or vice versa. Even if I thought the music was great, sometimes I couldn't get in touch with the artist because there was no contact information on the CD.

You should also have your material copyrighted before you send anything to anyone. I'm not talking about a "poor man's copyright" (mailing a copy of a song back to yourself), but an actual copyright Form PA from the Library of Congress. If you are sending actual masters, you may want to consider an SR copyright as well. (For more information about Form PA and SR, see Chapter 6, "Intellectual Property.")

Also remember that you may have to send out hundreds of these packages, and some will just be tossed aside. Don't spend too much money on them.

If you'd like the recipients to return your materials if they're not interested, make sure they have a return policy. If they do, include a self-addressed stamped envelope with your submission. Some people would send material to my law office, and not only did they expect me to spend my time reviewing their package for free, but they actually expected me to return their materials to them at *my* expense! This was inconsiderate of my time and money. I apologize to any prospective clients who may have done that, but I wasn't about to incur costs on their behalf with absolutely no hope of any return.

I always reviewed the material when I had the time, and if the act was good enough, I would write them or call them back. I received a lot of material every day, and 99% of it was not commercially exploitable enough for me to put my name behind it. Some firms or music companies might correspond with you for free and consider it a cost of business, but I feel that you should be much more considerate of other people's time and money. Remember, you are the one who's asking for something, so please don't expect people to go out of their way to help you. Make it easy on them.

Your biography should be short and simple. It should include a brief description of your experience in the music industry, and maybe some personal history, such as your age and where you are from. Stay away from hyperbole or overstating your ability. Don't use language such as "the greatest singer you've ever heard," "the best act in the country," or "the most phenomenal musician alive today." Be humble. Your music will speak volumes about your talent. (Besides, it can be a real turnoff to hear someone talk about how great he is, when in fact he has a whole lot more work to do.) Let the listeners make up their own minds about your abilities. If you put yourself in front of the right people, they'll know whether your music is right for their needs. If you say that you are "the most incredible musician ever" or some other hyperbole, you will end up being the office joke of the day.

Don't include all of the places that you have played or other irrelevant information. Nobody really cares if you've played the best bar in your town. If you have any press from a newspaper or other reputable publication, you can include that. But don't overdo it. If your music is good enough, the record label will handle your entire public relations and other matters, and your promo kit will no longer have any significance whatsoever.

As for your picture, try to get a professional photographer so that you will be seen in the best possible light (no pun intended) and at the best angle. A picture is worth a thousand words, and a bad picture will speak volumes about your professionalism. One 8×10 color or black and white picture will suffice. If anyone requests more pictures, you can send them later. Remember, it's a numbers game, and you may have to send out hundreds of packages over a period of years. Sending one photo will help keep your costs low and won't waste valuable photographs that could be used for other packages.

The most important thing is the music you submit. That's the truest representation of your work. The better your music sounds, the more likely you are to get a deal. Take some of the music you've recorded and play it on your favorite stereo system, in your car, or wherever you listen to music the most. Then listen to some recordings that have been done professionally or that you've heard on the radio. Do they have a similar sound quality—not just the singing and musicianship, but the quality of the recording? If not, the recipient will definitely take that into consideration. Sending the best-quality recordings is going to increase your odds of impressing someone.

Think about who is going to receive your package, and then plan accordingly. Are you a songwriter who has no interest in an artist deal, but is only trying to get a publishing deal? Include your best songs, performed by the best singer you can find and recorded at the highest quality possible. You may even want to include samples of all your work, as well as copies of your lyrics and any pertinent information about copyright and co-writers' credits.

Also consider whether you should send just a guitar/vocal or keyboard/vocal recording, because some people won't want to hear a heavily produced version of your song. They sometimes prefer to have a stripped-down version so that they can use their own experience and imagination to envision the song's potential. If you already know your stuff is going to be heard by a particular person, it may be best to ask what he prefers. Does he want full-blown demonstration recordings, simple guitar/vocals, or both? Always be ready to provide him with what he is asking for. This is not only a time saver, but very professional.

If you are going for an artist deal, you only want to send three songs that are the best representation of your music. It's a good idea to include a ballad, a mid-tempo song, and an up-tempo song. Anything more is asking too much of the person receiving your package. Trust me, if he likes what he hears, he'll get in touch with you soon to ask for more.

Having more material ready to go is also a great idea. I can't tell you how many times I've had clients with good material and the person that I was pitching to asked for more. If the client didn't *have* more material right then, the contact would lose interest as he waited for more material to be produced. This is not a good idea.

If you meet with someone in person, don't expect him to listen to all of your material at once. These people listen to music all day long, and they may not be in the best of moods. They may have other pressing matters to attend to. If they want to hear more, they'll ask you. But if you put them on the spot and they feel like they are being forced to hear your stuff, they won't take it very well. Most likely, you won't ever get a meeting with them again.

What Was I Looking For?

I've received hundreds, if not thousands, of promotional packages from all sorts of people trying to get a deal. These people were savvy enough to know that an entertainment lawyer or a reputable manager was the only way they were going to get their foot in the door. So, you might like to know what I was looking for when people asked me to help them get a deal.

QUALITY PRODUCT

I've had enough experience as a musician to know what it takes to make a living, get a gig, or attract someone's attention in the music industry. I also have plenty of experience in seeing how many opinions there are about "good" music. Early on, I realized that the music I liked and the music that ended up on the radio were not always the same thing. Therefore, when I began practicing entertainment law, I had to take an objective look at music. Getting someone a deal wasn't always about what *I* thought was good music. It was more about what was commercially exploitable.

So, the first thing I looked for was quality product. To the record labels, publishing companies, etc., musical talent is really just a product, a commodity—a widget, if you like. Therefore, I was always looking for an act or writer who was a total package, someone who labels or publishers could mold into something commercially exploitable. This meant my clients had to have not only talent, but depth of material and versatility. They also had to have a good attitude and be a team player.

DEPTH OF MATERIAL

One of the most important things I looked for when clients wanted me to pitch them for a major recording or publishing deal was depth of material. No matter how good their songs were, if there was any interest at all, I usually heard, "This is really good, but what else do you have?" If a writer has only a few good songs, he is less likely to get a publishing deal. In many cases, the publisher wants the writer's prior compositions as part of the publishing deal. The more depth of material the writer has before entering into a publishing deal, the more confidence the publisher will have of the writer's ability to turn in commercially exploitable material during the term of the publishing contract.

If you are looking for an artist deal or your band wants a record deal, you should have two to three albums' worth of material either recorded (demos, at least) or ready to record. This doesn't mean a couple of really good songs and 20 mediocre ones. You need at least enough for the record company to choose up to two full CDs of material. Record companies can go through thousands of songs just to find one that is right for a particular artist.

If you are lucky enough to get your first record deal, you will most likely be offered a "one and six" deal. This means you're guaranteed that the record company will put out one record with you, and then if they want to continue, they have the option to put out six more. If your first record is successful, you will have to top it with new material, which you'll need to come up with while you're touring in support of your first record. Depending on the timing and the record company's needs, your deadline could come pretty quickly. That's a lot of pressure. If you don't come through with a really good record, you could fall prey to the *sophomore jinx*. Your second record will be less than memorable, and you will end up getting dropped like a hot potato. Then you will have to go back to the rank and file of all other artists out there without a record deal. If you're really lucky, you may get signed by another label, but that almost never happens.

On the other hand, if you have enough material for two really strong albums right out of the gate, you won't have to worry about the sophomore jinx, and you will have even more time to come up with your third record. Furthermore, if you have enough really strong material for at least two to three CDs, you may be able to negotiate a "two and six" deal, which guarantees that the label will put out two records for you.

Using a Computer

If you don't have a computer, you really should get one. It will help with most of the tasks that are suggested in this book. You don't have to spend tons of money on a brand new one. You can get a used computer from one of your friends or a business that buys new ones regularly and really cheap. A used machine should have most of the software and other stuff that you'll need already installed.

I discussed getting organized earlier in this chapter, and I can't think of any tool that is more suited for the task. The computer is the most unbelievable tool at your disposal in the music business. I truly feel sorry for people who can't get over their fear or ignorance of them.

They're missing out on the greatest invention since the wheel.

I use mine for just about everything. I can do all of my correspondence, bookkeeping, bill paying, songwriting, music recording and production, graphics work, Web site design, research, shopping, and so much more on one little machine. Furthermore, since I have several computers hooked to my LAN (local area network), I can delegate which machines do certain tasks. That way I never have to wait for one computer to finish a certain task while I move on to another, which just increases my efficiency. I can't imagine being nearly as productive without a computer or two.

Keys to Success

Lastly, there are some very simple tenets that can be your keys to success and happiness.

Always think about how the things you do and say will affect other people. How you act and what you say can come back to haunt you. Be very careful, because you never know who is aligned with who. The music business is a tight-knit bunch of people who eventually run into each other. Be the person who's fun to be around, not the prima donna who nobody can stand.

Be supportive of others who attain success. Don't be jealous. There's enough success to go around, and they just might be willing to share. Remember the Golden Rule: Do unto others as you would have them do unto you. If you're only concerned with your own interests, you probably won't get very far. People enjoy doing business with others who are a pleasure to work with. Don't be the one who ruins it for everyone.

"Expect success and you may never attain it. Prepare for success and you'll be ahead of the game."—*Durphy Doucette*

Finally, think about how you'll handle success if it happens. It's really easy to get caught up in the bright lights of the big city and forget about who you really are and what's important to you. Keep yourself grounded and remember where you came from. Never forget about all the people who have helped you climb the mountain of success. If you do, you will meet them again on your way back down.

When you lose sight of the reasons you did something in the first place, it's no longer fun. It's work. And when work isn't fun anymore, you'd be better off doing something else. If you're in the music business for any reason other than your love of music, maybe you should move on.

Lastly, if you really want to make a small fortune in the music business, start off with a large one. This is a tough business, and fortunes have been lost time and time again.

Summary

If you follow most of these simple guidelines, you will get organized, do your homework, make yourself more memorable, and be totally prepared for whatever comes next.

Suggested reading:

▶ *The Greatest Salesman in the World* by Og Mandino

▶ *Music, Money, and Success* by Jeff and Todd Brabec

▶ All trade magazines about the music business

CHAPTER 6

Intellectual Property

"Protecting your rights...."

One could generally say that intellectual property law is the law behind protecting the work product of one's imagination or mind. But it doesn't just stop there. Not only does intellectual property cover copyright, trademark, and patents, but it also covers publicity and privacy rights, as well as trade secrets. One thing that is for sure is that intellectual property is one of the most important areas of the law that musicians, songwriters, artists, and others in the entertainment industry should understand. At the very least, a cursory knowledge of the law in this area can be a real asset and can actually help to prevent a lot of potential problems that can arise throughout one's career.

Unfortunately, learning all of the intricacies of intellectual property law can be quite difficult. Furthermore, intellectual property is the field of the law that I feel is the least understood by most general practitioners, and in some cases even less by the courts that sometimes hear these issues.

Finding a lawyer in Anytown, U.S.A., who really knows very much about intellectual property can be pretty hard, if not impossible. You will most likely have to find an intellectual property lawyer in the larger cities where there are federal courts. Fortunately, most intellectual property issues involve matters that are a federal question and thus must be heard only by a federal court. A federal question is an issue of law that is governed solely by federal legislation and statutes. But that does not mean that some state courts and judges won't have jurisdiction over intellectual property issues, because most states have some sort of intellectual property laws on the books, and some issues such as privacy must be heard by a state court only.

The good news is that for the most part, there are only a few general principles that you should be familiar with to make sure that you are able to protect yourself and your intellectual property. Also, in most cases, filing for intellectual property protection is something that you can do yourself, or in instances of publicity or privacy rights, you don't have to file for protection because you are protected automatically by law.

The three main branches of intellectual property are copyrights, trademarks, and patents. But there are also related areas such as trade secrets, publicity rights, and privacy rights that should be considered as well and will be discussed later in this chapter. But first, let's take a look at copyrights. We will discuss who they protect, what they protect, and how, because copyrights are the cornerstone of the music industry. However, be aware that all of the areas of intellectual property are definitely worthy of an entire book or even books for that matter. In fact, there are thousands of books out there on each subject, but the goal here is to boil a lot of that down into something that is easier to read and understand. To that end, this discussion is designed the hit the bullet points and to give you a basic understanding of the general principles involved.

Copyrights

Copyright law is designed to protect the creator of works such as songs, recorded music, writing, drawings, paintings, sculptures, and a host of other expressions of ideas. It is very important to understand this concept, so I will repeat it : *Copyright is designed to protect the creator of the works.* In the beginning of this great country, the framers of the Constitution created the right to copyright to protect the originators of works. But they were also concerned about the general public having access to these works, such as books, which were the main subject of the original copyright act, so that the general populace would be encouraged to read and to learn. That is why they limited the right to copyright to 14 years. However, they also provided for the right to extend the life of the copyright to a longer period by application. But there was still a limit so that publishers and owners of copyrights didn't end up with a monopoly over vital information.

As time has gone by, more and more expressions of ideas have come into the marketplace, and therefore the number of public domain works has increased as original copyrights expire. Therefore, with so many works available to the public, the laws have changed to reflect the state of the intellectual property world today. To add more protection to copyright owners, the legislature has extended the life of copyright to the life of the creator plus 70 years, for a number of reasons. What is important to know is that copyright protection won't change without new legislation, and to keep up with that, all you have to do is keep an eye on new copyright laws and how they will affect you.

International Copyright

There are a number of treaties to which the United States is a member or signatory party that can greatly affect your music career. The General Agreement on Tariffs and Trade (GATT), the World Trade Organization (WTO), and many more affect international business and finance, and there are many treaties that cover protection of intellectual property and copyrights. The main one that covers intellectual property rights is the Berne Convention for the Protection of Literary and Artistic Works. The World Intellectual Property Organization (WIPO) administers the Berne Convention along with the Rome Convention (the International Convention for the Protection of Performers, Producers of Phonograms, and Broadcasting Organizations). There is also the Universal Copyright Convention (UCC), and of course there are many more, but each of these treaties is very difficult to understand due to the nature of the subject matter, and the fact that each country has different laws and interpretations of the same laws. Suffice it to say that understanding these treaties and how they are covered is best left to professionals, unless you just happen to be interested in that field. However, I can assure you that if your music or other intellectual property happens to be good enough to be marketed to the international community, and you happen to have any success in this regard, suffice it to say that you will be able to afford the proper representation to guide you through this maze of law that has developed country by country.

Federal Copyright

Section 102(a) of the Copyright Act states that copyright is available to the following: "Original works of authorship fixed in any tangible medium of expression, now or later developed, from which they can be perceived, reproduced, or otherwise communicated, either directly or with the aid of a machine or device."

Section 102(a) further provides that the following works can be copyrighted: "Literary works; musical works; sound recordings; dramatic works; motion pictures and other audiovisual works; pantomimes and choreographic works; pictorial, graphic and sculptural works; and architectural works.

For anything to be eligible for copyright protection, there are three basic requirements: originality, expression, and fixation. Originality can be somewhat confusing because there are so many ideas floating around, but that doesn't mean that these ideas are copyrightable. Furthermore, the real crux of creativity is usually taking someone else's basic idea or perhaps style and making it your own and in your own way. After all, don't most musicians start out by learning cover songs? Pretty much. Don't most artists sound somewhat similar to some other artist? Yes, critics make these comparisons all the time. Isn't it possible that the original artist was a major influence to the sound-alike artist? You bet! Does that make the sound-alike unoriginal? Of course it doesn't, and it certainly doesn't pursuant to the copyright code. Perhaps you've heard the old expression in songwriting that "amateurs borrow and professionals steal."

Be that as it may, this leads us to expression, which requires that you can't just have an idea, but you must express it. This is pretty much self-explanatory. You can't just think it, but you must put the idea down in some tangible medium such as sheet music, a work tape, or something that allows someone to see or hear your work. And this leads us to fixation. Fixation just means that you must express your idea in a tangible medium so that others may listen to it, view it, read it, etc. So if you think about the basics, all you have to do is come up with an idea, and then express it some tangible way so that others will be able to enjoy it or hate it, because there is no accounting for taste. That's a very simplified version, but you should get the gist and if you are interested in learning more, I highly suggest that you read more about it, because copyright is a very fascinating subject! But again, there are countless books out there on this subject, and I would rather just hit the main bullet points for our purposes here.

Bundle of Rights

It is very important to understand that there is a bundle of rights exclusive to a copyright owner. This bundle of rights includes the right to reproduce, distribute, and perform copyrighted material. Furthermore, these rights can be exercised by anyone that the creator or original owner of the copyright authorizes to do so. Usually, to authorize others to use a copyright, the owner of the copyright will enter into some type of licensing agreement. As far as the music industry goes, the most common types of licenses are performance licenses, mechanical licenses, synchronization rights, and print licenses.

Performance licenses are usually granted to radio, television, concert venues, businesses, and other places so that they can play your songs publicly. The money you receive from these licenses is commonly referred to as a royalty. And we all know what that means: mailbox money! There are a lot of songwriters out there who will never have to work again because some songs they wrote a very long time ago are still raking in the money due to licensing and exploitation of those copyrights. In other words, when you hear a song on the radio, in a club, or some other venue, the performing rights societies (BMI, ASCAP, and SESAC) have negotiated a blanket license with that radio station, club, or venue so that these venues can play your underlying musical work as recorded music. A blanket license is merely a flat fee or pro rata fee that is charged by the licensing organization so that the copyrights in their catalogue can be performed publicly. The money from these blanket licenses is collected by the performing rights societies and paid both to the publishers of the music and the writers of the underlying musical works who are members of these societies, based upon a specialized formula from licensing organization to licensing organization. That is designed to pay out money to copyright holders based upon chart positioning, record sales, and a number of other factors.

When you go into the grocery store or are on an elevator and you hear the latest song by a new artist being covered by an elevator music band, the company that releases that elevator music is charging money for that elevator or grocery store to play its music. In turn, that music company has to pay a royalty to the writer of the underlying musical work for playing his songs. Furthermore, since Muzak and similar companies are creating derivative works, they have to obtain permission from the copyright owners. (See "Derivative Works" later in this chapter.) If you are an affiliated member of one of the licensing organizations as a songwriter, your performing rights organization will collect those performance license fees and pay the pro rata share to the writer and publisher of the songs. Your performing rights organization will also collect all other performance royalties from concert venues, businesses, and the like, and pay you and/or your publisher based upon the computation and pay schedule that your performing rights organizations uses.

Mechanical licenses are granted for the right to make mechanical reproductions in the form of sound recordings of the underlying musical work. They are usually granted to your record company or other artists so they can reproduce and distribute other versions of your underlying musical work on CDs, cassettes, and the like. These companies or individuals that make copies are required to pay the writer or copyright owner a percentage of the sale price for each mechanical copy that they sell. The amount that is due depends when you make the copies. The publishers and music industry negotiated a flat rate in 1998, and as of 2004 the rate is 8.5 cents per copy. In 2006, the rate will go up to 9.21 cents per copy, but the requirement to pay is statutory, and unless negotiated again, Congress will set the rate. Mechanical royalties are due monthly as you sell CDs, and failure to pay these royalties could cause any license you may have to be terminated, and worse, could make you subject to copyright infringement and all of the problems that can create. (See "Remedies for Infringement" later in this chapter.)

There is also something called the compulsory mechanical license that you should be aware of. The compulsory license was introduced under the 1909 Copyright Act to prevent publishers from having a monopoly on reproductions of music. The 1976 Copyright Act also made provisions for compulsory licenses, and the basic premise is that once a song has been released in a phonograph (or other reproduction), anyone has the right to reproduce or make a cover recording of that composition. It also provides that the copyright owner has the absolute right to control the first recording of that song. However, after the song has been released, the copyright owner cannot prevent anyone else from releasing his or her own version of that song. It's important to note here that the compulsory license only applies to non-dramatic musical works. If you want to release a cover song, you must obtain a compulsory license. To do so, you must file a Notice of Intention with the original copyright owner and with the Copyright Office. You must also pay the statutory mechanical royalties as set out previously. However, if you change the music substantially, that will be considered a derivative work and you will have to obtain permission from the copyright owner to do so. (See "Derivative Works" later in this chapter.)

It is important to note that many record companies do not want to have the accounting hassles of having to pay out money each month to the copyright owners, as provided for in the Copyright Act for compulsory licenses. Therefore, they will negotiate a mechanical license with the copyright owners so that they may make payments quarterly, and also so that they pay only royalties on actual records sold, and not just records made or shipped. They may also make provisions for reduced rates for record clubs or controlled compositions clauses. (For discussion of controlled composition clauses, see Chapter 9, "Why Sign a Record Deal?") Finally, many record companies, publishers, etc., actually use a mechanical licensing agency to collect mechanicals for them. One such company is called Harry Fox. Harry Fox collects a small fee for its services and can make releasing a record with a number of works from a number of publishers much easier on the record label, which only has to deal with Harry Fox to obtain all of the appropriate mechanical licenses. Harry Fox can be found at www.nmpa.org.

Synchronization rights are paid out as a percentage, but more often as a negotiated license fee for use of music in television, film, or commercials. It can be extremely lucrative to have your song placed in these markets. For instance, the theme music of a very popular television show can be a tremendous earner for the songwriter. But even if you have one of your songs played in the background in a movie, it is still a moneymaker and can give a tremendous amount of exposure to your band or your songs. For instance, let's say that the actors in the scene are walking down the street past a bar that has music blasting out of it. Rest assured, that song has been licensed, or they could not use it without being made a party to a copyright infringement suit.

Therefore, any use of your music in film, television, or commercials will bring you money in the form of royalties.

Print licenses are obtained for companies that produce sheet music or songbooks. Most of us musicians started out practicing with a songbook with the music and words printed out, so that we could learn the songs. Even though the chords and music are often changed from the original version or the tablature is not exactly perfect, the companies that produce this printed material still have to pay a royalty for every copy that they sell throughout the world. So whenever you see printed sheet music, lyrics, and chords, they represent money to the songwriters. It may not be a killing, but you can bet that it's still a good deal of money, especially if the song that is printed is an extremely popular one that is sold to schools, churches, music stores, and the like.

Of course, there are a lot of other ways that your song could earn money. If a portion of your song is put on a t-shirt, you can negotiate a royalty for that. In fact, if your song or even a portion of your song is used in just about any medium, you have the right to be paid for it.

Statutory Copyright

Prior to January 1, 1977, there were two types of copyrights: common law copyright and statutory copyright. The common law copyright was what existed with regard to a work before a copyright was published. However, determining if something was published was not very clear. The usual test was whether or not the work was publicly displayed, and there were many opinions about what constituted a public display. Furthermore, if you published your work without any notice of copyright, your work immediately fell into the public domain, which meant that anyone could copy or reproduce your work without any worry of infringement, and the creator of the copyright was out of luck should he desire to assess his rights or ask for protection. Statutory copyright was granted if the creator put a copyright notice on the work with a circle C (©), along with the date and the artist's name, in a reasonably prominent place sufficient to give others notice of the copyright claim. This afforded the creator with statutory protection for the life of the copyright. However, you still have to give notice of the copyright if you want to assert your statutory rights to prevent the work from falling under public domain after publication.

The new law that went into effect in January 1977 did away with common law copyright. After January 1977, the minute that you represented a work in a tangible medium, such as a poem, lyrics, a work tape of a new song, a finished Web site, a painting, or any other work of art, you were immediately protected under a statutory copyright. But statutory protection is not the same as protection afforded the person who actually files for copyright protection. If you go to the trouble to register your copyright with the Library of Congress, and you should, your registration provides you, the writer, with three *extremely* important rights: the right to file suit, the ability to recover statutory damages, and the right to ask the court to force the infringing party to pay your attorneys' fees if you prevail. Of course, injunctive relief may also be granted to prevent the proven infringing party from continuing to infringe on your copyright. But if you can prove infringement with a registered copyright, you can really rake in some damages depending on the scope of the infringement, and you will be able to find an attorney to take the case without having to pay him a ton of money up front, if at all—especially if the song that you can prove is infringing on your copyright is actually making good money.

Some people refer to the statutory copyright as the poor man's copyright. They also believe that if you mail a copy of a work to yourself, it somehow protects you more than just the statutory copyright. But that belief is quite unfounded. There are a number of reasons for this. Mailing something to yourself only creates a presumption that you created the work prior to the postmark date on the letter. However, that presumption can be overcome or is subject to rebuttal, thus switching the burden of proof to the other party, and that is where it gets tricky. If you are asserting that someone has infringed upon your work, the burden of proof is on you to show that your work was created first. What happens if you only have a mailed copy of your song as proof of the date of creation? Let's just assume that some unscrupulous person has a bunch of letters with an earlier postmark that he has mailed to himself, and all he has done is copy your work, either by copying the lyrics or just performing a similar version of your song onto a work tape. After that, he inserted his version into the steamed-open envelope. Now he has alleged proof that he created their work first. Obviously, he has switched the burden of proof to you, and you must show that he has steamed a blank letter open and added your song. Trying to prove that is very much like proving a negative, and when it comes to litigation, it doesn't matter what you know, only what you can prove. Furthermore, proving a negative is next to impossible. Therefore, in that scenario, there is a good chance that you will lose your infringement argument and therefore lose your right to copyright your song.

There is a saying in the legal business: "He who is first in time is first in right." This simply means that if you are making a claim or are headed for litigation, and you are able to show that you filed your copyright first, you have done all that you can to protect your work. So it is always best to file the appropriate copyright before you decide to send out your work tapes, demos, lead sheets, lyrics, or any other form of expression on which you have saved your music, so that you are completely protected by all facets of copyright law. Failing to take this simple step could be devastating, and the cost of filing is small indeed versus the cost of what you will lose in the end if you do not file for the appropriate copyright.

What Type of Copyright Form Should I Fill Out?

There are a number of forms you may need to fill out and file, along with the appropriate fees, with the Library of Congress to protect your particular type of work, but for our purposes here, we should focus on the two most important for musical works. First, there is the Form PA. This is what you fill out to protect an underlying musical work. This underlying musical work is the copyright to a particular song and *not* the actual recording of the song. In other words, if you play a song onto a work tape for the purposes of copyrighting the song, you aren't copyrighting the actual recording, but rather the underlying musical work. Form SR is usually reserved for master recordings, where you want to copyright the actual sound recording to prevent others from making copies of your masters. This type of protection is what most recording artist and record companies are worried about. Of course, with the Internet today, a lot of people are really into downloading or otherwise getting copies of outtakes, demos, or other non-licensed sound recordings of your work. So in some cases, it may be necessary to protect those types of recording too. The last thing you want are bad recordings of your songs being passed around for free.

Of course, there are a number of forms that may apply to your work, so you want to make sure that you get the correct one for the protection you are seeking. Again, please check with the Library of Congress for more information on the subject.

How to File for Your Copyright

Filing for copyright protection is really pretty simple. You can download the forms at www.copyright.gov/forms, or just write to:

Library of Congress
U.S. Copyright Office
101 Independence Avenue S.E.
Washington, D.C. 20559-6000

Or call them at (202) 707-3000. The forms are fairly self-explanatory, and there are easy instructions to follow. Once you have received your registration information, you are protected for your life plus 70 years. Again, it's important to note that a registered copyright gives you the right to file suit, the ability to recover statutory damages, and the right to ask the court to force the infringing party to pay your attorneys' fees if you prevail in an infringement suit, as well as the right to injunctive relief.

If you are concerned about the cost of filing a single copyright on every single song that you have written, you should consider filing a collection of your songs as a compilation work. However, you must meet certain requirements before you can fill out the Form PA for a collection of works. First, all of the works in a compilation that you intend to file must be unpublished. Second, the works must be by the same writer, or that writer must be have co-written at least part of each song, and the same party or parties must own all of the rights in the works and the collection as a whole. You must put the songs on one CD or other recording, labeled with the song titles and order, and you must give the compilation of songs a single title, such as *My Songs, Volume I*, or whatever you wish, such that the compilation can be uniquely identified.

But what if you co-wrote your songs? Who owns the individual copyrights? The established practice among professional writers is that if there are two writers, they each own half of the song. If there are three writers, they each own one-third of the song, and so on. Of course, you have to take into consideration who among your co-writers have signed publishing deals, and the nature of each publishing deal, so that you can discern who will end up with what portion of the total copyright. (For more information on publishing deals, please refer to Chapter 7, "Publishing.")

Sometimes when two people co-write songs, there is a lyricist and a music writer. In these instances, who owns the music and who owns the lyrics? This comes up quite a bit because some people are better at writing words and some are better at writing music. The work should be considered as a whole if the intent of the writers is to create one composition. Therefore, both writers will share in ownership of the copyright. Furthermore, the lyrics and the music will both be covered under the same copyright so that nobody can just copy the words or just the music. Of course, if the song is an instrumental, it's copyrighted and owned by all the parties who contributed to the song.

But what if you and your band co-write a song? This can get pretty tricky. Just because your bass player, lead guitarist, keyboard player, or other instrumentalist wrote their instrumental parts doesn't mean that they have co-written the song. If you completely write the lyrics and the music (chord changes, melody, and structure of the song) for the underlying musical work before you bring it to the rest of the band for them to work up their parts, they are not co-writers. They have just written their parts and/or arrangements to your song. Unfortunately, this can cause a serious rift between band members, as history has shown us. There are several acts out there that have had a good degree of success, only to find out a year or more later (the usual time before performance royalties start to roll in and after their initial success) that the songwriter or main songwriters of the band are making more money from the underlying musical works. You can rest assured that this has caused the breakup of many a band, but that is just how it is. The actual songwriters are the ones who are going to get those royalties, and not the band as a whole. However, if you and your band decide to co-write a song, each of the band members will get writer's credit. Under the Copyright Act, it takes two or more writers to be joint owners, and each must have the intent to create a joint work that is to be considered one work as a whole.

Word for a Third

Sometimes, you may write a song completely by yourself or with a co-writer, and yet some folks would like some of the publishing even though they are not your publishers. Furthermore, when you get into professional circles of songwriters, publishers, and producers, you may find out that someone in a position of power wants to change some of your lyrics or maybe a melody line or two. This is sometimes referred to as *a word for a third*. This just means that if you co-wrote the song, which is a very common occurrence, and then the person in a position of power makes a few changes, he expects to get one-third of the copyright for his meager input. Furthermore, if a major producer is going to place your song with a major artist, it is not uncommon for him to request part of the publishing rights to the song. Again, this is discussed in greater detail in Chapter 7.

Works for Hire

In some cases, you could be required to sign an agreement that all of the songs that you write will automatically become the property of the company for which you have written the song. This is the case when you are considered an employee of the company or you are commissioned to write a song for a particular entity. Whether or not you are considered an employee is subject to a number of considerations, such as the skill required to do the work, whether or not you use the tools of the company, whether or not you receive employee benefits, and the like. However, there are not that many companies that hire songwriters as employees. The work-for-hire situation usually applies to patents and not songs. Therefore, don't worry about it too much, unless you are presented with a contract with that language in it, which you must sign for the work-for-hire provision to be effective. However, you may see a work-for-hire clause in a publishing agreement if you are under contract with a publisher. In this case, you will not be considered to be an employee because you set your own time and places to write songs. Furthermore, you are not paid a salary, but rather an advance against future royalties if any of your songs are commercially exploited. Most likely, you will have to assign your publishing interests to your publisher, who will then own them for the term of the copyright. (For more information, see Chapter 7.)

Assignment of Copyright

Usually in a publishing deal, you will be asked to assign all of your rights to your publisher. All songs are broken up into a division of rights. The music business has, for reasons of simplicity, adopted the 200% method of ownership in copyrights. It is the industry standard for publishing agreements that the publisher ends up with ownership of the copyright but that you will receive 50% of the proceeds from the publishing deal. This just means that if you write a song completely by yourself, you own 100% of the writer's share, and unless you are in a publishing deal, you own 100% of the publishing. If you are in a publishing deal, you will retain your writer's share, but your publisher will own 100% of your publishing rights. If you co-write a song, you own 50% of the writer's and 50% of the publisher's share, and the other writer will own the other 100%. Confusing? Pretty much, but that is how it is done. This method has been adopted so that if you want to enter into a co-publishing agreement and retain part of the publishing, you can, or if someone wants a piece of the publisher's share, you can assign that to him. But you will still receive your writer's share, unless you have made a transfer of that right too. However, be advised that no assignment of copyright is valid unless it is in writing. In most cases, not only will it be in writing, but also you may be required to have a notary public attest to your signature for the assignment, just so that you won't have any problems in the future should someone say that he or she didn't really sign that particular assignment of copyright. Be that as it may, it is a good idea to get at least three copies of any assignment: one for you, one for the transferee, and one for the copyright registrar.

Termination Rights

Congress has tried to protect writers from bad publishing deals, and this is a pretty unique situation, because when you transfer other property rights, such as selling land or a car, you can't terminate the transfer. You're stuck with the deal you made. But you can with copyrights. The reason for this is that Congress understands the lack of bargaining position that a writer has when dealing with a publisher. So termination can be made for a 5-year period after the 35th and before the 41st year after transfer. There are unique rules for this, so you had better keep track of the date of transfer, as well as the date of first publication, and make sure that your successors, heirs, and assigns have notice of this in the event of your death so that they will know that they can terminate the transfers and therefore keep 100% of the copyright and thus 100% of the money from royalties on those songs. You must give written notice to terminate a transfer, which can be done 10 years before the date of termination and up to two years before the termination date, and you must also send a copy of the notice to the Copyright Office. It is strongly suggested that you hire an attorney for this, and if the song is really worth much money, you will be glad that you have someone to make sure all of the requirements and procedures are handled correctly.

Derivative Works

The Copyright Act refers to a derivative work as "a work based upon one or more preexisting works, such as a translation, musical arrangement, dramatization, fictionalization, motion picture version, sound recording, art reproduction, abridgment, condensation, or any other form in which a work may be recast, transformed, or adapted."

Simply put, a derivative work is when someone creates a new work by taking all or portions of an original work and incorporating it into the new work. But be advised that there are two requirements for a new work to be considered a derivative work. First, it must borrow a good deal from the original work, such that the borrowing is discernable, and second, it must change or adapt the work in some fashion. You see this all the time with the sampling in popular music today. However, you can't just create a derivative work without the permission of the original copyright holder, and he won't let it go cheap. In fact, he may retain the rights to the derivative work and make even more money off the new song that you have created. There has been an incredible amount of litigation over derivative works as more and more bands are using samples in their songs. So beware! Get permission first, and try to negotiate the best deal you can. If you're really lucky, you may get permission and not have to pay any royalties, especially if the original artist doesn't expect you to make any money off your song.

Infringement of Copyright

One of the calls that I received most often at my law office was a client who was convinced that someone had stolen his song. Unfortunately, more often than not, infringement just wasn't the case. You have to consider that there are so many songs out there… somewhere in the millions, if not hundreds of millions. Furthermore, it is not uncommon for many people to write about the same subject matter, and it is very common for people to come up with the same title. However, titles are *not* copyrightable. Finally, since most popular songs follow a similar formula, it is not uncommon for a song to be very similar to another song. However, to prove a copyright infringement case, you need to prove two important facts. First, you must first show that the infringing party had access to the song, and second, you must prove substantial similarity.

Unfortunately, proving access can be quite difficult, unless you are able to come up with witnesses who saw you hand the song to someone, or if you mailed your song return receipt requested. In other words, the party who intends to prove copyright infringement must be able to prove, by a preponderance of the evidence in a civil matter, that the alleged infringing party was able to get his hands on the song and thus be able to steal or copy it. Of course, there are a number of ways to prove access, but you will need pretty strong evidence to meet the burden of proof, and that can be a very slippery slope indeed. This is one of the reasons that record labels and major publishers refuse to receive unsolicited materials. In other words, if you are an unknown writer, or a publisher with a bunch of unknown writers, and you just blindly send in your material to a major publisher or record label, it will send your material back to you with a huge stamp that says "RETURN UNSOLICITED," or just refuse to accept it. If it did accept unsolicited material, it would be much easier to prove that it had access to unreleased songs.

Second, assuming that you can prove access, you must be able to prove substantial similarity. To do this, you usually have to hire an expert, who is usually a musicologist who can give an expert opinion to help prove substantial similarity. A musicologist is most often a professor of music or some other similar expert with a vast knowledge about music (usually a person who has a doctorate in music) who can say, based upon a reasonable degree of certainty, that your song is substantially the same as the song that you claim copied or infringed upon your work. Unfortunately, substantial similarity is a very difficult burden to prove. The musicologist will break the song down into very small increments, including the lyrics and melody, and then break it down into even smaller increments, so that he can show that the songs are basically the same, if not note for note and word for word the same. So the main thing to understand here is that the burden is on you, as the person claiming copyright infringement, to prove that the person who has allegedly infringed upon your song actually had physical access to your song and then copied your song almost completely verbatim and note for note.

REMEDIES FOR INFRINGEMENT

If you have filed for copyright registration and it is granted and you can prove that someone has infringed on your work, you will be entitled to injunctive relief, compensatory damages, statutory damages, costs, and attorney's fees. An injunction is simply a court order that prevents the infringing party from further infringement. In short, the court will rule that all infringing activity should cease immediately. Compensatory damages can be in the form of actual damages, which is the actual amount of money that the copyright owner did not make from the infringement. Damages are calculated by the fair market value of the goods, or in this case the music that was sold or misused. Also, you may be able to recover the profits from the entity that has infringed upon your copyright. However, you must be able to show how much of that business's profits would be directly attributed to your original work. Proving these damages can be quite difficult, and you will not receive any damages for emotional distress even though you may have felt that you have suffered considerably, because that is not provided for in the copyright code. If your actual compensatory damages don't amount to much, you can also recover statutory damages. For instance, if someone were to illegally copy one of your songs and only sell about 100 copies, your actual damages would be miniscule and not really even worth filing suit over. However, statutory damages may be awarded depending on the nature of the infringement. In some cases, the damages could be as high as $150,000 or as little as $750. Again, that all depends upon the nature of the infringement, whether or not the infringement was willful, and the amount of infringement that has occurred. However, the good news is that you will be able to afford an attorney to guide you through this maze of law. Under the Copyright Act, you are entitled to recover reasonable attorney's fees as well as all costs associated with a court case, such as court costs, expert witness fees, court reporters, transcription costs, postage, photocopying, etc., if you can prove your case.

STATUTE OF LIMITATIONS

There is a time limit for filing an infringement suit. You are required under the 1976 Copyright Act to bring suit within three years of the time that the infringement should have been discovered. This just means that you don't have to file suit within three years, but rather within three years from the time that the court determines that you should have discovered the infringement. Therefore, you don't have to constantly comb the airwaves or the Internet to find out if your song is being infringed upon and file suit immediately. However, to protect your rights, you should at least make some effort to do so.

FAIR USE

The Copyright Act has granted persons who do not own a copyright the right to use a copyrighted work for purposes of criticism, comment, news reporting, teaching, and research. Of course, this list is not inclusive, because there are numerous types of fair use, but the gist of the fair use doctrine is to allow others to use your songs as long as they are generally not seeking to exploit your copyright commercially. (For more info, see Chapter 8, "Digital Rights.")

The most important thing that you should understand about all of this copyright information is that you should file your copyrights with the Library of Congress if you wish to be completely protected. Failing to do so could prove to be disastrous. And now, we move on to protecting your name, which falls under the provisions of trademark law.

Trademarks

The second most important type of intellectual property protection for those of us in the music industry is trademark. Trademark law covers the right of a person, company, or other entity to file for protection for its logo, company name, catchphrase, and the like. However, unlike copyright, which protects the creator of a work, trademark is designed to protect the consumer and not necessarily the owner of the trademark. Although the person or entity that wants to assert any trademark rights will be the one seeking relief, ultimately the real test is whether or not a trademark causes confusion in the marketplace. In other words, when you buy a Coca-Cola, you know that it was bottled under the authority of the Coca-Cola bottling company. You know this because there is a registered trademark symbol (®) on the can or bottle with the classic logo. Also, if you buy the Coca-Cola in the original bottle with the unique shape and design, you also know that the product is a Coca-Cola because the shape of the bottle is also trademarked. Coca-Cola has also trademarked the slogan "Things Go Better with Coke" and many others.

TRADEMARKS AND SERVICE MARKS

Trademarks show the source of a product or good, while service marks show the source of a service. More often than not, a business will offer both services and goods. Such is the case with bands. They may start out offering services when they play live for parties, clubs, or other venues, and in time they begin to sell t-shirts, hats, and other products, and eventually they will start to sell CDs, tapes, or other recorded music, either at their gigs, in stores, or on the Internet. Therefore, it is a really good idea to think about both a trademark and a service mark. In fact, many businesses own several trademarks and service marks just so to be thorough and protect their brand with many different logo designs, slogans, or names.

FEDERAL VERSUS STATE TRADEMARK

Most states have adopted some sort of trademark statutes. These statutes allow persons or businesses in that state to file for protection of their trademark or service mark without applying for federal protection. This type of protection is good for a business that is not planning on offering its products or services outside of that state, or even outside of a particular city. This is a good thing to get in some states, because it is sometimes very cheap and quick. This means that you will be protected in that state, assuming that there was no federal mark that precluded you from obtaining state status. Unfortunately, states usually don't have nearly the budget of the federal government, and state protection is not the best way to go if you are in the music business, because you would hope to be able to sell your products or services throughout the United States, if not the entire world.

CLASSES OF GOODS OR SERVICES

If you are offering a number of products or services, it is a good idea to cover yourself with as many marks as you can. Under federal trademark law, there are certain classes of goods or services that you can file for trademark protection. Let's say that you are in a band and would like to file for protection. What type of protection do you need? Well, you are selling services to bars, restaurants, clubs, dances, etc., so it would be a very good idea to apply for a service mark for your band name. This would be under Class 41 for entertainment services. You may also be selling hats, t-shirts, or other articles of clothing, so you would want to file for a Class 25 clothing trademark with your band name and logo. You may also be selling CDs or cassettes and the like, so you would want to file under Class 9 for videotapes, audiotapes, compact discs, CD-ROMs, records, computer programs, or business software. For more information on the classes of goods or services your product or service fits for filing a trademark or service mark, you can go to http://www.uspto.gov/web/offices/tac/tmfaq.htm.

COMMON LAW TRADEMARK

If you use a mark to identify a good or service, you are automatically covered by common law trademark. This is especially true if consumers see the brand name as being associated with the source of the product or service. However, a common law trademark is limited to the geographic area in which the mark is used, within a certain zone of expansion. This zone of expansion means that your mark will allow you protection only in a slightly larger area to protect you as your business grows. Finally, common law trademark gives very little notice to others who wish to use a similar mark in commerce in relation to a similar class of goods or services.

FEDERAL REGISTRATION

Filing for federal registration gives you the ability to recover profits, damages, and costs for infringement, and in some cases treble damages (three times your damages). You may also recover attorney's fees if you are successful in prosecuting an infringement action. You also have the right to use the registered trademark symbol (®) with your mark. You also make it easier for others to know about your mark, so that they will not try to use a substantially similar or possibly confusing mark. After five years of registration, you achieve incontestable status, so that most arguments will fail if someone were to assert that you didn't have the right to use your mark. Finally, you have the right to actually file suit in federal court should someone infringe on your mark.

BRANDING

Your name is your brand, and any marketing guy will tell you that branding is the key to success. You will spend a great deal of time practicing and honing your act, only to be known strictly by your name. Your music will *only* be known by the name of the band. If band members come and go, and they do, you still have the band name, and that is what people identify with. Rare is the artist who leaves a band and becomes a household name. But it happens. If you put any money into advertising, marketing, and promotion for your band name, you would be well advised to protect it.

CHOOSING THE WRONG NAME

Choosing the right name can be such an important step but is often overlooked, at least from the standpoint of research. The right name has so many implications, so give it some thought and then some serious research, because if you choose the wrong name, it may come back to bite you. Case in point: There was a band from the Midwest that moved to Nashville to try to get some sort of a record deal. The band had played all over the country for years and was one of the top bands in the Midwest for several years. After moving to Nashville, the band played as much as posible, including playing a gig at a local club where the owner thought that it was another band that used the same name and actually did get a record deal. The club owner threatened the band members with arrest, and he wouldn't even let them get their equipment out of the club. To make matters worse, the club owner refused to pay them for the gig. Of course, he thought they were the other band that had a record out. So who was causing confusion in the market-place? Under the law, the other band that had the record deal was the infringing party. The original band ended up filing a case against the other band with the record deal, and the case was settled for a very substantial amount of money. The other band with the record deal had the choice of abandoning its name and losing a great deal of marketing and promotion that it had expended on that name, or paying a lot of money to the original band, which it opted to do.

TRADEMARK REGISTRATION

Trademarks are filed with the United States Patent and Trademark Office. You don't necessarily need an attorney to file a trademark, but it's a very good idea because filing a trademark is a lengthy and complicated process. You have to comply with every single requirement, dot your I's and cross your T's, or your trademark will not be granted. You also have to follow up with the application over a very long period of time, because trademarks are not granted immediately. If you would like more information or basic facts about trademark registration, go to http://www.uspto.gov/web/offices/tac/doc/basic/.

The materials that must be filed with the U.S. Patent and Trademark Office for trademark registration are:

► An application form containing a declaration of use.

► A single page that contains the name of the applicant, the address of the applicant, the dates of first use for the mark, the description of goods or services on which the mark will be used, the international classifications of the goods or services, and the mark itself.

► Three identical specimens of the mark in use.

► A trademark application fee in the amount of $245 per international class.

When an application is received, the Trademark Office reviews it to see if it meets the minimum requirements for obtaining a filing date. If the application meets the filing requirements, the PTO assigns it a serial number and sends the applicant a receipt about two months after filing. About four months after filing, an examining attorney at the PTO reviews the trademark application and determines whether the mark may be registered. If the examining attorney determines that the mark cannot be registered, the examining attorney will send the prospective applicant an office action listing any reasons for refusal and any corrections that are required for the application. Sometimes, the examining attorney will telephone the applicant if only minor corrections are required. Be advised that the issuance of an office action is pretty common and doesn't necessarily mean that the mark will never be registered. The applicant is required to respond to any office action within six months, or the application will be abandoned and the process starts all over again. If the applicant's response does not overcome all objections by the examining attorney, the examining attorney will issue a final ruling on the trademark application and a whole new set of problems will abound. The applicant may then appeal to the Trademark Trial and Appeal Board.

If the examiner does not make any objections to the application, or if the applicant corrects all objections, the examining attorney will approve the mark for publication in the *Official Gazette*, a weekly publication of the PTO. The PTO will send a Notice of Publication to the applicant indicating the date of publication. Any person or business entity that feels that it may be damaged by the registration of the mark has 30 days from the date of publication to file an opposition to registration. Even if no opposition is filed and the application becomes registered, it is still possible for a third party to object to the registration of a particular mark. This objection is usually made through a cancellation proceeding, which is similar to an opposition proceeding except that it takes place after registration.

Opposition and cancellation proceedings are formal proceedings similar to an abbreviated court trial, except that the proceedings are held before the Trademark Trial and Appeal Board (a division of the PTO) and the use of live witnesses is extremely rare. Usually, the party bringing the cancellation or opposition action is alleging that the mark being registered is causing confusion in the marketplace or is substantially similar to a mark owned by the opposing party.

If you file an intent-to-use application, it is necessary to file a proof of use of the mark before it will be granted registration by the PTO. If the applicant has begun to use the mark prior to the publication of the mark, the proof of use should be filed in connection with an Amendment to Allege Use. The amendment to the application must include a verified declaration of use signed by the applicant, and specimens showing how the mark is actually used. Once the Amendment to Allege Use is filed and accepted by the PTO, the application will be treated as if it were filed based upon the actual use of the mark in commerce. Next, once the mark has been published, it is not possible to prove use of the mark until after the opposition period has been completed. If no opposition is filed after the mark is published, the USPTO. will issue a Notice of Allowance. The applicant then has six months from the date of the Notice of Allowance to either use the mark in commerce and submit a Statement of Use or request a six-month Extension of Time to File a Statement of Use. There are certain circumstances when the applicant may request additional extensions of time. If the Statement of Use is filed and approved, the PTO will then issue the registration certificate.

A mark will be granted federal registration after the mark has been published, the opposition period has expired, and proof of use has been filed. The federal trademark registration is granted for 10 years, with 10-year renewal terms. However, between the fifth and sixth year after the date of initial registration, the registrant must file an affidavit setting forth certain information to keep the registration alive. If no affidavit is filed, the registration is cancelled. As stated before, anyone who claims rights in a mark may use the TM (trademark) or SM (service mark) designation with the mark to alert the public of the intent to use the mark and/or to file for registration, and it isn't necessary to have a registration, or even a pending application, to use these symbols. However, the registered trademark symbol (®) can only be used when the mark is registered with the PTO.

TRADEMARK SEARCHES

Since filing for a trademark isn't cheap and can take up a lot of your time, you would be well advised to do a complete search before you pay your money to file an application for trademark, only to find out that you will have to pay again just to file for protection on another name, since the one that you have chosen has already been taken or is likely to cause confusion in the marketplace. The cheapest place to search is the Internet, but just because you don't find any name that is like yours doesn't mean that you will be granted a trademark. You need to find out if there are any substantially similar names so that you know that the trademark office will grant you the mark that you need.

A good place to start is the phonographic log at your local music store. Most retailers carry this rather large book, which lists most records that have ever been released. But this is not an inclusive search. You can also check for any music business listings in different music business directories, but again, this is not very inclusive. Your absolute best bet is to hire a research firm that will research all business licenses, incorporations, trademark filings (state and federal), and many other resources. Several companies provide these sources, but two that I have used in the past are Thompson & Thompson at www.t-tlaw.com, and Government Liaison Services at www.trademarkinfo.com. There are a number of other services out there, so do your research and remember that you get what you pay for. Once you have done your research, you will be ready to choose the best name for your band, or at least you will know if there are any bands or businesses out there with the same name and in the same class of goods, which could cause you some problems in your quest for trademark or service mark registration.

INFRINGEMENT

Each state has its own statutes on the books with regard to trademark infringement, but be advised that they are often both civil and criminal in nature. So intentional infringement could have you paying some hefty fines, or you could wind up in jail! Federal trademark infringement also carries both civil and criminal penalties. If you feel that someone is infringing on your mark, you can send a cease and desist letter, and if they do not stop, you will have to take them to court to try to seek an injunction. Of course, if you can show that your mark was first in commerce, but have no registration, you may still be able to protect your rights and get the infringing party to stop, but you will not get any statutory remedies. However, if you have a protected mark, either by state or federal registration, you can seek all of the remedies that the legislation and courts will allow.

STATUTE OF LIMITATIONS

If you feel that someone or some business has infringed upon your trademark, you have only a limited number of years to bring suit before you are forever barred from asserting any claim. As with copyright, in some cases the statute of limitation could be tolled based upon when you actually noticed the infringement or should reasonably have been put on notice. Check with your state for any statute of limitation there may be, and for federal cases, you have to keep up with any changes in the law. Therefore, you will either have to hire an attorney or do your homework and keep up with any changes in the law.

Patents

Patents are somewhat like copyrights, in that they are the intellectual property right that is designed to protect the creators of inventions. However, they are somewhat like trademarks, in that there is a stipulation that the protection is only for a term of years so that the consumer can have a choice of buying that patented idea from another manufacturer. Therefore, when someone invents a new product, after 20 years, anyone else may manufacture that product, and this allows for competition, thus driving prices down and making that technology available to the consumer at a lower price.

A patent can be granted for a new or improved manufactured good, machine, chemical composition, process, computer software, business method, or other technology, whether for the Internet or elsewhere. What the patent allows you to do is to prevent anyone from copying, producing, using, or selling your invention unless some sort of licensing arrangement has been agreed upon. This means that nobody can take your invention and put it in the marketplace unless he is willing to pay you for the right to do it, and therefore, you can attempt to make money off your invention and try to recoup the costs that it took you to develop it. The test as to whether a patent will be granted is whether the new invention is unique, non-obvious, and in some cases useful.

An invention is considered to be unique or novel by the Patent and Trademark Office if it is different from all prior art (inventions). The invention doesn't necessarily have to be completely new, but it must have one or more parts that are new and different. The inventor must also show that he came up with the invention before any other similar invention was used in the public marketplace or was published in writing somewhere within one year prior to the inventor filing for a patent. This one-year requirement is also known as the one-year rule.

An invention is considered to be non-obvious by the Patent and Trademark Office if someone who has a good degree of experience and skill in the particular field of the invention would look at the invention as a surprising or unexpected development. Unfortunately, this means that the final test is a subjective one. In other words, not every patent examiner will have the same opinion about whether or not some new invention is a surprising or unexpected development in the field, so it can be a hit-or-miss situation. When one considers the time and energy involved in coming up with an invention, as well as filing the patent, it's not too hard to imagine how upsetting it could be if your patent wasn't granted just because you got the wrong patent examiners. Regardless of which patent examiners you get, it may take a while for them to get around to your invention, so they could still be influenced by newer technologies and inventions that have come about since you applied for your patent. Therefore, the patent examiners are supposed to go back and check what the standards were at the time the patent was applied for to get the most accurate information about whether your invention was non-obvious. Here again, you can see that it may be difficult to pass this test for any number of reasons, whether they are subjective or objective.

An invention is considered to be useful if it has some benefit or practical use, or helps people to perform tasks in their day-to-day lives. However, only an inventor who applies for a utility patent must show that his invention has some type of use. There are design and plant patents where the inventor does not have to show any use. A design patent can be granted to anyone who invents any new, original, or ornamental design. Unfortunately, the design patent protects only the appearance of an invention and is granted only for 14 years. Furthermore, the test for determining infringement in a design patent is a subjective one, in that the issue that must be determined is whether or not a design is similar, if not identical. Again, a subjective test casts your fate to the winds of opinions, which can vary from person to person as much as a fingerprint. Plant patents are granted to people who come up with new plant or animal (single-cell or multi-cellular organisms), and unless you are in that field as well as the music business, I wouldn't worry about it.

In years gone by, the design patent applications were considered to be a poor man's patent, in that you could file for a design patent much more cheaply and still have the same protection as a utility patent. Now, you can file for a provisional patent, which gives you protection for one year, but during that one-year period you have the same protection as a utility patent. But in the end, filing for the most protection allowed by law is usually the best way to go.

Finally, some patents can be granted even if they only have a humorous use, like a battery-operated light array on a guitar strap. Also, an invention doesn't necessarily have to work, but must theoretically be able to work.

Often and by necessity, people come up with ideas for things that can be quite useful for other musicians or just about anyone. You may have come up with something new that could possibly make you some money. If you have, you should contact a patent attorney. Of course, you can file for a patent yourself, but it is much more complicated than filing a simple copyright or even a trademark. For more information, contact the United States Patent and Trademark Office at 1-800-4-Patent (472-8368), or for more general information, go to www.uspto.gov/web/offices/pac/doc/general/. Filing a patent with an attorney can be quite expensive, but if your product is good enough and you plan to market it, you'd better get to it and quickly. The time limit can sneak up on you rather quickly, and if you miss it, all of your hard work and sweat equity will be for naught.

Trade Secrets

Here are a couple of scenarios. What if your employees want to use information that you have collected over a long period of time and through a good deal of hard work? Let's say that you have a booking agency and have developed a large number of contacts that you do business with to keep your acts working. Most likely, you have a large number of addresses either in your computer or on your Rolodex. If one of your employees takes your Rolodex and uses it to slowly steal your clients away, you may be able to make a claim for theft of trade secrets. A lot of producers, engineers, and the studios that they work in develop certain unique tricks and techniques to get their trademark sound. This has nothing to do with trademark law, but the sound they can get by using their particular equipment is a sound that people in the industry can determine to be unique to that studio. These studio tricks and techniques can be considered a trade secret, if you take the appropriate steps to make sure that your employees know that you are trying to keep your tricks and techniques secret.

Many states have adopted some form of protection for trade secrets. A trade secret may consist of any idea, process, pattern, formula, or compilation of information that provides the owner with a competitive advantage over others in the marketplace, and if the owner treats that idea, etc., in such a way by the owner that he can be reasonably expected to stop the general public or other competitors from learning about it without having stolen it. A really good example is the formula for Coca-Cola. Other examples are recipes that can't be copyrighted, marketing strategies, manufacturing techniques, customer lists, and many more. One thing about trade secrets is that you don't have to register them with any government agency, but rather, you simply have to take all steps that you can to keep them secret. If you make the secret available to the public, you lose any protection that you may have had.

If you are the owner or keeper of trade secrets, you can prevent your employees from disclosing or using trade secrets that they're exposed to as a part of their job. This type of trade secret protection is implied and is automatic. You can also prevent others from using your trade secrets if they obtain your trade secrets from people who have no right to disclose them, or from people that discover a trade secret by accident or mistake, but who must have a reason to know that the information was a protected trade secret. However, if someone comes up with a trade secret independently, he is entitled to use that trade secret even though you may feel you own it. Also, there is no trade secret protection if someone figures out your trade secret by reverse engineering. In other words, if people buy your product in the regular course of business, take it apart, and figure out how you built the product, they are entitled to use your trade secret. Regardless, the best protection that you can have to protect your trade secrets is to have all of your employees sign non-disclosure agreements.

Non-Disclosure Agreements

Your best protection is to have all people who are exposed to your trade secrets sign non-disclosure agreements, which are also known as confidentiality agreements. These types of agreements require your employees to promise not to disclose trade secrets without proper authorization. Even though employees are bound under an implied duty not to disclose sensitive information, all employees who come into contact with a company's trade secrets should sign nondisclosure agreements, because such agreements make it clear to the employee that the company's trade secrets must be kept confidential.

Non-Disclosure/Non-Circumvent Agreements

If you have an idea for which you have not filed for either patent, copyright, or trademark protection, or if your idea does not fall within the provinces of copyright, trademark, or patent law and therefore cannot be protected, you still have ways of protecting your rights. One of the most important things that you can do to protect yourself is to draft a non-disclosure/non-circumvent agreement. A non-disclosure/non-circumvent agreement prevents others from disclosing your ideas, and more importantly, from taking your ideas so that they may compete with you. Let's say that you have a great idea for a concert event in a venue that has never been used or even thought of before, but you can't really afford to put the whole thing on by yourself. This idea is really not copyrightable, even though your business plan may be protected under copyright. However, if you don't protect yourself *before* you approach any potential investors, they may just take your idea and run with it, thus leaving you out in the cold, and you can pretty much bet that if they can, they will. If you don't have a non-compete/non-disclosure agreement before you give away the idea, don't be surprised that more often than not, you'll be cut out of the deal. Your friend you shared it with will take your idea to his people and act like it was his idea all along. He somehow managed to get owner amnesia as to the originator of the idea, and is only concerned with making himself look good. A non-disclosure agreement is a basic contract such that the party with whom you share the idea will not share the idea with anyone else. A non-circumvent agreement is a basic contract that states that if you share the idea with other parties, they will not try to use your idea to compete with you. Of course, getting people to sign one of these agreements is an art that not many have mastered. You must make sure that they are not already using the idea first. So make sure to do your homework before you ask anyone to sign such an agreement.

Non-Compete Agreements

Sometimes, employers will have their employees sign non-compete agreements, since they know if one of their employees leaves their business and goes to work for a competitor, they are otherwise likely to divulge trade secret information to the new employer. To protect yourself, you can have your employees sign a non-compete agreement. These agreements are enforceable if they are not too restrictive. They must be for a limited time and within a certain geographical area.

To prevail in a trade secret infringement suit, a trade secret owner must show that the information alleged to be confidential provides a competitive advantage, and that the information really is maintained in secrecy. In addition, the trade secret owner must show that the information was either improperly acquired by the defendant or improperly disclosed by the defendant. The owner of the trade secret can seek injunctive relief or sue for damages, but damages may be very hard to prove unless you can show some economic loss due to the loss of the trade secret.

Intentional theft of trade secrets can constitute a crime under both federal and state laws. The most significant federal law dealing with trade secret theft is the Economic Espionage Act of 1996 (EEA) (18 U.S.C., Sections 1831 to 1839). The EEA gives the U.S. Attorney

General very broad power to prosecute any person or company involved in trade secret misappropriation, and punishes intentional stealing, copying, or receiving of trade secrets. Penalties for violations are severe: Individuals may be fined up to $500,000 and corporations up to $5 million. A violator may also be sent to prison for up to 10 years. The government can seize or sell all property used and proceeds derived from the theft. Several states have also enacted laws making trade secret infringement a crime. You should check your state statutes to find out what type of protection you may be afforded.

Publicity and Privacy Rights

Privacy and publicity laws are designed to protect completely separate and distinct interests from copyright or trademark interests, but are often very much interrelated by the media that are used to exploit these rights. As discussed earlier, copyright protects the copyright holder's property rights in the work or expression of an idea, while privacy and publicity rights protect the interests of the person or persons who may be the subject or subjects of the work or expression of an idea. Privacy and publicity rights come into play when someone wants to use photographs, audio, video, or prints or likenesses of individuals. Therefore, for someone to actually infringe on someone else's privacy or publicity rights, he generally must use some type of copyrightable art form such as a picture, video, audio, and the like.

Let's look at photographs and discuss the rights that are involved, because seeing a person in pictures is a very common situation that arises every day. When a picture is taken, the photographer is the person who has the right to copyright his pictures, because he is the person who creates the photograph and therefore should be able to have the right to protect his work. However, the subject of the photograph has rights too. You wouldn't want someone to use a picture of you on something that is for sale, would you?

If a recording artist wants to use a particular photograph for an album cover or other promotional material, and the photograph features some person or subject other than the artist, a couple of issues will arise. First, the photographer must grant a license to the recording artist to use the photograph, unless of course the photographer was paid by the recording artist to take the picture as a work-for-hire. In a work-for-hire relationship, the photographer is paid to take a photograph and is required to sign an agreement whereby he accepts payment for his creation of his intellectual property right (the photograph), and transfers that ownership in the copyright to the person who pays for the photograph and who now will have the exclusive right to file for the copyright and be granted all the rights that copyright entails.

As to the second issue with regard to use of a photograph, if you use a picture on an album cover or whatever, and you have not obtained the permission of the subject of the photograph, you may very well have a publicity or privacy right issue on your hands, and you may end up being liable to that person for your improper use for commercial gain.

Privacy rights laws with regard to the subject of a photograph or other medium are of a personal nature and are designed to protect the individual. Every person has the right not to have his or her personal image or likeness put out to the public without his or her consent. In other words, we all have the right to be left alone and not be exploited by the media in any way. However, some folks have signed up for a public life by their own actions. You may wonder how the paparazzi is able to hound rock stars, movie stars, and politicians, and continually take their pictures and sell them to the highest bidder. The reason is that people who put themselves out in the public eye for personal gain have waived certain aspects of their rights to privacy, because they have become public figures. Also, anything that is a matter of public record is fair game. Therefore, if you are arrested or involved in any court proceedings, unless there is a gag order by a judge or an agreement that a settlement will be kept confidential, anyone who can get to the courthouse has the right to read the entire file. Unfortunately, in this day and age where identity theft is so prevalent, the courts are going to have to make some type of change to the law so that addresses, Social Security numbers, credit card numbers, and other personal information will not be so readily available to would-be criminals or others with less than honorable intentions. In the end, if you really want to remain a completely private person, you may be well advised to never leave your house, because once you are in a public place, you are in the public.

Publicity rights laws focus on the protection of an individual's name or likeness. A likeness can be a sculpture, a drawing, a painting, a caricature, a photograph, or any other reproduction of the image of a person. In some cases, it does not necessarily have to be a person's face, but any part of their image that can be easily determined to belong to that person. The right of publicity gives people the right to prevent others from using their name or likeness for commercial gain without prior consent. The right of publicity is also very important to those in the entertainment and sports fields who use their name and likeness to make a living, and therefore, anyone who exploits that right without consent or compensation is taking advantage of that entertainer or sports figure's publicity rights, and preventing that entertainer or sports figure from reaping the benefits of his hard-earned success. But these rights are not the exclusive rights of celebrities. Thus people can sell their stories for made-for-TV movies, tabloids, and the like, because these studios or magazines cannot use these individuals' names and likenesses without consent and in many cases without placing the highest bid for the right.

There is no doubt that star power can enhance the commercial value of goods or services with which they are associated. In fact, commercials for a wide variety of products now have endorsements from celebrities and sports figures. Before Tiger Woods had ever even teed up a golf ball as a professional, he was already worth tens of millions of dollars in the form of product endorsements, for which he had to make appearances, wear certain logos on his clothing, and appear in certain commercials. Celebrity wields so much power that advertisers now even have celebrity voices delivering the voiceovers to hawk certain goods or services, due to the warm and fuzzy feeling we get when we hear a familiar voice.

Unfortunately for the entertainers and other public figures, along with huge paychecks for commercial endorsements comes an incredible demand for news stories, articles in gossip rags, interviews, biographies, and the like. Permission is not necessary to use a celebrity's name or likeness in a news report, novel, play, film, or biography, because the life stories of celebrities are for the most part public domain and as such belong to everyone, and therefore they can be related by anyone, even if there is a profit to be made. This is exactly how the tabloids are able to get away with what they do. However, there is one huge caveat that lies in the area of tort law: You cannot make any statement that is defamatory. Disseminating either written (libel) or spoken (slander) statements that are not true can be actionable by law, even if you are able to show that your statements were made by reasonably relying on the truth. Therefore, if people make up stories that can be proven to be false, you may have a cause of action for defamation. However, the burden of proof for the plaintiff in a defamation action is very hard to meet. You must show that the alleged defaming party had a duty not to make false statements, that they breached this duty and actually made false statements (which isn't that hard to prove), and that their false statements have actually and proximately caused you damage. This last tenet can be very hard to prove. First you must show that but for the actions of the alleged defamer, you would not have been harmed, and if you can actually meet this test, you must prove how much you were in fact damaged. Regardless of the burden of proof, there is always a risk when periodicals or newspapers hold up people to ridicule or put them in a bad light, especially entertainers with deep pockets who can afford high-dollar attorneys to represent them. At the very least, these high-dollar attorneys can make the tabloids think long and hard before printing potentially damaging stories.

Another thing to remember about reporters, newspapers, periodicals, and other media is that they will often hide behind the First Amendment. Although I am a firm believer in and staunch supporter of First Amendment rights, I don't believe that anyone should be able to report or print just about anything they want just to sell copies of their rag, especially if what they print or report is damaging to people and is not true. Reporters, writers, and the like should have some degree of morals and ethics, and also should be held strictly accountable when they represent things falsely. But who should be able to dictate public morality? This is a difficult question, to say the least. Be that as it may, there isn't much that you can do when they take sound bites from your statements and seemingly twist them so that they have more mass appeal and some degree of sensationalism. After all, that's what sells newspapers and advertising for the news, so there really isn't much you can about it.

It is important to note here that copyrights and trademarks are federally protected rights, while publicity and privacy rights are not. Publicity and privacy rights are the exclusive provinces of state laws. While many states do have publicity and privacy rights laws that one can look to when seeking redress, some states do not have any privacy or publicity laws on the books. However, these rights can still be protected under general common laws of misappropriation, misrepresentation, and/or false presentation. In some cases, the federal Lanham Act that covers trademark law can be used for claims for unauthorized use of a person's identity to create false endorsements and the like. Also, it important to note that fair use can be a defense to copyright infringement, but the fair use doctrine was specifically written for federal copyright law and does not apply to publicity and privacy rights. Regardless of the issues, if you feel that you have a claim against someone, you are best advised to find a very good intellectual property lawyer to represent you, because the law is very complex, and you will need someone who is very skilled at these types of arguments if he is going to convince an extremely subjective judge or jury to rule on your behalf and grant you the justice that you feel that you deserve.

Finally, for the most part, your privacy rights end when you die. However, your publicity rights that are associated with the commercial value of your name and likeness can continue long after your death, and can be passed to your heirs so that they control those rights long after your death. The best example of this is the Elvis Presley estate, which has complete control of Elvis's name and likeness, and the estate guards and protects them like they were pure gold, which is exactly what they are.

Summary

As you can see, intellectual property is a fascinating subject, and there are many twists and turns. But if you have a basic understanding of it, you will at least know when you need to hire an attorney or not.

CHAPTER 7

Publishing

"Where the real money is.…"

Music is everywhere. It permeates almost all places in our society, so much so that it is hard to imagine our world today without it. Music is on the radio, in bars, in shopping malls, in grocery stores, in elevators, in your home, in your car, on airplanes and trains, on television, in movies—everywhere. And you can bet that anytime you hear music, there is someone behind the scenes collecting money, or at least making a claim for money.

The ones who are collecting the money are the owners of the copyrights. If you want to see who makes a good chunk of the money in the music business, take a good look at publishing companies and the hit songwriters who create these valuable copyrights.

The life of a copyright currently lasts for a very long time. If you are lucky enough to have a song that is played on the radio and performed live, you will be getting plenty of royalty checks for years and years to come.

It's pretty cool to think that you could still be making money from a song that you wrote a very long time ago. In fact, you can look at publishing royalties as a nice little retirement fund.

Unfortunately, there are always people who think that they should not have to pay just to listen to music. Many of these people own bars, restaurants, retail outlets, etc. They argue that music is merely ancillary to their business, and therefore they should not have to pay to play music in their businesses for the enjoyment of their customers. But could you imagine going into a supposedly "hip" bar or retail outlet that played only public domain music, such as classical music or really old music? It would drive customers away. The music that is playing over the stereo, radio, or television in any business helps to set "the tone" and can define what type of clientele that business is targeting. You won't hear punk rock in an upscale bistro, nor will you hear easy listening in a rock club. In fact, if you go a bar and there's no music playing at all, you'll probably wonder what happened to the stereo system. After all, who wants to hang out in a bar and only listen to other people talk the whole time?

With that in mind, we should take a very long and hard look at exactly how publishing money is made, how it's distributed, and many of the other aspects of music publishing.

If you are a published songwriter, you should give some serious thought to joining a performance rights organization. What constitutes a "published songwriter" depends on the organization and its requirements. But usually the main requirement is that your song has been performed on the radio or at a live performance, or released on a recording. The three performing rights organizations in the United States are ASCAP, BMI, and SESAC. They will collect your performance royalty money, so make sure that you get to know these people. They can be an asset to your career. Their job is *not* to get you cuts or to handle any aspect of getting you a deal, but they can be very helpful in a number of ways if you take to the time to get to know the right people.

If you are a publisher, you still need to join a publishing company. You will have to submit a list of possible names for your company, and if your name is cleared, you can set up your company with that name. Of course, you should also make sure that any name you choose does not infringe on any other company's trademark. (For more information, see Chapter 6, "Intellectual Property.") Once you have a cleared name, you will need at least one writer (which can be yourself) who is affiliated with you for that particular licensing organization. Also, you can join each licensing organization as a publisher if you have songs in your catalogue from at least one writer who is affiliated with a particular organization. However, as a songwriter, you can only affiliate with one licensing organization.

So, now we move on to how money is made in publishing. To do that, we need to look at copyrights and what role they play in the music we hear. Copyrights, as discussed in Chapter 6, are the cornerstone of music publishing, so we need to focus on how copyrights are created, portioned, and exploited. Some of this information may be repeated from Chapter 6, but it's so important that I don't mind the risk of repeating myself. Based upon the bundle of rights, copyright owners are the sole persons or entities who have the right to perform their songs, make copies of their music either in print or audio/visual media, or even allow others the right to perform or copy their songs. You may decide to transfer this bundle of rights to a publisher because it's the most sound business decision, or you may decide to become a publisher yourself. If you are able to sign a publishing deal, you will have a lot of help to get your songs out there. However, if you do decide to become a publisher, the first steps that you will want to look into are setting up your business and acquiring your catalogue.

Setting Up Your Business

As with any other business, you will have to choose a business structure and you will be well advised to have a business plan. (See Chapter 2, "Choosing a Business Structure," and Chapter 3, "Making a Business Plan.") The benefits of having your own publishing company can be great, but unless you can dedicate a great deal of time specifically to your company and not just to writing songs, you may want to reconsider running your own company. It can be daunting, especially if the revenues from your publishing company are going to be your sole means of income. Publishing is very much a "hit or miss" business, and misses don't pay much money!

Major publishers employ many people with various and sundry skills, because there are a number of tasks that must be mastered in order to have a profitable publishing company. If you are thinking about starting your own company, you may also want to consider whether you will be able to get others to work for you, at least as subcontractors or even part-time, because you may find that you can't handle the entire workload by yourself. You will need to take care of many tasks, such as submitting all clearance forms, handling all copyright administration, handling all general accounting, drafting and negotiating contracts, and much, much more. You will most likely find that some people are more suited to particular tasks than others. A person who's good at math may be best for the bookkeeping and administration work, the more creative types could be better at pitching, and the folks with more organizational skills would be better suited for running and overseeing the overall enterprise.

However, you can do it yourself if you are willing to really work hard at it and be willing to wear a number of hats. You must know when you need to get extra help, such as when to hire a lawyer to review your contracts, an accountant to make sure that you are getting your figures right and paying all of your taxes, a song plugger to pitch your songs, and an outside consultant to make sure that you have all of your ducks in a row. But again, you can do it solo, and I've seen plenty of people who have had a great deal of success on their own.

In fact, my mentor when I was starting out had over 100 album cuts and got them all pretty much by himself. He was an artist/songwriter/producer who could write great songs, get them to a number of his contacts, and actually get cuts from his own personal efforts. He would utilize his large number of friends who were artists, managers, and A&R people so that he could constantly keep pitching his own songs, or songs that he acquired from other writers. He kept getting cuts, which led to a good deal of his success.

However, before you can even start to think about running a company, pitching, and getting cuts, you have to think about how you are going to acquire a song catalogue.

ACQUIRING A CATALOGUE

If you have written a bunch of songs, either by yourself or with others, you may already have a catalogue of songs that you can include in your publishing company. Furthermore, if you have already set up your own publishing company and you have co-written a lot of songs with unsigned writers, that may be a good window of opportunity to acquire some if not all of the publishing rights to those songs, especially if your co-writers don't have the knowledge or desire to start their own publishing companies. You may also be able to work with other writers who don't necessarily want to be their own publishers, or perhaps don't have enough good songs to get their own publishing deals. This could be a good opportunity to grow your catalogue, even if it is just one song at a time.

If you are going to be pitching songs to anyone for just about any type of project, the more quality songs you have in your catalogue, the more likely you are to be able to get a cut or place a song. I've seen many people who came very close to getting songs placed, but just didn't have enough depth of material. The people they were pitching couldn't find the exact right song. In short, quality is better than quantity, but the more quantity you have, the more likely you'll have a song that someone will want. The last thing you want to hear is, "This song is really close to what we want, but it's not quite right for the project. Have you got anything else?" Being that close to getting a cut is a great ego boost, but not getting the cut is no different than never being considered in the first place.

Now that we have discussed setting up your business and acquiring a catalogue, let's look at getting some cuts or placing your songs with different types of projects.

PITCHING YOUR SONGS

The most critical part of any publishing company is getting cuts, getting songs placed, or finding other ways to generate income from your song catalogue. You can't expect hits if you aren't getting any cuts recorded by artists on the major record labels, even if they're only companion cuts. A *cut* is simply a song placed on a record that will be released by a recording artist with any type of record deal. A *companion cut* simply means that your song will be placed on a record but not released as a single. If the song is not released as a single, you or your publisher are at least guaranteed to get mechanical royalties from the sales of records. Obviously, getting a companion cut with a major recording artist would be better than getting a single cut with an unknown artist on an unknown record label. However, what any publisher is always looking for are hits, or single cuts released by a major recording artist that hit the charts. If your songs become hits, you will not have nearly as much of a problem getting them used in film or television, or in other ways that generate revenues. Furthermore, if you are not getting your songs recorded by either yourself or other artists, you won't be generating *any* income, and therefore you could go out of business rather quickly.

If you are trying to get songs cut, the most important thing you can do is pitch songs constantly. You will need to keep up with as many trade magazines as you can, because knowing who is doing what is the key to knowing where there are people looking for songs. If possible, get pitch lists so that you will know who is looking for songs at any particular time. *Pitch lists* are compilations of acts, artists, managers, A&R staff, etc., who are looking for songs to record for their upcoming projects. You should also establish a good rapport with A&R executives at the major labels, artist managers, and signed artists.

I know a lot of songwriters who were able to get cuts that eventually became number-one hits without their publishers' efforts. This doesn't mean that your publisher's efforts aren't important. In fact, having a reputable publisher in your corner has many, many benefits. But just because you have a publishing deal doesn't mean that you should rest on your laurels and wait for your publisher to get you a cut. Join as many organizations as you can, network with as many people as you can, and always be out there with a copy of your best songs. You never know when that one chance to pitch will come. The last thing you want is to be unprepared for the moment that could change your life forever.

SONG PLUGGERS

If you do not have adequate staff at your publishing company who can spend most of their time continually pitching songs, or if you are not signed to a publishing deal, there are a number of individuals or companies that offer their services as *song pluggers*. These song pluggers can be a good source of information and leads, because they're out there gathering information about who needs which type of songs for particular projects. If they are good at their game, they can help you to keep your catalogue in the minds of the people who will decide which songs will be placed on which records. Song pluggers are paid in a number of ways. They may require a weekly fee, they may want a piece of the action, or both.

If you are considering hiring song pluggers, you need only ask about their track record. If they have been getting cuts for a number of publishers or writers, you may want to hire them in some capacity. If they have no track record at all but seem very eager and professional, you may consider giving them a chance. But the publishing business is risky enough without taking chances on unproven people, so be very careful about how you spend your money and who may be representing your company. The last thing you want is for some agent of your company to go out and represent you in a bad light. Contacts and relationships are the keys to success in this game, so be careful not to burn any bridges.

MANAGEMENT

If you have your own publishing company, you need to decide how you are going to handle the management. Someone needs to decide who should be hired, who will handle the day-to-day operations of the company, and who will oversee the employees and make sure they're living up to their job descriptions.

ADMINISTRATION

This part of your publishing company is probably the most tedious, but certainly one of the most important. Someone has to make sure that all copyrights are filed, any applicable extensions are applied for, all clearance forms for licensing organizations are filled out, all other important paperwork is handled, and all moneys are being received, and much, much more. In short, without good administration, you will not have much success as a publishing company.

Publishing Deals

Let's assume that you are not going into business for yourself, but are thinking about signing a deal with a publishing company. We should move on to how different types of publishing deals will work. We'll start with the split, or how the rights to copyrights are divided up amongst the players that are involved.

THE SPLIT

As covered in Chapter 6, when a writer sits down and writes a song, he creates a statutory copyright that gives him 100% ownership of the copyright. Furthermore, once the writer files that copyright and receives registration from the Library of Congress for that song, not only does he have 100% ownership of the entire copyright, but also 100% of all the rights that are attached to that copyright. However, when you talk to publishers and other music business aficionados, they often to refer to a copyright in terms of 200%. In other words, the copyright is split into 100% of the publisher's share and 100% of the songwriter's share.

The writer's share is simply how much credit a person gets for writing a song. Therefore, if you write a song completely by yourself, you get 100% writer's share of that song. If you co-write a song with one other person, you get 50% of the writer's share, and so on. However, there is also the publisher's share. This only comes about if you plan to publish your song, which I'm sure that everyone wants to do. If you sign with a publisher, you will assign 100% of the publishing to the publisher. You will retain 100% of your writer's share, and if you are able to negotiate well, you could end up co-publishing with your publisher and retain a portion of the publisher's share. Even though you may technically assign 100% of the song or entire copyright to the publisher, you will still retain your writer's share. Even though you are giving up half of the proceeds to your songs, a publishing deal is a very good thing. If you are an established songwriter or have a record deal, your publisher may offer a higher percentage of the split or even enter into a co-publishing arrangement with you. (See "Co-Publishing" later in this chapter.)

No matter how the split works out for you, major publishers will have the contacts, the staff, the funds, and many other resources to best exploit their song catalogues. If you are fortunate enough to gain interest from a publisher, you will definitely be asked to sign a contract, because transfers of copyrights must be in writing. You may be asked to sign either single song agreements or an exclusive songwriter's contract. And each of these types of agreements may divide the bundle of rights so that certain rights can be assigned to one or more parties. In other words, mechanical rights, performance rights, print rights, and synchronization rights can be assigned to different parties. However, most publishers will insist that they obtain all of the rights to a song for a single song contract, or for all songs that are part of an exclusive songwriter's contract.

SINGLE SONG CONTRACTS

In some cases, you may have an opportunity to get a single song published instead of signing a long-term publishing contract. This can be a good thing, because you don't necessarily need to give all of your songs (and your trust) to a company that may not be willing or able to work your entire catalogue. Signing a single song agreement is a good way to see how well that company will work your material, and whether you may be interested in signing an exclusive writer's contract with it. However, be very careful, because you don't want to assign your rights to a company that is not going to do anything with your song other than increase its catalogue. Make sure that you learn as much as you can about your potential publisher so that doesn't happen to you.

Single song contracts can be expanded to include any number of songs. However, they may or may not require that any advance be paid against royalties, or that any money be paid to the songwriter for the rights to the songs. If there is little or no money transferred as consideration for acquiring your songs, the publisher will usually agree to use its time and efforts to exploit the song, as well as to pay to have a demonstration recording made for some if not all of the songs that are transferred. Of course, the publisher may request that you pay for all or just part of your demo costs. If this is the case, there will be less money to recoup if you get a cut, but if you are paying for any costs, you should try to enter into a co-publishing agreement. On the other hand, a single song agreement can be a good choice for a publisher, because it can cherry-pick the best songs of a particular writer and not be on the hook to pay a monthly advance to that writer to turn in songs that have yet to be written. This way, the publisher knows what it is getting and may be much more likely to work those songs.

A single song agreement will have many of the same clauses as exclusive writer's contracts, such as the term, consideration (which could be nominal consideration in the form of $1.00, along with a promise to pay royalties), territory, accountings, right to audit, indemnification of the publisher for any breach of warranties by the writer, right to use the publicity rights of the writer, jurisdiction, and more.

Most of the language you will see in a single song agreement will be fairly standard, However, there are a few clauses that should be of concern to any writer.

First of all, any royalties that are called for under the contract are always a concern. You will want to get as much royalties as you possibly can for piano copies, printed editions, collections of works that include your songs, mechanical royalties, and synchronization rights. If you do not understand what you should be getting, you should hire an attorney or find someone who can explain whether you are getting a fair deal. If you have some degree of negotiating power, you may be able to get increased royalty rates and increase your foreign royalties from 50% to 75%, but you will have to allow the publisher to assign its rights under the contract to its foreign affiliate or subsidiaries. Just make sure that you don't get caught up in a situation where the affiliate or subsidiaries take a percentage (usually 25%) to collect foreign royalties. Make sure that you receive the full percentage that is paid at the source of the royalties (for more information on source royalties see the section "At Source Royalties"). Otherwise, you could be losing 25%

each time one of the publisher's affiliates or subsidiaries passes along the collection money from company to company before the money even hits the United States.

I have found that writers and publishers that don't pay very close attention to their foreign royalties end up not getting paid substantial sums. Many people think of foreign royalties as a sort of bonus, but in today's worldwide market, the world is becoming a smaller and smaller place. Remember, in foreign countries you get royalties in the form of a percentage of ticket sales if your song is played in a motion picture, as well as other considerations that are not paid in the United States.

You want to clearly define what advances you will be responsible for, as well as how those advances will be recouped. Make sure that you know whether you will be on the hook to your publisher for anything other than demo costs, such as copyright registration fees, lead sheets, printed materials, copying costs, or advertising. If you have to pay back these fees, make sure that the publisher is spending your money wisely.

You may also want to limit the number of professional copies or free goods that the publishing company will give away for advertising or promotional purposes, or at least keep track of them. Of course, your publisher will have to advertise, market, and promote your music, but you don't want your publisher giving away free goods when there is no need to.

Creative control can be a real thorn in the side of the songwriter, especially if the publisher insists on the ability to change the title, lyrics, or music, prepare derivative works, or more. To make matters worse, the publisher will want the ability to hire someone else to make these changes, and you'll end up in a co-writing situation without any input on the co-write. You should at least ask the publisher to allow *you* to make any changes requested. But the publisher may insist that they retain total creative control, which means that they may not even ask you before they change your song.

The publisher will also insist on the right of assignment, which is necessary for foreign subpublishing. But you should limit the publisher's ability to assign your song or songs to a third party that you do not approve of. The publisher should at least try to exploit your song or songs with the same degree of professionalism as your original publisher. Otherwise, if your publisher goes out of business or cannot continue to be your publisher, your songs could end up in the hands of someone that you absolutely do not want to do business with, or that doesn't want to work with you. And that publisher will still own your songs.

EXCLUSIVE SONGWRITER'S CONTRACTS

An exclusive songwriter's contract is the standard type of contract that you will see between songwriters and major publishers. However, I don't really believe that there is such a thing as a "standard" contract or agreement. Each company has its own agreements, which cover different issues in different ways, and each agreement will vary based upon the negotiating positions of the parties. Unfortunately, a new songwriter doesn't really have much negotiating power. The publisher probably thinks the songwriter is lucky to be offered any type of songwriting deal in the first place.

Be that as it may, an exclusive songwriter's contract may be offered to a new or established songwriter so he'll write exclusively for that publisher. Depending on whether you sign a single song contract or an exclusive songwriter's contract, you will see many of the following types of clauses.

Advances

You are normally offered some sort of advance, so that you can dedicate most of your time to songwriting and still pay your bills. You may get a lump sum or payments in increments. The amount varies from deal to deal and from one publishing company to the next, but it will usually be just enough that you won't have to go into debt just to survive. You won't get a much better deal than that, unless you are an extremely established songwriter with a very good track record of writing charted hits. Of course, many agreements will allow for increases in subsequent option years, so the advance will increase with cost of living increases, etc.

You probably won't be considered an employee of the company, and you will not be providing songwriting services. Rather, you will be assigning your copyrights to the publisher, which often is an outright sale of your entire bundle of rights. In return, you get an advance against royalties that the publisher hopes to recover by getting your songs cut by other artists, or you may have some type of artist development or major record label recording contract.

However, some companies will want to treat you as an employee, and all of the songs that you will turn in will be considered works for hire. If this is the case, you can't reclaim your works that are tendered to the company under that agreement. Of course, sometimes you may be commissioned to write a song for a particular purpose. If this is the case, there is no exclusive relationship, and the relationship ends as soon as the song has been tendered to the person or entity that commissioned the song.

Getting back to advances, they are usually paid out monthly or sometimes biweekly, and are incorporated with any costs that the company may advance to have your songs made into demonstration recordings, or other costs incurred so that the songs may be pitched to any interested parties. Again, you should be careful to define clearly what advances you will be responsible for, as well as how those advances will be recouped. Make sure that you know whether you will be responsible for costs such as copyright registration fees, lead sheets, printed materials, copying, advertising, or marketing. If you do have to pay back these fees, you'd better make sure that the publisher is spending your money wisely.

Regardless of what advances you are responsible for and will be recouped by your publisher, once any of your songs begin to generate income, you will begin to collect performance royalties directly from your licensing organization. However, before you get any of the mechanical, synchronization, or other royalties that are paid directly to the publisher, the publisher will recoup all of its advanced costs from these royalties until you have fully recouped all advances.

Recoupment

Since you will receive your performance royalties directly from your licensing organization, whether it's ASCAP, BMI, or SESAC, you may not have to worry about recoupment coming from performances, but check your contract to make sure. In most cases your recoupment will come from mechanical, synchronization, or other royalties. Therefore, before you receive any moneys from these sources, your publisher must have recouped all moneys that have been advanced to you in the form of cash advances, demo costs, or other advances, which are outlined in your contract. However, make sure that you know exactly how any moneys that were advanced will be paid back, and keep a handle on the total amount of those advances. Then you'll know when you are supposed to begin seeing future royalties from sources other than performances.

Once you have recouped all moneys that have been advanced, make sure that you are not incurring any further advances or costs that you don't need to live on, or that do not need to be spent on behalf of your catalogue with your publisher. In other words, once you are in the black, you may request that all future advances cease, so that you can live off your royalties and not have to worry about going further into debt with the publisher. Of course, if the publisher is holding you responsible for copyright registration, costs of lead sheets, marketing, etc., you should keep a close eye on how your money is being spent.

If you are in a co-publishing type of agreement, your publisher may want to recoup any advances from any publishing royalties that you are due as part of your co-publishing rights. This is a fairly common practice in co-publishing or participation agreements. It will be up to you whether you want to try to prevent this. However, keep in mind that if you are lucky enough to get a co-publishing deal and you can recoup all advances quickly, you will end up with more money in the end. Allowing your publisher to recoup from your co-publishing rights may not be such a bad thing.

Cross-Collateralization

To ensure that publishers can recoup all advances for songs that they have acquired from an individual songwriter, the publishers will often ask for cross-collateralization. This means that if the publisher has advanced X dollars for song A and Y dollars for song B, and song A never makes money, it can take the money that is being earned from song B to recoup the money lost on song A.

If your negotiating position is strong, you may be able to get out of cross-collateralization, but it's rare in a first-time contract. However, you can always try to put the onus on your publisher, whose reputation rests on being able to pick hits, not to take songs that have less chance of making money. In other words, if the publisher doesn't think that song A is a hit, don't ask for an assignment on that song. Just take the ones that you are sure will be hits, and that way you can assign your other songs to other publishers who do believe in them. Of course, if you are in an exclusive songwriting contract, this probably won't be possible, because the publisher will want to retain all rights to your songs in the hopes that these songs may find some degree of commercial success in the future.

Power of Attorney

Usually you'll have to sign a limited power of attorney, giving the publisher (or any person that the publisher may direct) the right to execute, sign, transfer, acknowledge, or deliver any instrument necessary to grant to the publisher any rights that are granted pursuant to contract. This means that the writer will grant to the publisher the right to carry out business or legal matters on behalf of the writer, such as the right to file for copyrights, issue licenses, etc. Also, be very careful as to what rights are granted under any limited power of attorney, because you don't want to sign over any more rights than the publisher needs.

Right of Publicity

This will allow the publisher to use your name, image, or likeness in any manner that is necessary to market or advertise you or your songs successfully. This includes using your name for printed works such as songbooks and folios, or even your picture or likeness. You may have to agree to be reasonably available for photography sessions and the like.

Right to Indemnity

You will have to make certain warranties when you sign an agreement. One is that you are not encumbered with any other contract that could prevent you from signing with the publisher. Second, the songs that you turn in must have been written by you and by no other party, other than a co-writer. Therefore, if any other company asserts that it is your exclusive publisher, or if any other writer or publisher asserts that any song you have turned in infringes on the works of another, you agree to indemnify and hold your publisher harmless for any breach of warranty on your behalf. This means that you could have to pay for any lawsuit for copyright infringement that may be brought against your publisher in regards to your songs.

Right to Change or Adapt

As mentioned in the section on single song contracts, the publisher will want to retain the right to change, adapt, edit, and prepare derivative works based on the songs that you turn in. In fact, the publisher will try to retain the right to hire someone else to make these changes, and you will end up in a co-writing situation without any input on the co-write. You should at least ask the publisher to allow you to make any changes it has requested. But the publisher may insist that it retain total creative control, which means that it may not even ask you before changing your song. Obviously, this can be a real problem, because you may have to share in any royalties for the rewrite. You should try to get the publisher to at least allow the original writer to make any changes, and if he can't do that to the publisher's satisfaction, you should try to negotiate that no royalties will be paid to the third-party writer.

JURISDICTION

Jurisdiction will set forth the situs of the contract and under what laws the contract will be governed by. In other words, if you sign a contract in California, the laws of California will usually govern that contract. However, you could sign a contract in New York or Nashville that will call for the laws of the state of California to govern the contract, or vice versa. This will usually occur when a company in New York or Nashville has its parent offices in California, or vice versa.

If you're signing a songwriting contract in Nashville, you want the laws of the state of Tennessee to govern, so that any suit regarding the contract would have to be brought in Tennessee. If you have to sue over some contractual dispute, you don't want to go through the expense of traveling back and forth to California to make court appearances just so that you can protect your rights.

Territory

The territory of your contract will usually be throughout the world, and sometimes even throughout the known universe. If you have sufficient negotiating clout and are an experienced writer, and if your publisher does not have affiliates or subsidiaries in foreign territories, you may want to limit your territory to the United States and Canada so that you can negotiate your own foreign rights. However, you need to be extremely experienced and have relationships with many foreign companies to negotiate your own foreign rights effectively. In most cases, if you are with a large publisher, you should allow the publisher to collect foreign royalties.

At Source Royalties

If you do allow you publisher to collect foreign royalties, you should try to get at source royalties. This means that if your publisher collects royalties from the United Kingdom or other foreign territories, you will not be paid the net royalties received after the foreign territory has collected its usual 25%. In other words, if the UK subpublisher charges 25% of all moneys collected and pays 75% to your publisher, you end up with 50% of 75%, instead of 50% of 100% collected at the source. Since the publisher and subpublisher are in fact affiliated, or possibly even owned by the same entity, you will end up losing money that you should be earning.

And again, foreign royalties should be watched very closely. You especially don't want to get into a situation where Germany collects money and deducts its 25%, and then sends the money to the UK affiliate that deducts its 25%, and so on. You could end up losing a considerable amount of foreign royalties without ever even knowing it. You would need to audit all of these foreign countries, which could be extremely expensive.

Reduced Rates

This also applies to the publisher issuing any reduced mechanical royalty rates or any other types of licensing deals to other companies that are affiliated with or owned by the publisher or its parent company, such as with at source royalties. You may see language that says the publisher must deal at arm length with any of its affiliates, subsidiaries, or even the parent company. That means they must deal with these companies as if they were just like any other company. This way, you maintain the same royalty rate that you would enjoy with any other company.

Term

The exclusive songwriter's agreement is for a fixed time or term, which can vary from one to five years depending on any options (see below), how good a songwriter you are, and how much commercial exploitability the publisher feels that it can attribute to your future and/or existing catalogue, which you will be required to turn in. In other words, the publisher is taking a big chance that it will be able to get cuts based upon your unproven ability to write songs for it. Of course, this risk is much less with an established writer, but there are lots of writers out there who have had a good deal of success before they sign a publishing agreement, and then never even get another cut. So the risks for the publisher are pretty great. Nobody can predict the future, and the publisher stands to lose a great deal of money unless it can find a future for your songs.

Options

In some cases, the publisher will want to retain the right to pick up options to extend the term of a songwriting contract. In other words, the publisher has the right to let you go after the first year. But if the publisher decides that you have a good shot at success, or has been able to get cuts for you or otherwise make money from your efforts, the publisher will want to keep you bound contractually for as long as possible.

There may not be much a new songwriter can do about the option part of the contract due to lack of negotiating power. However, it's a good idea to word the contract so that the publisher has to give you notice before the option is picked up, instead of the option being exercised automatically. This way, if the publisher isn't paying close attention to the contract, it may miss the required notice and you'll be free of any further contractual obligations. Of course, you may wish to continue the contractual relationship, but if not, the contract will be terminated when the publisher fails to pick up the option. It just depends on each individual situation as to whether you or the publisher will want options to the contract.

Prior Compositions

You may be required to turn in your prior compositions, which are the songs that you have written prior to entering into the agreement with the publisher. This is usually a good point of negotiation for the new writer with no track record. You may have written quite a few songs over the years before you sign a publishing deal. The more songs you bring to the table, the better the deal you will be able to negotiate for yourself.

However, the offer to write for your publisher may be conditioned upon your prior works, and therefore you may not get any extra consideration for those prior works. You should negotiate some sort of signing bonus for these prior songs, if you can. Otherwise, you will have to sign away your rights to your prior compositions as part of the entire consideration of the contract, and you will get nothing extra for turning in your prior compositions.

Minimum Commitment

You will also have a minimum commitment of songs that you must turn in every calendar year. The average number is usually 12 songs, and it could be less if you are a recording artist with additional time constraints.

Meeting that requirement very much depends on whether the publisher accepts the songs that you turn in. If you co-write a lot of songs, you would have to co-write 24 of them to meet your minimum commitment of 12 songs. Or, if you had two co-writers, you would have to write 36 songs. In fact, I used to think that I would never need to use algebra in my legal career, but the first publishing deal that I negotiated for one of my songwriting clients had language setting forth numerators and denominators so that one could figure out the number of songs that needed to be turned in pursuant to the minimum commitment clause of the agreement.

Be that as it may, make sure that you completely understand what the publisher expects in regard to your minimum commitment, especially when it comes to what songs the company will accept. You don't want to turn in 100 songs only to find out that your publisher will accept fewer than 12 of them, and therefore you have breached your agreement. Therefore, it is very important to understand what level of songwriting is expected of you.

Unfortunately, whether someone likes a song is entirely subjective. You could feel like you have turned in some of your absolute best work, only to have it rejected by your publisher. This can be a very tricky thing to deal with, because the language in the contract will call for songs that are deemed to be satisfactory for commercial exploitation. But again, the publisher will make that decision.

To make matters worse, the publisher will also want to retain ownership of the songs that you turn in that are not deemed to be commercially exploitable. You should at least retain some type of reversion rights, or try to keep all songs that are not accepted by the publisher as part of your minimum commitment. But again, a new songwriter will not have a strong negotiating position, so ask for everything that you can get and see how the publisher deals with your requests.

Accounting Periods

Your publisher will not want to go through the time, trouble, and expense of doing an accounting and providing it to you every single month. Therefore, the publisher will usually do a semiannual accounting, and in some cases a quarterly accounting, and provide you with a statement along with your royalty payments. However, many publishers will not send out that statement or the royalty checks for a period of 30, 60, or even 90 days after the accounting has been completed. Obviously, as the songwriter, you would expect to get paid as soon as the publisher receives money on your behalf. However, unless you are an extremely lucrative writer for your publisher, this just isn't going to happen.

It's in the best interests of publishers to hang onto their money for as long as they can. In fact, publishers keep all of their funds that eventually will be dispersed in an interest-bearing account so that they can maximize their profits, and it's perfectly legal. Obviously, this interest adds up quickly and adds extra income to the publisher's coffers. But the time between when a publisher receives the money and when it's paid out is a source of constant friction between writers and publishers. The only thing you can do about it is to negotiate these points up front, or you will be waiting for your money just like everyone else who's signed with your publishing company.

There is usually a long time between when a song hits the charts and when you get the money for performances and for all other royalties. Your performance royalty money has to come from blanket licenses from radio, foreign licensing, etc. That money will be collected by your performance licensing organization (ASCAP, BMI, or SESAC), and that takes time. Once the licensing organization has received the money, it has to do some serious calculations as to who is entitled to the money based upon its own pay scale plans, and *then* it sends the money to you. As far as what your publisher receives, sometimes synchronization fees are negotiated and paid up front, but still moneys must be collected from overseas and other sources. In short, it will be a long time before you see any money, even if you have a number-one hit.

However, there are many banks that cater to the music industry, and they are more than willing to give you a loan based upon collateral in the form of assignment of royalties you will be paid for having a charted hit. The bank knows that a charted hit is money in the bank for the writer, and therefore will be willing to make a loan so that you can buy a house, a car, or whatever you feel you deserve as the fruits of your labor. But unfortunately, you will end up having to pay interest on that loan, so try not to go crazy once you get a hit.

If you do end up with a hit song, or even a string of hits, manage your money wisely. This way you'll be sure to have plenty to last you for the rest of your life, because those hits will generate money for years to come. But the money won't flow forever, so plan accordingly. I once had a client who wrote a check for a house for one million dollars. He was single and had no tax deductions, and he would have been much better off making payments on the house and deducting the interest. But he went ahead and bought the house outright just because he could!

Right to Audit

Your publisher will grant you the right to audit the books, but just like with a record company audit, you will have to give notice and conduct the audit during normal business hours and at reasonable times so that you don't interrupt the day-to-day business affairs of your publisher. Again, the contract will most likely specify that you can only audit its books with a licensed CPA present, and there may be restrictions on the number of times that you can audit your publisher during the term of your contract.

Once you have signed away your rights pursuant to your publishing contract, you are pretty much stuck with that agreement. However, there are a few situations where you can get your songs back, especially if you are not getting paid any money or your songs are not being exploited in any way.

Termination of Rights

As stated in Chapter 6, you can terminate your assigned rights for a 5-year period after the 35th and before the 41st year after the initial transfer. So, you had better keep track of the date of transfer and the date of first publication, and make sure that your successors, heirs, and assigns have notice of this in the event of your death so that they can terminate the transfer and keep 100% of the copyright. Also, you must give written notice to terminate a transfer, which can be done between 10 and 2 years before the termination date. Remember that you must also send a copy of the notice to the Copyright Office so that your rights are protected.

You could also ask a court to rescind your contract if your publisher isn't paying you moneys that you are due. Of course, the more that the publisher pays, the less likely you will have an action against your publisher. Furthermore, if there have just been some minor accounting errors or late payments, your chances of getting out of your contract are not very good. However, sometimes the amounts paid versus what is owed are so different that you could file a legitimate suit and win. The courts are becoming much more understanding of the disparity of negotiating position between a writer and publisher. If the publisher is breaching the contract by failing to pay moneys that are due, you could make a good faith argument to rescind the contract for non-payment and ask for all of your copyrights to be reassigned to you.

Retention Periods

As stated above, you can terminate the rights assigned to your publisher after 35–40 years. However, in some cases you may terminate these rights upon the termination of the contract, if the contract calls for it. If so, the publisher won't really have any incentive to work any of the songs assigned under the terms of the contract during the last year or two of the contract. The publisher will therefore have a right of retention for a year or two, to extend the period that the publisher will be able to collect moneys from songs that were exploited during the last years of the contract. This is only fair when you consider the time that it takes to get paid and the fact that the publisher should be paid for its efforts in exploiting your catalogue. However, unless you are a very established writer, you won't have to worry about this because you will assign your rights for as long as the publisher can get them.

Performance Clauses

You may be able to get your publisher to agree to certain terms that require the publisher to get your song or songs placed or cut on a record or released as sheet music, or obtain a synchronization license for film, television, or advertising jingles within a certain time limit. This is especially negotiable if you are receiving a very low advance. This way, the publisher has some affirmative duty to get results with your material, and cannot just dally around and never exploit your songs.

Of course, if you have received a large advance, the publisher has extra incentive to exploit your catalogue, because the publisher will want to recoup its investment. So, you will have to negotiate this provision based upon the amount of your advance and the publisher's willingness to agree to time restraints for performance. Again, the more negotiating power you have, the more likely you will be able to get your songs back if the publisher is not working them. But if the publisher will not agree to give your songs back after the time limit agreed upon, you could ask for a larger advance so that publisher will have more incentive to exploit your material. If the publisher is not able to get any of your songs exploited during the term or option periods of your contract, you should ask for a reversion.

Reversions

A reversion clause in a contract is simply a way that you can get your songs back, pursuant to the terms you have negotiated in your publishing contract. A reversion clause basically states that if the publisher is not able to exploit the copyright that is assigned within a reasonable amount of time, such as two or three years, the song will revert back to the writer or writers. You will usually see a reversion clause in a single song agreement, but not nearly as often with an exclusive songwriter's contract. The publisher is going to be paying you advances in the form of cash for living expenses, operating expenses that can be attributed to your catalogue, and demonstration costs that are paid to studios, musicians, etc., so that your songs can be in a form that is worth being pitched. However, that should be the risk that the publisher takes. If the publisher can't do anything with your songs, you absolutely need the right to be able to get your songs back so that you can find someone who can exploit your songs, assuming that you can't exploit your songs yourself.

Buy-Back Clauses

Since your publisher has expended money in the form of cash advances against future royalties, demonstration costs, and the like, you may have to buy back the rights to your songs, but only if the publisher is so inclined. Your contract with your publisher is irrevocable unless you can show some other defense to contract (see Chapter 12, "General Principles of Contracts"). Therefore, your publisher has no duty whatsoever to let you buy back your copyrights.

If and only if your publisher agrees, you can buy your copyrights back by paying costs advanced, and in some cases more, to cover operating expenses incurred on your behalf. But if your publisher will not allow you to have any reversion rights in your contract, you can at least ask for a buy-back clause. If you feel that one, a few, or all of your songs that have not been exploited by your publisher could have potential, you want to be able to get your songs back, even if it means paying money.

Of course, all of this will depend on the success of any songs that are exploited. If you have a song or two that have made money such that your publisher has recouped all moneys advanced, buying back any songs may just be for the costs of any demos advanced on those songs.

Third-Party Assignment of Copyright

As discussed earlier in the chapter, you will be required to assign all of your rights, title, and interest to your songs to your publisher. In effect, you sell the publisher the rights to effectuate this transfer of copyright for prior compositions, and the right to file the copyright for songs that you turn over to it in the future, pursuant to the terms of your agreement with the publisher. However, there is the back end of the assignment that may be of interest.

Sometimes your publisher will want the right to assign the rights given it, pursuant to the term of your agreement to a third party. In some cases, this could be a good thing for you. For instance, you may sign a publishing agreement with a new publishing company that is just getting started, and it gathers some steam and forms some sort of alliance with an even bigger publishing concern. You would then have all of the resources of the major publishing company at your disposal to exploit your copyrights further, and that type of assignment could be very beneficial to all of the parties that are involved. However, your publishing company could be facing some financial difficulties, and could be looking to assign its rights to your catalogue to a third party that may not be that reputable or even that experienced in publishing matters. If this is the case, you could be getting bought out by a company that is merely looking for a major tax break and that has no intention of working your catalogue. Obviously, this is a really bad thing! There are ways to get around this, one of which is to ask for a key man clause.

For instance, you may have signed an agreement with a publishing company because you were particularly interested in one or more people who brought you into the deal in the first place. You expect to be working closely with them for the entire term of your agreement. You believe in their ability, and they believe in yours. If those people are replaced, the replacements may not see the value of your songs or songwriting ability, and therefore your interests could be put on the back burner or forgotten about completely.

You can always ask for a restriction that allows you to get your songs back, a reversion, or a buy-back of your songs. However, you may have to come up with some money to do it. After all, the publisher has advanced money to you so that it could acquire your copyrights in the first place. But on the other hand, the publisher takes the risk that it cannot get a song placed or cut, and therefore if it fails to do its job, it should not be able to keep your songs.

Exclusions
Depending on your negotiating position, you may be able to restrict the use of your songs, or ask for certain types of exclusions so that your songs will not be used for certain purposes that are against your wishes. If you are an artist who writes your own songs, you may want to ask that the publisher give you the right of first release. This will allow you to release the songs that you have written on your own records before they're offered

to other artists. The publisher may wish to restrict this amount of time for you to exercise the right of first release, in that you may not ever be able to get some type of an artist deal and the publisher just can't wait forever for you to get that deal. What is going on with your career and the amount of interest that you have from the record labels will be a large factor in deciding the amount of time that your publisher will allow for you to exercise any right to first release.

You may want to restrict your publisher's right to make changes to your songs, or to exercise total creative control over your song catalogue. As stated earlier, if the publisher insists on total creative control, including but not limited to the ability to change the title, lyrics, and music, and to prepare derivative works, the publisher can hire someone else to make these changes. You will end up in a co-writing situation, as well as having to share or split royalties on the song without any input on the co-write whatsoever. You should at least ask the publisher to allow you to make any changes it has requested. But the publisher may insist that it retain total creative control, which means that it may not even ask you before changing your song.

You may not want your songs to be associated with certain products, political campaigns or parties, or any number of other things that you feel are morally objectionable or that offend your personal beliefs. You may have objections to your publisher licensing your songs for pornography, or some other use that could be embarrassing to you or perhaps prove ruinous to your career. Negotiating for these exclusions is usually fairly easy as long as your requests are reasonable. But remember that you are writing songs for your publisher so that you can both make money. Try to be fair, open, and honest about any objections you may have.

Administration Deals

In some cases, if you have a fairly large catalogue that is generating cash flow, you could consider signing an administration deal. With this type of deal, you can contract with a third party so that it will handle the collections and other administrative duties that a large publishing company would normally do, but you don't have to sign away all of your publishing rights. In most cases, you will have to assign 5, 10, or even 15% of your copyrights in return for these services. But that really isn't a bad deal when you consider that you won't have to worry about the financial end of collecting your royalties, or paying out mechanicals and performances, etc.

However, you should also know that in an administration deal, the administrators have no duty to exploit your catalogue or pitch your material to anyone. It will be up to you to make sure that your catalogue is exploited and that you are pitching your songs. If you can, try not to assign your publishing rights by contract, but rather assign a percentage of the money collected by the administrator. This way, if you want to terminate the agreement, you will be able to do so much more easily, and of course, you will still own your publishing rights in full.

Co-Publishing Contracts

Co-publishing can be a great way to divide up the work, as well as take advantage of the resources of another publisher. This could mean more chances at getting songs placed, and a whole lot more. If a smaller publisher enters into a co-publishing agreement with a larger publisher, there is usually more money and clout. That can be a real benefit to the smaller publisher, or even the writer who retains part of his publishing rights.

Co-publishing agreements can come about in a number of ways. But basically, the parties agree to divide up the work, consult with each other in regard to the copyrights, and share in the proceeds. Of course, one co-publisher could agree to handle all of the administration and provide an accounting to the other publisher, or to divide up other tasks in a fair and equitable manner. The only downside to a co-publishing agreement is that there is always the risk that the other side will not hold up its end of the bargain. That works both ways. If you enter into a co-publishing agreement, you are still required to hold up your end, so don't expect the other publisher to do all of the work for you. You will still be required to file all copyrights, send in all clearance forms, and be responsible for continuing efforts to exploit the catalogue that is the subject of the co-publishing agreement.

Now that we have discussed the basic ins and outs of publishing, let's focus on how money is actually made from the exploitation of copyrights.

REVENUE STREAMS

The royalties that you receive from your publisher will be the same from most publishing companies, with slight variances depending on the deal and your negotiating position. As stated before, you will receive your performance checks directly from your licensing organization. All other moneys will come from your publisher, after it deducts any moneys that are due from advances and for recoupment. To that end, your main revenue sources are as follows.

Mechanical Rights

Mechanical rights are paid for the right to make copies of any sound recording. The Harry Fox Agency, which is operated by the National Music Publisher Association, is the main mechanical rights society in America. Harry Fox is very much involved in protecting its clients from music piracy and other copyright infringement (For more information on mechanical rights, see Chapter 6.)

Performance Rights

Performance royalties are collected by ASCAP, BMI, and SESAC, and then paid out to the respective writers and publishers. They are collected from blanket licenses to radio and television, live performances of your songs in clubs and bars, jukebox plays, and background music that is played in grocery stores, elevators, and the like. This is how the lion's share of money is made in the music business. Literally millions of dollars are generated each year from performance royalties and distributed to the writers and publishers. You should learn as much as you can about how you're getting paid by your licensing organization, because each one calculates payments differently.

Synchronization Rights

Synchronization rights come about when music is combined with video to create an audiovisual work. They are negotiated for a number of uses, such as film, television, promotional music videos, theatrical uses, commercial advertising, and non-commercial uses, such as business training films and the like.

Once a license has been issued, it is the responsibility of the publisher to obtain a cue sheet from the user of the song, setting forth the name of the program, how the song was used, and the duration of each use. The publisher should also notify the licensing organization and any foreign licensors of the use so it can be logged.

Finally, it is important to keep track of any administrative duties so that the money is collected, and that any contract options are kept track of so that any renewal notices will be sent to the appropriate parties in a timely fashion.

Print Rights

Print rights are basically the rights to reproduce your music in songbooks, sheet music, educational books, different arrangements for different types of bands (concert, brass, marching, stage, and other types of bands), fake books, and folios, which will combine songs from a particular artist or from a particular record. Print rights also include the rights to put your lyrics in popular fan magazines or other periodicals, as well as on the Internet or in certain books.

Grand Rights

Grand rights cover dramatic musical works that are created for the live stage, such as on Broadway. While performance, mechanical, synchronization, and print rights are known as *small rights*, grand rights cover musicals, opera, operettas, and ballet. The nice thing about grand rights is that if your music is used for such purposes, you get a piece of every ticket sale for those shows. If you're lucky enough to get a song placed as a grand right on a long-running Broadway musical, you will be seeing some pretty hefty royalty checks.

However, you should be aware that dramatic uses are not the same as grand rights. Dramatic uses or performances are when someone performs a song "as a song" in a dramatic sense. This does not mean that the song is a part of a collective work in its entirety, which is required for a grand right to come about. For a song to be included as a grand right, it must be interwoven into the story or plot line. Thus, in a sense it carries the dramatic work, or becomes so much a part of the work that the work would lose its meaning without the song. Therefore, if your song was merely part of a collection of works on Broadway, that would constitute a small right. However, if you wrote a song that was used to tell a larger story and became the central focus of a Broadway musical, you would be entitled to grand rights.

There is often a good deal of dispute over whether a certain use constitutes a grand right, especially since the performing rights societies have no part in the collection of money for dramatic licenses, only for non-dramatic uses. The publisher has to negotiate directly with the theatrical agency that is producing the work. Obviously, the user of your work would much prefer to pay a small right non-dramatic license rather than a grand rights license. Thus the reason for the disputes. But if you can show that a certain use is a grand right, you will make a good deal of money if the dramatic musical use has any measure of success.

Jingles

If you are lucky enough to have a very popular song, any number of large companies may want to use your music to market their products or services. Of course, your song doesn't have to be a charted hit to get a commercial licensing deal, but it helps.

You should always be on the lookout for ways to place your song in commercials. Moby, the techno artist, found a brand new market for his music by offering it to advertisers for all types of products. Not only did he make money from these deals, but he increased awareness of his music and therefore drove album sales, live appearances, etc.

Of course, if the jingle use is for an audiovisual work, this will be covered under synchronization rights. But if the song is used for radio, a performance royalty will be in order.

Foreign Licensing

As stated before, foreign licensing or subpublishing can be an extremely lucrative source of income. In fact, as our world becomes more and more connected through technology and outsourcing of work to foreign countries, the world is slowly becoming one giant marketplace. Foreign subpublishers often work your catalogue in their particular markets by trying to get cover recordings by local artists, promoting your recordings in that marketplace, putting out printed editions of your songs, protecting your copyrights from infringement, and generally exploiting your catalogue just as your publisher would.

Miscellaneous Uses

There are a number of miscellaneous uses that people may have for your songs or lyrics. One of the more common uses is parody, such as what Weird Al does with other people's music. Another use is sampling, which is very prevalent in hip-hop and dance music, and can be very lucrative depending on the nature and length of the use. In fact, Sting negotiated with P. Diddy for the use of

"Every Breath You Take" and kept all of the royalties for the use of that song. Medleys that incorporate more than one song are another source of revenues.

There are also a number of new media that use songs, such as with MIDI (Musical Instrument Digital Interface) files. These MIDI files are used so that a computer, sampler, or other MIDI device can play back a song in its entirety, or even samples of the music, so that the music can be played back without a human ever touching the keyboard or other instruments. Karaoke is another form of new media that incorporates your music and lyrics into their applications so that others can sing your songs. Since karaoke is often performed publicly in certain bars, there is a performance royalty included, as well as a mechanical royalty for the copying of the music and a print license to print the lyrics.

Greeting cards that use your lyrics would have to pay a royalty, which would fall under print licensing. But if the greeting card features a small sample recording of your song, that company would have to pay a mechanical royalty. If a board game uses your lyrics as part of a trivia question or some other use, the manufacturers have to pay a print license. If your lyrics are printed on a t-shirt, each shirt sold will generate a royalty. If a doll or other children's toy uses your music in some way, you're entitled to a mechanical royalty. Video games can also be a fairly lucrative market. In fact, the uses for songs increase every day as more and more items become interactive or feature music in some way.

You and your publisher should always be thinking outside of the box and continuing to look for new and inventive ways to exploit your song catalogue.

Summary

When you get into the publishing game, you will begin to see the vast amounts of money that can be made through the exploitation of copyrights. But the publishing business is extremely competitive, and there are thousands of writers and publishers out there who are starving. Just because you can write and/or publish songs doesn't mean that you will make money at it. If you're lucky enough to get offered a publishing contract, you should seek a competent music attorney before negotiating.

Whether you are going to be your own publisher or you sign a publishing deal, if you approach the publishing and writing game just like any other business, and with a great deal of hard work and enthusiasm, you may find yourself sharing in all of that gold!

CHAPTER 8

Digital Rights

"The future is uncertain...."

There is probably no issue in the entertainment industry that causes more dispute today than digital rights. This is the area of copyright law that deals with materials that have been developed with newer digital technologies. With the advent of newer and faster technologies, especially computers, just about anyone can copy CDs that they have legally acquired and then burn copies to give to their friends. This is copyright infringement, plain and simple.

With the explosion of the Internet, almost anyone can copy, distribute, and share text, images, music, and video files with impunity. It is so easy to engage in copyright infringement that anyone who can turn on a computer and connect to the Internet can access just about any content he wants, anytime he wants, and basically for free.

All of this is done despite the fact that copyright laws unquestionably protect much of the content that is available for copying or downloading. The common perception seems to be that any files from any source should be absolutely free, which flies in the face of the copyright code and the intent of the framers of the Constitution, who intended to protect the creators and owners of copyrights.

Unfortunately, the only way to police the situation is most likely to infringe upon the privacy rights of people who are copying CDs or who are downloading them from the Internet, which gives rise to a whole set of other legal arguments and issues. The problem lies in finding a balance between the absolute right of copyright owners to be paid for their work and the right to privacy of consumers. How do you give consumers access to legal file sharing without the federal government having to step in and police the situation?

The issues in the chapter are very important to those of us in the entertainment industry, because they are going to shape how the music business is conducted in the future. Many argue that file sharing has a direct effect on copyright owners' ability to make a living. They further argue that the more income that is lost to file sharing, the less money will trickle down to those who are even remotely trying to make their living in the music business.

On the other hand, Koleman Strumpf, a professor of economics at the University of North Carolina, has done a statistical analysis of file sharing trends and suggests that there is no empirical data that they have any effect on the music business whatsoever. Professor Strumpf suggests that other market indicators are responsible for recent losses in record sales, such as changes in consumer demographics and the state of our economy. He further suggests that there is new competition on the market that takes up consumers' time and money, such as video games and cell phones. Also, some suggest that during the boom of the early '90s, a good deal of the increased music sales could be attributed to the advent of the compact disc. It allowed older consumers to purchase some of their favorite music on the new and different media, which was allegedly better in quality than cassettes or LPs.

Although there are a number of problems that need to be addressed regarding music pricing, delivery, availability, variety, marketing, promotions, etc., many see the number one problem facing music copyrights today as file sharing over the Internet.

File Sharing

In today's world of computers, file sharing via peer-to-peer technology (P2P) is fast becoming the norm. The problem is rapidly growing worse each and every day, as more and more people get on line and start downloading music files or other copyrighted materials. Through file sharing software such as Kazaa, Music City Morpheus, Bearshare, and many others, you can search vast numbers of remote computers, networks, and databanks by merely searching for filenames, artist names, and/or the title of any song, video, or other copyrighted material. Once you find the files, downloading them has never been easier. All you have to do is point and click, and you can get just about anything you want for free. In fact, with broadband, you can download a song quicker than you can listen to it. Why should anyone go buy a CD when he can get any music off the Internet for free?

At any given time, Music City or Kazaa can have a few million users connected and sharing trillions of files. More than 300,000,000 people have downloaded some type of file sharing software, and millions of them are out there grabbing files for free as you are reading this. If you translate that into lost revenues for the record labels, the artists, and the songwriters, millions and millions of dollars could be lost every single year. And the problem is getting worse as each day passes. (See "Lost Revenues" later in this chapter.)

To share files on the Internet, you just need to get some sort of CD ripping software, which you can usually find for free just about anywhere on the Internet. Once you have your ripping software installed, you just rip your CDs onto your hard drive. Ripping a CD is simply the process of extracting the raw audio files, which is completely legal if you have purchased the CD. All you have to do is insert any CD into your CD-ROM drive, open the ripping software, and extract the raw files straight to your hard drive. The files that you rip will usually be .wav files, which in some cases are too big to send across the Internet. However, you can easily find free compression/decompression software (codecs) on the Internet that will allow you to convert large .wav files into MP3 files, and vice versa. MP3 files are basically the same as .wav files, but are compressed by a factor of about 10. A 50MB (megabyte) .wav file is converted into a 5MB MP3 file, which makes that file that much easier to share. In some cases, your ripping software will convert your raw audio files to MP3s.

The next step is to download peer-to-peer software, which usually will create a "shared" folder on your computer automatically. You can move all of your ripped MP3s or any other files into that shared folder, and you are ready to share them with anyone who's connected to that peer-to-peer network. Since many people are using broadband, they are connected to the Internet as long as their computers are turned on. Therefore, they are allowing people to take files off their computers 24 hours a day, 365 days a year.

You don't even need to own any CDs to get tons of music for free and then share those files with others and in fact, most file sharers never buy CDs. To find music files on a peer-to-peer network, just type in the artist's name, song title, or even lyrics, and you can usually find just about anything that you are looking for. Once you find the file you want, point and click, and you are downloading the file immediately. Since these songs are placed in your shared folder automatically, the more files you download, the more files you make available for others to share.

So it's easy to see that illegal file sharing grows exponentially as more and more songs are moved from place to place, and as more and more songs are made available in the shared folders on more and more computers. If one person downloads 10 songs to his shared folder, and then 10 people download them from that person, and then those 10 people share those songs with 10 people each, and so on, the possibilities for infringement are almost unlimited. The only enforceable restrictions are the collective conscience of the people who are doing the sharing. Of course, the laws are changing, and only the future will tell what will happen if you are caught sharing lots of files.

Once you have all of these MP3 files downloaded, what do you do if you want to play them on any standard CD player? To reverse the process of converting .wav files to MP3s, just use the codecs from your free ripping software and then decode the MP3s to .wav format. Then just burn then to a CD, and you can listen to that illegally obtained music in just about any standard CD player. Also, MP3 players are becoming much more prevalent, and most newer players will play CD-R, MP3, CDA, and other formats. A standard CD-R disk can hold 17 or 18 songs in .wav format, and 10 times that many MP3s, for about $0.25. That's over 11 hours of music on a single CD, and for all intents and purposes for free.

It is no surprise that the RIAA is cracking down and suing some of the people who are sharing large amounts of files. However, since many of these file sharers are young, they don't really have any concept that what they are doing is illegal. The more they do it, the more they resent having to pay just to download a song. Does this mean that these file sharers will start downloading from only the people who are offering their music for free? Not if the RIAA can possibly stop it. It doesn't want *any* file sharing whatsoever, even if the artists want their music to be available for free, which is true of many artists. Of course, the RIAA isn't concerned about representing the little guy who wants to promote his music via file sharing. It is only concerned with the almighty dollar and the record companies it represents. If the RIAA had its way, you could be sued or possibly arrested if you download music that is free or whose copyrights the owners do not wish to enforce. As it stands now, the vast majority of the files being downloaded are from the artists with the highest record sales. Go figure....

If people keep getting sued for file sharing, or even start going to jail, there are going to be some pretty upset fans out there. The recording industry is in a real public relations nightmare, and hopefully these issues will be resolved very soon, perhaps by new legislation or even education. Unfortunately, technology will most likely stay one step ahead of the lawmakers. Whatever legislation may be in place, people are going to use technology to find ways around it, even if these file sharers and creators of technology are breaking the law or subjecting themselves to civil sanctions.

In fact, there are already newer technologies coming out. Some versions of non-standard peer-to-peer applications use random floating nodes to allow access to software, movies, music, and the like. With this technology you don't really connect to someone else's computer to download an entire file. You specify the file that you are looking for, and it sweeps the Internet looking for packets of information to download that will eventually make up that entire file. Therefore, nobody is actually stealing or downloading files from one particular file sharer, but gathering packets of digital information from many sources on the Internet until that entire file has been completely reconstructed. I'm very interested to see how the lawmakers propose to police this type of random packet sharing.

There is also open source code, which is non-commercial and is written by anonymous code writers, that allows for connecting peer-to-peer so that you can share files with impunity. If the Inducement Act, which is designed to impose criminal sanctions on peer-to-peer software, is passed into legislation, how is the Justice Department going to find the people who write this open source code? (See "The Inducement Act" later in this chapter.)

Of course, you may have heard the argument that MP3s don't sound nearly as good as regular CDs, but I doubt that most of the buying public, or rather the non-buying public, can tell the difference. I doubt that anyone who's getting his music for free really cares that it's not CD-quality. Here is a small test that you can try. Convert a song on CD to an MP3 file. Play the song off the CD, play the song in MP3 format, and compare them sonically. If you have a decent stereo system and some fairly good speakers, you should be able to hear a difference, but not necessarily a *huge* difference.

Another problem with MP3s is that the codec that somebody uses to rip a song may not be the same as the codec you use to convert the MP3 back to .wav (or .aiff for the Mac). But again, when you weigh the loss in sonic quality against getting the music for free, most people couldn't care less.

To make matters worse for the copyright owners, when you look at the legal notices on these file sharing sites (the really fine print that hardly anyone reads), the file sharing software companies place the onus on the people sharing files to decide if they're violating any copyright laws. Let's face it, most folks have never read the copyright code, nor are they very concerned that they could be stealing. I'm sure that many of these people think gathering these files is perfectly within their rights. Most of them probably don't realize how their copyright piracy could be affecting all of the people who make their living from the music business. In fact, many of them think that music should be completely free, and they question why they should be lining the pockets of the big bad record companies. After all, you can hear music for free on the radio all the time, can't you?

Most folks who are not in the music business don't understand that radio is a huge source of income for songwriters and copyright owners, in the form of performance royalties, as well as a huge source of music promotion for the record labels. But with radio, you only get to hear what the stations want you to hear. With file sharing, you can hear what you want to hear, when you want to hear it.

Also, most people don't realize that the file sharing software companies are selling download information to the labels so they can track market trends. When the labels receive information that shows a large number of downloads in certain areas of the country or in major cities, they will put more promotional money into those markets to get radio stations to play those songs and increase record sales.

To make matters worse for the artists, the record labels are refusing to pay full royalties to artists and producers for download sales. They're paying reduced rates (in most cases 50% less) to artists and producers for downloads, because they fall outside of what the labels deem to be normal retail channels (namely record stores). Download royalties are calculated at rates like those of budget line records or record clubs. Furthermore, the labels are taking deductions for things such as packaging and breakage, even though file downloads don't require any packaging and can't necessarily be broken in the traditional sense, which further reduces payments to artists and producers. The record companies are sticking it to the artists and producers once again, while raising all kinds of sand about file sharing. It seems like they want it both ways. They want to stay on top and rake in as much money as they can, even if it means taking advantage of the artists and producers who actually make the records, as well as punishing the very people who buy them.

It is important to note here that record sales dropped by well over 85% when radio hit the market way back in the early part of the 20th Century, and the recording industry was understandably up in arms about that loss. Since radio was offering music for free, the labels worried that they would be put out of business. But of course, that didn't happen. In fact, the record companies are now paying radio, albeit indirectly through independent promoters, to play their music, even though payola was outlawed years ago. Seems kind of funny how times change, and yet the record labels are still insisting on staying on top of the money chain, doesn't it? To some, it looks as if the record industry would like to have its cake and eat it too. Isn't file sharing just another means to promote music? Isn't it possible that it could be another boom to the music industry, just like radio was, and that the RIAA and the record labels are looking at it in the wrong way? Won't the market bear itself out without resorting to putting people in jail? This is certainly some food for thought.

Unfortunately for the RIAA, these file sharing networks take the moral high ground. Even though they know that their software is being used for unlawful purposes, and the vast majority of the files being shared are protected by the copyright code, they state that they only make file sharing possible and do not encourage or endorse illegal file sharing. Are these file sharing software companies involved in a conspiracy? Perhaps. In order for a conspiracy charge to stick, two or more people must decide to break the law and then take one step toward doing so. So the argument could be made that the file sharing companies are engaging in an illegal conspiracy.

Of course, we all know what happened to Napster, but that was a different sort of software application and was only exposed to civil sanctions and injunctions. However, the RIAA is pushing Congress to enact laws that would allow for jail time for peer-to-peer software creators. Will this mean that gun manufacturers are next and will be held liable for crimes committed with their products?

These file sharing software companies are not actually agreeing to allow illegal file sharing to take place, any more than gun manufacturers intend for murders to take place with their products, but they are indeed taking some action by making this software available. But unless the federal authorities step in, there isn't much that anyone can do about it. Besides, wouldn't shutting down peer-to-peer networks infringe upon our right to free association? Shouldn't the peer-to-peer networks just be sued by the RIAA, like Napster was? Couldn't the peer-to-peer networks be required to monitor their subscribers, or even educate them about copyright infringement, instead of setting up themselves and their users to be sued or perhaps even jailed?

But we must remember that file sharing doesn't always come about in the form of downloads.

Copying CDs

I have seen a lot of people who will make copies of CDs for other people, and they actually scan the cover art and all of the other graphics work, put all of that into an entire package, and then sell it to someone at a much lower cost than the original CD. This is absolutely music piracy, as well as copyright infringement of the cover art. In fact, if you are caught with copies of illegally acquired CDs when you are driving around in your car, especially if you have a large number of them that would add up to a market value of over $2,500, you could be arrested on the spot and taken to jail. (See "No Electronic Theft Act of 1997" later in this chapter.)

At any rate, this direct copying is a real problem here in the United States, but it's even more prevalent in Russia (the "one-disk country") and Asia, where copyright laws are not as developed and copyright infringement is much less of a priority than more serious crimes. In fact, when I was working in Moscow, you could buy just about any software program, CD, or DVD at kiosks on almost every single corner. Unfortunately, until some type of international governing body has some control over it, this type of theft will continue to take place. Good luck to the RIAA if it thinks it can control copyright infringement in markets throughout the entire world. I doubt that the ICJ (International Court of Justice) will care whether anyone has had a million illegal downloads of his songs in foreign countries. It has enough to deal with in regard to basic human rights, war, and many other issues.

Many people feel that protection of copyrights and some sort of public relations effort by the music business are going to be crucial, as opposed to putting people in jail for file sharing or copying copyrighted materials. People are going to have to understand that making copies and handing them out is wrong, but stopping that is going to be even more difficult than stopping downloads. Downloading music for free should be actionable in some way or another, such that it would be much easier just to buy music legally than to face being sued. However, if the RIAA continues to sue people for file sharing, won't the federal courts get tired of hearing so many cases over such small amounts of money? Should downloading expensive software programs be stealing as well? A number of issues need to be resolved, but does there need to be a catch-all law that could possibly put half the country in jail? Whatever happens, people should know that the creators of the copyrights need to be paid! But how?

Should File Sharing Be Legal?

Is it legal to steal a few slices of bread from a grocery store? Maybe you are really broke and need only a few slices of bread so that you can survive. Shouldn't we all have the right to eat? Of course not. The grocery store looks at taking a slice or two from a loaf of bread as stealing the whole loaf. And even though that loaf of bread may cost the grocery store only pennies on the dollar, it is not about to allow any type of shoplifting. You will be prosecuted and go to jail, plain and simple.

Of course, the people who own the land that grew the grain that was used to make the bread aren't worried about you stealing one slice of bread, because they've already been paid for the grain. Furthermore, the bakery that made the bread won't care if you steal a slice from the grocery store, because it has already been paid for every single loaf of bread that the grocery store bought. But this is *not* how the music business works, because making CDs is not paid for in the same way as most other commercial goods.

The owners of sound recording copyrights that make CDs for profit make money from the sale of CDs only when the consumer buys them. The record stores have the right to return stock that does not sell to the distributors, who in turn charge back these costs to the record labels (even though that may not be at the full wholesale price). The record labels in turn charge back those returns to the artists, and no money is paid to the publishers or songwriters on units that are shipped but not sold. Usually, there are no returns for overstocks in other commercial enterprises that sell commercial goods. Once you buy goods to sell at your retail store, those goods are yours to sell whether you make a profit or not. This means that a retail business will need clearances or other sales to move its stock, but in most cases it won't be able to return the products it is not able to sell to the manufacturers.

Perhaps the music business should change the model it uses to make money. But how? There is no simple answer, but whoever comes up with a new delivery system that allows file sharing for free and still generates money for the copyright owners will most likely be a very rich person. That certainly is food for thought.

In short, many owners of copyrights feel that stealing copyrighted music should be as illegal as stealing physical property, and if you are caught you should be prosecuted. But do we really need to be filling up our jails with people who are caught downloading music, especially if most of them are not even 18 years old? Should they be held civilly liable for infringement, along with all the monetary penalties that entails? How do you expect to collect money from a 14 year old, unless parents have to pay for the acts of their children? Do we really want to start arresting people over approximately $0.082 cents a song? Of course, if someone is sharing thousands of files, that makes a really big difference. Unfortunately, this is a really huge problem and there is no easy solution.

Let's apply that same standard of shoplifting food to stealing music. Even though music is not required for survival, it still plays a major role in our day-to-day lives. Of course, we can hear music for free anytime we want if we just turn on our radios, but we have no control over what we hear and when. It is important to note that radio stations are paying a blanket license for the ability to play the music that you hear, and all of that money goes directly to the songwriters and the publishers through performance licensing organizations. The record labels are getting promotional value for acts on their labels, but they are paying *huge* sums to radio through independent promoters to get them to play the music. As stated before, the recording industry was up in arms about radio when it first came out. Record sales dropped considerably. But there were huge problems with the economy at that time, because the country was in the largest depression in history. Regardless, the recording industry was freaking out, and rightfully so!

It had empirical data to enforce those feelings. But look what has happened. The record companies are now paying radio up to $50,000 for three spins a day for only two weeks in major markets.

So for those who don't want to rely on radio and wish to hear what they want to hear when they want to hear it, they can either purchase the music legally or continue to engage in illegal file sharing. And if they engage in illegal file sharing, they are definitely taking money directly from the copyright owners, which could be considered to be theft.

Under common law, theft consists of the following elements: There must be property that belongs to another which is appropriated, with said appropriation being dishonest and done with the intention of depriving the other of the property. You must have the actus reus and the mens rea for the action to be a crime. *Actus reus* is the action that, when combined with the *mens rea* or guilty mind, makes the act a crime. But this would seem to mean that borrowing is not a crime but rather a civil action, which it really is. But if a couple of kids borrow a car to go on a joy ride, with the intent of bringing the car back later, they are still going to jail for grand theft auto… you can bet on it.

Although theft is considered to be an intent crime, proving intent is next to impossible. How can you possibly prove what someone is thinking, especially whether the person intends to return the property? Many states let the act speak for itself and will not try to prove intent. They use the "ignorance of the law is not an excuse" argument. Otherwise, the state would have to prove that a person accused of theft knew that the act was illegal.

You are supposed to be innocent until proven guilty by law, but the reality is that if you are caught stealing or removing property, you are really guilty until you prove you are innocent.

Despite all of this legal meandering and semantics, many argue that every single time someone copies or downloads a song without paying a royalty, this equates to taking a slice of bread from the mouth of some hungry songwriter or his kids. And worse, this is not just being done by one or two people, but by thousands and thousands, if not millions. And remember, the songwriters and the artists are the ones who aren't going to be able to survive due to these lost revenues. Sure, the record companies are losing large amounts of money too, but let's not forget about the little guys. Everyone even remotely connected to the music business will have to pay the price eventually due to these lost revenues. If you don't believe it, take a trip to Nashville, drive up and down Music Row, and look at all the businesses that have closed. I'm sure that New York and Los Angeles are feeling the pinch as well.

But is this downturn really the result of file sharing? It's hard to say for sure. All newer technologies are having their effect on the music industry, including the affordability of home studios and the proliferation of other products that make demands on consumer dollars, but money *is* being lost one way or another. Furthermore, if you look strictly at the copyright code as it stands right now, file sharing is in fact copyright infringement.

If you ask your local grocery chain whether it would allow anyone to steal even one slice of bread without having to pay for the entire loaf, it would say that if these shoplifters were caught, they would be prosecuted. What would the grocers do if they knew that their stock in their own company was being stolen by anyone who could push a mouse button and download a loaf of bread? They would be outraged and they would want those people prosecuted! Of course, we can't move tangible property over the Internet, but we can sure move intellectual property. And there really isn't any difference between a physical property right and an intellectual property right. The law protects them both from theft.

But intellectual property *is* different from physical property. So shouldn't this be a civil matter? After all, some say there is no real proof that copyright owners have been deprived of their property, which is an element of theft. In fact, one of the reasons that file sharers have not been put in jail in the past is that many of the files being copied were given away as promotional goods before they were offered for sale. To some, it seems that the promotional value of downloads is in fact working in favor of the record companies. But you can bet that the RIAA doesn't look at it that way, and neither do the record companies. And again, let's not forget about the songwriters, artists, and producers.

Lost Revenues

There is really no way to figure out exactly how much money is lost each day as file sharing continues. Of course, some argue that no money is being lost at all, because they feel that file sharing has a great deal of promotional value. But we can do some math and look at some possible figures.

LICENSES ON BLANK CDS

Each blank CD that you purchase contributes to the Sound Recording Fund and the Music Works Fund. In fact, 2–3 % of the retail sales of blank CDs are paid to the labels, artists, publishers, and writers. (For more information, see "AHRA—The Audio Home Recording Act of 1992" later in this chapter.) However, if you take the cost of a single blank CD, which is around $0.25, and multiply that by 2%, you get half a penny ($0.005). That is to be split by the labels, artists, publishers, and songwriters. That's not a whole lot of money. And this is designed to pay for copies that are made from other copies of legally acquired CDs and the like. But if you are not paying for the actual music first, it's very easy to see that large amounts of revenues are lost.

For every song that is downloaded, the record label should be making around 66 cents ($1 minus 1/3 to the download company such as iTunes, which I will use for this example). The label has to pay a mechanical royalty to the publisher/writer of the song, so that's about 8.2 cents. That leaves the label with $0.578, and it has to pay the artist about 5% of that (due to reduced royalties for downloads, and if the artist had recouped to the record label). That means the record labels are losing about $0.5491 per song, and the artist is losing about $0.0289 per song. If you consider that 200 MP3 files can be put on a single CD, multiply that by $0.5491 and you get $109.92. That's how much the labels lose per 200-song MP3 CD that is burned, while the artists lose $5.78. Multiply those figures by millions of people, and you get tens of millions in lost revenues. Of course, for each blank CD that's sold, the artist and label get to split $0.003 from the Sound Recording Fund. So it's easy to see that the labels and the artists are losing a lot of revenue!

As for the publishers and writers, right now the mechanical rate to the artist is $0.082 per song. If you consider that 200 MP3 files can be put on a single CD, the labels, artists, publishers, and songwriters are losing $16.40 (200 times .082) for each MP3 CD that is burned, less $0.00125 (.25 times .005 to SRF), which is still $16 total or approximately $8 apiece. That adds up to a lot of lost revenues just to the publishers and writers.

It is very easy to see that the labels, artists, publishers, and artists are losing a lot of money. No matter what anyone says, this is a real problem and something should be done. But do we really want to put people in jail? I'm sure the RIAA doesn't want to pony up the money to sue all of the different peer-to-peer networks or all of the people who are downloading music. Eventually, the federal courts would be filled with civil copyright suits, and there would be no room to hear other important federal civil suits. If the RIAA has its way with the new Piracy Act and/or the Inducement Act (see below), the Federal Justice Department will be overrun with thousands if not millions of criminal cases.

Furthermore, what is to be done about people outside the United States who are engaging in file sharing? Even if every single American quit sharing any files whatsoever, what about the millions of people outside of the U.S. who are sharing files illegally that are owned by U.S. companies or citizens? How do we plan to bring these people to justice? Are we going to extradite millions of people from overseas just to prosecute them in our Federal Courts?

But this still leaves us with the problem of how the record labels, the publishers, and the RIAA are going to police file sharing. You can bet that they are going to try to do away with the Bill of Rights to the Constitution of the United States.

Right of Privacy

One of the bigger problems with file sharing is that it's very hard to police what is being sent from one computer to another without violating people's right of privacy. Should criminals be allowed privacy rights as well? There is a lot of discussion about these issues, especially with regard to terrorists who use the Internet to gain access to information and engage in illegal activity. With terrorists running rampant and using the Internet to communicate, lay plans, and carry out their crimes, the government is really in a quandary as to what to do. It has been cracking down, and our privacy rights are going to go down the tubes because of it. The FBI and other offices of the government have been given complete authority to carry out their tasks of investigation in the name of the war on terrorism, despite our rights to personal freedoms. The bottom line is that the federal government is absolutely going to impinge upon people's rights to privacy during times of war. It has been doing it for the last two centuries, and history shows that the United States has had very little downtime when it has not been at war. In fact, we have been carrying out the war on drugs for a very long time now.

But where does one's right to privacy end and the government's power to restrict illegal activity begin? The law states that if there is a compelling state interest, the government has the right to impinge on people's civil liberties. These are incredibly difficult issues to resolve, and you better believe that the government is doing things it most likely should not be doing, in the name of national security. Are we going to allow the government to do the same when it comes to music piracy? Do we want the government to have the right to come look at highly personal information on our computers in the name of stopping illegal file sharing?

There is some proposed legislation to outlaw peer-to-peer networks and to impose greater penalties, including jail time, for those who engage in file sharing. But how are the federal authorities going to police the situation? More likely than not, they are going to impinge on the civil liberties of individuals and actually engage in unlawful search and seizure, which is prohibited under the Fourth Amendment, as well as invading people's right to privacy, which is guaranteed by certain parts of the Bill of Rights as well as by federal legislation.

Under the Fourth Amendment, the federal government needs probable cause to look at the information on your computer, unless you give the authorities consent to search. Or, if you put files in a shared folder that's open to anyone on a peer-to-peer network, in essence that does not necessarily afford you full protection or guarantee of any right to privacy.

The Fourth Amendment stipulates that "no warrants shall issue, but upon probable cause." Probable cause, also required for a warrantless arrest, is an objective standard rather than a function of subjective opinion or suspicion not grounded in fact or circumstance. However, the facts or circumstances need not be of the nature of certainty necessary to establish proof in court.

This is *very* subjective, to say the least. It all depends on how one looks at probable cause. It usually depends upon a judge deciding whether a warrant to search shall be issued. However, if an officer of the law has probable cause to believe a felony is being committed, in some cases he does not have to get the approval of a judge.

Furthermore, according to the law, any individual's right of privacy must be balanced against the state's compelling interests, which would give the state the right to take action despite the Fourth Amendment. Such compelling interests include promoting public morality, protecting the individual's psychological health, and improving the quality of life. Is the protection of copyrights a sufficient compelling state interest to violate one's personal liberties, such that anyone can look at your personal information on your computer? Personally, I don't think so. However, others may beg to differ. If the RIAA had its way, it would be able to get inside your computer and look for copyrighted materials. Obviously, this is a serious violation of the Bill of Rights, unless there is some probable cause. But what would that probable cause be? Just because you are connected to the Internet, anyone can look at your personal files? I hardly think this is right. Of course, if you have files in your shared folder that you are making available to anyone who wants them, you could be in trouble. When it comes to the U.S. Constitution and the Bill of Rights, I believe that everyone's right to privacy, as well as his right to be protected from illegal search and seizure, should be absolute. However, I don't want just anyone to be able to take any person's copyrights without paying for them. This, I believe, is going to be the real crux of the argument, and there is no way to predict what will happen.

There has got to be a way that copyright owners can come up with the equivalent of the bar code security feature that you find at any grocery store. It shouldn't affect what you do on your computer, just like moving things around in the grocery store is perfectly legal… just so long as you don't walk out the door without paying. Of course, there are a number of other possible solutions to this growing problem, some of which I will discuss later on in this chapter.

Will File Sharing Ever Stop?

No matter how the federal government eventually decides to protect the owners of copyright, the profit streams from music are going to change continually. The entire music business is in for a big wake-up call if we can't find a way to protect ourselves and find newer economic models that will provide income from our work. Although the purveyors of copyright may be able to protect themselves by lobbying for stiffer penalties in the copyright code to scare people away from file sharing, it's here to stay. The hole in the dike cannot be plugged that easily and has turned into a flood of copyright infringement. You may be able to stop peer-to-peer file sharing networks, but it's nearly impossible to prevent people from using e-mail, FTP (file transfer protocol), or even secure FTP or encrypted e-mail to pass copyrighted files from server to server. You can't do with without some violation of each and every individual's right to privacy.

You are also going to have a really hard time stopping hackers or curious kids from figuring out ways around any protection scheme you try. But if there is a way to make buying music more attractive than risking arrest or serious civil penalties, you may see the tide turn eventually. Of course, don't forget about the new and different applications that will allow people to share files in packet form.

New Models

Let's look at different models for making profits. In the first days of the Internet, there were a lot of pay services that were offered with the three main bulletin board systems: AOL, Prodigy, and CompuServe. A trend that you may be seeing more and more will be pay services that are not only affordable but also completely legal. More and more music sales are being logged on the Internet every year, so there is a trend that is moving in the right direction. But as far as the RIAA is concerned, it's not moving fast enough to protect the owners of copyrights.

Some argue that you should just give up your right to copyright, give your music away for free, and use it as an advertisement for your live shows or merchandising, which is how most artists make the bulk of their money anyway. But you have to consider the costs associated with writing songs and making records. Songwriters must work on their craft for years. They continually write and play their instrument until they write that one really great song that could make their years of hard work pay off. Countless dollars are spent on guitar strings, piano tunings, music lessons, etc. If you take away songwriters' ability to make money for their work, you take away their incentive to create their music.

The same is true of the artists. They also spend years working on their craft. They may spend considerable amounts of money on instrument lessons, vocal lessons, and/or equipment so that they can play live shows to work on their craft. If you take away these artists' ability to make money from the sale of their music, you are taking away their incentive to become good enough to be commercially acceptable.

If artists are not making money from the sale of their recorded music, they will be forced to drive up the ticket costs for their live shows and the price of their merchandise. You may have to pay a higher price just to get into even a small show, and if you want to buy a t-shirt or whatever, it will cost 10 times or more what it's actually worth. In short, the market will pass those lost revenues to the consumer, which just drives up prices for everyone.

If we do away with copyright protection for music, what happens to copyrights for software, books, paintings, and other copyrighted material? Also, what about patents and trademarks? Do we just do away with those too? I doubt that really big businesses that make billions of dollars from their intellectual property rights will stand for losing their intellectual property rights too.

What Is Legal?

Now that we have discussed what could be illegal or subject to civil sanctions, and what revenues could be lost, let's talk a little bit more about what *is* legal. What are you allowed to do with music that you buy legally, and what can you do with legally acquired copyrighted material under the fair use and the first sale doctrines?

FAIR USE

As discussed in Chapter 6, "Intellectual Property," the Copyright Act has granted persons who do not own a copyright but have purchased copyrighted material legally the right to use it for purposes of criticism, comment, news reporting, teaching, and research, without fear of an infringement action. The gist of the fair use doctrine, with regard to normal consumers, is to allow others to use your songs (or other copyrighted materials) as long as they are not seeking to exploit your copyright commercially.

If you interpret the fair use doctrine with regard to copying music or CDs, people who have legally acquired copyrighted materials have the following rights:

▶   They can make back up copies of anything that they have legally acquired. This just means that they can make extra copies in case the original gets damaged or destroyed.

▶   They can time-shift content that has been acquired legally. This means that they can record video or audio for later viewing or listening.

► They can space-shift content that is acquired legally. This means that they can use any content in different places, as long as each use is personal and not for commercial gain. Therefore, they can copy a CD to a portable music player.

► They can play their music on the platform of their choice. They can listen to their music files in the car, on their computer, or in their portable music player.

► They can convert their legally **acquired music** files into other form**ats, such as** MP3s. However, if you are a D**J who plays** MP3s in clubs or you are playi**ng music** at parties for profit, you could be enga**ging** in illegal activity.

► They can use existing or future technology to exercise any of these rights.

As you can see, you have the right to do what you wish with music or other copyrighted content that you have purchased or acquired legally. But again, once you try to make money from this content or use it in a commercial way, you will be breaking the law and severe penalties can be imposed. (For more information on penalties for infringement, see Chapter 6, or see "New Legislation" later in this chapter.) Unfortunately, the new digital rights laws are slowly but surely chipping away at fair use as well.

There is also another doctrine that is important in this discussion: the first sale doctrine.

THE FIRST SALE DOCTRINE

Once you have legally acquired or bought a copyrighted item, such as a book or a CD, you own that item. However, that does not mean you have acquired any ownership to the item's copyright. The first sale doctrine allows you to lend the item to another person, or resell the item to another person or business, such as selling a CD to a used record store. You can even dispose of the item by throwing it away or destroying it. However, you have absolutely no right to copy the item in its entirety for commercial use. In many cases, you don't even have the right to take a substantial portion of the copyrighted item and copy it for other uses, such as sampling.

File sharing is not like letting someone borrow a CD you have purchased. In fact, people who are illegally sharing files are doing so with people they have never even met. They are not letting friends borrow CDs, but are in fact co-conspirators to theft. They are allowing "mechanical" copies of files to be placed on other computers without paying for the privilege.

Possible Solutions

So what can copyright owners do about file sharing? There are a number of possible solutions, but one thing is absolutely for sure: The recording industry is having one heck of a public relations problem that must be addressed immediately. Is the answer arresting the alleged perpetrators of copyright infringement? Most likely not, but it could be perfectly within the bounds of the law. After all, when you take something that isn't yours, it's stealing, isn't it?

But copyright infringement is a federal action, and the Justice Department already has its hands full with much bigger problems than people downloading songs. Furthermore, federal prosecutors have the absolute and unqualified power to decide what they will and will not prosecute, especially if they feel that justice won't be served. I doubt that the federal courts want to prosecute a bunch of kids. Also, if the owners of copyrights file tons of small copyright infringement actions, they will clog up the courts and waste valuable time and money that could be better spent elsewhere. If file sharing is prosecuted with jail time, our jails will be filled with file sharers. Is that going to help? That just means *all* citizens will be paying for this problem, with increased tax revenues spent to jail file sharers.

The problems that may arise as a result of civil or even criminal penalties will be enormous, but something must be done. The RIAA has targeted some offenders who are sharing thousands of files, and has filed civil suits and has even gotten some pretty hefty judgments. However, that has caused a pretty serious public relations backlash among the general populace. Furthermore, taking an active stance against file sharing, like Metallica did, can alienate your fan base. The last thing you want is to alienate the very people who support your music in the first place.

Personally, I feel that education is part of the fix. The general public must be educated about the seriousness of illegal file sharing. They must know that they are not just keeping the big record companies from making money, but they are actually taking money from the artists and songwriters, even if it's just pennies at a time. For each copy of a song that is illegally downloaded, the songwriter is losing around 8.2 cents. When you stop to think about the millions and millions of songs that are being illegally downloaded, that adds up to millions if not billions of dollars. And you have to consider that if the record labels are losing money, those costs will be passed along to the legal consumer who still goes out and buys CDs at record stores or downloads songs legally.

If the general public understands that copyright infringement is illegal and that there are serious repercussions, they look for legal ways to get their music. One possible solution is to charge a small fee for every download. Once the customer has paid, he owns the song and can do he wishes with it, as long as hisr use falls within the fair use doctrine.

Pay Per Download

One of the best solutions to the file sharing problem is for people to pay for the songs they download as they go. If the price is appealing, say a dollar a song, and you know that you're getting a good-quality file, what's the big deal? Also, having to buy a whole CD is becoming less and less appealing due to the cost. Also, many people will buy a CD for one or two songs and are very disappointed with the rest. People like the idea of making their own CDs with all of their favorite songs. As long as they have paid for all the songs, they have the absolute right to do so.

Subscription Services

Back in the late '80s and early '90s, the World Wide Web didn't exist. There was the Internet, but you had to access it through telnet or similar connections. Then there were the bulletin board companies, such as AOL, CompuServe, and Prodigy. These companies had an interesting way for people to access information. You had to pay a basic connection fee that allowed you to send e-mail and access some files and basic information, but you had to pay for premium services to access more useful information. This type of plan worked for a while, but once the Web came about, that pretty much did away with pay-per-access sites. However, there is something that can be learned from this older model. Perhaps the copyright owners could license their copyrights for on-demand downloads or streaming in premium forums or services.

Blanket Royalties for File Sharing Sites

If people want to download and listen to files without copying them, they could pay a blanket license, just like radio stations do, but for a much cheaper price. Napster has come up with a new program that was instituted at Penn State University. The students can download as much music as they want, and the university pays the blanket license for performance royalties. It's just like listening to the radio, except they don't have to wait to hear what they want to hear. No more calling the radio station to make a request and then waiting for the station to play it.

However, if the students want to burn copies of what they've downloaded to CD or move them to other media players, they have to pay a small fee (less than a dollar). Then they own the songs and can time-shift them, space-shift them, or exercise any other rights that are legal under the fair use or first sale doctrines.

There are also a number of payment choices. Students can download music legally, listen to music with commercials, or listen to commercial-free music. However, since much of this music is digital, can they record it for later use? Should this be legal? The answer depends on a number of factors.

ISP Use Tax

I've heard some folks propose an ISP use tax. However, if you levy a performance and mechanical download tax on everyone who connects to the Internet, what about all of the Internet users who don't download anything and merely use it to conduct their business? Obviously, this is not a very good solution to the problem. However, your ISP could negotiate a deal with the record companies, just like every other download service is doing, and try to give its customers a reasonable rate for broadband streaming and downloads.

Encryption and Password Protections

Encryption is certainly one way to go. Cryptanalysts believe that computers are going to make their jobs obsolete, and there is code being written that nobody will be able to break, not even supercomputers. But how do you incorporate that into protection of DVDs or CDs?

As it stands now, the owners of copyrights, such as the record labels and now the movie companies that are putting out DVDs, have not been able to implement any type of encryption protection successfully. One company put millions of dollars into a CD protection scheme that put a smattering of code at the beginning of each CD so it couldn't be copied. It didn't take the hackers long to find a low-tech solution to this high-tech problem. To bypass the encryption code, all they had to do was run a felt tip pen around the inside edge of the CD and blank out the code. Then they could copy the CD with ease.

Apple's iTunes and the iPod have implemented a digital rights management (DRM) protection built into legally purchased digital music to prevent any type of copyright infringement. But there are inherent problems with this system as well. Different on line stores will use different types of DRM codes, and this means that legally downloaded materials sometimes won't play back in all players. If you legally download music for your iPod, the music won't play on any other device. Until some type of universal scheme is implemented so that all music will work on all devices, you will see a fractioning of the markets, which is not very fair to the consumer.

However, if there's a universal DRM scheme, that will become a huge target for hackers, just like any operating system such as Windows from Microsoft. Because Microsoft is such a huge target, more and more hackers are trying to wreak havoc with computers using its operating systems. So the real question is, can any encryption or protection scheme finally put a stop to hackers? Only the future will tell.

Hardware Keys or Dongles

Some software will not work unless you have the proper hardware. This is true of Pro Tools and other digital input/output (I/O) devices that allow you to record music on your computer. If the music industry would come up with a hardware device you could plug into your computer, the same way as a USB key or dongle, you could play your music without the record companies or copyright owners worrying about whether you acquired it illegally. But there would have to be a standard device that would accept all types of protection schemes. Otherwise, you would never know whether what you've bought will work with most players.

Unfortunately, this type of solution is fraught with problems when it comes to protecting music, and perhaps would be better used for software protection. And no matter what protection schemes come up, there's always going to someone who figures out how to get around it.

Software and Site Regulations

Perhaps another solution to stem the tide of illegal file sharing is to place the onus on the software manufacturers to police the users of their software. These companies could be forced to place notices on their software to educate the consumer about copyright infringement and thus try to prevent illegal file sharing. Some say that's like asking the fox to watch the henhouse, but there could be an administrative body created to help monitor these sites or software applications. That would be a whole lot cheaper than paying the judicial system to prosecute these matters, and then the penal system to house and feed the violators. Shutting down peer-to-peer networks and similar sites, or even making the development of this software illegal, will open up a whole host of problems for both the consumers and the manufacturers.

One has to consider the number of bands that do not wish to protect their music from file sharing, and that want the promotional value they get from people sharing their music. Are we going to stifle their ability to be successful in the name of the RIAA and the record labels that oppose file sharing? What about bands, duos, and solo acts that download music only to learn that song and then go play it live, thereby exposing that song to more and more people? Doesn't that have some inherent promotional value to the original artist? Isn't covering another artist's song the sincerest form of flattery? Are we going to arrest the creators of fan sites with song lyrics, chord charts, and lead sheets that allow the fans to learn their favorite artists' songs? Obviously, some of this new legislation to criminalize even the smallest amount of alleged infringement is overreaching and draconian.

Despite all of these suggestions, which may or may not be feasible, let us not forget about legislation. If there were good legislation on the books and a good way to enforce that legislation, it would be much easier just to go ahead and pay for music rather than acquire it illegally. The legislature should be able to come up with a decent solution that protects copyright owners without using draconian measures or imposing such stiff penalties that the rest of the citizenry has to pay for the expense.

New Legislation

One of the problems with digital rights is that the technology is so new and continues to change so quickly, there is just no way for the law to keep up. The legislature must go through the paces of drafting proposed legislation and discussing it openly on the floor of the Senate and the House. If the bill passes these tests, it may be signed into law. Unfortunately, it takes so long to get a bill passed that by the time it's enacted into law, the digital landscape has already changed and the bill may not have any real significance anymore.

To make matters worse, most of the politicians who are voting on these issues don't really know or care much about musicians and artists but for some reason are willing to listen to the RIAA. These lowly musicians and artists don't have the political muscle, much less the cash, to contribute to the political action committees that put so much money into these politicians' favorite programs.

However, you may see some serious changes now that the movie industry is beginning to feel the pinch from illegal copying. Don't be surprised to see a whole lot more pressure on Washington to do something about illegal file sharing and copying. Once DVDs are as commonplace as CDs and people can download entire movies in a short period of time, you will see a lot more legislation. But unfortunately, time marches on, whilst the legal system crawls on its hands and knees through the shattered glass of the hopes and dreams of all the songwriters and other copyright owners.

Will the Market Bear Itself Out?

Many argue that the market will just bear itself out. File sharing will subside or at least even out, and more money will be made by legal downloads, etc. For the most part this is true. As more and more content becomes available over the Internet, people will either allow advertising to drive revenues or decide to pay for the content that they feel is most important. As it stands now, the major labels are pretty much in control of the radio markets. Therefore, to maximize profits, they promote a small number of top-selling acts, and a lot of very talented bands get left by the wayside. Unfortunately, this leaves us, the consumers, with homogenized corporate music on the radio and in the stores. Furthermore, this current system makes it very difficult for bands that aren't on the major labels to break out in bigger markets and gather larger fan bases.

However, the Internet is quickly changing our current landscape and making music more and more available. Up and coming bands can distribute their music over the Internet and reach markets throughout the world. Unfortunately, the Internet is such a huge place that the problem is not finding music but rather finding the music that you like. As more and more portals or communities crop up, the easier it will be to find the types of music that you like, while at the same time more variety will be available. This will also change the current marketing schemes for standard record stores. They will have to offer customized compilation CDs on demand or risk going out of business.

However, the real questions is, how is the law going to affect what people can do with their music?

Where Is the Law Headed?

There is really no way to predict which way the law is headed. In fact, the law will usually stay several steps behind technology, which will continually evolve at incredible rates. The law cannot dictate morality and expect the people to follow like lemmings. People are always going to find new and inventive ways to circumvent existing protection schemes, and they'll continue to engage in what many of us deem illegal activity.

There will need to be some serious changes in the way the music industry looks at its business structure. Just because change is resisted doesn't mean that it's a bad thing. Just like Wal-Mart has put tons of smaller stores out of business, smaller businesses that provide good content through the Internet are going to put a major dent in the major record labels' sales. There is just no way to say that you have to do business a certain way and the market will change with the technology. Unfortunately, the law is always going to be one step behind.

One thing that we can do is look at recent laws that have been passed, so that we can begin to understand where we are, as well as make some informed guesses as to what the future will bring.

DRM—Digital Rights Management

This is not a law, but rather a means to determine if the law is being broken. Many content providers have developed software that enables them to ensure safe and secure distribution, and to prevent illegal distribution of paid content over the Internet. This type of technology is called Digital Rights Management, and it's being developed to protect purveyors of copyrights from file sharing. It's designed to allow creators to maintain a close watch on their intellectual property, and to determine the means by which content can be used, reused, purchased, copied, and/or distributed by the people who acquire it legally.

AHRA—The Audio Home Recording Act of 1992

In 1992, Congress passed the Audio Home Recording Act (AHRA), which was an amendment to the federal copyright law. This amendment basically states that all digital recording devices must incorporate a Serial Copy Management System (SCMS). This allows digital recorders to make first-generation copies of digitally recorded works, but doesn't allow second-generation copies. In other words, you can make as many backups from the original disk as you want, but you can't make copies of the copies.

The AHRA also places a royalty tax of up to $8 for new digital recording machines, and 2–3% of the cost of digital media such as audiotapes and discs. To support this tax, the owners of copyrights waive any claim to any copyright infringement against consumers using audio recording devices in their homes. It's important to note that computers are excluded from this tax. The royalties that are collected from these revenue sources will be paid to the Sound Recording Fund and the Music Works Fund. The Sound Recording Fund receives two-thirds of the money, while the Music Works Fund receives one-third.

The Sound Recording Fund distributes royalties to artists and sound recording copyright owners, while the Music Works Fund pays royalties to the songwriters and publishers, who are the owners of the underlying musical works.

The Federal Anti-Bootleg Statute of 1994

This statute criminalizes the "unauthorized fixation of and trafficking in sound recordings and music videos of live musical performances," also known as *bootlegging*. In effect, this makes it illegal to tape-record a concert and then distribute copies. A number of bands actually encourage bootlegs, because they believe it's a promotional tool and brings the band and the fans closer together. The RIAA is not having it, though.

Digital Performance Right in Sound Recording Act of 1995

The DRSRA is the first time that public performances of sound recordings have been protected. This act is designed to cover royalty payments for digital transmissions, which include streaming audio, downloading, and uploading. Thus, copyright holders of sound recordings (Form SR) now have the exclusive right to perform their work publicly through digital transmission. However, television and radio broadcasts are exempt from this act.

World Intellectual Property Organization Treaty of 1997

The WIPO Treaty extends copyright protection for computer programs and compilations of data, or other materials such as databases, in any form that has copyrighted information or files. The WIPO protects against circumvention of any technological measures to prevent unauthorized performance, reproduction, adaptation, or display of copyrighted materials. The WIPO provides for civil and criminal sanctions for violators, with some exceptions for innocent violations and for libraries, archives, and educational uses. The treaty also provides for protection of ISPs that allow people to connect to the Internet, and limits the ISPs' liability to injunctive relief.

No Electronic Theft Act of 1997

The NET Act imposes criminal liabilities on people who willfully infringe on copyrights by electronic means. Any person who distributes one or more copyrighted works with a total value of $1,000 or more will be guilty of a misdemeanor, with jail time of up to one year and a fine of $100,000. If anyone distributes one or more copyrighted works that have a total value of $2,500 or more will be imprisoned for up to three-five years and be fined $250,000.

The law further includes a more detailed definition of financial gain to include anyone who "receives, or expects to receive, anything of value including the receipt of copyrighted works." Therefore, anyone who's giving away files for free, but not on a large scale, would not be subject to criminal sanctions or remedies, but would be subject to civil suits. This means that innocent infringement of a few files by any individual would not be prosecuted. But if you are giving away large numbers of files, you could end up in jail.

Digital Millennium Copyright Act of 1998

The DMCA of 1998 makes it a crime to circumvent any anti-piracy measures that are built into most commercial software. It also outlawed the manufacture, sale, or distribution of code-cracking devices or key generators used to copy illegally or install illegal software. However, the DMCA does allow the cracking of copyright protection devices to conduct research, assess product interoperability, or test computer security systems.

The DMCA also provides that ISPs can't be held liable for copyright infringement for simply transmitting information over the Internet, but must remove suspected infringing materials from their Web sites. It further requires that Webcasters pay licensing fees to record companies and/or publishers.

Digital Media Consumers' Rights Act (DMCRA)

This law gives the Federal Trade Commission control over labeling of CDs for the benefit of consumers. In short, this law requires that all CDs must be labeled prominently if they have any form of copyright protection that could prevent them from playing in any standard CD player or being recorded on any standard blank CD-Rs. The law exempts DVDs and super-audio CDs from this, because they are already labeled as such.

The law also provides certain limitations, such as giving consumers the right to circumvent some restrictions if their use is not considered to be copyright infringement. This law actually allows you to hack, which is *not* criminal but is the nature of figuring things out for yourself. However, you are not allowed to crack, which is criminal.

The Piracy Deterrence and Education Act of 2004

There are currently two versions of this act that are being considered for enactment into law. As of September 2004, the House Judiciary Committee has approved a law that would make the sharing of copyrighted music, movies, and software a crime. This law will also target peer-to-peer software companies, both from a civil and a criminal standpoint.

Some argue that there's no evidence that those who download music would not have purchased the songs anyway. Therefore, there is no proof that these people are depriving the original owner of the use of the material, which has been a traditional legal element of theft. They feel that since there's no theft, these matters should be left up to the civil courts and should not be prosecutable by criminal sanctions. In short, many of these people feel that this is a moral issue, and that the state should not be able to dictate morality to its citizens.

The Inducement Act

This proposed legislation was recently shot down but will most likely be redrafted and revisited before long. In short, the bill called for any product or entity that intentionally aids, abets, induces, counsels, or procures others into any action that would constitute copyright piracy to be found criminally liable for copyright infringement. Naturally, this bill was aimed at peer-to-peer file sharing software and Internet downloads.

One problem with this bill was that if any product or software that could be involved in copyright infringement is found to be engaging in copyright piracy, the makers of the product could be jailed even though the consumer is the one who's actually engaging in copyright piracy or infringement. This could have meant that TiVos, VCRs, CD-RWs, DVD-RWs, and a whole host of other new technologies could have been taken off the shelves, because manufacturers would not want to risk being arrested.

The Future Is Digital

No matter what happens with file sharing or other copyright infringement, you can bet that the future is digital. Convergence is the wave of the future. The line between your television and your computer is becoming blurred. There will be more and more content on the Internet in the years to come, such as film shorts, live Webcasts for music, and a whole lot more, all ready for download or streaming.

How is all this going to be paid for? When radio first came out, people were amazed at the technology, but nobody could figure out a way to pay for it. It wasn't long before advertisers capitalized on that. It was the same thing when television came out. It wasn't long before sponsors were paying for the production of shows. Regular commercials came along soon after that. Now you have a slew of TV channels on cable, such as Food Network, Speed Channel, ESPN, CNN, and many, many more. As markets continue to grow, more and more targeted advertising will be paying for these individual cable channels. And you are going to be seeing more and more of this new content on the Internet. But will people want to pay for content if it means they won't have to deal with advertising? It's becoming more and more prevalent. Personally, I would rather pay a small fee for ad-free Internet content than have to deal with a barrage of unwanted pop-ups, pop-unders, or other annoying advertising.

Summary

The music businesses, as well as all other owners of copyrighted material that can be freely sent over the Internet, are in for a long haul. The times are changing, and we in the music business cannot continue to rest on our laurels. Those who can adapt and overcome will end up with a larger chunk of the market share.

Protection of copyrights has never been an easy thing. It is virtually impossible to know when someone is making copies of materials and distributing them to friends. But I doubt that putting people in jail is the answer. Some feel that if the government continues to control every issue in our lives, Big Brother has arrived and we will not be far away from the thought police. If we as citizens are faced with the loss of our personal rights, the turn to the dark side will be complete. We need to start thinking outside the box and come up with a new model that will not only protect the copyright owners, but also allow legal downloading and file sharing. And we can't resort to draconian measures just to protect the record labels that continue to use their power against the very artists who make money for them.

CHAPTER 9

Why Sign a Record Deal?

"Can't I just do it myself?"

One of the most important decisions a new act must make is whether to sign a recording contract. If you are lucky enough to be offered a deal with a major record label, you may think, "I've finally made it!" But have you? The answer depends on a number of factors.

When the music industry was in its infancy, countless artists got taken by unscrupulous companies or individuals. Unfortunately, many of these artists sold the rights to their music outright just for a new car or for very little consideration, only to find out later that they had lost out on millions of dollars. When you think about the money that is made by the re-release of old recordings on CD, you can see that the music companies further increased their earnings with no little or no money going to the original artists.

Thank goodness those days are over for the most part. Artists are much better informed now, but getting a good deal still isn't a sure thing. In fact, just because you get a record deal doesn't mean that you're going to make a whole lot of money. This chapter will discuss what can happen if you get a major record deal, if you sign an independent record deal, and if you just do it all yourself.

Deal Point for a Major Record

A *major record label* is any label that garners a very large percentage of all annual sales of records and that has its own distribution system. The Big 5 record labels are Universal, EMI, BMG, Warner, and Sony, and the distribution companies are WEA, BMG, Sony, UMVG, and EMD. Also, each of these Big 5 has a number of smaller labels that they have either affiliated with or acquired through the years.

Most artists and bands will be very lucky to even be considered for a major record deal, much less get one. Even if you do, the terms probably won't be that appealing unless you generate such a strong buzz in the music business that the record labels start a bidding war against each other. You will quickly find out that the record label has all of the negotiating power and that you have next to none. Record companies are in the business of making money, and to do that, they don't get themselves into bad deals.

This chapter will discuss some of the deal points that you may see in new artist/band contracts, as well as the points you can try to negotiate.

Options

The *one and six* deal is the most prevalent type of offer you will see. This means that the record company will only guarantee to release one record, with the option to release up to six more, depending on how well the records sell over the term of the contract. (You may also see a *one and eight* deal.) The option to release more than one record is solely at the discretion of the label.

Sometimes, if artists can show a depth of material and a proven track record of sales, either by themselves or with an independent label, the record label may promise to release two records with the rest subject to their option, but that is quite rare. Obviously a *two and six* is most advisable, because if your first record loses money and you get dropped, getting another major record label to pick you up is next to impossible. It does happen, but very rarely.

Also, sometimes an act can get dropped before its first record is even put out, so watch out for any terms that could allow the record company to do that. It's always a very good idea to be totally prepared before you go looking for a major record deal. The more depth of material, experience, and marketability you have, the better the deal you will be offered.

Number of Releases

If the record company decides to pick up your options, it's going to make sure that you put out a record every so often. In fact, you could be required to put out a new record almost every single year. This means that as soon as you put out your first record, you will immediately need to go on tour to promote it. Then you need to write and record your second record in a very short time, possibly while you are still touring. Make sure you're not forced to put out an inferior second record due to time constraints. Don't fall prey to the sophomore jinx.

On the flipside of that coin, you may not be able to put out your second record for a very long time because the record label has other interests it wants to pursue. More specifically, the label may want to put it time, money, and energy toward other artists, or similar artists on other labels may be releasing their records.

The best way to avoid the sophomore jinx is to be as prepared as you can and have at least two records' worth of material before you even look for a record deal. As for what the label decides to do about any of your options, you are pretty much out of luck. The label's going to do what it feels is best, and there just isn't much you can do about it. If the record company decides to drop you, you will have to go back to square one.

You should ask how many records the label releases per year. You don't want to sign with a label that releases too many records, because it will have only so much time, money, and energy to put into the marketing and promotion of those records. You don't want to get lost among a lot of other records put out by the label that month, that quarter, or even that year.

Term

The *term* is how long your contract is going to last. Unfortunately, this is where a record contract can be much like some type of indentured servitude. In fact, many state laws prohibit contracts that will keep an employee tied up for more than seven years, but in most cases the record labels have gotten exceptions to these laws. Therefore, if you are signed to an agreement that has six or more options, you could be tied to your label for 20 years or more. If you stop to think about it, that will most likely be your entire career. Of course, you could try to sign for a number of *years*, but the record company would prefer that you were committed to a certain number of *records* and the corresponding options.

Exclusivity of Services

The record company will want all of your services to be *exclusive* to it. This means that you can't record with any other label, or possibly even perform or appear with anyone else from a different label. Record labels will give you permission to record with other major artists if it suits them, but they will retain the *right of first refusal*. This means they will have the option to approve any recording that you do. Therefore, you should ask for a sideman clause in your contract, and perhaps for the members of your band if they're signed to the recording agreement. This will allow you or other members of your band to record with other acts, produce other projects, make appearances at live shows with other acts, or any other type of work.

You want to make sure that exclusivity is very well-defined, so that you know exactly what you can and cannot do outside of your record label. Obviously, you should try to get as much freedom from the label as you can. However, if the label is holding the reins too tight, make sure your contract states that its permission cannot be *unreasonably withheld*. The label at least needs a very good reason to withhold its permission. If the label will not grant you permission and you have to take the matter to court, the court will use the *reasonable man* standard to interpret what is reasonable or not. (For more information on the reasonable man standard, see Chapter 12, "General Principles of Contracts.") Remember, if you are tied too closely to your label, it could prevent you from working on interesting projects. More importantly, it can be bad for your overall cash flow, as well as your publicity and marketability.

Territory

You will find that your contract covers a very large *territory*. In fact, most likely it will state that your services are exclusive throughout the world. I've even seen contracts that gave the record company the rights to someone's recorded music and exclusive services throughout the known universe and beyond. This may seem a little bit ridiculous, but if aliens land next year and want to take your music back to their home planet, the record company wants the absolute right to sell it to them, all of their friends, and any other beings in the universe. You never know, it could happen.

Creative Control

Unless you are very lucky, you will not have much, if any, *creative control* at the very beginning of your career. This is going to be a real thorn in your side. The label will want the power to override any decision you make in regard to picking songs, styles, a studio, producer, engineer, etc. You will be forced to perform the material that the record company wants you to perform, even if someone else wrote it.

Some folks are fine with this and can just go with the flow. Other folks like to think that they are true artists and don't really need any input from anyone. In fact, many an artist has been dropped from a label purely over creative differences.

Obviously, you want to work with the label to get as much input as you can. But at the same time, the label people have a great deal of experience in the music business. They wouldn't be working at the label if they didn't have pretty good ears and didn't know the politics of the music business, which can be incredibly difficult to learn.

The label will also have some basic ideas about what the buying public is looking for, based upon marketing research and other empirical data. But there is no guarantee that the label will have its finger on the pulse of the public, or that it can predict the newest trends and the next big thing. Just make sure that you get as much input as you can, but don't be difficult to work with. You will have a lot of people to satisfy all the way up the chain, from the junior A&R staff to the president of the label. So be ready to make some creative sacrifices, or you could get dropped before you even get started.

Ownership of the Masters

The record company will most likely insist that it exclusively owns the sound recording copyrights to all of your masters. You may even make your records as works-for-hire, in which case you might *never* get your masters back, even if you are dropped from the label. You may also be considered an employee of the label.

To that end, you need to make sure that you can define your exact role at the label. Do they pay your withholding? Do they supply you with the tools of the trade? Do they set the times and dates for you to work? Depending on the state you live in, many of these factors will define your exact role at the label. You could be an employee, a subcontractor, or merely contractually bound to the company in one way or another. Make sure to ask your lawyer about every single detail of your status at the label.

You also want to find out whether you can get your masters back if the record company drops you or fails to release any of the records you make for it. The label may even try to prevent you from rerecording and releasing those same songs for the life of your contract and any extensions.

Make sure that you cover every possible contingency, and that you know what you can and cannot do if the label drops you or doesn't release your records.

Co-Publishing

The record label may want to sweeten its deal by taking part of your publishing and assigning it to certain people at the label or one of its publishing arms. (It can even request a co-writer's share for someone at the label who helps you to fix your songs.) So, you may be lucky if you keep all of your publishing rights. Obviously, you want to keep as much of your own publishing as you can, because those royalties could be worth a lot of money.

Controlled Composition Clause

Even if you can negotiate for all the rights to your publishing, the record label will most likely ask or even demand a *controlled composition clause*. This is just one more way for the label to reduce the amount of money you can make, even if you successfully retain all of your publishing rights. How the record companies ever get away with this is a mystery, but they do it all the time. It's just one more way for the labels to stick it to their artists who have little negotiating power.

Controlled compositions are also known as the *3/4 statutory rate*, it means that you will not be paid 100% of mechanical royalties for songs that you or your band write for any of your records. The label is *supposed* to pay any of the writers of the songs and/or their publisher a statutory rate to mechanically reproduce the masters, which are the subject of any underlying musical work. However, if you write any of the songs on your record, the label won't agree to pay you what is supposed to be paid by law. (That's what statutory means. There is an actual statute, or law, on the books.) In this case, by federal law labels are supposed to pay the full rate to all songwriters. But they get around this with the controlled composition clause and will only agree to pay you 3/4 of that statutory rate. So if you sell 1,000,000 records for the label, under the current rate it should be paying you $0.082 (2004) for each record sold. This means you and/or your publisher should be getting $82,000 per song for writer's and publisher's shares. Instead, the label will pay you only $61,500. So that's $20,500 per song that the label will keep just because you wrote your own songs.

These controlled composition clauses should not be allowed, but the only thing you can do is write your federal or perhaps state legislators to stop this practice. It's just not fair to recording artists who write their own songs. In fact, many feel that there should be some type of extra compensation for a writer/artist who writes his own songs.

It's a travesty, in my opinion, but the labels get away with it all the time. Try to avoid this if at all possible. You'd be surprised how much money could end up going to the label instead of directly to you and/or your publisher.

All-In Rate

The *all-in rate* means that your royalties and your producer's royalties will be lumped together. If the record label gives you a 12-point all-in rate, this means that the label will only pay you or your band about 8–9 points, with your producer getting 3–4 points. The label usually picks the producer and also negotiates the producer's salary per side (song). Depending on the producer, that fee can be between a few thousand and tens of thousands per side. Of course, eventually you'll need to pay the label back all the money for the producer as part of your recoupment.

Even if you and your producer are the hottest things since sliced bread and you're in the middle of a bidding war, you will be extremely lucky to get a 20% all-in rate. However, once you have sold a ton of records for the label, your negotiating position will definitely change. You should renegotiate your contract so that you will make more money for each record sold. Garth Brooks was able to do this, but then again, he sold tens of millions of records for his label. If the label hadn't renegotiated, Brooks could have jumped ship, so it was more than happy to oblige him.

But a situation like that doesn't come around very often. The label is going to stick to its guns and try to keep your royalties as low as it can. In fact, the labels' position is that it costs millions of dollars to break a band, and they have many acts that never make even a single penny of profit. The labels are taking a huge chance on any act that they sign.

By the way, you should also know that your producer will be paid royalties subject to recoupment of any advance received, and subject to any deductions, etc. So you aren't the only one who the record company is going to be chipping away at. And speaking of chipping away, let's look at what actually happens with all of those royalties you are supposed to get.

Royalties and Deductions

An artist will have two main royalty sources from the record label: artist royalties and mechanical royalties. As far as artist royalties are concerned, the royalty rate will be based upon a percentage of the standard retail price for all CDs that are sold through normal retail channels (NRC). However, you will get a reduced royalty rate for CDs sold outside of the United States, usually around 75% of retail, and a reduced rate on all discounted CDs that are sold anywhere. Furthermore, you will get a reduced rate for CDs sold through record clubs, often half of what you would normally get. It isn't that hard to figure out why. Have you ever seen an advertisement to join a CD club that offers you 12 CDs for the price of 1, or 12 CDs for $1? I'm sure that you have. Of course, the catch is that you have to buy one CD a month from that label's club at regular price. If you do the simple math, that's 24 CDs for close to the price of 12. Thus the reason for the reduced rate. Unfortunately, a lot of your sales outside of normal retail channels will be generated like this.

The record company will not pay you any artist or mechanical royalties for free goods, including the hundreds, if not thousands, of your CDs that it gives away to radio stations, independent promoters, record company personnel, and a host of others. You will not get one thin dime for any of these free goods. In fact, you will be charged for those costs unless you can negotiate otherwise (which is very rare). Of course, the label may offer you a small number of free goods, but you won't be able to sell them because they will be marked Not for Sale—Promotional Copy Only.

You will also get quite a few deductions for various and sundry reasons, which will further reduce your royalty rate. One of the main deductions will be for packaging, which can run from 15–30% of the normal retail price. So in essence, you have to pay for the packaging of all of your CDs, including free goods, and that will reduce a 12% royalty rate to 9%. And don't forget that your producer will get 3 or 4 points. Thus, your total royalty rate will end up being 5–6%. If you figure in sales outside of normal retail channels, you will only end up with a 3% royalty rate for record clubs and discounted CDs.

The bottom line is that, by the time all deductions are taken out, you will only get about a buck per record sold. Furthermore, you won't see any of that money until you recoup of all moneys spent by the label to break your career, which can be in the millions of dollars. In fact, many acts *never* make a dime from record sales, because they never recoup enough money to pay back the label's investment. It's pretty easy to figure out that you won't be seeing much money from the label unless you can sell millions and millions of records. All your money will come from touring and merchandising, so get ready to hit the road.

There *is* one consolation: If you ever recoup all of the money from your record's total budget, and you continue to sell your music in the years to come, you will be getting some nice "mailbox money." If the industry changes to a new format, such as the transition from LPs to cassettes to CDs, your recordings can be resold in that format, thus generating more cash for all involved.

Reduced Royalty Rates for Digital Rights

One more instance where the labels are going to stick it to the artists and producers is reduced royalty rates for digital rights. This can be a huge loss for the artist and producer, because more and more people prefer to download their music legally one song at a time. The record labels have decided that legal downloads don't fall under the NRC provisions of their agreements. Therefore, they only pay a rate of 50–75% for all songs sold via the Internet.

Tour Support

Record labels will most likely offer some sort of tour support, and they should if they want to protect their interests. Without touring, record sales can fall off and an artist can slowly disappear from the public eye. So, the label will want you out there touring and promoting your records everywhere you can.

Make sure the label gives you the support you need so that you can launch a decent tour and reach as many people as you possibly can. If you do get good tour support, this will also be considered a loan from the record company that is recoupable. However, after the label gets its money back, all of the other money that you make from touring is yours to keep. To that end, you need to make sure the label will recoup any tour support funding from record sales, and *not* ticket sales or merchandising.

Furthermore, you can make more of a profit if you play larger venues or even hit the coliseum tours. Just make sure you don't borrow the money from the label only to play to empty arenas. You and your label need to pack the houses to maximize your profits. You will find that you prefer to play to a capacity crowd in a small venue than a relatively small crowd at a larger venue. Playing at larger venues will require more overhead, and unless there are large crowds, your tour could have trouble breaking even.

Merchandising

The label may want a piece of your merchandising, or maybe even all of it. Naturally, this is a huge income stream for you, especially if you are touring all of the time. You should try to keep all of your merchandising, because if you're doing really well, you'll need to hire someone to keep up with all of it. You're much better off striking a deal with an outside company that can handle all of the manufacturing, distribution, and sales of your merchandise. That way, you'll end up with a much larger slice of the pie.

If the label doesn't ask for a piece of your merchandising, your manager probably will, as he gets a piece of your gross. Regardless, since you can see that the label is getting its money and the manager's getting 15–20%, you want to make absolutely sure that you keep as much of your merchandising rights as you can.

Recording Costs

You obviously want to make the best-sounding record you possibly can, but recording costs can go through the roof quite easily. So be very careful, and remember that the money you get from the label to make your record is considered an advance. It has to be paid back solely by you or your band from record sales until the label recoups the entire budget.

With the right people and the right studio, you can make a great-sounding record for a very limited budget. (See Chapter 10, "Making Demos Versus Masters.") But if the record label is going to spring for the bill up front, it is going to insist on using the best studios, engineers, and producers. It will be much less likely to foot the bill, in the form of an advance, if you pick a lesser-known studio, engineer, or producer.

Regardless, you should negotiate with the record label to keep costs as low as you can. Otherwise, you may never recoup your recording budget, and you could get dropped from the label. The more experience you have in the studio and the more prepared you are to record the better, because it will reduce the actual time spent recording and therefore the overall budget (see Chapter 10).

Video Budget

A video is an incredible marketing tool, and there are lots of video channels that can make you a whole lot more accessible to a very wide market base. Therefore, you want to make absolutely sure that the record company will put out a video, especially for your first singles from each record.

However, videos can cost hundreds of thousands of dollars. Since doing a video serves both the label's interests and your own, you should ask the label to pay 50% of the budget, as non-recoupable. If you don't, you'll end up paying back every penny that the label spends on the video, which will just push your recoupment date that much further away.

Marketing and Promotions

As discussed in Chapter 4, "Advertising, Marketing, Promotion, and Distribution," you won't get very far without those things. So, make sure the record company markets, promotes, and distributes your record in every possible way it can.

Before you sign a deal, you should know how many acts are on that label, and what type of acts they are. You also want to find out how many records the label plans to release during the same quarter as your record. You don't want the label to put most of its money and energy into another act.

You will be paying back all the money that the label spends on your behalf, so make sure your money is not wasted on anything less than a stellar marketing and promotion package that will ensure your success. Remember, just because you put out a great record doesn't mean that anyone is going to hear about it. And if people don't hear about it, they won't buy it or show up for any of your gigs.

In the same way that a video is a great promotional tool that serves the record label well, so is money spent on marketing and promotion. In fact, a large portion of money spent on your behalf will be for marketing and especially promotions. Record labels can spend tons of money just to get their artists' songs played on the radio. They even call radio airplays "ads." However, the record company will not split these costs with the artists. In fact, the artist has to pay back the label every single dime that is spent on marketing and promotions. It's unfortunate for the artist, but that's just the way it is.

Advances

You are going to need money to live on while you are making your record, doing any preproduction, pre-promotional work, etc. The record company is likely to be less than generous and only pay you enough to eat, pay your rent and utilities, and very little else. Of course, it would be nice to get a million-dollar advance, but just remember you have to pay back every dime before you start to make any money off record sales. If your advance is small, you will recoup faster. Then again, if your advance is large, you will at least have money in the bank that you can count on instead of waiting for any royalty checks to roll in, especially if you never break even. It all depends on your particular circumstances.

Record companies have learned not to just write a huge advance check to an artist or band, because they know that the chances are against an act garnering much commercial success. The labels may want to set up a recording fund, which is usually the artist's or band's advance and the studio budget all rolled into one. If the band cannot deliver its record under budget, it gets no money to live on before it hits the road to tour. Naturally, this tactic will make sure that artists don't waste time and money making their records.

So, should you take a large advance, or just wait for your royalty checks? It's purely a judgment call. If you get a large advance, at least you will have cash in hand. If you wait for royalties, you may never get paid. There is no simple answer, so you'll have to weigh your options.

Budget/Recoupment

The record label is going to spend a certain amount on your budget, but it is going recoup every single penny unless you can negotiate with it to split some of the major costs. In other words, every single dime that the label spends on you, including but not limited to all clothing for awards shows, limousine rides, little parties for record executives, etc., will be advanced to you, and you have to pay it all back. Fortunately, if the label doesn't make back all of the money, you won't have to pay it back out of your own pocket, and this is one of the reasons why the label makes so much profit from hit records.

Some argue that this is grossly unfair, and in some cases it really is. However, consider the alternative. Who else would be willing to invest so much time and money in your music and risk losing it all if you end up going lead, aluminum, or copper instead of gold or platinum?

But if you do make a lot of money for the label, you can renegotiate and get more points, advances, or other concessions. The last thing the label wants is an unhappy artist who's made millions of dollars for the label. Knowing when to renegotiate will depend on a number of factors, but if you are successful, you can hire the best lawyers and they will steer you through the quagmire that renegotiation can be.

Since the record labels are taking such a huge risk, you won't be seeing the returns that you would if you entered into some type of venture capital deal. I've had some experience in investment banking and many independent projects that required raising investment capital, and I have never seen a deal where the creators of the projects received so little return for their hard work and talent. If a mall developer needs seed money to build a mall, he may pay up to 50% to his investors until he has earned back all of his money and a nice tidy profit, but the percentage is very rarely that much. It will more likely be 30% for a term, and the investor usually knows that all of his money could be lost. He is happy to get his investment capital back with his profits, because these types of deals are more profitable than investing in the stock market, t-bills, or bonds.

Compare that to a record deal. No business could stay in business for very long if it had to pay back all of the money that it borrowed plus over 90% of its profits to its investors. That wouldn't leave much to make a decent living. Furthermore, it wouldn't leave much capital to invest in advertising, marketing, and the like. But unfortunately, record deals are nothing like investment deals. You may be surprised to find out how many artists never even turn a single dollar of profit for their label. That means the label needs other artists who *are* turning a profit if it is going to stay in business for very long.

Regardless of what moneys are advanced or what costs are split with the record company, you will still need to pay back a lot of money before you see a profit from your record deal. To make matters worse, you may only get up to 10% in artist royalties. The record company is going to make 10 times that amount before you are in the black with your recoupment. Furthermore, the record company will allow you to recoup your percentage only as money is being made. In other words, the record company won't count all of the first moneys received toward your recoupment, but only your particular royalty percentage of what it receives. Therefore, only 10% (or whatever your royalty rates are) of all moneys received by the label will go towards your recoupment, which means that you won't get to full recoupment for a very long time.

Since you get only a small piece of the pie, and the record company will continue to spend more and more promotional money to push your record if there is even a small measure of success, you probably won't ever get into the black unless you're a multi-platinum artist. Multi-platinum records are a very, very rare thing indeed in this business. Only a small percentage of the top recording artists ever achieve this.

It would be nice to see the labels allow a 50/50 split of all moneys received until everything has been recouped, and then lower the percentage to a decent royalty rate. That way, the artists wouldn't be in debt to the labels for so long. I doubt this will happen anytime soon, but you never know. The way the music business is changing, and the way the Internet market share is slowly starting to climb, you could see some pretty drastic changes on the horizon. If the record companies don't start to rethink their old ways, they may end up paying a huge price. In fact, they already are. (For more information, see Chapter 8, "Digital Rights.")

Cross-Collateralization

Cross-collateralization means that the record label has the right to pay for your first record from the proceeds of your second record, if it picks up your option and if your first record never makes it into the black. In other words, if you don't make enough money to recoup the budget of your first record, the label will take the money from your second record to pay for the loss. This also applies to your third or fourth album, and so on. If you don't recoup the entire budget on all of your records, you don't make a penny on record sales—ever. A number of platinum-selling artists have never made any money whatsoever from record sales, because all of the money went toward paying for their first or subsequent records, along with all of the money that was spent to market, promote, manufacture, and distribute those records.

There is one upside to this, however. If your first record is not much of a success, but you sell more of your second or subsequent records and your career is really starting to take off, you can ask the record label to wipe out your bill for your first record as consideration for the increased sales on subsequent releases.

Publicity Rights

You will need to assign your publicity rights to the record label in some fashion, because the label will need permission to use your name or likeness for promotional purposes. You should go along with this, but you may want to specify that they cannot be used for purposes that may offend any political, religious, or moral beliefs. For example, you probably don't want your name, likeness, and music to be licensed for pornography or other things that could be offensive to you. If you have any objections, get that in your contract.

The label may also request ownership of your Web site domain names, but you want to keep control over your Web site if at all possible. Of course, the label should have its own Web site, on which it can put a whole section about you. But if you give up the rights to your Web site, what will you do after you are dropped from the label? You'll have to get another domain and then drive traffic to your new site. It's best to keep as much control of it as you possibly can. Of course, if the costs of building a very good site are not within your reach, you could always try a coop deal or a joint venture with the label if it's absolutely necessary.

Since you and the music you record over the term of your contract will be the exclusive property of the label, they won't want you selling records from your Web site. They may even want a piece of the merchandising you sell on the site. However, you should definitely try to retain all rights to your site, domain, trademarks, and any other intellectual property rights that should follow you when you leave the label. You don't want to get into a position where you can't capitalize on the name you have built while working for the label, especially if you get dropped and still need to make money from your brand.

You may be surprised at how behind the times some of the older folks at the labels are about digital rights. Even some of their attorneys don't really get it, but they are starting to catch on. So if you can keep all digital rights to your music, you should. If the record company doesn't bring it up, you will have a whole other outlet to bring your music and merchandise to the buying public.

Reasonable Appearances

You will have to promote your records at a certain number of public appearances, such as trade shows, radio promotions, in-stores at record stores, festivals, fan gatherings, and the like. You will have to make reasonable best efforts to appear, which basically means if the label says jump, you ask how high. You really shouldn't miss any of these opportunities unless you can't make it due to illness or some other major emergency. But rest assured, this will take up a good deal of your time, because it is absolutely necessary to the furtherance of your career.

You may be required to make appearances at events that you do not approve of, such as political rallies or events for sponsors that sell products you dislike. If you have any particular religious, ethical, or moral beliefs, or other valid reasons that would prevent you from participating, make absolutely sure that you inform the record label up front and have that included in the language of your contract. Otherwise, you may have to make these appearances regardless of your objections.

Unions

The record company will usually ask that you join a union such as AFTRA/SAG or the AFofM. This is pretty much standard, and if you read Chapter 17, "Organizations," you will see that there are plenty of advantages to being in a union. Just make sure you know which unions you're required to join and find out as much about them as possible. Keep in mind that the unions rely on their strength of numbers to help out their individual members.

Assignment of Contract

The record company is going to want the ability to assign, sell, or otherwise transfer all of the rights, duties, and obligations it has under its contract with you to a third party. But you can't assign any portion of your contract to a third party, because your services are unique. This is a fairly common practice. Just make sure that if the label does assign the contract, it doesn't sell the rights to a smaller label that cannot do for you what the major record label can.

One way to ensure that any assignment by the label won't stick you with an inferior company is to restrict the right of assignment to another major label, or to an independent that has sales of 1,000,000 or more records per year. Of course, this 1,000,000 sales figure is merely an example. You will have to negotiate this with the label up front, and most likely it will be fairly open to any of your suggestions. After all, it is signing you so that it can make money with you. However, circumstances can change, and the label may be forced to assign you or may be bought out by another company. Regardless of the scenario, if you have spelled out any limitation to assignment, it's less likely you'll be stuck working for another company.

Key Man Clauses

The record company may insist that if any member of the band leaves for any unforeseen reason, the record company has the right to drop the entire band. This could be a huge concern, because you never know when a band member may have some sort of family emergency, personal problems, or any other contingencies that may require him to leave. You should try to get some clause in your contract that gives you the right to bring in a replacement, assuming that the missing band member is not completely key to the entire act. The record company will retain the right to veto any prospective band member, and especially a member of a duo, but you should try to add some language to the contract so that the label can't refuse to accept any new member without some extremely good reason.

If you're part of a duo and your partner leaves, the label may not release your solo records. It all depends on the strength of the individual artists in the duo. But if you lose your drummer or some other musician who never really sang much or contributed to the songwriting, you may stand a better chance of not being dropped. It all depends on what the label feels that the band or act has lost by losing one or more of its members.

Similarly, you may sign with the label because of a particular person in the A&R department or someone else at the label who is your biggest supporter. At the very least, you should find out as much as you can about the A&R staff and others at the label who will be working with you. Find out who they've signed, who they've worked with, who they've worked for, how long they have been at the label, and what they did before they got to the label. If there is a key person that you know will be your biggest ally, you may request that person to be on your team at all times. And if that key person is terminated or leaves for another job, you may want the rights to get out of your contact or at least renegotiate. Remember, if you lose your key man at the label, you might not get the attention that you need or feel you deserve. You could get dropped because nobody is left at the label who actually believes in your talent.

Indemnification

When signing your contract, you will make certain warranties, such as that you have the ability to enter into your agreement with the record company. You will also need to state that you are not encumbered with any other deals that may affect your deal with the record label. You may have to assert that you have written your own material and own your own band name, or make any number of assertions that you have the right to carry out any of the provisions provided for in your contract. If you do not have these rights and the record company is sued because of your incorrect assertions, the record company will have the right to be held harmless and completely indemnified by you if it is sued by any third party. In other words, if you make assertions that turn out to be untrue and the label gets sued because of it, you will have to pay the label's attorney's fees and any damages that may be awarded. This could be devastating to your career and to the label, and most likely it will drop you quicker than you can ask, "What happened?"

In short, don't make representations that are not true. If you do what you're supposed to do pursuant to the terms of your contract, and you don't make any untrue assertions as to your copyrights or ability to enter into an agreement with the label, you won't have anything to worry about. Of course, there is not much you can do if some old manager or other party whom you may have worked with rears his head up and starts demanding money. Labels don't take too kindly to getting sued, even if they win the lawsuit because it has no merit. So be up front with the label and with your attorney.

Suspension Clauses

If for some reason you or your record label can't perform as per the terms of your contract, the record label will suspend the contract until such time as either of you can perform. As far as the label is concerned, the only reasons it may not be able to perform under the terms of the contract would be some type of natural disaster, war, or other act of God. Of course, the record label could go into bankruptcy or even go out of business, but if you are with a major label, the chances of that happening are pretty slim.

As far as the artist is concerned, if you become ill for an extended period of time or have to go into rehab, the record label will consider you in breach or suspend your contract until you can perform as per the terms of your contract. This can be a real problem, because it will further increase the amount of time that you are signed under the term provision of your contract.

Furthermore, if you have an extended leave of absence for some particular reason, you could be bound to the label for life. Of course, the law does *not* allow contracts for the life of one of the parties. But you will find out pretty quickly that record labels have a lot of negotiating power in regard to the term of your contract. Unless you are pretty crafty, you'll be stuck with the term that you signed for.

Accounting

The label will agree to provide you with an accounting so that you can see what has been earned versus what has been spent on your behalf. Make sure you have an accountant help you with this, especially if you don't understand any part of your royalty statement. There will be a lot of different revenue streams, deductions, and a whole lot of other stuff that may be difficult for you to understand. You would be well advised to meet with the royalty department of your label or publisher and have someone explain every single part of your statement to you. If he can't explain everything to your satisfaction, or won't meet with you at all, you could have a big problem. Obviously, the more you know, the better you can protect yourself.

You may also try to find someone besides your accountant who is very familiar with these types of statements, to make sure the record company or publisher is not padding its expenses or bills, spending money in ways it shouldn't be, or failing to pay you the money that you are owed. If you don't take care of your royalties, later you may find out that you aren't getting what you deserve. You never know unless you ask, and it's better to be safe than sorry. You should never just expect the record company to take care of everything. People make mistakes. All it takes is a misplaced 1 or 0 and you could end up losing a lot of money.

Right to Audit

Most label deals will automatically give you the right to audit. If yours doesn't, you had better get that clause in your contract. If you find a discrepancy or think that you are not being paid what you should be, you'll definitely need the right to audit the books. You may be able to do so only with a CPA, and only at reasonable times that are dictated by the record label, but you absolutely must be able to see what is going on with your money. After all, *you* are the one who's paying for almost everything. You may be quite surprised at how much money you're owed.

Most Favored Nations

You may find a *most favored nations* clause in your recording contract. All this means is that the United States has granted preferential trading status to certain countries, who benefit from lower tariffs on goods exported from the United States. Most countries have MFN status with the United States. However, some countries have refused to recognize the basic human rights of their citizens or have implemented what the United States deems harsh governmental policies, so these countries don't have MFN status. Examples of such countries are Afghanistan, Cuba, Iraq, Libya, and North Korea. This type of clause is really nothing to worry about, but you should be aware that it exists.

Termination

Unfortunately, you can't just *terminate* your recording contract unless you have an extremely good legal reason, such as impossibility or performance or frustration of purpose (see Chapter 12). If you are terminally ill or there's some other circumstance that prevents you from fulfilling your contract, you should able to get out of it. Also, if there's civil unrest, war, or some other natural disaster that prevents the contract from being enforced, you could possibly get out of it. However, the courts are very reluctant to let someone out of a signed agreement, especially if they were advised to have adequate representation before signing it.

In fact, your recording contract will probably state that you've had the opportunity to seek legal representation, and that you are entering into the contract of your own free will and without any duress. Once you sign your name, getting out of the contract will be very difficult. Even if you do, you probably won't own the masters to the songs that you recorded with the label, and you may not be allowed to record for a set period of time after the termination of the contract.

If you can get out of your contract, you need to know what rights, if any, you have concerning your music, brand, trademarks, etc. The more rights you assign to the label, the less likely you will be able to take those rights with you when you leave. As for your copyrights, if you have signed a work-for-hire agreement, you will never get back the rights to your masters. (For more information, see Chapter 6, "Intellectual Property.")

If you take into consideration all the pros and cons of deal points that were listed earlier, you can see that a major record deal is not always the best deal for the artist. I don't want you get the wrong impression or think that I look at major record labels as the enemy. In fact, quite the opposite is true. They definitely have their place. But I do wish that they would be a little more creative with the choices they offer, put out some different music, and be a little more respectful of the artists and producers who actually put money in their pockets. It sometimes feels like the accountants and lawyers are making the creative decisions about what we hear, and sometimes the cookie-cutter mentality that seems to so prevalent in music today makes for limited choices when it comes to what you hear on the radio.

I also wish that radio wasn't so corporative and over-commercialized, and that more independent records were played so that our musical landscape was as diverse as the actual music that is being made throughout this great country. However, as long as legalized payola in the form of independent promoters exists, there won't be much change on the regular airwaves anytime soon. Fortunately, there's always the Internet, and satellite radio is coming on strong, so at least there are new avenues for consumers, artists, and independent record labels to explore.

Be that as it may, the real upside to signing with any of the major labels is that they have the money for big recording budgets, tour support, and the like. Also, the Big 5 labels have the marketing and promotion muscle to make sure your record is played on the radio in all major markets. However, the major record labels are a lot like a big cruise ship—once they get moving in one direction, they have a really hard time stopping or turning in other directions, such as niche markets that can be very profitable for all those involved. So even if you can't get a deal with a major record label, you should not give up, because there are always the independent labels.

Deal Points for an Independent Deal

An independent record label is basically any label that is not affiliated with any of the Big 5, and that uses different distributors than the major labels to get its music to the retailers. An independent label may be the only place you can go for a record deal, especially if your music is not in the mainstream or doesn't have huge market potential.

But this doesn't mean that these independent labels can't help you out. In fact, often they're better suited to niche markets and can adapt more readily to changes in the marketplace. Furthermore, an independent label may be much more willing to take a chance on developing an act even after the majors have passed it.

Unfortunately, these independent labels have limited budgets, and therefore have a hard time keeping up with the deep pockets of the major labels. Obviously, lack of appropriate funding can be a hindrance to breaking an act worldwide. But on the other hand, if an independent record label sells 1,000,000 records, it is going to make a lot more money than a major record label can due to its lower overhead.

If you are offered an independent label deal, you will find many of the same deal points that you will find with a major record label, but there are some differences. You want to make sure the independent label has the money to make a first-rate record, to market and promote that record, and to distribute it in the retail stores. You can make a really good record for a fairly good price these days, but don't skimp on making a great-sounding record or you will end up with an inferior product.

As for marketing and promotions, if the independent doesn't have much money to put behind your record, you won't be getting much radio airplay, and therefore you won't sell many records. Furthermore, if there is no video budget, you won't be getting as much television exposure as you will need in major markets, so you will have to rely on touring to get your music across to the masses. Therefore, it is very important for the independent label to help put you on tour, or to find some sponsors to help with the costs. If it can't do much to help you with marketing, promoting, distribution, and tour support, you are pretty much on your own. You may be better off putting out your own record.

Just like with the majors, your contract will have a term with options and a guaranteed number of releases. Your services will be exclusive to the independent label, but you can more readily negotiate appearing on other labels, making appearances with other acts, etc. The label will want as much creative control as possible, but you will have a little more negotiating power and may be able to retain more control over your career. In other words, there won't be whole divisions of the record label putting in their two cents as to what would be more marketable. The label will want to sign you based much more on what you *are* than what they feel that you can *become*.

The independent record company may ask for a piece of your publishing or merchandising so that it gets a larger piece of that action, but you may be able to avoid any controlled composition clauses. It may require part of your publishing because it won't have the same amount of revenue coming in as the majors do, and it has to make money so it can afford marketing and promotions. And the more money it spends on marketing and promotions, the better your chances for success. Just make sure the label doesn't try to tie in your publishing rights so that it keeps your mechanicals as part of your recoupment. You at least need *some* money coming in for songs that you have written.

You may also want to limit the number of options an independent label can get, so that you won't be stuck with that label if a bigger and better deal comes along. If you have a relative degree of success with your independent label, you will have a better negotiating position to get a better deal with the same independent, with another independent that has more money for promotion, marketing, and distribution, or maybe even a major record label.

Everything will depend on the success of your music and the efforts of the independent label. But you will find that an independent label will make you feel much more part of a team than simply a product, because you will be one of the few artists on the label. You don't want to sign with an independent that has too many artists or too many different types of acts on its roster, or you could get lost in the shuffle. In other words, if you are a rock band that gets signed to a hip-hop label, it may not have the requisite experience and contacts in the rock world to work your record with maximum efficiency.

Make sure the independent label you're considering has in-house staff that will budget time and money to promote your records to radio, or money and significant contacts with independent promoters that can get you airplay in the major markets. You should find out what other artists are on the label, and see if any of them have gotten radio play in the past. If they haven't, you probably won't either, so you won't sell a lot of records. You should also ask about the label's advertising and marketing budgets. Again, if you aren't getting any support in these areas, you won't be selling many records.

You may sign with an independent just because of one person's total commitment to you or your band. If this is the case, make sure that you get a key man clause in your contract. Otherwise, if that person leaves, your stock with the independent label could drop quite rapidly and you could find yourself at the bottom of its priority list.

Finally, you should insist that you get some type of tour support. You'll need to tour relentlessly to get your music heard, and unless the record company helps you out, you'll have a hard time coming up with the cash to finance a decent tour so that you can reach as many people as you possibly can. An independent label should be able to think outside of the box and come up with new and different ways to get sponsors for your tour, or other ways to bring in the needed capital to finance your efforts.

Despite these common issues, there a few deal points that are especially important if you decide to sign with an independent label.

ASSIGNMENT OF CONTRACT

This clause is even more important with an independent label than with a major recording contract. Make sure that if your contract is going to be assigned to another label, it will be a step up, rather than sticking you or your band with a company that can't do much for you. Make absolutely sure that any assignment will go to a major record label or an independent with gross sales that are comparable to the largest independent labels out there. If you get assigned to a label that doesn't sell many records, you could be tied to that label for many years, depending on the options that you gave to the original label you signed with. You should ask to be let go from your contract completely.

JOINT VENTURES

Another real upside to an independent label deal is that you can sometimes get better terms for royalties and the like. And if your independent label can sell enough records, it may get a joint venture deal with a major label. Then you get the benefit of the major label's money, marketing, promotion, and distribution, but still get the terms of your deal with the independent label.

Of course, the majors aren't exactly bad businesspeople, and they understand the strength of their negotiating position, so they may ask to renegotiate the terms of your original contract so they're more in line with their terms. Even if that happens, at least you will now be on a major label. Your chances for success will increase exponentially, even if that success doesn't come in the form of royalties.

ASSIGNMENT OF TRADEMARK

When you sign a deal, the label may want to register your band's trademark under the label's name! This doesn't happen very often, but it used to be a problem with some labels or management companies. This point is absolutely non-negotiable. I know of a lot of bands that have gotten themselves into bad deals, and when they were dropped from the label or their management team, they had to deal with some other guys out there touring using their original band name. Nothing adds insult to injury more than seeing less-than-talented people capitalizing on your good name and knowing that there is nothing you can do about it.

Register your band name and logo with the U.S. Patent and Trademark Office, and never assign it to anyone. Your name is your brand, and you don't want to end up building a fan base all over again under a different name. (For more information on trademarks, see Chapter 6.)

So now that we have discussed the "take it or leave it" mentality that is so prevalent in the major record labels today, and the benefits and downsides to signing with an independent, let's look at what could happen if you just do it all yourself.

What If You Do It Yourself?

If you really want to take a proactive approach, doing it yourself will give you a whole lot more control over your career, and you'll be the one collecting most of the money from your record sales. But going it alone is a really tough proposition. You won't have much money to put into promotions, and you will have to learn how to be a guerilla marketer so that you can continue to build your fan base and sell more and more records.

A lot of bands out there have continued to gig and continued to expand their markets by playing farther and farther from home. If they can garner a loyal core following that buys their CDs, they can make a pretty good living. If a band has four members and they sell just 10,000 records each year, that's about $100,000 the band can split evenly. If they play about 150 dates a year (less than three shows a week) at $500 to $1,000 a night, that's $75,000 to $150,000 a year from touring. Include another $25,000 in profits from merchandise, and the total is between $200,000 and $275,000. Then subtract about $75,000 in overhead and expenses, and you get $125,000–$200,000 total profit, or $31,250–$50,000 per member. They won't get rich, but they can make a fairly decent living. It certainly beats a minimum-wage job at the local fast food eatery.

Of course, those figures can grow if you sell double the number of CDs, double the amount for your shows, and double the amount of merchandising, which should be a definite goal. Quite a few bands have taken this route and have been extremely successful at it. Furthermore, if you include any writer's royalties, or any other publishing income that you can get from exploiting your songs, these numbers can continue to grow and you will also have a back end in the form of mailbox money.

But you may ask, "Where am I going to get the money to even get started?" You are going to need money for equipment to tour with, and money to make your first record. Unfortunately, it's pretty hard to find anyone to pony up a bunch of money to finance a band, but it can be done. You will just have to be very professional and creative so that you can find solutions to the problem. You can finance equipment through music stores, or even banks if you can show that your business is making money. Also, if you are careful with your credit, slowly build your borrowing power, and pay off your debt quickly, you can get some equipment and finance your touring costs until you can build some steam. Once you are gigging a lot, you should start to make enough money to get started on your first record.

You can always start out with one-, two-, or three-song CDs, which don't cost as much, until you can afford to put out a full-length CD. Also, take into account that your local station may play only one of your songs, if any, so you don't really need a full CD just to get some airplay. Furthermore, the FCC is bringing legislation to allow for new low-power radio stations that will focus more on local programming, so the chances of getting some airplay are looking better. Regardless, you need to think outside of the box and be very creative so that you can afford to build your business slowly but surely. With a great deal of hard work and persistence, you may be surprised at how far you can go.

Another way to raise capital is to presell packages to your existing fan base. If you can get 100 of your fans to put up $100 each, you could raise $10,000, which should be enough to make your first record, print up some t-shirts, hats, and posters, and book a bunch of shows. In return for the $100, your fans will get a signed CD and discounts for any subsequent releases, a poster signed by everyone in the band, a t-shirt and/or hat, and a laminate that gets them free admission and backstage access to all of your shows for the next year or two.

Of course, you need to make sure that your band is truly committed to staying together. If you break up after your fans have given you all that money, they're going to be pretty upset and you could be faced with lawsuits. Once you've presold the packages, you need to get in and out of the studio quickly. You also need to check on all of the manufacturing costs for t-shirts, hats, and CDs. If you deliver as promised, and quickly, it could work really well for all involved.

If you have a larger fan base and can get 1,000 fans to put up $100 each, you could have substantially more money at your disposal. You could make a better record or two, and offer better-quality swag. This is a very creative solution, but it will take a good deal of planning and professionalism. Remember, the more you have your stuff together, the more others will believe in you. After all, isn't that what fans are, people who believe in you and your music?

Even if you can't presell packages or find other means to finance your music, you have so many options that just weren't around even 10 years ago. The Internet is creating new opportunities every single day.

Online Deals

There are many on-line music companies in business, and more and more of them are popping up every day. It's easy to get some type of deal with these companies, because they're playing a numbers game and hope to get as many acts as they can. Some will promise to pitch your music to major record labels, and some have actually had a good deal of success. Unfortunately, you don't get much for free, so you may be required to put up some money for these types of deals. Be very careful. Don't give any company a bunch of money unless it has a proven track record and you're sure you'll get what you pay for.

On the other hand, some of these on-line companies are quite artist-friendly. In fact, many are non-exclusive, which means that you can sign with other companies that offer similar services, as well as sell records on your own. There are so many other companies out there with similar services that on-line companies would not sign many acts if they insisted on exclusive rights. The more companies like this that you can sign up with, the better results you'll get.

However, if you are signed to an independent label, there may be restrictions that prevent you from using these types of companies. Check your contract to make sure you are under no restrictions, or you could wind up in court. But if you run your own label, you can do whatever you like. In short, if you put out your own records, you can be the master of your own destiny.

With most of these on-line deals, you still own your copyrights, which leaves a lot of options open to you. But you will have to indemnify any on-line company if you assign, sell, or otherwise grant rights that you don't own. So make sure you're not making representations that can get you into trouble. Get your clearances, file your copyrights, and protect yourself as best you can.

Many of these on-line companies offer some fairly decent payment terms and royalty rates. And if you aren't seeing much success with a company, you can usually terminate your agreement rather easily. Again, *read the contract* to make sure what you can and cannot do. Don't get stuck in a contract that you wish you hadn't signed.

Even though these on-line companies can seem like a real bonus to your career, there are some downsides. Some of these companies will want the right to edit your material in any way they deem appropriate, so that they can remove any controversial or offensive material. They also may want to give away promotional copies as free goods, or enter into joint-venture advertising deals that use your name and likeness or your music to sell certain products. If you have any objections to your music being used to sell products or being involved in any political advertising, don't give up those rights. Furthermore, offering your stuff for free is not going to put any coins in your pocket, but the upside is that you will get some much-needed exposure. You will just have to find out as much as you can about any potential on-line deal, weigh the pros and cons, and then make an informed decision.

Another downside to on-line promotions is that it's easy to get lost in the crowd. With so many bands on-line, it's not easy to rise to the top of the heap.

Summary

No matter what type of deal you're offered, remember that you alone determine your self-worth. Don't get discouraged. With years of hard work building your fan base, and with some pretty decent record sales, you can position yourself for a bigger and better deal or even a joint venture. The more that you know and the more that you can do by yourself, the more that you will be prepared to climb the ladder of success. Make a plan, stick to it, and never give up. If you apply all of the principles in this book and really work hard, you might be surprised at what you can do on your own. But nobody is waiting on you to do a thing, so get off the couch, never give up your dream, and get to work! The music business is changing each and every day, and who knows what the future will bring? Just remember, success is definitely out there somewhere, but it's up to you go out and find it.

Making Demos versus Masters

"In the land of the blind, the one-eyed man is king."

If you have decided to take a proactive approach and make your own CD or demo, you will definitely want to read this. Making a demonstration recording or a full-blown master recording will involve a number of important issues. After all, this recording can make or break your career, so you shouldn't take it lightly. Also, making good-sounding recordings isn't as easy as it looks, much less as easy as it sounds.

If you plan to release your CD by yourself, you will need to consider a number of other steps. Whether you are making a master or a demo, you need to pick a studio, negotiate a price, get a contract, know your completion date, figure out what it's going to take to get to that point, and many, many more issues.

You also want to think about who is going to produce and/or engineer your CD or demo, and how much that will cost. If you decide to put out your own record, you need to set up your business correctly, obtain all the proper clearances, get the rights to any artwork, include appropriate credits, and a host of other issues. In short, making your own full-blown CD or demo is a rather large investment in your career and should not to be taken lightly.

Of course, if you have been lucky enough to sign a record deal, the label will advance you the money for your recording. You'll have very little control over the actual budget, though. The label will pick the producer, and the producer will pick the studio, engineer, etc. Plus, you will be expected to pay back every penny spent on your behalf.

Even if you haven't been lucky enough to sign a major record deal, don't let that discourage you from giving it your best shot or trying to make the next hit record! You'll never know unless you try, and these days it's a lot more affordable than you might think.

Home recording studios are cropping up all over the place due to the proliferation of new technologies, especially hard disk recording on home computers. These home studios can compete with larger studios that have the most state-of-the-art gear, due to home computers' incredible versatility and ease of use, and the great sound of digitally aided recordings. In most instances, these home studios can offer much better rates while still delivering radio-ready recordings.

Home studios or smaller recording facilities don't necessarily need to pay commercial real estate rates for the rent, lease, or purchase of a place to record, nor the extra expenses that many commercial studios have to pay, such as increased insurance, phone, electric, etc. Therefore, some of these smaller studios can give you a quality product for less money.

Commercial rates are always much, much higher. The major recording studios are always having to "keep up with the Joneses." They need to buy the latest, the greatest, and the most expensive gear to attract major recording artists, and also to justify their incredibly high fees. On the other hand, many people have converted their garages, basements, or rooms in their homes into basic recording studios, and therefore can offer very affordable rates with a very high-quality sound. With just a single isolation booth or two, you can record drums, bass (direct), guitar (direct and/or with amp), and keyboards (direct) on basic tracks with very little bleedthrough, and then overdub the rest of the tracks later. With digital editing, automated mixing, etc., a home computer can give you a really professional sound. There are plenty of songs on the radio that have been recorded at home studios.

Of course, you could always buy your own studio equipment, computer, hardware, software, microphones, and microphone preamps, and make your own records right in your own home. However, the learning curve for many of these software applications is quite steep. If you don't have much computer experience, it could be a long time before you can actually make decent-sounding recordings. Making studio-quality, radio-ready recordings is no small task. It can take months if not years to learn the ins and outs of recording before you can put out something that sounds good enough to shop around. Remember, if you shop bad material, you probably won't be able to go back to that company or contact person again.

If you don't have your own studio and aren't planning on buying the equipment, you need to put some serious thought into picking a studio.

Picking the Studio

What should you consider when choosing a place to record? First of all, you should ask for a copy of something that was recorded at the studio. Listen to the overall sonic quality of the recording. If you have the capability, try to A-B compare the recording to some professional recording that you want to sound like. To truly A-B compare, you will need some way to play two CDs at a time, and then switch back and forth between the studio demo and the professional recording. This will allow you to compare the two in real time. That way you can hear the differences much more easily than if you rely on your memory.

If you can't do that, at least give a really good listen to the professional recording and get used to the overall sound. Then put in the studio demo and see if it stands up to the professional recording. Remember that your recording is much more likely to sound like the studio demo than the professional recording. You need to really focus on what you are shooting for, or you will not be happy with the overall sound of your final product. If you don't think the studio can give you the quality that you need, don't waste your money recording there.

If you are satisfied with the studio's demo, or you just don't have too many other studios in your area, you may be ready to proceed further. You should ask some very important questions. First, find out what recording equipment or software/hardware the studio uses. If you are not familiar with studio gear, find a friend who is and have him explain what's needed to make a good recording. Or you can always search the Internet for more information. Of course, digital recording is not necessarily the only way to go, but you will find that it can save a ton of time. You can fix things such as errant notes or drum hits, and you can also cut/copy/paste parts together without having to resort to the old splicing method. These and other shortcuts aren't available on analog or even digital tape recording machines such as ADAT recorders.

Next, ask about their microphones, their microphone preamps, and other outboard gear, such as signal processing. The better the quality of the microphones and microphone preamps, the better your recording will sound. If you don't know about microphones, you can always search the Internet for more information. You can ask questions in newsgroups, discussion forums, or even the Web sites of the manufacturers. Most companies are happy to explain their products if they think there is a sale in the making. But remember that most manufacturers are going to say *their* stuff sounds the best! You can always try to download sound snippets to compare different products. Do your homework and learn as much as you can. You'll be glad you did.

Now let's move on to one of the most important aspects of recording in the studio: Who will be working the recording equipment?

Picking the Engineer

You need to know whether a prospective studio provides an engineer. If so, find out how much experience the studio engineer has, and more importantly, how much experience he has with that particular recording equipment or facility. This can be a huge factor in how long it takes to complete your recording, and in the overall sound. The more experience the engineer has, the less time it will take to make your recording and get a final mix.

If the engineer comes with the studio, it's a really good idea to ask for a meeting with him, as well as for copies of materials that he has recorded in the past. At this meeting, you want to ask as many questions as you can about the entire recording process there. Establishing a rapport with the engineer is crucial, because you will be locked in the studio with him for quite a long time. Make absolutely sure that you get along with the engineer and he has the ability to capture your artistic vision. You should also ask what will happen if the main engineer is not available. The last thing that you want is to work with some replacement engineer if the main engineer is unavailable.

The engineer may be included in the price of the studio, may be paid a flat rate per song, or may be paid by the hour. You need to know these costs up front, or you might not be able to afford to finish your CD.

Finally, an engineer with any experience will want to negotiate his credit on your recording. As long as his demands are not unreasonable, by all means, meet them.

Once you feel good about your engineer, you need to give some thought as to who is going to be producing the recording.

Picking the Producer

Picking the right producer can mean the difference between a really good record and a really bad one. Even though you may have to pay a producer to work with you, this could actually save you money in the long run. You'll probably get a much better product, and in less time, than if you try to do everything on your own. You may want to consider producing the CD yourself anyway, but having a third party there who can give you some objective opinions can be invaluable. Furthermore, if you choose a well-connected producer, he may be able to help you get a record deal, or at least open some doors for you so that the right people will hear your music and possibly sign you.

Your producer will assist you in a number of ways. He helps you choose the right material to record and assists you with all facets of preproduction. He makes sure you're completely prepared to make the maximum use of your studio time, which saves you money in the long run. He may help you with arrangements, if needed, and he'll make sure that all of the work that needs to be done actually gets done, both before you get to the studio and while you're in it. He may even be able to help you pick a studio and an engineer, which is really good because he will be the one in the control room working with the engineer most of the time. He can arrange for any other musicians you may need, organize recording times to make sure everyone will be there, and get any extra gear you need for the recording sessions. He will also be at all of your studio sessions to guide you through the recording process, and will help settle any minor disputes or problems that may come up.

He may also be able to play certain parts or instruments to fill up any holes in the sound, or he can get you, your band, or other studio musicians to play or sing parts that will add to the overall production value of your recordings. He will know when to keep some of the mistakes that are made during the recording process, which can really add a human feel to the tracks. Or he will know what can be fixed in the editing process to save time and money. He will also assist with the mixing process and make sure to master your CD so that it stands up to other commercial releases. At the very least, the producer should have very good people skills so that he can keep everyone working together and keep the whole process moving along.

A producer is usually going to be paid by the number of *sides*, or songs, that he produces on your record. This often means that he will be paid a flat fee per song. The amount of money required for his services will depend on a number of factors. First and foremost is the size of your recording budget. If he is a well-seasoned producer, he could be quite expensive. He will also be asking for *points* on the deal, which means that he will expect a percentage of all records that are sold. The number of points on the deal depends on your producer's skill and experience.

If you get a record deal with a major label, your producer will usually be included in the *all-in rate*, which is the amount of artist and producer royalties paid by the record company. A really seasoned producer usually gets 3–4 points, and the artist usually will get 8–12 points. If you consider the all-in rate, you and the producer will end up with 12–16 points. Of course, different deals can come with different rates. A producer who is in extremely high demand will be paid a very hefty flat fee per side, and may be able to command a much higher point payment schedule.

A seasoned producer will definitely have provisions in his contract that specify how he will get credit on the record. In some cases, he may not want to share credit with you or your band, as that could be grounds to reduce his producer's points, so make sure you discuss that up front. Furthermore, a producer may insist that he produce all tracks on the record or he won't work with you. He may not want to have his name associated with another producer, or with other songs on your record that he has no control over. Make sure to discuss all of these points beforehand, assuming that the producer doesn't already have his own production contract.

If the producer is doing some type of development deal or you can't really afford to pay him much money on the front end, he'll ask for points on your first record or two. He may also ask for a percentage of your advance if his work helps you get a record deal. Be very careful with these types of arrangements. They can be a hindrance to you actually getting a record deal, especially if the producer wants to sign you to some type of development contract. Record companies sometimes don't want to deal with a particular producer, or may have other reasons not to pay a third-party producer. You could consider a buyout clause or a percentage of your advance to get you out of any deal with a producer who has agreed to work with you as part of a development contract.

However, sometimes a record company won't sign you if it means being forced to work with your new producer. This is especially true if your original producer wants the rights (or even the right of first refusal) to produce the first one or two new CDs with a major record label.

Executive Producer

The executive producer will assist in the overall production, but doesn't necessarily share in any technical aspects of making your record. He handles all of the business and/or legal issues involved with making a record, such as song clearances, contracts, etc. An executive producer can be superfluous if you already have a really good producer. Also, you may have an attorney or business manager who may be able to handle these matters, so that you have someone who's completely on your side when it comes to money matters.

Studio Musicians

If you already have a band, you won't need to worry about getting any studio musicians. However, a lot of bands actually have studio musicians play on their records, which can make a big difference if your band is not that experienced in the studio. Just because a player is a good live musician does not necessarily mean he's a good studio musician.

If you are going to hire studio musicians, obviously you want to make sure that they are top-notch players. However, the first thing you need to find out is whether they belong to the musician's union. If so, you will need to tell them up front whether you are making demos or masters, because the pay scale for each of these types of recordings is very different. Demo scale is much cheaper, whereas you may have to pay triple scale for master sessions on a CD that's going to be released nationally. Make sure to check with the musician's union (the American Federation of Musicians) to see how much each player is going to cost for the amount of time that you will need him. You might also need to pay money to the players' pension fund or other payments, depending on how you plan to release the recording. The upside is that really good session players will be extremely experienced in the studio and will often play great parts, sometimes on the first take.

Of course, if the musicians you use are not union players, you can negotiate with them for a set price per song or perhaps an hourly rate. But paying per song may be the best way to go. You also want to make sure that the musicians have had time to work up their parts so they don't waste a lot of studio time.

When it comes to really good musicians, it boils down to the old adage: You get what you pay for.

Recording Budget

Once you have decided on a studio, an engineer, and a producer, it boils down to money. You need to ask some very important questions to get the most for your money and negotiate a better price. (This information can also help the studio owner understand how to prevent any miscommunications with his clients.)

If you are like most people, you are working within some kind of a budget. You need to get as much information as you can from a prospective studio so you can negotiate the best price, and so there will be no financial surprises when you get the bill.

Here are some points that you may want to consider:

▶ How much does the studio charge?

▶ Does it have a day rate?

▶ Does it have an hourly rate?

▶ Does it charge for load-in and setup?

▶ Does it have different rates for setup, basic tracking, overdubs, and mixing?

▶ How long do you expect the session to last, and therefore how much will it cost?

▶ Does it offer a flat rate for a certain number of songs?

▶ How much will it cost to get your mixes just the way you want them?

▶ What incidental charges are there for things like tape, hard disks, blank CDs, and so on?

▶ Can they master your recording, or will you have to hire a mastering studio?

▶ Are there any other issues that could crop up before your product is ready for duplication or manufacturing?

Some studios will charge a day rate. And in some cases, this can be a good thing, depending on the rate and the hours. A day rate can be figured into blocks of 4, 6, 8, 10, and 12 hours, or any other combination of blocks of time. It may or may not include the payment to the engineer, so make sure you know what you are getting before you start to move in your gear.

For sessions that can take days, block rates may be a good way to save time and money. This way, the studio knows that the facility will not be idle for the days that you have booked it. The owners will be much more willing to make financial concessions, especially if you are planning on paying for a lot of studio time from the start.

Some studios may charge an hourly rate and nothing else. If that is the case, you'll need a very good approximation of how many hours it will take to record, mix, and perhaps master your entire project to your complete satisfaction. If you don't get this approximation right, you could end up with an unfinished project and some empty pockets. You will have to rely on the studio to quote you an overall price, which can be a daunting task because it's impossible for anyone to foresee the future. If the studio quotes a flat rate for your entire project, it could end up making much less money than if it charged the normal hourly rate.

However, if the studio doesn't know approximately how long the project will last, and you don't know how long you'll need to work on it, you could end up running out of money before you finish. A flat rate can be the riskiest proposition for the studio and probably the best deal for the act, because any number of problems can affect the amount of time needed to make a great product.

This may be your only chance to record this material, and the last thing you want to do is compromise the overall sound because you run out of money. Remember that the music business is very competitive. If you are shopping a demo and/or trying to get a record deal from these recordings, you had better make the absolute best record you can. People in the industry are very spoiled, and they expect quality product.

If you can get the studio to stick to its original quote for the time allotted to complete your project, you may not have to pay for any extra studio hours past the original estimate. To that end, it would be wise to draft a formal agreement setting forth all of the terms that you have agreed upon. This way, the studio can't change the terms after you have already started the project. Get it in writing, or you could get hit with a very large bill that you can't pay and never receive your masters.

All studios want to stay booked every hour that they possibly can, because that is how they stay in business. In fact, the studio may have a session booked right after your session closes. Make sure you know exactly what time you have to quit. If not, you could be in the middle of some of the best playing you've ever done, and yet you will have to quit to make room for some other band that's booked the studio. You may never get to that place in the creative process again.

Furthermore, if another band is coming in, you may lose any non-automated settings on the mixing board or other outboard gear. It's always much harder to come back to something in the studio if things have been changed than it is to just knock out what you need to do before anyone else comes in and moves everything around.

Now it's time to get prepared so that you don't waste a lot of time and therefore money in the studio.

Be Prepared!

The best way to save time and money in the recording studio is to be prepared—and I mean *completely* prepared! I have seen so many bands that just can't get it together in the studio for one reason or another. Either they haven't put much thought into how difficult recording can be, or they just can't pull everything together like they can at their live shows. These bands can waste a lot of studio time trying to come up with parts or arrangements, or even fixing problems with their equipment, and all of this wasted time could be prevented. They end up spending way more money than they should have, leaving less money for manufacturing, advertising, and promotion of their record. In some cases, they never finish their record because they can't afford the costs.

Remember, this is a business, and controlling costs is the key to any business. Some simple steps, such as thoughtful preproduction and being prepared for as many contingencies as you can, will go a long way toward controlling costs.

Preproduction

Learn your songs, and practice, practice, practice. Invest in some type of tape recorder (cassette or microcassette) to get down ideas and record the band during rehearsals. Have the singers learn their background vocal parts by singing along with the lead parts, instead of trying to learn them on the spot in the studio. Break each song down into small parts and make sure that you've got it all down pat, and you'll find that the studio session will go much faster.

Remember that rehearsing for the recording studio is not like rehearsing for a live gig. You will be stuck with this recorded performance and sound for years to come, so you had better be able to play your parts right every single time. The studio is not the place for ad-libbing or going off on tangents, unless you can afford it.

If you are a solo artist who plans on using studio musicians, make sure you have a very clear idea of what you want each musician to play. Have all of your lyrics written out or typed up with chord changes, and make extra copies for everyone who will be in the studio. Record your guitar/vocals, keyboard vocals, or whatever, and then use that tape to work up any background vocals. Continue to practice the background vocals so that you can lay your parts down very quickly. I can't tell you how many times background vocals have taken way too long because the singer wasn't prepared, which just ended up costing more money.

If you are in a band, make sure that everyone knows his individual parts cold. Print out all lyrics with chord changes, and make sure to have extras for the engineer and/or producer. Also make sure that all of your equipment is in the best shape possible. If your drummer needs new drumheads, change them and get them tuned to everyone's satisfaction before you get to the studio. Take care of any extraneous rings, squeaks in the drum pedal, or unwanted sounds on the entire kit. Have your drummer play the entire kit, and walk around it listening very closely for any unwanted sounds that could end up on the recording.

All guitars will need new strings and time to stretch, so make sure that's done before you get to the studio. Don't forget your tuner, and figure out beforehand whether you are all going to record all songs at A-440. If your guitar player is going to use alternate tunings, consider bringing an extra guitar with fresh strings to save time. If your guitar player's amp or effects boxes are making a bunch of noise, that will be recorded, so get it fixed before you get in the studio. Bring extra guitar cables to take care of any hums, as well as extra fuses, batteries, or any other necessity that may go on the blink. You don't want to have to stop a session just because your gear isn't working like it should.

Load-In and Setup

You should always ask if the studio charges for load-in and setup. *Load-in* is moving all of your gear into the studio and setting it all up. This includes setting up the drum kit, getting it tuned, and getting rid of any bad rings or errant sounds that may show up on the recording. *Setup* is the actual process of getting sounds into the recorder. Be aware that this can take an incredible amount of time as you tweak all guitar settings, figure out the best microphone placement for all instruments, and make sure that you aren't getting any bad signals that could affect the overall sound of the recording. The most challenging part will be the drum sounds, which can sometimes take hours and hours, if not days. Some studios include this in the day rate, giving you a little more time to get your recordings done. However, hourly studios may charge for the setup if not the actual load-in time, because they make money by the hour. Make sure you ask in advance what you are being charged for, so that you can plan your budget accordingly.

Time is money when you are in the studio, so make sure you don't spend too much time on the wrong things. Your equipment must be set up the way each musician prefers, but each instrument/amp also needs to have its corresponding microphone set up for the best possible signal to go to tape or hard disk. Headphones must also be set up so everyone can hear everyone else, and so each musician feels good about his headphone mix and will be able to play at their absolute best. If the drummer prefers a click track, that signal must be set up so that the drummer can hear it clearly. The rest of the band may or may not want a click track, so that has to be decided and set up before you can proceed. If you are not using a click track, you may have some serious timing issues. Your song could speed up or slow down, which won't bode well for the overall feeling of the song (unless you do it on purpose). If all of this is not set up right, your recording session will not go well and may even be a total waste of time and money.

Make sure that the vocalist and all players have time to warm up. You don't want to start recording before you feel good about what you are playing. If you can, do this before you get to the studio. However, by the time you get everything set up to your satisfaction and it's time to start recording, you may have to warm up all over again. Of course, the singer is going to need the most time to do any vocal exercises and so forth, but he or she can be doing that while the rest of the band is setting up their instruments.

Sometimes it's a good idea to get everything set up the day before you record, if you can afford it and the studio is available. This way you can take the time to get really warmed up, and then go into the studio and cut your tracks when you feel that you are at your best. Also, during setup there could be a host of problems that you cannot predict. There is nothing more frustrating than dealing with technical problems and then suddenly having to put on your creative hat and sound great on the spot.

Basic Tracks

After you get set up to everyone's satisfaction, including the engineer's, and you're sure that all instruments are getting good signals to tape or hard disk, it's time for the basic tracks. This is where you will actually record all of your parts. If you have a band that plays each entire song together, and the studio is equipped to do this with complete separation of all instruments, you can move along at a fairly quick pace. In fact, this can be the most predictable part of your recording schedule, if you are prepared. You may have to do several takes of each song, but if you're prepared, it shouldn't take very long at all. If you figure in three takes per song, you should be safe. Then, if you know how long each song is, you can calculate the amount of time it will take to record the basic tracks:

Song 1 (3:20) × 3 takes = 10 minutes

3 minutes between takes

10 minutes to listen to each take

7 minutes per song for breaks and other downtime.

You should be able to record one song every 30 minutes or so.

Don't forget that by using digital recording, you can fix the odd cymbal miss or any sound that doesn't belong there. If there is a glaring mistake, try to figure out if it can be fixed during editing. If not, you will need to rerecord a small part of the song, if not the entire basic track. In editing, you can copy and paste other parts that may be perfect to fix those parts. This can be a huge timesaver, so consult with the engineer to make sure that he can fix it later on. Sometimes, though, the only way to know if it can be fixed is to do it right then.

If you're using analog, your basic tracks had better be perfect, because you won't be able to fix much if anything later on. Splicing is nearly impossible on individual tracks. If you make a mistake with splicing, the whole recording can be completely lost. This has happened to plenty of seasoned studio veterans. The worst feeling an engineer will have in his professional life is calling up a band or producer and explaining that a song is completely gone and cannot be recovered.

Overdubs

You may want to consider doing your overdubs while the first song is fresh in your mind, but some people prefer to move on to the other basic tracks and worry about overdubs later. This way each musician is warmed up and can get his parts done in a smooth fashion, without breaks or time to second-guess his work.

Once the musicians have laid down their parts, they can leave the rest of the players to finish up. If band members decide to stick around in the main room after they're done, make sure that they are quiet, attentive, and don't distract the engineer and producer from the work that needs to be done. This also applies to girlfriends or friends of the band. The more distractions there are, the more likelihood of mistakes or other problems. In fact, some studios have a "closed studio" policy and don't allow people hanging out in the control room.

Whether you do your overdubs as soon as you finish the first song or wait until all basic tracks have been completed is up to you, the engineer, or the producer. It also depends on the number of songs you plan to record at that time, as well as any number of other factors. Some people prefer to go ahead and do their overdub parts while the song is still fresh in their minds. It can also depend on whether there is more setup to be done, such as bringing in new guitars or amps, etc. If so, doing overdubs before moving on to new tracks could be the best choice.

Once again, calculating the time for basic tracks can be fairly simple if you are prepared. This can also be true of your overdubs. If you have all of your lead guitar parts worked up, the vocals and background vocal parts are sorted out, and keyboard pads or lead parts have been learned, doing the overdubs for these can be very quick. If you give all of this a good deal of thought before you get in the studio, everyone will know what to expect. Turning in a track sheet is a very good idea, so that the engineer will know exactly what will be recorded next. That way, he can set up for each of those parts to be recorded as he goes.

If the creative process sweeps you up at any point during recording, that is absolutely welcomed. However, the more you go off on a tangent, the harder it will be to get back to your basic plan. So try to keep a tight rein on things. Remember that unless you can afford it, the studio is not the best place to be coming up with new ideas, writing new parts, or going off in different directions looking for that awesome sound.

Mixing

Now that all of the parts are laid down and you feel good about everything that was recorded, you can move on to mixing. A good mixing engineer is worth his weight in gold! Anybody can get a decent board mix shortly after the basic tracks and overdubs are done, but that is a far cry from a truly professional mix that will stand up to all those professionally recorded songs you hear on the radio. In fact, in most music circles, a board mix that doesn't take very long is called a *demo* and certainly not a *record*.

There are so many factors that go into a good mix, and one of the most important is patience—especially on behalf of the artist. You can expect to pay the studio for about four or five hours of mixing time, if it is not included in the day rate. For a really good mix, it can take even longer. Also, just because something sounds great in the studio, that doesn't mean it's going to sound great on your home system, in your car, or any other place where you are accustomed to listening to music. To make sure that your music sounds the way you want it to sound, it's a very good idea to bring in a CD of something that you think is a great mix. Then the engineer can A-B your recording to that outside recording. This gives you a reference point so that your mix doesn't go off on some sonic tangent that could end up sounding muddy or just plain bad.

In some instances, the producer or engineer may have a particular recording that he prefers to use for A-B purposes, but that may not be the sound you're looking for. You probably have a good idea of how you want to sound, based upon other music that you like. Just remember that if a band has put in a few million dollars and several months in the studio, you may not be able to duplicate its sound on a low budget. Don't expect miracles!

But this is where the home studio can keep up with the big guys. Most digital editing software applications have a plugin that takes the place of a whole truckload of outboard signal processors, and you can use that plugin on as many tracks as you want. This allows you to add compression, noise reduction, noise gates, reverbs, delays, and a whole host of other signal processing without having to run patch cords, so you can achieve that perfect mix. But again, don't expect miracles. You need to put in some time and experiment to see what will suit your sound best.

Mastering

Experienced mastering engineers have the edge over most home studio engineers. Mastering engineers have years and years of experience at their craft, which is an artform unto itself and completely different than just mixing a recording. They also have state-of-the-art equipment in their completely isolated and tuned rooms, so they can discern even the slightest difference in sound. They know when to leave well enough alone, and when to add the right amount of equalization, compression, or any other signal processing to your overall mix. They know all the tricks of the trade, and they can make the difference between a decent-sounding record and a phenomenal-sounding record. They also can deliver your masters in the proper format for manufacturing and/or duplication so that you can be assured of the best-quality CDs.

However, mastering can be very expensive. If you cannot afford mastering, try to get your recording studio to master your CD. To that end, you should make sure that all of your songs have the same level and equalization. Make absolutely sure that there is no clipping on any of your masters, and no distortion of any kind. Also make sure that each track flows into the next track and there are no major differences in the sonic quality of the songs. If you don't do this, the CD may sound like it has been recorded in two different places, or some songs won't sound as good as the rest. If you don't fix these differences, you will have a very sketchy product at best, especially if you are trying to shop a deal. You never know which song on your CD will be someone's favorite, so make sure all the songs sound equally good.

Negotiation Points

There are many deal points you may want to negotiate. Ask the studio for its standard recording contract, if it has one. This contract should have all the information the studio needs to protect itself, and each party should have a clear understanding of what it must do to fulfill the terms of the contract. It should include the dates and times for the recordings, studio rates, and any other issues that the studio deems appropriate. Make sure that you read the entire contract, and ask questions about points that you don't understand. Also, if you see some terms that you don't agree with, negotiate those terms so that the agreement is mutually beneficial. If you're not sure you can afford the day rate or hourly rate, you may want to consider booking studio time at night when it isn't so expensive. If the studio doesn't offer a written contract, draw one up yourself or hire an attorney to do one. At the very least, you should set out each party's rights, duties, and obligations. (For more information, see Chapter 12, "General Principles of Contracts.")

You should ask what will happen if the engineer screws up and loses a bunch of your work. You should not have to pay for that time, nor the time it takes to get you back where you were before the mistake. Also ask what happens if the studio gear goes on the blink. You shouldn't have to pay for any downtime while the studio gets its gear fixed.

You should make it absolutely clear that you need your product by a certain date. If you have to deliver your recordings to a third party, or need to have your CDs by a certain date for a release party or gig, you'd better let the studio know. It can be a serious bone of contention if your product is not ready on time. An experienced studio will give you a specific date when the project will be done. If it can't deliver your product on that date, you may not want to use that studio.

You should also ask the studio, engineer, and producer what ancillary services they offer, if any. Does the studio have some type of deal for getting product manufactured at a better price? Can they refer you to people such as graphic artists and the like? Do they have any other contacts in the music business that might be interested in your product? Again, ask as many questions as you can. They should be more than willing to help if they want your business in the future.

Finally, you need think about how the studio makes money, and look for ways to help it out if you can. You may even be able to trade out for services or goods so that you can save money. You never know, so don't be afraid to ask.

Clearances

If you have decided to do any cover songs or use any samples, make sure that you have obtained the correct clearances before you go into the studio. You will need to contact the owners of the copyrights for those songs so that you can request derivative works permission (if applicable) or a compulsory license. (For more information, see Chapter 6, "Intellectual Property," and Chapter 7, "Publishing.") The last thing you want is to have to recall records that have already been shipped or get sued for copyright infringement.

Of course, if you have written all of your own songs, you won't have to worry about this task. But you *will* want to send in any clearance forms to your licensing organization, such as ASCAP, BMI, or SESAC. This will ensure that all songs on your CD will be catalogued for radio licensing and so forth.

Who Owns the Masters?

Now that you've recorded your CD, you should make sure that you have absolute right, title, and interests in your masters. Remember that there is a difference between the sound recording copyright and the underlying musical work. Whoever creates the sound recording has the rights to it, while whoever writes the songs owns the rights to the underlying musical work. Your producer will not own any part of your copyrights, unless that's part of his contract based upon his contribution to any co-writes of the underlying musical work. Furthermore, he cannot make any claim to the copyright for the actual sound recording, even though he assisted you in making it. However, he could be paid points from the sales of the CD, and that must be negotiated on the front end.

What If You Can't Pay for Your Recording?

If you can't pay for the work that has been done, the studio may not turn over your masters until it is paid in full. Depending on the amount of money due, the studio may file a *material and workman's lien* on the masters. It can legally keep you from releasing your masters until you have paid for it in full. In some cases, the court can issue an injunction preventing you from taking any action with your masters. If you try to do anything during this injunction, you could be held in contempt of court and held accountable. So don't mess around, because the judge has the power to put you in jail if you don't comply. The best policy is to pay for what you get from the studio, and then get a release from the studio so that it won't make any claim to the masters or try to cloud the sound recording copyright. Then you can do what you want with your masters.

You may have borrowed money from a bank (highly doubtful) or from a private investor to make your CD. If that is the case, the bank or the private investor can get a lien against your masters to ensure that it gets its money back based upon the terms of the loan agreement. If you have to borrow money to create your masters, make sure that you get a signed release from the lender after you have paid back all that you owe. This will protect you from any future claims by any investor in the event that your record is a hit. You will be surprised at how many people come out of the woodwork and ask for more money if they were involved in a project that is making millions of dollars all of a sudden. If you cover all of your bases, pay for what you get as you go (or at least as soon as you can), and get the appropriate releases from anyone who could possibly make a claim for moneys that he thinks he's owed, you will have a much better defense against demands for money or even lawsuits.

There is really no way to prevent people from filing lawsuits if they think they have a legitimate claim. But if you have all of your documentation and have done everything that you were supposed to do, you can make the lawsuit go away by simply filing a *motion for summary judgment*. This means that the court will rule as to whether the plaintiff has a legitimate legal claim or a material issue of fact that can be tried. If the court finds that there is no material issue of fact (in other words, that you have covered all your bases), the lawsuit will be dismissed and the other side will have to pay all of the costs for filing the lawsuit. Furthermore, if you can prove that the other side didn't have a good-faith reason for filing the lawsuit, you may be able to get it to pay your attorney's fees and other costs. In some cases, there are even penalties for filing a frivolous lawsuit. (See Chapter 16, "If All Else Fails, Sue.")

Bootlegs/Unfinished Masters

The studio and the artists should be very careful about letting copies leak out during the mixing process. There is no way to tell how your rough mixes are going to sound outside of the studio, unless you take them to the places where you usually listen to music. If you do that, though, there's a greater risk that the songs will be leaked. You may want to institute a policy that all rough mixes taken out of the studio will be turned back in or destroyed, and never copied or distributed to friends and family. You don't want people to hear a rough mix that is in the process of becoming a great mix, and then make a snap judgment about the quality of the act's or studio's work.

A lot of records have gotten into the wrong hands and have been leaked to the Internet before they were even finished. There's nothing worse than finding out your material has been "released" before it's even finished, so take all precautions to keep your masterpiece from getting out before it's done. One precaution is to set forth some type of *liquidated damages clause* (for more information, see Chapter 12, "General Principles of Contracts") in your recording contract, specifying a dollar amount for the damage you could suffer if someone at the studio steals a copy of the mixes and puts them out for the whole world to hear.

Graphics/Content

Now that you have your masters, it's time to think about packaging. I'm sure that you have thought about how you want your CD to look, but have you given much thought to how much it's going to cost? Have you thought about all of the information that should be included on the CD cover and inserts? You should collect all that information before you even talk to the graphic artist.

Of course, you may be able to do your own artwork by using Photoshop or some other graphics program. If you can, that's great. You could save yourself a good deal of money. But you still need to check with the CD manufacturer so that you will have the proper specs.

The covers and inserts will need to have the name of your band, obviously, as well as the song info. This includes who wrote the songs and their respective publishing affiliation. This information is important, because you want it to be logged at radio stations so that you can get your performance royalties. You also want to provide the song runtimes so that radio stations will know how much time each song will take to play. Make sure that you include all copyright and trademark notices as well, because you don't want your stuff to fall into the public domain.

You should include all appropriate credits for everyone who worked on the record. This is very important, so make sure you discuss it with the studio, the engineer, the producer, the musicians, and everyone else involved. If nobody asks for credits, or that issue is not even discussed, you may want to bring it up beforehand. If you don't give everybody credit for the work they did, there really isn't much they can do other than get pretty upset about it, and most likely they will.

However, most people will make sure to have proper crediting written into their recording agreement, production agreement, and the like. If they do, and you don't give them proper credit, you *will* be hearing about it. It's extremely important to these people, so always give credit where credit is due.

The CD cover should have your logo, or at the very least your name or band's name, as well as the name of the CD. If you are releasing your own CD, you may need to set up your own label. You could just do business under your band name, but having your own label could lend an air of professionalism. (If you are concerned with setting up your business correctly, see Chapter 2, "Choosing a Business Structure.") However, before you turn the CD over to manufacturing, make sure that you own the rights to your name. You don't want another label or band to claim that you are causing confusion in the marketplace and therefore infringing on their name. (See Chapter 6, "Intellectual Property.")

You should also include as much contact information as you can. People may lose your card, so make sure the CD label tells people how to contact you. If you have a Web site, put your domain name on the CD so that people can get more information about you and your products, and get in touch with you if they want to book you or talk about a record deal.

Once you have compiled all of your information, your logos for the label and the band, and any photos and other graphics, you are ready to meet with the graphic artist. You should consider having the artist sign a work-for-hire agreement so that you will own the rights to the artwork. Otherwise, the artist will retain the copyright and could sue if you use his work without permission. If the artist won't agree to work-for-hire, you may be able to get him to sign a release of copyright or license the artwork. Ownership is what you are after, though.

Also, don't use any picture or artwork that you do not have the rights to use, or that are not in the public domain. You don't want to get sued for infringing someone's copyright. Also, if you are using a picture of a person, make sure that you have the license for the publicity rights to use that picture. You don't want to have to recall all of your artwork just because you didn't get permission to use a graphic or a person's likeness.

The graphic artist may charge a flat rate or an hourly rate. Since art is a very subjective thing, the graphic artist may be willing to give you a few ideas so that you will know what direction he is heading. He may even do this without charging you. However, remember that just coming up with basic ideas will take up a good deal of his time. If he is willing to do this for you, that's a good thing, because you can stop him if you don't think he's headed in the right direction. But recognize that he is taking up his valuable time to give you something that you can use. The more understanding you are about the needs and concerns of your graphic artist, the more likely you are going to get quality artwork.

The Graphic Artists Guild (www.gag.org) is a good source for information about graphic artist guidelines, pricing, ethical concerns, and other information.

UPC Codes

Uniform Product Codes, or *barcodes*, are an absolute necessity if you plan on selling your CDs in retail stores. Therefore, you need to get the proper coding for your CDs. You can go to the Uniform Code Council to apply for your own unique six-digit company identification number and become a member of the UCC. It will provide you with a list of suppliers that can provide camera-ready barcode symbols you can include on all of your products. Once you have your own company number, you can assign a five-digit product code to each of your products. Furthermore, if you are selling items that come in different sizes, such as t-shirts, you will need a unique number for each size.

Unfortunately, the initial fee to become a member is over $3,000.00, and you will also need to pay a yearly fee to maintain your membership. If you have a business license, you've probably registered your company name already, but the UCC doesn't require it. In fact, you don't even need to be incorporated to get a membership. However, since the fee is so high, you may want to forego this individual product code and see if you can piggyback your UPC codes with another company. There are a number of CD replication and duplication houses that will give you a UPC number code and then assign your personal product code to the number of the manufacturer.

Finally, you want to register your UPC code and CD information with SoundScan, a company that tracks retail music and video sales in the United States. It collects sales data from point-of-sale cash registers and a variety of other sources. You can download the membership form from www.soundscan.com. Nielsen SoundScan also reports all sales to the Billboard charts, so you should seriously think about getting onboard. You never know when your music will hit the top of the charts.

You may also want to register your recording with CDDB. Gracenote licenses this proprietary technology to developers of consumer electronic devices and on-line media players like Winamp, iTunes, Napster, and RealOne Player. It allows just about any digital player to recognize the name of a song, the artist's name, and other information. You can contact Gracenote at www.gracenote.com. Since the Internet is such a growing market for music, you will be doing yourself a favor when you register.

Manufacturing

Once you have your master CD in hand, you need to get it manufactured. There are plenty of companies out there that would love to have your business. But be very careful, because you don't want to pay a bunch of money for poor-quality CDs. Also, not all companies provide you with silver CDs that will work in every single CD player. Some companies offer CD-Rs that will work in most players but are not the industry standard. CD-Rs are usually cheaper, and you won't have to buy as many to get a decent deal.

Make sure that you ask what processes they use to make the CDs and print all the artwork. Ask what types of masters they require so that you won't waste time submitting something they can't use. Also, you don't want to incur any extra mastering fees so that they can duplicate or replicate your CDs. There is a lot of information out there on the Internet, so do your homework. You will save yourself a good deal of time, hassles, and money!

Starting Your Own Label

If you are putting out your own record, you should consider starting your own record label. It will lend a good deal of professionalism to your CD. You will have to set up your business, as discussed earlier in the book, and also clear your trademark for both your band and your record label. Once you have written your business plan and manufactured your CDs, you must implement your marketing and promotions plan, and look for some type of distribution. If you are willing to work hard and use what you've learned from this book, you should start in the right direction. (See Chapter 2, "Choosing a Business Structure," Chapter 4, "Advertising, Marketing, Promotion, and Distribution," and Chapter 6, "Intellectual Property.")

Distribution

Once your CDs are manufactured, you need some type of distribution deal so that you can sell your records in music stores. There are a number of distributors out there, and you can make all sorts of deals. However, most distributors won't want to pick you up unless you have some sort of track record for selling CDs. After all, they don't want to stock a bunch of stores with CDs that never sell. You may need to show a prospective distributor your books to prove that there is a market for your music.

Your distributor may want to deal with you exclusively, and may also ask you not to sell any records on consignment once you have a deal. They won't mind if you sell your CDs from the stage, but they want to maximize their profits just like everyone else. Distributors are going to get a percentage of your sales, from around 30% up to 50% of retail or some wholesale figure. Get to know as much as you can about a prospective distributor, including what other clients they handle, what type of sales staff they have, and what type of distribution deal they are offering. You may need to give the distributor a lot of free goods to pass along to the retailers to help them decide if they want your record. And you will have to be ready to accept all returns if they can't sell your record.

You will need to keep up with all marketing and promotions, because this is *not* the distributor's job. You will need to provide the distributor with all of your marketing and promotions efforts, along with list prices, barcodes, and catalogue numbers. You will also need to work with your distributor to arrange in-store appearances and furnish any posters or other point-of-purchase graphics for the stores.

If your business is doing exceptionally well, you may be able to get a deal with the major distributors. The National Association of Independent Record Distributors (NAIRD) has an annual directory that lists independent distributors in the United States. Do your homework and ask as many questions as you can, and you could get a really good distribution deal that will help you sell a lot of records!

Shopping Your CD or Demo

Let's assume that you have completed your promotional package and have finished a really good record, whether it's a demo or a master CD. Now what are you going to do with it?

You should set up meetings with as many managers and attorneys as you can, as well as any contacts or prospective contacts at record labels. You need to hit the ground running to get your product out there. At the very least, you will learn what the labels are looking for. Always remember, you will never know unless you ask.

Joint Ventures

If you've made a really good record and have been able to sell a substantial number of CDs on your own, you may be able to set up a joint venture with either a major record label or a larger independent label. They may be willing to offer you help with promotion, marketing, and/or distribution. This could be a really awesome deal, because you will then have some serious clout behind you. With that extra push, your record could hit the charts and make everyone involved a whole lot of money.

Unless you are experienced with these types of deals, you're better off hiring an attorney who can handle this for you. Make sure to find one who has done these deals before, or you could end up getting burned.

Internet Distribution

If you decide not to place your CDs in regular retail stores, there are a number of other ways to get your product to the marketplace. Of course, you should consider using all of the avenues at your disposal to get your music out there, but sometimes that isn't economically feasible. If you research the Internet, you will find all sorts of new companies that offer these types of services. But remember that this new market is changing quickly and companies come and go. Research them thoroughly, and you can get your music all over the world.

Summary

If you are really serious about a career as a recording artist, or want to start your own record label, nothing is more important than making quality recordings. Even if you have great songs, it won't matter if they're not recorded well. Make sure that you pick the right studio, the right engineer or producer, and the right equipment, and learn as much as you can about the recording process. Make sure that you and your band are completely prepared before you go into the recording studio, and the whole process will go a lot smoother.

You'll need to get your material mastered professionally if you expect to be competitive. Make sure that you take care of the legal and business end of making CDs, starting your own label, or trying to get a record deal, and you won't have anything come back to haunt you. If you can't get a record deal, make sure that you can raise the capital, stick to a budget, and reserve cash for manufacturing, marketing, and promotions, and you will stand a much better chance of making money. You should be able to make at least enough to afford to do your next record. However, if you don't have an overall business plan, you could end up with thousands of really expensive CDs collecting dust in your closet.

One thing is for sure: If you don't take a chance and buy a ticket, you won't ever hit the lottery!

CHAPTER 11

Management—
Ancillary Services

"How your slice of the pie gets smaller...."

Surrounding yourself with a good team is incredibly important if you want to minimize the number of extraneous tasks you have to deal with. If you want to put yourself, your band, or your business in the best possible position for continued success, you are going to need a lot of competent help. A major recording artist can have a whole entourage of people to take care of just about every need. Of course, these artists are making enough money to afford the best of everything, and not everyone in the business is going to be that fortunate. In fact, only a lucky few ever get to that point.

However, if you run your affairs like a business, you really can't afford to do everything by yourself. There just aren't enough hours in the day to do all that needs to be done to further your career. It really boils down to what you can afford, as far as paying for these important service providers, and what you can't afford, in regard to doing without their services. You may find that if your slice of the pie is not very big to start with, you may end up with only crumbs. You will need to be making some pretty decent money before you can hire all of the support that you need, such as a personal manager, business manager, road manager, booking agent, publicist, accountant, entertainment attorney, personal assistants or secretaries, etc.

Everyone needs a whole lot of help to truly make it to the big time. But you can't afford that kind of help in the beginning. The best way to approach this catch-22 is to learn to do as much as you can on your own. By the time you can afford to hire a good team (albeit one service at a time), you will know what needs to be done and thus can manage the team. You will also understand how well your personal team is performing its duties. If you *don't* understand the jobs of each person on your team, you are setting yourself up for someone to take advantage of the situation. You do not want to get into that type of position if you can possibly avoid it.

The first person that you may want to consider hiring is a personal manager.

Personal Manager

A *personal manager* can be a great asset, and most successful acts can't live without theirs. The manager acts as a buffer between the artist and the outside world. He handles all matters and disputes that arise in the normal course of business. Believe me, there can be a lot of fires to put out when you're as busy as a major recording artist.

If you start out with a reputable manager who really knows the business, his advice and counsel can help you to develop your act, hone your image to make it more marketable, and avoid the many pitfalls that lie in wait for the unsuspecting artist. He can help to put together a good team of professionals, such as a lawyer and accountant. He should also be able to find a booking agent to keep those gigs coming in, market your act to the right people, and do many other important tasks that you don't have time to deal with or can't do yourself. After all, when you're dealing with all of this stuff, you have less time to be the creative artist that you want to be, and you'll have to fend for yourself in an extremely competitive and unforgiving business. It's also very professional to have someone else in your corner who has your best interests in mind and knows what is best for you. If you can find a very knowledgeable manager, he will know exactly how to position you for optimum success.

Most management agreements usually require only that your personal manager give such "advice and counsel" as needed by the artist or band. He doesn't agree to do a whole lot more than this, because it's hard to define all of the duties and obligations of a manager. He doesn't really have an absolute duty to do much of anything, which borders on failure of consideration (see Chapter 12, "General Principles of Contracts"). In fact, in many management agreements that I have seen or negotiated, the manager usually had *no* duties to book the act he was managing. However, I have always taken exception to this provision in most management contracts, and have opted for a "seek and see" clause. This means that the manager at least has to look for a booking agent, and for any other work that makes the artist money. In the end, if you have a reputable manager, he will want you or your band to be making as much money as possible. Otherwise, the manager won't be making much either. A percentage of next to nothing is not very much.

Your manager will usually get about 15% to 20% of your gross take, so he has a vested interest in making you more money. You may try to get him to take 15% to 20% of net profits, but there are so many ways of calculating net profits that you probably won't find any experienced manager who's willing to accept such an offer.

Also, the percentage that you pay your manager can sometimes be based on an escalated scale. This means that you'll pay a larger percentage if you become more successful based upon the efforts of the manager. In other words, the manager is paid an increased amount during a calendar year when the artist is grossing over a certain amount, or if the artist reaches certain milestones in gross income.

On the other hand, the management agreement could be set up with a declining scale, in which the manager gets the full 15% of any moneys made up to a certain dollar figure. But if you're making large amounts of money, such as $5,000,000.00 a year, the manager will be dropped down to a lower percentage. Since a smaller percentage of a larger amount of money is still a pretty hefty sum, you may be able to get a manager to agree to this. However, the manager will probably have the best incentive to make the most money for both of you with an escalating scale.

On the other hand, if you're making less than $100,000.00 a year, no experienced or reputable manager will be willing to work very hard for less than $15,000.00

or $20,000.00 a year. Of course, he might if he was managing 5 to 10 acts, but then you'd only get 1/5 to 1/10 of his time and attention. However, if you're grossing $1,000,000.00 a year, the manager may be quite satisfied with his percentage of that amount. Then there is the manager who can position you such that you're grossing over $10,000,000 a year. Obviously, that manager may be entitled to higher percentage of the gross take.

In some cases, an act can get so big as to require *two* managers. If each manager is only making 7.5% to 10% of gross, they may not be making enough to survive and won't want to continue. Ten percent of $1,000,000.00 is only $100,000.00 per manager per year, but an additional 5% could be all that is required to keep those managers working. So you should try to look at it from the manager's side. Unless you're making considerable money, the manager doesn't make much, especially if he's working long hours trying to help you become more successful.

Sometimes a manager may be willing to work with acts before they even sign a deal or have any real income from the entertainment industry. This is sometimes referred to as a *development deal*. In this type of deal, the manager understands that you won't be able to pay him much from your local gigs, but he's willing to make his money on the back end *if* he gets you some type of deal that will pay some pretty good money over time. In this situation, the manager may ask for a higher commission because he is taking a higher risk.

Furthermore, since you are unsigned and probably not making much money, the manager may have to put up some of his own money or perhaps some other investor's money, which can be a very big risk. There are only so many deals being handed out each year, and the chances of getting any act signed are fairly small. So finding a manager to help you develop your act can be a very good thing, but if he is asking for 40% or more of your gross income, you may want to wait until you are further along to find a manager who's willing to take less.

Remember, if you sign a bad management deal, you could be stuck with that manager for many years to come, which could be the death knell for your career. You could be prevented from furthering your career for the entire length of your management contract. In a business that places an emphasis on youth, your career could very well be over, or at least put on hold for a long time.

Since the manager doesn't really have many duties other than giving advice and counsel during the term of your management contract, he could just do very little and still make a claim for any moneys that you make. Of course, you could always pay your manager the 15% under the original management agreement and then hire another manager who will actually further your career, but then you would be paying yet another manager a large percentage of money to work with you. Many artists have had to pay an old manager a lot of money once they made it big, even though that manager had little or nothing to do with obtaining that artists' success.

A manager who does development deals may not have any intention of being your full-time manager. He may have other business concerns that could prevent him from giving you his full attention once you are firmly on the road to success. His intention may be to get you a deal and then transfer his rights under your management agreement to another manager who will have the time to dedicate to you. You can bet on this if the first manager has a rock-solid contract that will allow him to take big chunk of your advance, and maybe retain some of your merchandising or other income over a long time. He will then transfer the rights to your contract to a third party (most likely without your approval) so that he can be compensated for his work without having to forego other business opportunities he would not have to time to attend to if he were working for you exclusively. In this instance, you definitely want to make sure you have some type of *key man clause* in the management agreement. This will make it clear that the reason you are signing with this manager is that you want to work with him and no one else. Therefore, it's a good idea to restrict the development manager from transferring the rights, duties, and obligations of your management contract to an unknown third party unless you have approved such a transfer.

Business Manager(s)

Many successful artists and writers have business managers who take care of all the day-to-day financial aspects of their business, and sometimes their personal life. Such a manager maintains your business accounts and sometimes your personal bank account(s). He handles all of the bookkeeping, pays all of the bills of the business, and sometimes handles all of your personal bills as well. He helps with defining budgets, making payroll to your entire entourage, and making investments, and can even help to secure lines of credit with the bank to finance things like new equipment, tour buses, or whatever it is you need. He may ask for a percentage of your income if it's fairly substantial, he may bill you an hourly rate, or he may be paid a flat fee per week or month. Rest assured, if both you and your personal manager are busy enough to need a business manager, it can save you a good deal of time and energy. He can also be a strong voice of reason when it comes to controlling costs and managing the bottom line of your business.

Your business manager can be a great asset who will allow you to keep a checks-and-balances system between you and your manager. If your manager is getting all of the money and then paying you from that, pursuant to the terms of your management agreement (a really bad idea), who is going to make sure that your manager is paying you what you're supposed to get? This type of situation has been going on for years and years, so be aware of it. Your business manager can make sure that all the money is being taken care of, and then disperse money to you, your personal manager, and the rest of your organization.

Road Manager

Before you hire a personal manager, you need a good road manager, especially if you're gigging or touring constantly. A road manager will make sure that all your gigs run as smoothly as possible. He will put out fires and make sure that you can dedicate your time to the show and other appearances. He makes sure that all the hotel reservations are taken care of and all the bills for the tour are paid. He makes sure that you get where you are supposed to be, and once you get there, he helps with tasks such as CD sales and merchandising sales. Depending on the level you're at, it's a really good idea to have a road manager who knows a good deal about lighting and sound. Also, depending on his degree of skill and your needs, he can make sure that your sound system and lighting are working properly. In fact, if you're a smaller band, your road manager can be your sound and lighting guy, as well as the person who sells your t-shirts and CDs. If he is really adept, he can help you set up interviews with radio stations and in-stores at the record shops.

And most importantly, the road manager will be the one who collects your money at the end of the night. If there are any problems with the payout, he can be the person who settles disputes, which prevents you from having to come off as the bad guy. In short, once you have a good road manager, you are going to hate to live without one.

A road manager is usually paid a salary per week, and in some cases a per diem. Of course, all of this is negotiable. But you have to remember that the road manager's job can sometimes be harder than being in the band. If you are in an unsigned band that is trying to go to the next level, you should consider making your road manager an equal member of the band until you can afford to pay him a decent salary. The more importance that you attribute to your road manager's job, the more likely that he will stick around and help take your act to the next level.

Road Crew

If you're gigging or touring a lot, at some point you're going to need people to help you get all your stuff to and from the shows, and to make sure that your gigs go off without a hitch. If you are lucky enough to play only venues that already have sound systems, you may not need a crew. But then again, just getting all of your band's instruments and other equipment to a gig can be a rather daunting task, especially when you need to conserve your energy for the show. Furthermore, what happens if something goes wrong while you are onstage? It can be crucial to have people there who can help with sound, lighting, cartage, changing strings, and the like.

Unfortunately, these guys don't come cheap, unless they are huge fans of your band and are willing to work for free or very little. You need to pay these guys some sort of wage, either by the hour, by the job, or by weekly salary. Most likely you'll also need to pay them a per diem for their basic road expenses like food, gas, and lodging. If you can enlist some part-time help, or just get some help moving your gear, that is always going to be welcome. But you're going to have to give some serious thought to your needs and do some financial calculations before you decide whether you can afford a road crew.

Before you even think about a road crew, you need to get the gigs in the first place. To that end, you should look at a booking agent.

Booking Agent

A booking agent is an absolute must if you're trying to break out. He will keep you working and keep bringing in cash flow. Booking agents normally charge from 10 to 15% of each show that they book. When you consider how many promotional packages you would have to send out on your own, and how many cold calls you would have to make, just so you continue to have gigs to play, you can see that a really good booking agent can be worth his weight in gold.

A booking agent's most valued assets are his knowledge of music, his ability to market and sell his acts, and his Rolodex with all of his contacts throughout the music industry. A good booking agent has his finger on the pulse of what is happening with all types of gigs, and he knows where to put his acts so that they can make the most money. He has a great rapport with all types of clubs, festivals, and medium and larger venues.

Not only does he handle all aspects of getting gigs, but often he makes sure that you get paid, because he's the one who has the contracts with both you and the venue where you'll be playing. Since he gets a piece of the action, it's in his best interests to get you as much money as possible.

But you will have to decide if you can afford to work with a booking agent full-time. For instance, if you are playing gigs for only $500 a night, and the booking agent gets 15% ($75) for booking the gig, neither of you will make much money. You will only have $425.00 to pay the band and all of your expenses, so the band could be making less than $50.00 a piece per night, which is less than the booking agent.

But I have always looked at that situation this way: If you are a working band, you should take as many gigs as you possibly can. In time, you will begin to make more and more money as you grow your fan base and expand the areas where you play. When you are starting out, even if you make only enough money to survive for that day, it's better than being stuck at a day job.

In most instances, the booking agent will require a deposit from the venue so he gets at least get some of the money for the gigs he sets up, just in case there is some unforeseen circumstance such as weather problems. Your contract with the booking agent should cover what happens to that non-refundable deposit if the venue needs to cancel for any reason. Your contract should also cover what types of gigs you will take and how much money you require for all of your gigs. This way you will ensure that your gigs are actually profitable for you. It is also a good idea to get some type of performance rider to set forth all of your band's needs, such as how much equipment you need, how much power you require for your equipment, the size of the stage, a place to setup a merchandise stand, etc. If you have your needs set out in writing in a performance rider, you are much more likely to have what you need when you get to the venue, and much less likely to encounter any problems, such as insufficient power to run your equipment.

Your main concern should be that your booking agent believes in your act and is going to keep you working! Unfortunately, some booking agents require that you sign with them exclusively. After all, they don't want to compete with another booking agent to coordinate your schedule. You should not sign any exclusive agreement unless you know that the booking agent is going to keep you working. If you sign an exclusive booking agreement and you are not working much, you could be missing a lot of opportunities. Furthermore, even if you get gigs on your own, your booking agent may expect to get paid for those gigs. If the booking agent demands an exclusive arrangement, you should insist that you be working a certain number of dates per week or month. If the booking agent can't deliver on that promise, don't sign!

Publicists or Public Relations Firms

As stated in Chapter 4, "Advertising, Marketing, Promotion, and Distribution," a publicist or public relations firm is hired specifically for the purposes of promoting your career. It helps to get you across to all types of media so that you can increase your exposure and sell your records, merchandise, services, or whatever.

A publicist should be very knowledgeable about the music industry and have a lot of solid contacts and relationships with all types of magazines, radio, television, newspapers, and other media sources. He should be a very personable and tenacious guy who doesn't like to hear "no." And if he's really good, he'll work with you to make sure you are constantly in the public eye. He'll help you promote your music by getting interviews with everyone from college newspapers all the way up to *Rolling Stone*. He'll also arrange other appearances on radio or television, and other public events. Again, if you get a good publicist, you'll be very glad that you did.

However, you are going to pay for this service, and it can be fairly costly.

Personal Assistants (PA)

Personal assistants take care of just about anything that you don't have time to do. You will need to be making some pretty good money before can you afford a PA full-time, but if you're crafty, you can find someone to help you out with just about anything you need and sometimes for next to nothing. The more people you have helping you with the day-to-day tasks, the more time you will have for the things you do best.

A personal assistant is paid by salary or by the hour, depending on his skills and experience. Of course, you may be able find an intern to help you with certain tasks, just so he can learn more about the music business. However, make sure that any personal assistant signs a confidentiality agreement so that he is legally bound not to exploit his knowledge of your personal life.

Accountants

Your business manager may be able to handle your taxes and other financial matters, but you still may need an accountant to make sure that all of this is done correctly and in a timely fashion. If you set up a business structure, your accountant will be an extremely valuable asset because he can help you with the tax returns for your business, as well as your individual taxes.

You may be able to find a pretty good accountant who will work for about $100/hour. But remember that accountants are just like everyone else in the service industry. They will bill for every single hour that they spend working for you, and that can add up fairly quickly. If you have both your business and personal accounting to do, you could be looking at some pretty serious accounting bills every tax season. To save money, keep meticulous records of all your expenses. Furthermore, if you learn to use some sort of accounting software, at the end of the year you can turn that information over to your accountant to finalize your taxes. Again, the more stuff you know how to do yourself, the more money you will save.

Another function of a really good accountant is to audit the books of your publisher or record label. You never know if the accountants or bookkeepers at your publishing company or record label are doing their jobs and keeping your best interests in mind. I have had artists or songwriters who thought they weren't being paid as much as they were supposed to for one reason or another. Once they'd put their publisher or label on notice that they were doing an audit, and before their accountant had gone in and audited the books, they were surprised to find an "updated" accounting from the label or publisher with a very fat check enclosed. Once the accountant had done his thing, the books were actually balanced. A really good accountant can go in and make sense of your publisher's or record label's books, and make absolutely sure that you are getting every single penny that you deserve.

Unfortunately, accountants don't come cheap. Hiring one just to make sure that you get the money you're owed can be cost-prohibitive, and therefore you may never get paid. So be very careful, and make sure you know as much as you can about when, how, and how much you should be getting. Don't get so far behind that you can never afford to catch up!

Attorneys

As discussed in Chapter 1, a really good entertainment lawyer can be very beneficial in furthering your career. He should have many connections in the music industry and can be invaluable in shopping a deal for you, getting you in to meet the right people, or any number of other issues. He can help you with the maze of contracts with just about every deal that you sign, and can help steer you clear of any problems that you could be facing in the entertainment business.

Ancillary Services and Products

There are a host of other services and products that you will need to grow your business steadily . It's all about finding the right balance between what you can afford to buy, what you can do yourself, and what you can't afford to live without. Don't forget that you will always be incurring costs for touring, such as buses, trucks, vans, or other transportation. You'll have a constant need for the tools of the trade, such as musical gear, recording equipment, and instruments, as well as constant repairs on these items. Food, lodging, gas, and other basic costs of living will have to be planned for, even if you live on the road. Of course, if you have a home base such as an apartment or house, you will have to make enough money to afford the rent or house payments, utilities, and other costs, such as car payments, insurance, etc.

So you really need to keep up with all of your costs and plan for the future. This is a business, after all, and unless you can afford to pay all of your bills, you won't be able to stay in business for long. (For more information, see Chapter 3, "Making a Business Plan.")

Summary

You don't need a record deal to make a living in the music industry. In fact, you may find that you can make more money in the music business than at a basic day job. But are you willing to do what is necessary to keep yourself working and earning the money you need? You will have to ask yourself, "How much can I live on?" Figure out your expenses and costs of living for the road and for home, and then you will know how much you need to earn in order to survive and even grow your business. Of course, you should also keep some sort of emergency fund for repairs or other unforeseen expenses.

Next, ask yourself, "How much do I make working at my day job?" If you don't have any skills other than music, you might be making minimum wage, or you might need to do some other type of unskilled labor that pays $10 an hour with no benefits. If you really work hard in the music business, you can make much more than minimum wage. In fact, finding a gig that pays fairly well isn't that hard to do, if you work at it and are professional in every aspect of your business. However, take into account that you may be working just a few hours a day, and you won't be working every single day. Therefore, the real problem is getting enough work to keep everyone in the band in the black, especially since most jobs as a musician will last for only one night or one week.

You will also find that your slice of the pie will get smaller as you hire more and more people to help you with your career. But if you take a proactive approach to your music and treat it just like a job, you will be surprised at what you can do all on your own.

CHAPTER 12

General Principles of Contracts

"Hope for the best, plan for the worst!"

....

Now that we have discussed recording, record contracts, management deals, and the like, we should take a look at what actually makes up a contract. Understanding contracts, or at least having a working knowledge of contracts, can be extremely useful when you're doing just about any type of business venture. You can't always trust the people you are dealing with, and getting something in writing can save a ton of hassles later on. People are quick to say that their word is their bond, or that you really don't need a contract, only to turn around and change the deal on you at almost every turn. Don't let this happen to you. Get it in writing!

It takes two whole semesters of law school to even begin to cover contracts. And after that, it can take many years of studying, reading, and drafting contracts to appreciate their finer points and intricacies. The most important thing you should get from this chapter is that contracts don't have to be written by lawyers. In fact, many are not.

Entering into a contract is almost an everyday occurrence. Contracts govern almost every aspect of our lives. Often they're referred to as *agreements*, which is a term I prefer to use. Contracts don't have to include a bunch legal jargon or legalese such as "whereas" and "heretofore," and you don't need to know the importance of *Hadley vs. Baxendale* or any other court precedent. However, the more you know about contracts, the better you will be prepared to protect your rights and keep from being taken advantage of.

The problem is that contracts can be extremely complicated, and each contract is different. So be prepared. Do your homework. Ask as many questions as you can. If both parties fulfill their end of the bargain, you should do just fine.

The musical roadside is littered with artists, bands, and songwriters who have signed bad agreements. Either they didn't read their contracts before they signed them, or they failed to hire adequate representation to help them understand and negotiate their agreements. Many of these people never got paid, or weren't paid nearly what they should have been. They had to watch someone *else* make all the money.

So beware! Whenever someone wants you to sign something and says, "You don't have to read it," you could be getting yourself into some real trouble. You'll never know what it says unless you read it and understand everything in it. Never sign an agreement that you don't understand unless you get someone who is 100%

in your corner to tell you what it means. This is especially important if it's a recording or publishing deal.

There are so many contracts in the day-to-day life of musicians, artists, etc. When you buy your music gear, you enter into a contract, either a sales agreement or a finance agreement. When you form a band, there is a sort of implied contract. In fact, there are several of them, such as agreeing to show up for practice, agreeing to play a gig, etc. When you book a gig, it's a contract. When you sign anything with a record label or publisher, it's *definitely* a contract. When you do just about anything that involves other people transferring goods or services, there is some type of contract even though there may be nothing in writing.

It would be almost impossible to have a lawyer follow you around every day to approve all of your personal contracts, but there's no reason you can't do a good deal of your contractual work yourself. It's important to understand the basics and always to think of as many contingencies as you can.

Contract Basics

A contract is an agreement between two or more parties. Contracts come in many different forms. They can be written or oral, implied or express, fair or unfair. Most contracts do not have to be in writing to be completely legal. Unfortunately, oral contracts are only as good as the people who make them. People often have selective memories, so having a written document that's been signed by both parties will go a long way toward clearing up any misunderstandings.

Contracts are promises that the law will enforce. In fact, a promise can be a type of contract, if there is a mutual exchange of promises between two parties. The law provides remedies if a promise is breached, and recognizes the performance of a promise as a duty. Contracts also arise when a duty comes into existence because of a promise made by one of the parties. To be legally binding as a contract, a promise must be exchanged for *adequate consideration,* or a benefit or detriment that a party receives or suffers that reasonably and fairly induces him to make the promise or contract. For example, promises that are purely gifts are not considered enforceable, because the personal satisfaction the grantor of the promise may receive from the act of giving is not considered adequate consideration. If someone says, "You can have this," the item is yours. However, in limited circumstances, certain promises that are not considered actual contracts may be enforced if one party has relied to his detriment on the assurances of the other party.

State statutory law and common law, which have been developed by court rulings over time, mainly govern contracts. There is also case law and private law. Case law is developed similarly to common law, in that these cases show the holdings of previous court cases over time. Private law principally includes the terms of the agreements between the parties who are exchanging promises. This private law may override many of the rules otherwise established by state law, and in some situations "case law." However, statutory law may require some contracts to be put in writing and executed with particular formalities. Otherwise, the parties may enter into a binding agreement without signing a formal written document.

Oral versus Written Contracts

Oral agreements are just that, agreements between two parties that are made verbally and never reduced to writing. They are just as legal as any written agreement. The big difference is that with a written agreement, both parties must sign it, and then it will be controlling when it comes time to perform or there is a dispute. In other words, if there is a dispute over the terms of an agreement, you look only at the written agreement and nothing else. Furthermore, oral contracts are extremely difficult to enforce and in some cases very difficult to prove. Both parties to an oral contract will often change their minds, if not their statements, as to what was said or done.

If there's a dispute over the terms of an oral agreement, the judge, jury, or arbitrator will have to listen to the facts of the case and decide who to believe. This will definitely be a "he said, she said" situation. Reducing your agreement to a written document will help any third party to understand all of the terms of the agreement. In fact, having a written contract is the best way to define each party's rights, duties, and obligations up front before there are any disputes.

Here's an example: Let's assume that six people, three guys and their dates, go to a football game in the fall. Three of the people are cheering for one team, and the other three are cheering for the other team. If they came back six weeks later and each give an account of what happened, I can assure you that their accounts will vary. This doesn't mean that any of them are lying, but rather that they each have their own perceptions of the truth. Men will look at situations differently than women, and that's just the way it is. If you are a party to a lawsuit and everyone is a little emotional about the issues, you can bet that each story will be different from the others.

So the lesson here is to get it in writing! If you don't, you could be arguing over what the agreement actually was, or even whether there was ever an agreement at all.

Parole Evidence

Learn to read the fine print!

Parole evidence is simply any prior or contemporaneous statement or statements made by either party that are not included in a written agreement. Such evidence is inadmissible when you have a written contract. In other words, any statements someone makes about the subject matter of an agreement, or any other promises that are made but are not included in the actual contract, will not be considered part of the contract. You must look to the "four corners" of any written agreement to see exactly what the parties have agreed upon.

I've seen some pretty unscrupulous people who will try to make you believe something's in an agreement when it isn't. The whole time, they're telling you not to worry about this or that, but trust me, you *should* worry. They may even go so far as to tell you what the contract says (as if you don't know how to read), so that you will agree to all of their terms. However, it doesn't matter what they *say* is in the agreement, only what the actual contract contains.

Some contracts must be in writing or they are *void ab initio*. In other words, they were not valid contracts from the very beginning and can be set aside by operation of law. This just means that the law has made provisions for this scenario and will not uphold a contract that isn't in writing. This concept is called the *statute of frauds*.

Statute of Frauds

This applies to contract for the sale of goods over a certain amount of money. The amount depends on each state's law or certain contracts that cannot be performed within one year, which in both circumstances require a formal written agreement. Therefore, whenever you buy a big-ticket item such as an expensive guitar, the contract for sale should be in writing or it can be set aside.

Furthermore, if you enter into an agreement for something that cannot be performed in a period less than a year, such as songwriting for a publisher, that contract must be in writing. Also, any contract that transfers copyrights must be in writing for it to be valid. If you are not sure whether a particular agreement must be in writing, get a formal written agreement anyway. Then you will be covered whether the contract falls under the statute of frauds or not.

The Parties

Any adult person or any business entity has the right to enter into contracts. However, some people may *not* have the capacity to enter into an agreement. In order for a party to enter into an agreement, he must be at least 18 years of age and must not be suffering from some mental infirmity. If he's not old enough or sane enough to understand the agreement, the agreement will not be enforceable.

Agency

Sometimes others are given authority to contract on behalf of another party, and this is known as *agency*. This is often the case with a band that contracts with others to perform. One person in the band usually has authority to deal with clubs, booking agents, and the like, to bind the others in the band into having a duty to perform under the terms of the contract.

Agency will be either implied or express, so that one party has the authority to bind some third party. In other words, a contract may specifically state that Joe Guitar, a partner in Joe's Guitar Band, has the right to bind the rest of the band members to play a certain date. If the contract doesn't expressly state that, it will be implied that Joe has the authority to bind the rest of his band to that contract, and therefore all members of Joe's Guitar Band must play the gig.

You may also have a booking agent who will enter into contracts on your behalf so that you can keep working. Your booking agent will have the authority to bind your band to a contract, and you'll have to play the gig.

Signatures

If you have a written contract, both parties must sign it or it's not binding. Furthermore, wherever you have written any part of a contract by hand, such as if you're using a boilerplate booking contract with blank spaces that you've filled in with the date or the amount to be paid, both parties must initial the handwritten portions. You should also have both parties initial every single page of your agreement. This will prevent anyone from disputing any handwritten part, or asserting that you changed the terms by slipping in other pages that were different from the original contract.

Another reason a signature is required is that it meets the provision that a contract must be *executed* to be valid. By signing, you have given legal notice of your acceptance of the terms, and therefore you are bound by the contract.

Term

Every written or oral agreement must be for a *term certain*. In other words, they cannot last forever. There has to be some sort of time limit, or that contract will be void on its face.

A friend of mine is a music publisher in England, and he has a bar napkin on his wall with a songwriter's signature on it and the words, "You will be my publisher forever." This is completely unenforceable. These two guys are completely honorable and really don't need a written agreement, but I doubt that you'll be able to find someone to honor an agreement like that in this day and age. Therefore, any agreement should set a term for a certain number of years. If the parties want to renew the agreement for another term, they are free to do so.

You may also find some agreements that allow for *options*. In other words, one or more parties may reserve the right to enforce a contract option, which may renew the contract for another term and may require additional consideration. However, you cannot have indefinite options. There must be a beginning and an end to any contract, or it's not enforceable.

Implied or Express Contracts

Some agreements can be enforceable even though the parties never actually make a contract. In other words, there's nothing written, and the parties never even shake hands (not that a handshake is binding, because it's not) or even state that they have an agreement. However, a contract is *implied* by the actions of the parties. For instance, if you see your lawyer to get some legal advice, it is implied that you will pay for his services. There are many different types of implied contracts, but usually they're when one party has received a benefit for which he hasn't paid any consideration.

On the other side of that coin are *express* contracts, where the terms of the contract are in fact written down. You should always get agreements in writing, especially if you expect to get paid. Just because *you* may deem something to be a benefit doesn't mean the other party will feel that he got something useful.

Quasi-Contracts

Sometimes an implied contract is called a *quasi-contract*. The courts have decided that a contract is implied if the alternative is that one party will be unjustly enriched by the actions of another. For instance, if you are in jail and call your lawyer to get you out, and he does so before he sees you to get paid, it is implied that you will have to pay your lawyer. Otherwise, you would be unjustly enriched by his services for free. You have an implied contract with your attorney, and you will have to pay him a reasonable fee.

This is also true if you're asked to play a gig for a friend. If you move your equipment, set it all up, and then play the gig, there's a quasi-contract and your friend will have to pay you a reasonable fee. However, you should avoid this situation at all costs. At the very least, you should try to come up with an agreement as to what you will be paid if you play the gig.

Elements of a Contract

There are a number of important elements to a contract that you should know about, such as offer, acceptance, and consideration. Also, there must be a meeting of the minds, the parties must deal in good faith, and the contract must be reasonable in its scope.

OFFER, ACCEPTANCE, AND CONSIDERATION
Let's first discuss what makes up a contract: offer, acceptance, and consideration. These are the absolute basics that you have to understand.

One party must make an initial *offer*. It could be "I'll sell you this guitar for $1,000," or "I want you to play at our club next Saturday for $1,000." After the offer, there must be *acceptance* of that offer. In the first instance, you can accept the offer by pulling out your $1,000 and paying the man for the guitar. The $1,000 is your *consideration* for the contract. In the second instance, you accept by making a promise to play the gig next Saturday. The promise is your *consideration* to support the contract. You're giving up something of value, or making a promise to give up something of value, whether it's cash or your time and effort.

The consideration for these two scenarios is different. Your consideration to buy the guitar is the $1,000 you pay, while the consideration from the man selling the guitar is the actual guitar. In the second example, your consideration is your promise to play, and the club owner's consideration is his promise to pay you $1,000. One contract calls for actual transfers of tangible items, while the other is simply an exchange of promises.

Another example is if you ask your guitarist to drive a very long distance to play a gig with you. In fact, you offer him $50 just to show up. The guitar player's acceptance doesn't have to be expressed. He doesn't have to say a word, and his consideration is the act of getting in his car and starting to drive to the gig. If he shows up, you have to pay him the $50, even if he doesn't play the gig. If there is an offer, acceptance of that offer, and consideration, there is a contract.

MEETING OF THE MINDS

In order for a contract to be enforceable, the two parties have to come to a *meeting of the minds*. This simply means that both parties must agree to the same terms.

For instance, if you agree to play a club gig on the first of the month and the club owner agrees to pay you $1,000, you have a contract. However, if you think that you are only supposed to play for two hours and the venue expects you to play for four hours, obviously there hasn't been a meeting of the minds. If there is a written contract, you look to the *four corners* of it. In other words, you consider the terms in that agreement and nothing more. So if there is nothing in the written agreement about how long you are supposed to play, you have a real problem.

You're also going to have some problems if there is no written agreement and just the statements of the two parties to rely on. The venue is going to say that it was implied that you'd be playing for four hours, and you should have known that. The managers could say that all the bands they hire play for four hours. Or they could just lie and say that they told you it would be four hours. Of course, you will say that you never agreed to play for four hours at that price, or that there was no way for you to know that four hours was the standard for that venue.

There are only two ways to resolve this issue: Negotiate a reasonable solution to the mutual satisfaction of both parties, or go to court. Of course, what's likely to happen is that you won't get paid if you don't play the four hours, and you won't be playing in that club again. The club will have the stronger negotiating position.

The absolute best way to avoid this type of situation is to discuss every possible deal point before you agree to do something for someone. And you need to make sure that neither side changes any of the terms based upon selective memory or some other misunderstanding. Again, get it in writing! If you think through every possible contingency, you will have a rock-solid contract. You should include the date of the gig, the time you go onstage, how long you are supposed to play, what type of music, etc. The more you include in the contract, the less room there is for miscommunication, and the better off both parties will be if there are any discrepancies. You do what you are supposed to do, and then the club has to pay you.

GOOD FAITH

This is a fairly easy principle to understand. It merely means that the parties who enter into an agreement must do so in *good faith*. In other words, the courts may look to the intentions of the parties when deciding whether a contract is fair and equitable. If either or both parties take advantage of the other party by making misleading statements or otherwise trying to get one over on the other party, the contract could be set aside as unenforceable.

However, proving the intent of another party can be quite difficult, especially if the party lies about it in court. Or the party may just have a different understanding of what was supposed to be done. Again, get it in writing. Set forth all the terms that each of the parties are supposed to live up to, and you won't have to worry about the good faith of either party.

REASONABLENESS

Because it is virtually impossible to predict all of the problems that can come up between two parties, the courts have created the *reasonable person* standard. This just means that a judge or jury will have to decide whether a reasonable person would have believed that a contract existed based upon the actions of the parties. No contract will be upheld if a reasonable person would not have recognized an implied contract under those circumstances.

For instance, let's say you get a little upset with your lead singer one night at a gig, and you jokingly say to your sound guy that you'll give him $1,000 to turn off the singer's microphone during the next set. If the sound guy does so, do you owe him $1,000? Probably not. A reasonable person wouldn't think that you were serious, or that the sound guy would be entitled to $1,000 just for turning off a microphone.

But it could happen. So watch what you say, or someone could end up feeling like you owe him money for something that you never intended to pay him for in the first place.

Expectation, Reliance, and Forbearance

Now let's discuss the interests that each party to an agreement may have: expectation, reliance, and forbearance. Each person in a contract may have a claim for one, two, or all three of them, which means that the damages if either party breaches the agreement could be much more than you ever expected.

We'll use the preceding example to keep it simple. If a club owner asks you to play his club next Saturday for $1,000, you both automatically have an *expectation interest*. Your expectation is that you will be paid $1,000 if you play the gig, and the club owner's expectation is that your band will play the gig for $1,000. Of course, it's reasonable to assume that the club owner is hiring you because he expects you to draw a crowd and make the club some money—at least enough for him to pay you the $1,000 and still clear a profit. Whereas you expect to get paid whether people actually show up or not. If there are no conditional promises, you must be paid whether the club owner lets your band play or not, as long as you have shown up and are willing to perform. The expectation interest is what the parties expect to get out of the agreement, whether it's cash or something else of value.

What happens once you have a reasonable expectation to get paid, as per the terms of the agreement? It's reasonable to assume that you'll need to take certain steps to prepare for the gig, and therefore you're relying on the club's promise to pay you. You have a *reliance interest* because you're expending money or time in preparation for the gig. In other words, if you have relied to your detriment and the gig is cancelled, you could be out not just the expectation interest of $1,000, but also your reliance interest for the money and time that you've expended.

Of course, the real measure of your damages is not your reliance interest *and* your expectation interest, but just your expectation interest. However, if the club owner has some legitimate reason for cancelling the gig, you can at least recover your reliance damages. For instance, it's reasonable to assume that you'll need to change the strings on all of your guitars, which could cost you up to $50. Therefore, you have relied to your detriment on the club's promise to pay, to the tune of $50.

Furthermore, even though you and the club owner have never discussed advertising, it's reasonable to assume that your band will print up some fliers so that your fans will know that you're playing at the club, and maybe bring in some new people to see your band. So let's say that you've spent $50 on the fliers and the gas to drive all over town putting them up. You have now relied to your detriment for a total of $100, and that doesn't even include the time that you could have spent doing other things to make money. You wouldn't have printed the fliers or spent any of the gas money if you hadn't been expecting to make $1,000. Your total reliance damages are $100, and perhaps more if you include your time. In short, any reasonable money and time that you expend in expectation of playing the gig could be included in the damages if you're not paid by the club owner.

On the other hand, let's say the club owner wants to bring in as many people as possible, so he takes out print or radio ads to the tune of $300. Then you don't show up. By paying for the ads, the club has relied to its detriment on your promise to play. The club owner could be out a lot of money that he expected to make from your gig, and he's definitely out the reliance damages for the money he spent to promote the show. Therefore, a reliance interest is when either party has expended time and money, or given something else of value, in the expectation that the agreement will be honored. Relying to one's detriment just means that if the contract is broken, either party may have lost even more than the actual money agreed upon.

The lesson here is that even though you may have an agreement for a sum certain, other damages can be incurred if either party spends money in reliance of a promise.

Now let's look at *forbearance interest*, which is when either party has passed up other opportunities in the expectation that the current agreement will be fulfilled. This is where it can get complicated.

Let's say that after you and the club owner agree on the gig for next Saturday, your band gets an offer to play a frat party on the same date for $2,500. Obviously, that's $1,500 more than you were going to make at the club. What should you do? Your band can't play two gigs at the same time, so you have to forego that opportunity to make more money if you intend to honor your original commitment to the club.

Next, let's say that between the time of your agreement and the time you're supposed to play the gig, the club owner gets a call from a bigger band about playing on the same night. Unfortunately for your band, this bigger band is on a major label. The band has a stopover gig due to a cancellation, and really wants to play that club. The club owner is sure that this band will draw a considerably larger crowd than your band, and that he can double the cover charge. Unfortunately for the club owner, he has to forego this opportunity if he intends to honor your contract.

So, both parties will have to forego the better opportunity if they're going to honor their original commitments. But will they? We live in a greedy world, and more often than not, people are enticed by the lure of more money and therefore will not honor their commitments.

But what's the two parties' total exposure to damages? Let's look at more facts to see how this could play out.

Let's assume that your band really wants to play this club, and really can't afford to blow off the gig to play the frat party. That's a one-time thing, whereas the club may let you play there several times over the next year. The extra $1,500 wouldn't be worth missing out on those other gigs because you left the club hanging without a band. Due to this bargaining disparity between you and the club, your band decides to play the club gig and blow off the frat guys.

Unfortunately, the club decides to go ahead and book the major-label band, *after* you've already told the frat guys that you can't play their gig. Unfair? Yes, but it happens all the time. Now you're out $1,000 in expectation damages, and $100 or more in reliance damages for the new strings and advertising. To make matters worse, a lot of your fans will go to the club only to find out that the cover charge is too high just to see this major-label act, and they can't see your band at all that night.

What's the solution? Well, you can ask the club to pay your expectation interest of $1,000 because you had a contract. You could ask for an additional $1,500 because you weren't able to play the frat gig either. You could also ask for the $100 or more for your guitar strings and advertising costs. By law, the club could be forced to pay any of these costs, up to the full $1,500 that you could have made if it had cancelled your gig in time for you to get the frat gig. If you don't ever expect to play that club again, by all means, try to get your money.

Your best bet is to negotiate with the club owner and get what you can. If he's fair (which is unlikely), he'll pay you something, especially if he made a lot of money off the bigger band. However, you don't have a very strong negotiating position because you want to play that club again, so you may want to take the high road and just move on. Then again, the frat may never call you again because it would rather call bands that will actually play its parties. It's a really bad situation for your band and a great situation for the club.

What if you take the frat gig, and the club owner turns down the bigger band that could make him more money? He could sue you for the $1,000 that you were supposed to get. And of course, he may have expected to make even more money than that from food and beverage sales. He could even make a claim for his reliance interest of $300 for radio and print ads. If he sues and wins, you'll have made $1,500 from the frat gig minus the $1,300 or more that you have to pay the club owner. To make matters worse, you probably won't ever play that club again.

So it's very easy to see that if people don't honor their commitments, it can create a lot of problems. But there are a lot of things you can do to fix these situations as they come up. First, call the club and see if they'll let you play the frat gig. You can even offer to get another band to fill your spot if the club can't find one on short notice. If you have a good relationship with the club owner, he'll want you to take the better deal. As long as you can find him a decent band that will draw well enough for the club to make money, you will be fine. Of course, you'll be out the cost of your fliers, and you'll have to let people know that your gig at the club has been cancelled. You shouldn't ever forget about the folks who have seen the fliers and are ready to expend time and money to show up at the club. You could even ask the club to make a list of all the people who do show up to see you, and then offer them a discount for the next show.

But if the shoe is on the other foot, the club isn't going to give you much consideration unless your band is a pretty strong draw. If you leave the club hanging, you've pretty much shot yourself in the foot. The best thing to do is always honor your commitments. If you lose out, at least ask the club for a few more gigs to make up for the lost frat gig and the lost club gig. If the owner is fair, he'll help you out. If not, you may want to just sue him and be done with it. If the club gets into the habit of messing with bands like this, you can always get all of your friends in other bands to boycott that club.

But you really can't afford to burn any bridges. If you have a rock-solid written contract, the club will be much less likely to book any other band. That's just bad business. There are other things you need to do when you find out a contract may have been breached, but let's save that discussion for a little later in this chapter. First, let's take a look at some other types of contracts.

Conditional Contracts

Most contracts have some conditions in them. In fact, many of the terms in a contract are referred to as *conditions*. For example, a contract might say, "As a condition of the contract, you are required to do this...." In some cases, certain conditions must be met before you can decide whether there is in fact a valid contract, while in other cases, a contract can become invalid based upon certain conditions.

CONDITION PRECEDENT

A *condition precedent* requires that something must occur before a contract will be considered valid. For example, let's say you promise your guitar player that if your band gets a gig this weekend, you will pay him $500. If you get the gig and he plays, you and your guitar player have a contract and you must pay him the $500.

If you don't get the gig, you don't have to pay your guitar player. Pretty simple.

CONDITION SUBSEQUENT

A *condition subsequent* is when a contract can become invalid if a certain event occurs. For example, on Monday, you tell a friend who plays guitar that your regular guitar player has been really sick lately and doesn't think he'll be able to make it to your next gig this weekend. You promise to pay this replacement guitar player $500 to play the gig this weekend. You now have a contract with the replacement guitar player, but it's subject to a condition subsequent—the chance that your original guitar player gets well before this weekend. If he does, your contract with the replacement guitar player is invalidated and you don't have to pay him.

But don't forget that the replacement guitar player may get other offers between Monday and the weekend. If he turns down another gig before you tell him that your original guitar player is okay, you may have to pay his reliance damages and perhaps even his forbearance damages. If he gets another offer and he calls and tells you he can't play, at least you have notice to find another replacement guitar player. Again, if you keep everyone informed, you can solve most of these problems.

Obviously, contracts can get very complicated. None of us live in a vacuum, and circumstances change all the time. But again, there are certain things that you have to do to prevent damages from getting out of control, as discussed in the following section.

Option Contracts

Option contracts also involve conditions. For instance, an offer doesn't have to stay open indefinitely, unless there is an option associated with that offer. An *option* means that a contracting party has paid some consideration to either buy or perform on a contract, but no obligation to buy or perform on the contract.

For instance, if you sign a record deal, the record company will guarantee to release at least one record, two if your are lucky. However, the record company also has the option to put out even more records with you, up to a certain number. Usually it will ask for six to eight records. If the record company decides not to put out anything after the first record or two (if it doesn't *pick up its option*), there is nothing you can do. Furthermore, the option is solely for the record companies. You can't force the company to pick up its option to release any more records than it has to.

Another place you see option contracts is in real estate. Someone may pay a certain amount of money for the option to buy a house. If he decides not to buy the house, he forfeits the money he paid for the option. It all depends on the type of option and the consideration there is to support the option.

Oral versus Written Modifications

No contract lives in a vacuum, and circumstances can change at any moment. So, the terms of your contract may need to be changed, modified, or waived in whole or in part by a subsequent agreement, which can be either oral or written. If circumstances change, you may enter into another agreement that will allow for those circumstances. However, if you have a written agreement, you should try to get another writing to modify, change, or waive any portions of the previous agreement. Again, with a written agreement, the parties are less likely to have different opinions as to what was agreed upon.

Also remember to take into consideration the statute of frauds. If the original agreement must be in writing, any subsequent modifications must be in writing as well.

Attorney's Fees and Cost Clauses

Every single written agreement that you draft should include an *attorney's fees and costs clause*. It should clearly state that if either party breaches the agreement, the non-breaching party is absolutely entitled to receive attorney's fees, court costs, and all other reasonable costs associated with the successful prosecution of any action.

This can be important for two reasons. First and foremost, if you sue for breach and you are successful, the other side will have to pay your attorney for bringing the case. They will also have to pay all court costs and all reasonable costs that you incur, such as depositions, court reporter fees, subpoena fees, expert witness fees, private investigator's fees, or any other costs that the court may deem necessary for you to bring your case.

The second reason why this clause is important is that it can give you real negotiating power if someone breaches the agreement. You can call the other side and request that they pay you what you are asking, or go to court and risk paying all that plus additional costs. This is a great way to gain some leverage, and you might be able to talk some sense into the other side. They'll probably want to pay you now, instead of dealing with all of the expense and aggravation of going to court *and* possibly having to pay you, your attorney, and all of your related court costs and other expenses.

However, if there is no attorney's fee clause that is signed by both parties, neither side will be awarded its attorney's fees unless there are some truly special circumstances.

Arbitration or Mediation

You may want to include an arbitration or mediation clause in your contracts to prevent either side from having to solve any disputes in court. If you're not the one drafting the agreement, but are given an agreement that calls for arbitration or mediation, you need to understand what that means. For a more detailed discussion, see Chapter 16, "If All Else Fails, Sue."

Breach of Contract

A contract can be breached in a number of ways, including failure to perform, failure to pay, or failure to live up to any provisions in the contract. You can take a number of steps to remedy this situation. If these steps don't work, you will have to seek other remedies for breach, or assess your damages and try to collect them.

ADEQUATE ASSURANCE OF PERFORMANCE
This is where we get back to what happens when you find out that circumstances have changed and therefore the terms of the contract need to change.

Let's go back to the club gig example. If you have a $1,000 gig booked for next weekend and you find out that the club has hired another band, you need to take immediate action. Once the club has informed you that it doesn't intend to pay your band to play, the club is automatically deemed to be in breach of contract. At this point, you have the right to demand adequate assurance of performance. What about your expectation of making $1,000? What about your reliance to the tune of $100? What about your band foregoing the $2,500 opportunity to play the frat gig? These issues will resolve themselves only after you have taken all reasonable steps to get another gig, which is also known as the *duty to cover*.

DUTY TO COVER

Once the club owner tells you he's not going to let you play that night or pay you anything, you have an absolute duty to *cover*, or mitigate your damages. You have to try to get the frat gig immediately. If you can't get it, you have to try to get another gig for that night as quickly as possible. As long as you have used your reasonable best efforts to get another gig, you have done all you can.

Of course, all of us in the music business know how hard it is to get a gig, much less to get one at the last minute. But you absolutely have to try in this instance. If you can't get another gig, you have other remedies for breach, but you may need to act quickly.

SPECIFIC PERFORMANCE

Specific performance is the right of one party to demand that the breaching party be ordered by the court to perform his duties under the contract. This can be awarded instead of monetary damages, and in some cases *in addition to* monetary damages if the contract can still be performed and the payment of money cannot make the non-breaching party whole.

The courts rarely order specific performance. They might, though, when a particular service or product may be considered unique, such as if you hire an artist to do the artwork for your CD, and there are no other artists available who could possibly produce artwork of that type and quality.

Furthermore, getting a court date in time for a judge to rule that your band should be allowed to play the gig will be next to impossible. It will also cost you a hefty sum to hire an attorney to draft a complaint and everything else that would need to be filed with the court to ask for specific performance. And even though your band may be unique, your service of playing the club is not unique, and therefore specific performance would not be a remedy. But you could file for injunctive relief.

INJUNCTIVE RELIEF

If you're suffering damages that are ongoing, or if you need someone to stop doing something he's doing, you may be able to request *injunctive relief.* This is a court-ordered restraint that prohibits a party from taking or not taking a particular action, and it can be granted in lieu of, or along with, the payment of money.

Often, injunctive relief is requested at the very beginning of a legal action, because time is of the essence in these matters. If you get an injunction, the court will determine how long the injunction will last and under what terms. For example, let's say you have an agreement with an ex-employee that he won't contact your clients. If he starts calling all of your clients, you can seek injunctive relief to stop him. In the case of the club cancelling your gig because it has booked another band, you can seek injunctive relief to prevent the other band from playing.

But filing any court action, even an injunction, can take time. If you can't get to court in time to get an injunction, you are out of luck. However, the court could still award you damages. Even if you do seek an injunction, the court could just award you damages and let the bigger band play the club. Either way, you probably won't ever play that club again.

RESCISSION

Rescission is a remedy that actually voids any existing contract and restores the parties to their respective positions prior to entering into it. If one party has paid any money to the other, the court can order that money to be returned.

Rescission usually occurs as a result of innocent or fraudulent misrepresentation, mutual mistake, lack of legal capacity, impossibility of performance, or duress. For example, if someone sells you a guitar, and later you find out that the seller really didn't own the guitar, the contract could be rescinded. In the example of the club owner not letting your band play for $1,000, you would not want to be put back in the same position you were in before the breach. So this type of remedy would not be for you, because you would want your contract to be enforced.

Repudiation

If a party has not fulfilled certain terms of a contract, the other party may *repudiate* the contract. However, repudiation is a breach of contract too, so you must have a good faith reason to do so.

Repudiation is also called *anticipatory breach of contract*. One party knows that the other party is not going to fulfill the terms of his contract, and therefore decides to repudiate the original contract and enter into another agreement. In other words, when the club owner cancels your gig and schedules the bigger band, you can anticipate the club's breach and go find another gig. The club owner can't come back against you if the bigger band cancels at the last minute. The club has already breached, and you've repudiated the contract. Therefore, you are free to sue the club for breach and/or get another gig. In fact, you have a duty to get another gig under the duty to mitigate. In other words, if you know you are going to incur damages, you have a duty to limit the amount of damages.

Damages for Breach

In the club gig example, let's assume that you weren't able to cover by getting another gig. Now we can talk about what types of damages you may be entitled to. In many cases, the only way that you can be made whole by the party that has breached an agreement is to award you monetary damages. These damages can be compensatory, consequential, punitive, nominal, and liquidated. And of course there are your expectation, reliance, and reasonably foreseeable damages such as your forbearance damages.

COMPENSATORY DAMAGES

Compensatory damages are intended to make you whole, or in other words, to put you in the same position as you would have been if all of the terms of the contract were fulfilled. These types of damages are also awarded to reimburse you for any costs incurred as a direct result of your loss due to the breach. They come in the form of a money judgment so that you are paid for your loss.

In the instance of the club breaching the contract for you to play, your compensatory damages would be $1,000. Since you would have spent the reliance damages as well even if you did play, you would only be entitled to the $1,000. However, if you can prove that you would have made $2,500 for the frat gig, you could be awarded $2,500 from the club.

CONSEQUENTIAL DAMAGES

Consequential damages are sometimes referred to as *incidental damages* and come in the form of money for losses that were reasonably foreseeable in the event of breach. For damages to be foreseeable, each side must have reasonably known that, at the time of the contract, there would be losses if there were a breach. Consequential damages include, but are not limited to, loss of use and loss of profit.

The purpose of measuring damages by the reliance interest is to put the plaintiff in as good a position as he would have been in if the contract had not been made, by compensating for losses caused by the plaintiff's reliance on the contract. In other words, your reliance damages are your consequential damages. But of course, you may have incurred other damages as a consequence of the club breaching its contract with you, which could include any lost CD sales and merchandising sales that you would have made if you had played the club gig. (But this is hard to prove unless you have sold a lot of CDs at the club before.) Also, if you can prove that the club knew about your frat gig and still cancelled your club gig, it's more likely that you will recover the amount that you would have made if you had taken the frat gig.

PUNITIVE DAMAGES

Punitive damages may be awarded on top of compensatory damages if the defendant's conduct is found to be intentional, willful, wanton, or malicious. They are intended to punish the defendant and to discourage that type of conduct. They are not often awarded in contract cases, but if the defendant's conduct is extremely outrageous, the court could award punitive damages to discourage that behavior in the future. In short, punitive damages are intended to add extra punishment for any behavior that the court feels should not be allowed in any business relationship.

Therefore, if the club knew about your frat gig, let you cancel that gig, and then cancelled your club gig, the court could say that the club's breach was intentional, willful and/or wanton. Therefore, the court could make the club pay punitive damages in that amount so that the club would not do that to other bands in the future.

NOMINAL DAMAGES

Nominal damages are awarded when the court wants to make sure that the defendant won't repeat the same conduct, but they're not necessarily designed to punish the defendant. An award of nominal damages may trigger the ability to collect punitive damages, legal fees, and costs. In our club scenario, the court could make the club pay for the costs that your band paid to advertise the gig as nominal damages, as well as the original $1,000. The nominal damages would be tacked on, just to prevent the club from trying to get away with breaching its contracts with other bands in the future.

LIQUIDATED DAMAGES

These are damages that must be specified in a written contract that will be payable if there is a breach. They are similar to penalties, but penalties are not allowed. Therefore, they have to be agreed upon before the contract is executed.

An example where liquidated damages may come up is if you agree to record a radio commercial project for someone who's planning to sell it to a company that needs the advertising. If you can't get the recording done in time so that the advertisement can be aired before the big sale, it is reasonable to assume that the advertiser will lose money. Since it is impossible to tell how much business the advertiser could lose, you would pay a sum certain for each and every day that you were late.

You often see these types of damages in construction contracts. For instance, if a contractor is building a mall and falls behind schedule, the owner of the mall will lose money for each day that his tenants can't open their businesses and therefore make money to pay their rents.

Pain and Suffering

The courts are very reluctant to award any damages for pain and suffering if someone breaches a contract. You can ask for them, but you probably won't get them. However, don't forget that you can ask for punitive damages.

Unfortunately, everyone suffers when contracts are breached, and pain and suffering remedies are usually reserved for torts. A *tort* is when someone has caused a civil wrong to another, such as a trespass, assault, battery, defamation of character, car wreck, and the like. That's a whole other area of the law that really doesn't have much place in a discussion of contracts.

Defenses to Contract

There are a number of defenses to a contract that you should be aware of. They include mistake of fact, misrepresentation, deceptive conduct, duress, lack of capacity, unconscionability, violation of public policy, statute of frauds, impossibility of performance, and Force Majeure.

MISTAKE OF FACT

Mutual *mistake of fact* is when both parties have made a mistake about what they were contracting over. For example, let's say you purchase a really old guitar that you and the seller both think is a piece of garbage, only to find out it's actually worth a whole lot of money. The contract could be set aside, because you would be unjustly enriched if you bought the guitar for $200 when it was really worth $20,000.

If there is a unilateral mistake, the contract can also be set aside. For instance, if you know that the guitar is worth $20,000 and the guy selling it doesn't, he can get the guitar back if he finds out its real value. If there is a unilateral mistake of fact, you interpret the contract based upon the rights of the person who did not know about the mistake, because allowing one person to take advantage of someone else's mistake would not be allowed by law.

MISREPRESENTATION OR DECEPTIVE CONDUCT

Misrepresentation or deceptive conduct can also void a contract. If a guy is selling a really expensive guitar and tells you that it's a collector's item, but it's really a fake, you can get your money back.

DURESS

If you're forced to sign a contract under *duress*, that contract can be voided. In other words, if someone holds a gun to your head and forces you to sign a record contract, you're not bound by that contract.

Duress could also be if someone is using financial constraints or other means to get you to sign a contract that you would not otherwise sign. This would be less than honorable, and therefore you wouldn't have to honor the agreement.

LACK OF CAPACITY

As discussed before, if you are not of age or are not completely sane, you *lack capacity* to enter into agreements and therefore will not be bound by them.

UNCONSCIONABILITY

Unconscionability merely means that someone has engaged in conduct that would utterly shock the conscience of a reasonable person. So if your grandmother, who isn't all there, is sold a piano with a finance agreement that will end up costing her 10 times what the piano is actually worth, the contract could be set aside.

However, this defense won't work with pawn shops and other finance companies that sometimes charge 25% or more per month. Don't pawn your stuff, and you won't have to worry about losing it. And don't try to take advantage of someone who has less information than you, such that some reasonable person would say that the deal is completely unfair. This does not mean you can't get a great deal; it just means you can't take advantage of someone. However, it is up to the court or perhaps a jury to decide that.

VIOLATION OF PUBLIC POLICY

If you contract for something that's illegal or violates public policy, such as buying a ton of illegal drugs, that contract will not be enforceable. So if somebody rips you off over a drug deal, don't go to court trying to collect your money. Not only won't you get your money, but you'll most likely end up in jail.

STATUTE OF FRAUDS

If what you are contracting for requires a writing, there must be a writing or the contract will be void.

IMPOSSIBILITY OF PERFORMANCE

If it becomes impossible to perform on a contract for some reason, the contract will be set aside. For example, if you have a club gig coming up next week and the club burns down, the club will have no duty to pay you because now it's impossible for you to play there. This is also known as *frustration of purpose*.

FORCE MAJEURE

Force Majeure clauses usually excuse a party from liability for a contract if some unforeseen event prevents the party from performing its obligations. This usually applies to acts of God such as natural disasters (flood, fire, or other bad weather). Sometimes it can apply at times of war, civil unrest, riots, and the like.

Illusory Promises

An *illusory contract* is one in which at least one party makes an illusory promise. This can also be considered a defense to contract. If one party promises to do something that he may or may not have to do, he really hasn't promised anything at all. Therefore, his promise is not sufficient to be considered adequate consideration, and there is no contract.

For instance, let's assume that I run a record store and you're a local band selling CDs. If we enter into an agreement whereby I promise to buy as many CDs from you as I need over the next year, I have made an illusory promise. As you can see, I may not ever need any of your CDs in my store, and therefore I've never really promised anything. If that is the case, you don't have a contract, because there is no real consideration.

Transfer of Contracts

Pay careful attention to any assignment clauses in a contract. Any contract can be assigned to another party unless the contract terms expressly prevent it. By *assignment*, I mean that any rights, duties, and obligations for any party under an agreement may be completely assigned to a third party.

For instance, let's say you have a contract with your booking agent to play a gig next month for $1,000, and you get a call from a frat to play for $1,500. Unless there are any provisions in your agreement with your booking agent, you can assign that entire contract to another band so that you can take the higher-paying gig.

There are some cases where this just can't be done, especially if the performance expected is unique and cannot be done by anyone else.

Assignment can be a really bad thing for some parties in certain types of contracts. For instance, if you sign a record deal with a particular company because the A&R guy is a big fan, and then he leaves the company, you could be really screwed. Unless someone else in the A&R department is willing to take over and help you with your career, you could be in for a short relationship with that record company. It will put out your record because it is contractually bound to do so, but it may not be willing to market and promote that record. You will be dropped as soon as you hit your options that the record company will not pick up.

So again, be wary of assignments or you could end up working with someone with whom you never intended to work. You could wind up very unhappy or leave the business altogether.

CYA Letters

What if you enter into an oral contract and then you write a letter setting forth the terms of that agreement? Even though the other party may not have signed that letter as acceptance of the terms, you have at least covered your rear and you will have evidence that you understand the agreement.

This will not constitute a formal contract because both parties haven't signed it, but you can use it to negotiate or possibly prove any possible issue that is in dispute. At the very least, it's a good piece of evidence if you have to sue to enforce any part of your oral agreement. It creates the presumption that what is in your letter is the understanding of the parties, and therefore the actual terms of your oral contract. If you can show that the other side received your letter by hand delivery, and you can produce the witness who put it in the hands of the other party or his agent, you will have a much easier time showing the court that the other party accepted your terms. You may also send the letter by return receipt requested mail, which is absolute proof that the other party received your correspondence. If the other side does not respond and refute any portion of your letter, he can be deemed to have accepted all of the terms included in it.

John Q. Artist
13 Starving Lane
Anytown, ST, 00000

Name of club
Address
City, state, Zip

Dear Club Owner:
RE: Booking

My band, the Club Players, will play your club next Saturday night. We will bring our own PA and will play from 10 p.m. until 2 a.m. We understand that we are to play at least 75% cover tunes, but are allowed to play up to 25% of our original music.

You will provide print and radio advertising. You will provide a 30x50 foot stage and lighting, along with eight separate electrical circuits within 25 feet of the stage. You will turn off all TV monitors and video games near the stage area during the show. You will provide a doorman and security for our equipment, and allow our road manager to assist with watching the door and counting the number of people who pay to get into the club. You are allowed to have up to four guests, but all other patrons must pay the cover charge unless they are on our guest list.

If your understanding is different, or you have any questions or comments, please notify me as soon as possible by contacting me at the above number, address, or e-mail address. We appreciate the opportunity to play at your club, and we look forward to seeing you around 4:00 in the afternoon for load-in.

Sincerely,
John Q. Artist

You should also be aware of the *mail box rule*, which states that if you are corresponding by mail and you post your letter of acceptance to a contract, it's just as though you put that acceptance in the hands of the person the letter is addressed to. Therefore, you could make the argument that when you put your letter in the mail (the U.S. Post Office being their agent), the other side has accepted your terms unless and until it notifies you otherwise.

Yet another way to handle this situation is to write yourself a letter as if were from the person with whom you wish to enter an agreement. Set forth all of the terms of the agreement and enclose a self-addressed stamped envelope. All the other side has to do is sign the letter and return it to you. This way, you have his signature and he doesn't have yours. He is bound by those terms in the letter, even though you may not be. Of course, he can always say that *you* wrote the letter for him and then he signed. Therefore, you should be bound by the terms of the agreement as well, and if you are honest and fair, you should be. But it does give one pause for thought.

Negotiating Tips

Learning how to negotiate is an extremely important element of contracts. If you're a good negotiator, you can get the best deal possible every time you enter into an agreement. Remember that information is power, so ask as many questions as needed until you feel that you understand exactly what you are agreeing to. In fact, the next chapter is on this very subject.

Summary

I have covered only the basics of contract law. There are many other important points, but they are the subject of thousands of books. However, you should now be able to see that contracts are fraught with problems, especially if they are not in writing. Furthermore, if you have to sue, you will burn bridges and spend a whole lot of time and money trying to set things right, especially if you don't have an attorney's fees clause in writing. Of course, in some cases you have no choice but to sue, because you don't want to get a reputation as a pushover. But if you get anything out of this book, it's that when you have a contract, get it in writing.

CHAPTER 13

Negotiating

"Look for the win–win situation.…"

Negotiating is an artform unto itself. It is the process whereby two or more parties with different goals, wants, or needs try to work together to find a mutually agreeable solution to a particular problem, issue, or circumstance.

Many of us look at negotiating as an uncomfortable process that's fraught with conflict, but it really doesn't have to be. It can be a calculated decision-making process whereby all parties can express their concerns in a civilized and friendly way. It's an opportunity to find common ground so that deals can be struck and future business is not jeopardized. It should not be viewed as an obstacle in the way of you getting what you want.

The more you know about the process of negotiating, the better you will be at it, and the more likely you will be able to negotiate fair and equitable solutions. Furthermore, if negotiations are successful for both parties, it's likely that they will negotiate with each other again. That's how you gain long-term clients and ensure the future of your business.

Just because you know what you want doesn't mean that you will be a successful negotiator in the long term, even if you get exactly what you're after. Remember the old saying that you can shear a sheep many, many times if you take care of it, but you can only fleece it once. Just because you have successfully negotiated one issue in your favor doesn't mean that both sides have a win–win situation. Therefore, you may not be able to negotiate with that party again. You must learn to think in the long term and choose your battles.

Negotiation is a tool that once learned will serve you well throughout your business and personal life. Negotiations are always going to come up, whether you're negotiating a night out with the guys, getting the best deal when you're buying a car, entering into a contract, or just about any other scenario you will encounter in this life. The most important thing to remember is that negotiating doesn't necessarily mean you are going to get your way. It's more about give and take, and finding the parameters that will define an agreement between two parties. More to the point, it's about trying to come up with solutions, not creating more problems.

Negotiating Tips

Many things come into play when you're negotiating, such as doing your homework, preparing your options, not being confrontational, avoiding emotions, understanding personalities, soliciting responses, being clear about what you want, looking for positive signs, negotiating upward, understanding the give and take, being creative, not tipping your hand, and knowing when to quit. But first, you must determine who is making the offer and what exactly the offer is.

WHO IS MAKING THE OFFER, AND WHY?

First, you must understand who is making the offer and why. Is it a person or persons, or is it a business? Does the party making the offer have the authority to make it? Try to understand why he is making the offer and what he is looking for. Once you know this, you can proceed, but be careful. You never want to lay all your cards on the table, draw a line in the sand, or shoot yourself in the foot by opening negotiations with a lowball offer that the other side accepts too quickly.

But sometimes, you just can't start the proceedings without at least laying out a general idea of what you're looking for. If you are the one making the offer, you should know exactly what you are looking for and why, but you may not want to tip your hand. The best way is to be very general and put across what you are offering without any hard-and-fast figures.

Furthermore, if you are making an offer as an agent of your company or partnership, you should know exactly what it is looking for and why. Sometimes this can be vastly different from your own personal expectations. Don't just assume that you know what your partner or company wants. Make sure to consult with your business associates before you make any offers to third parties, so that you don't extend an offer that you have no authority to make. The more you discuss your offer with your associates, the better prepared you will be to represent their interests and define your goals.

Once you have determined what your side is offering, try to understand how your offer is going to benefit the other side. Ask yourself, "What could they possibly want or need from me, and does my offer address those needs?" Therefore, it's a good idea for you to learn as much as you can about who you're making the offer to.

Are you dealing with an individual or a large company? If you are dealing with an individual, you should try to figure out how your offer is going to benefit that individual. However, if you are dealing with a large company, you want to know what position the person you're dealing with holds in that company, and what his authority is to deal with you. Someone who's working for a large corporation should always have the best interests of the company in mind. But then again, he may have his own agenda for one reason or another, and it's your job to find that out. To that end, you should ask as many questions as you can.

If the other side is making the initial offer to you, you still want to figure out what entities are making the offer, why they are making their offer, and how their offer is going to affect both parties. Obviously you'll be most concerned about what you are getting, but you need to know what the other side is trying to get as well.

WHAT IS THE OFFER?
No matter who is making the offer, you must know exactly what the negotiation is going to be about. Of course, if you are making the offer, you will have had time to prepare. However, if the offer has been made to you, you still need to understand exactly what the offer is and all of its ramifications. The best way to do this is to ask as many questions as you possibly can. There is no

such thing as a bad question, only bad answers. If you are sure that you will never have to deal with the other side again, you may not have to be as careful not put yourself in a bad light, or as concerned with trying to get the best deal that you can. But always keep in mind that you may be doing business again with the other side. The last thing you want to do is burn any bridges, especially in a business relationship.

You need to do as much homework as possible on the subject of your negotiations. If an offer is made to you and you don't feel prepared to accept it, by all means, thank the other side for his kind consideration and then ask if you can get back to him. If he needs an answer right away, he may be desperate or operating under some timeline. If that is the case, tell him that you can call him back in a few minutes, but you need time to think about it or discuss it with your associates. Either way, you should at least take some time to reflect on the matter. If it's very involved, you should be as prepared as possible.

Now that you understand who is making the offer and what the offer entails, it's time to do some homework.

DO YOUR HOMEWORK

In some cases, the issues can be quite simple. For example, someone may call and ask you to open a show for another band on a particular date. Do you accept? Perhaps. After all, there really isn't much to think about. Or is there? You may want to think about the following questions:

▶   Is this a "take it or leave it" type of offer?

- ▶ Who is the show for?

- ▶ What type of show is it?

- ▶ What type of audience is expected to be there?

- ▶ When is the show?

- ▶ What time are you supposed to be there?

- ▶ How long are you to play?

- ▶ What time are you supposed to start?

- ▶ What time are you expected to quit?

- ▶ What equipment do you need to bring?

- ▶ How big is the stage?

- ▶ Does the venue have lighting and sound people?

- ▶ Is there going to be a good monitor system?

- ▶ If not, can you bring your own?

- ▶ What type of material is the venue looking for?

- ▶ Will you have a dressing room?

- ▶ Are you allowed to bring guests?

- ▶ If not, how much is the cover or ticket price?

- ▶ Is the venue going to advertise your name?

► If so, how prominent will your name be displayed on the bill?

► If not, can you advertise and use the venue's logos and/or trademarks?

► Can you sell your CDs from the stage?

► Will the show be recorded?

► If so, will the venue want to record you?

► If not, can you record your own show?

► How much will you get paid?

► When will you get paid?

► Is that negotiable?

► Is the price negotiable if you give up other concessions?

► Is there going to be a contract?

As you can see, there may be a whole lot of questions you need to ask. Depending on your experience as an opening act, you may know all of the questions that you need to ask. On the other hand, if this is brand new to you, call up a friend who has experience doing that type of gig. Find out what you need to know so you don't get yourself into a bad situation.

But notice that all of these questions address only *your* concerns. If you are trying to get something that the venue is not offering, you may want to figure out *its* concerns. Usually, you're trying to get more money for your efforts, or perhaps free tickets for your friends or family. If that is the case, ask yourself the following questions:

▶ Can the venue get anyone else to open the show?

▶ Does the venue have others in mind if we don't accept?

▶ What do other bands get for the same type of deal?

▶ What is the standard at the venue or for that particular headliner?

▶ What is the normal number of guest tickets that the venue usually gives out?

Obviously, you won't be able to answer all of those questions, but you can do some simple research or ask the contact person who made the offer. Try to get as many answers as you can so that you can make an informed decision.

You always want to discern exactly what is going on by researching the issues that you are confronted with. For example, if you are being offered a record deal, you don't just want to ask, "Where do I sign?" Since most recording contracts are very involved, this will require a great deal of research and work on your behalf. Do as much research as you can about record deals, and ask as many questions as you can to your lawyer, manager, etc.

But before you can even begin to negotiate any of the issues that you have researched, you need to ask yourself some of the following questions.

► What is the motivation of the other party?

► What is the actual intent of the other party?

► What benefit will they get?

► What benefit will you get, if the other side gets what it is after?

► Can the other side get someone else to provide what you have?

► Do you have some special expertise that very few others possess?

► Is there a timeline involved?

► Does the other side have a much stronger negotiating position?

► What issues are of the most importance?

► Can you make concessions on some issues and not others?

► Can the other side make concessions, and how will those concessions affect him?

► Are there any other issues that you may have forgotten?

If you think you may have forgotten about something or you don't completely understand what is going on, by all means, ask someone you trust who knows about your particular situation. Ask your bandmates, your family, or anyone who can help. Keep an open mind and try to think outside of the box. There are no hard-and-fast rules here, so use your common sense.

Here is a scenario: It's raining hard, and as you drive by a bus stop, you see an old lady who looks like she's about to die and needs to go to the hospital. You also see an old friend who once did a huge favor for you. You *also* see the prettiest girl you've ever seen and you know that she's perfect for you.

What do you do? Do you take the old woman to the hospital and perhaps save her life? Do you give the friend a ride? Or do you pick up the girl who's perfect for you? You have more options than you may realize at first. Think about this for a moment before reading further.

If you are thinking outside of the box, you may have come up with the answer. Give the keys to your friend and have him take the woman to the hospital. Then stay behind with the girl of your dreams. By the time your friend gets back from the hospital, you should have had time to get to know the girl.

This is a fairly simple solution, but one that requires thinking outside of the box. So you can see that creative thinking can be a good tool to use.

PREPARE OPTIONS

If someone has made you an offer and given you time to think about it, prepare as many options as you can before you call back. Be ready to make suggestions, if your solution is not acceptable to the other side. Prepare yourself for any opposition your suggestions may get, and be ready to come up with alternative solutions. There is no way to always anticipate the other side's offer, but you have to be ready for him to throw something different at you that you did not expect. This will require some serious time and consideration. Make a list of options and alternative solutions so that you won't have to think on your feet or forget the points that you feel are important. The better prepared you are, the more likely you will find a reasonable solution.

DON'T BE CONFRONTATIONAL

Again, negotiating is about coming up with solutions, not causing problems. No matter what you are negotiating, neither party would be at the table if there weren't some hope for a mutual understanding. Both parties have some reasonable expectation that can be attributed to their respective needs, wants, or concerns. Remember, negotiating is not about a battle of wills. The attitude that you take from the beginning will set the tone for the rest of your negotiations. If you take a hostile or uncooperative stance, you may end up with nothing.

Furthermore, if you immediately come on as confrontational, you will be setting yourself up for a good argument, and neither party will benefit from that. However, if you agree to the offer too quickly, you may miss your chance to get more than what was originally offered. In short, don't get stuck with your acceptance and then try to change the terms to suit your needs later on. This can cause friction between the parties and could end up ruining the deal.

IT'S NOT ABOUT WINNING OR EMOTIONS

If there is a "winner," that implies there is a "loser." That is *not* the way to negotiate successfully. You must always try to find common ground and solutions to problems. You just can't view negotiations as a contest, but rather a challenge that you are up for. Furthermore, if you are more concerned about "winning," your emotions may get the best of you. Try as hard as you can to keep emotion out of it, or you can lose your focus and say something that you regret or that kills the deal. Try to focus on being constructive and helpful, because getting upset won't really help anybody. It might make you feel better, but after you have time to cool off, you may regret what you did in the heat of the moment. If you disagree with something, by all means let the other side know, but try to be gentle yet assertive, and never be demeaning. You don't want to get into a power struggle.

UNDERSTAND THE OTHER PERSON AND HIS PERSONALITY

Try to understand what the other party wants or needs. If you take the time to learn more about the other person and how he perceives what's going on, you may find that what he wants isn't too different than what you want. If there is a personality conflict, you should focus on the issues and not how much the other side is getting on your nerves. Also try to avoid putting the blame on anyone if the negotiations aren't going well. Try to take responsibility for any problems, even though it may not be your fault. Cooperation, rather than aggravation, will go a long way toward finding a solution. After all, if you are going to be doing business with someone, the problem should be a *mutual* problem. If it's not, there may be a lack of mutuality in the agreement in the first place, and therefore you should not enter into it.

SOLICIT RESPONSES AND CLARIFICATIONS
While you are negotiating, you always want to get as much input as you can and make sure that you completely understand the position of the other side. Ask him what he think about the points you're making, and about any concerns he has. Once he has expressed his concerns, make sure he knows that you understand. This will help to clear up any misunderstandings from the get-go. You may want to say something like, "So you are saying *this...*," or perhaps, "Correct me if I'm wrong, but what you are saying is *this....*"

BE CLEAR ABOUT WHAT YOU WANT
Sometimes it's not only important to be very specific about your goals or needs, but about *why* you need something. You may be surprised how often two parties are in disagreement about the *method* of resolving an issue, rather than the issue itself. If you are very crafty, you can make one of your ideas become the other side's idea, and it can be one of the very best ideas he has ever had. It all depends on how you go about selling your idea. After all, it doesn't really matter who gets the credit for the idea, as long as you are getting what you want or need.

LOOK FOR POSITIVE SIGNS
While you are in the middle of a negotiation, you should always be aware of what the other side is doing. Look and listen for any positive signs that things are going your way, and use that information to your advantage. Watch the person's body language to see if he is open

and receptive to you and your ideas. If he is on the phone, pay attention to his tone of voice and what he is saying. If he doesn't seem to be interested, or if he seems to be distracted by something that is out of your control, you may want to reschedule or call them back later. Pay attention when he's trying very hard to sell you on his idea, calling you back often, or seems anxious to close the deal. The more anxious he is to close a deal, the better your negotiating position.

NEGOTIATE UPWARD

This may go without saying, but you never know. Try not to be the first one to make an offer of final figures, because you never know if the other side has a higher offer in mind. But once you have the other side's position, you can make your counteroffer. Try to be mindful of where his offer is, and try not to so much higher as to appear greedy, but make it so that you will at least know when the other side has reached his final position. Remember, unreasonable demands can hurt negotiations or even kill the deal. It never hurts to ask, but don't insist.

UNDERSTAND THE GIVE AND TAKE

Each side should be willing to make certain concessions, so try to go with the flow. Also, be aware of whether you are the only one who can provide what the other side is looking for. If you have a strong negotiating position, press your advantage. If the other side has the advantage, back off and accept what is being offered. But always keep in mind what will be fair to all parties, and don't try to take advantage of the situation unless you absolutely have to. Remember that the other side may have to take your offer to a higher-up at his company.

That person may realize what you are trying to do, and you may end up with nothing.

BE CREATIVE

Always look for different ways to achieve your goals, and be willing to make certain concessions to increase the value of the deal. Remember that being creative also encompasses the way you present your offer so that it appears the most acceptable to the other party. Look for points that you can trade off with other points, so that each side has made a certain number of concessions. Being inflexible and expecting everyone to see it your way is not very creative.

DON'T TIP YOUR HAND

You don't ever want to offer more information than necessary. After all, information is power, so don't get nervous and start running your mouth. You could tip your hand too quickly and be stuck with what you said in the heat of the moment. You have no obligation to talk about everything that you know, so be careful about what you say and how you say it. Offer only the information that is absolutely necessary to achieve your goals, and think about how that information could be used or perceived. Furthermore, think about how you will be perceived by the way you answer questions. Check your ego at the door, and try to be polite but never evasive. If the other side asks a lot of questions, answer him to the best of your ability. But if he asks you for the time, don't tell him how to build a watch. Be clear, concise, and to the point.

KNOW WHEN TO QUIT

The best way to lose everything you've been able to nego-tiate is to try to get too much. There is usually a point in your negotiations where you've gotten everything you're going to get. After that, you risk the principle of dimin-ishing returns, or you may just put the kibosh on the entire deal. You should always play to your strengths and be aware of your limitations. More importantly, you had better know when to quit. Just because you have to quit negotiating doesn't mean that you've lost. Furthermore, you will be surprised how differently you think about the situation after you have had time to reflect.

PUT YOUR AGREEMENT IN WRITING

In my experience as an entertainment attorney, most of my negotiations for my clients or myself involved contracts that had already been drafted. If there was no contract, what was being negotiated was to *become* a contract if the parties could agree. Therefore, it is a good idea to draw up a contract if one hasn't been drawn already. The contract should address every single aspect of what was negotiated and should leave nothing to chance. Just because you think an issue is minor doesn't mean that the other side feels the same way.

If you are not going to draw up a formal agreement, you should at least send a letter to the other side of the negotiations outlining in detail your understanding of your agreement. This way you can state point by point exactly what the rights, duties, and obligations of each party are going to be. By taking time to write down your side of the negotiations, you can make sure that you understand all of the issues and agree with all aspects. If the other side doesn't have any objections to your letter, you can assume that he agrees to all of the terms set forth in your letter.

If you can, make sure to get some sort of evidence that the other side has received the letter, by hand-delivering it or sending it by certified return receipt requested. If you can't do that or it seems inappropriate under the circumstances, mail one copy to the other side and CC someone on your side. You want to make absolutely sure that you have covered all of the issues and try not to leave anything to chance. After all, when you are in the process of an intriguing and exhilarating debate, it is very easy to overlook certain issues or details.

Summary

If you are aware of what you need to do and how to do it, as well as what *not* to do, you are much more likely to find a win–win situation in just about any negotiation. Furthermore, if you do your homework, prepare your options in advance, don't be confrontational, avoid emotions, try to understand differences in personalities, solicit responses, be clear about what you want, look for positive signs, negotiate upward, understand the give and take, be creative, don't tip your hand too quickly, and know when to quit, you have done all that you can to strike a mutually beneficial deal. And if both parties win, the likelihood that you will be doing business with that other party again increases substantially. And isn't that what you are trying to do in the first place?

Suggested reading:

You Can Negotiate Anything by Herb Cohen

How to Win Friends and Influence People by Dale Carnegie

CHAPTER 14

Questionable Practices

"Caveat emptor (Let the buyer beware)."

There are a number of unscrupulous people and companies that are more than willing to prey on unsuspecting musicians, songwriters, and artists. It's easy to take advantage of people who want to be in the music business, for a lot of reasons. The most obvious is that unsigned acts or songwriters lack bargaining power and knowledge about the music business. Needless to say, some unscrupulous people and companies are very aware of this. They also know that many hopefuls who are just starting out in the business will do almost anything to make their dreams come true.

The music business is very complicated, and there are many things you must know to protect yourself. Unfortunately, these unscrupulous people and companies know the rules of the game and are always looking for loopholes or other ways to take advantage of the unsuspecting. Most unsigned artists, musicians, and songwriters don't have connections in the business, so they can't get their material heard by people who can help them get signed. When anyone shows some interest or makes some promises, they are ecstatic at having a chance to realize their dreams.

The thought of having a hit song is seductive enough to make many people sell their souls. They feel that they have worked hard at their craft, and when someone shows interests in their work, they think their big break is around the corner. The chance to get one of their songs on the radio is the payoff that most writers are looking for. But the fact is that less than 52 songs per year become number-one hits. Your chances of hitting number one are less than your chances of being struck by lightning. (According to the National Weather Service statistics, the average number of lightning fatalities in the U.S. for the last 10 years was approximately 70 people per year.) When you think about how many folks are out there making music, the chances that you will see any of them at the next Grammy show or on the legitimate music charts are pretty slim indeed.

People who are truly successful in the music business are in a pretty exclusive club. They seem to have an exciting lifestyle that is far from the day-to-day lives of the rest of us. Most of these people live in New York, Los Angeles, or Nashville, the major centers of the music industry. Of course, there are other cities where you can make it in the music industry, but they're usually larger metropolitan areas such as Chicago, Atlanta, Austin, etc. That means the musicians, writers, and artists who live in smaller towns all over America don't really have much of a chance to fulfill their dreams, unless they quit their day jobs and move to where the action is.

And when these undiscovered people are offered a chance, they fall for it hook, line, and sinker. There are thousands and thousands of people vying for that brass ring, whether they're from small towns or big cities. Unfortunately, many of them can be blinded by empty promises of fame and fortune.

Song Sharks

Song sharks are people or businesses that solicit amateur songwriters, poets, and lyricists to submit their material. These sharks advertise in trade magazines, newspapers, and other publications, asking for submissions. Usually they have some official-sounding name, such as The Songwriters Publishing Association. They may also contact writers directly by getting membership lists of local songwriter organizations, or lists of writers who have submitted material to the Library of Congress for copyright registration.

These sharks promise that even if you don't play an instrument or write music, they can have your material set to music and made into a song. They may even call your work a *song-poem*. Although this term is not really an accepted industry term, it can be used for poems that are set to music. For people who write music, the sharks promise to have lyricists put words to their music.

These sharks claim that they are major publishers or can get songs directly to major publishers and major recording artists who will record them. They may claim to get your songs played on the radio, or make some other offers of success. But there is always some charge for their services, which they claim is to help them with costs associated with making your material a success.

Once they get their initial fee, they may ask for additional fees to have your material put to sheet music, arranged for a large band, or to perform any number of other services. They may even ask you to pay to have your music recorded by these companies. Sometimes it's legitimate, because there are a lot of talented writers and musicians who do this type of work to help pay the bills, but more often than not it's a complete scam.

The most important thing is to find out as much as you can about these people and companies. Ask for references, call the Better Business Bureau and find out how many complaints have been filed against them, ask for samples of their work, etc. Don't get taken to the cleaners.

All reputable publishers are swamped with legitimate material already, so they don't actively solicit outside writers for songs via newspapers or magazines. In most cases, they put good writers on staff and pay them an advance, or draw, against future earnings from the songs they write. These staff writers must turn in a certain number of songs each year, usually 12, during the term of their contract. The publishers are betting that they will recoup their payout to their writers by getting songs cut by major recording artists. For the price of a draw, the publishers get 100% of the publishing rights to the songs for the life of the copyright, or, if the writer is lucky, for a set time period, after which the rights revert back to the writer. But the writer usually doesn't have to pay for any costs associated with getting a song published, such as demo costs, lead sheets, etc.

Sometimes, the writer may have a co-publishing deal with the publisher, which means that the writer retains a portion of the publisher's share. The writer can split any costs associated with his songs, but gets to keep more of the money that the song makes if it is successful. Therefore, a co-publishing deal can be really good thing, and sharing the costs is only fair. However, any company that keeps asking for more money to do this or that with your music, but never produces any real results, needs to be treated with a good deal of skepticism. But if you are a lyricist who needs your songs to be put to music, you can find reputable people to work with. Just be very careful.

The Numbers Game

The main thing about scam artists is that they are playing a numbers game. They may just have a staff musician who spits out generic tunes and melodies that really aren't commercially viable, and then you are stuck with your great lyrics set to some substandard music. Remember, the more people these scam artists can get in and out the door for a certain dollar amount, the more money they make, and the more disgruntled people they leave in their wake. Do your homework.

Not all of these outfits are scam artists, though. If you have song lyrics but can't play an instrument, and you can't find anyone near you to write music, there are legitimate companies that provide this service. Keep in mind that these songwriters will probably just crank out some chord changes and a melody for your lyrics, which could be what you are bargaining for. However, you may be better off finding a good musician to collaborate with. If the music writer were really that good, he would most likely have his own publishing deal and spend all of his time writing his own songs. Also keep in mind that if the writer does that sort of thing all day long, just how original could his work really be? He's bound to run out of ideas after a short while. Therefore, you're probably going to get substandard work.

If someone charges a fair price to record your material to a demo (demonstration recording) or a CD, go for it. Just watch out for companies that make promises of stardom if you just send more money. The most important thing is to find out how much they charge for all of their services, and more importantly, how your money is going to be spent. Ask how much the studio time is, how much the musicians make, how much for the engineer, how much it costs to actually make the CDs, etc. Of course, in order for legitimate people or companies to make a living, they have to make a profit, so it boils down to how much profit they make versus how much service or product they provide. If you can't get a budget that lays out all costs, you may want to consider doing business with someone else. If you do get a budget, you may want to call around to see if the prices are reasonable.

Custom Label Deals

Also known as a *vanity deal*, this type of record deal can be good or bad, depending on the label and your particular circumstances. Basically, a *custom label deal* is when a label (certainly not a major label, or even a really good independent label) offers to make a record for you if you pay for everything. Depending on the custom label, it may offer you all sorts of promises, such as getting your record played on the radio or at least shipping it to all the major radio stations throughout the country. The label may also promise to get your songs onto certain independent music charts. (See the discussion of independent music charts later in this chapter.)

In many cases, the custom label companies will offer to put your songs on a CD (often a compilation of 10 or more artists who have paid them money, just like you), which they promise will be shipped to all the radio stations. They may even guarantee that your song will be played on the radio. Most likely, the custom label has some type of payola or promotional deal with a local station, and the song is played once or twice during off-peak hours and then sent to the round file (the garbage can).

In some cases, a custom deal could be good for you. If there aren't many good recording studios where you live, you may need to pay someone to make your CD. If you don't have access to skilled musicians and you've never really recorded before, you really need some assistance. If you have lots of money because you are independently wealthy, just won the lottery, inherited a bunch of money, or perhaps have backers with loads of cash to burn who think you're the greatest act since the Beatles, by all means, make your CD. However, be very careful. Making records does not come cheap, and making great-sounding records that live up to the standards of today's marketplace can be extremely expensive. Watch out for companies that will take all of your money without giving you much in return, especially if they make empty promises of stardom.

First, ask for a simple budget. Ask how much they want you to pay, what you're paying for, and how your money will be spent. More often than not, you will never hear from that company again. The last thing these companies want is for you to check them out with the Better Business Bureau or find out how their operation runs, especially if they haven't delivered what they've promised to others before you. If you do your homework, you won't get burned. If you just hand over large sums of cash based upon promises that someone is going to make you a star, you're probably throwing away good money for little or nothing in return.

In short, it takes a whole lot more than just recording a CD to make you a star. In fact, even the major record labels with huge marketing and promotions budgets have many acts that never turn a profit. These acts get dropped and fall by the wayside. Although they're very talented, they never see anything close to stardom.

Custom Producers

Custom producers are very much like custom labels. They offer to make you a demo or even a CD for a specific price. They may also promise to get your music to the major record labels, publishers, and the like, but be very wary. Often they will use inferior studios with inferior players so that they can squeeze out the most profit. You end up with an inferior product that is pretty much useless. Furthermore, you'll probably find that nothing ever happens with your music once you've paid out all of your hard-earned money.

A custom producer may have produced a hit song 20 years ago, which can be enticing. But most likely, he really isn't a major player in the music industry today.

He may like to do a lot of namedropping to impress the unsuspecting with his alleged contact lists and accolades.

Fortunately, it's not hard to do some research and find out how legitimate these people are. If you speak with an A&R person at a major record label, he may have never even heard of that producer.

Again, the best way to protect yourself from these people is to do your homework and ask for a budget. You want to know exactly what you are paying for and how that money is going to be spent. Find out who that person really is, if he has any legitimate contacts in the industry, if his claims of success are true, if he's going to use a good studio and good players, and whether you're getting what you pay for.

Independent Music Charts

Some custom label houses and other unscrupulous people will promise to get your music on some music chart. Just remember that if it's not Billboard (which gets its chart information from SoundScan and retail sales) or Radio & Records (a radio-driven chart based on singles airplay), it's not going to do you much good, especially if want radio airplay to generate album sales.

There are a number of music charts besides the Billboard and R&R that are completely legitimate. Some are used to track certain aspects of niche markets, such as pop, rock, hip-hop, rap, dance, country, and the like. However, many charts may look legitimate but don't really mean that much to anyone in the music industry. These bogus charts are specifically set up to make aspiring artists think they're making some headway in the music business. Legitimate industry people look at many of these charts as a joke. Major labels aren't going to pay attention to some manufactured chart that people pay money to get on.

A lot of these unscrupulous companies or people pay a little money to a chart company (assuming that they don't own it), and the charts are printed and then shipped to the unsuspecting consumer. The charts may even include some of the top acts in the country to add an air of legitimacy. However, these charts are only about getting as much of your money as possible. Remember, these people just want to make you feel important so you'll pay them. They're not giving you anything of value at all.

Internet Companies

We all know that the Internet can be a very dangerous place. Just about anybody can set up a fake company on the Web and make all kinds of claims about what they can do for you. Be very careful when dealing with these companies. Check with the Better Business Bureau, read as much as you can about the company and the people who own it, and make sure that they are legitimate, or you could be wasting your money.

Bogus A&R Services

A number of companies will promise to set up *listening events*, where you take your material to a conference and have people in the music industry listen to it. These events may have a few A&R people or hit songwriters there to lend an air of legitimacy. However, these people are paid big bucks to listen to everyone's songs, and it is extremely rare for anything to ever come from it. If you stop to think about it, the A&R person will have to listen to hundreds of bad songs that day, and the chances of your song standing out from the crowd will be minimal at best.

Of course, you could get some very valuable feedback that helps you out with your songwriting, but you never know. You need to decide whether it's worth it to pay a lot of money for a chance to have your songs heard by a professional and perhaps picked up by a major label. You may be better off just buying a lottery ticket.

Bogus Talent Scouts and Talent Agents

Many people out there call themselves "talent scouts." They come to your town and hold open casting calls or talent searches. They advertise in the local newspaper or radio station and lure unsuspecting people to a hotel conference room or convention hall to showcase their talents. They may even say that they have worked with a number of new talents who are successful in the music, acting, or modeling fields. But how do you know they actually had anything to do with making those people successful? They may have worked with those stars in some small capacity, but not necessarily in a way that advanced their careers. So be very wary!

These scouts hold their casting calls and then select a lucky few. If you check, you'll probably find that just about everybody who auditions is accepted. They invite you to attend one of their seminars or workshops to train you for your chosen profession. Then they promise to place you. They ask you to pay a fee up front, with the balance due when you get to the seminar. Furthermore, you will have to pay for all of your own travel expenses, food, and lodging. When it's all said and done, you come back with no record deal and a lighter bank account. Meanwhile, the scouts have made a ton of money and may only have found one or two people whom they're willing to work with.

This is not to say that *everyone* out there is trying to scam you. Many of these people are legitimately trying to make a decent living in the business and find the next big act that can make their careers. However, the legitimate scouts usually don't ask for money up front. You should ask for their credentials and some references, and make a few phone calls to find out if they're legitimate.

Remember, if it sounds too good to be true, it probably is. If they want your money, be very careful and don't get duped. Try to stick with reputable people if you possibly can.

Bogus Seminars

Just like the "talent scout" scam, a number of bogus seminars lure the unsuspecting into paying money to learn more about the music business. These are extremely rare, but they do take place. These bogus seminars may advertise an "expert" who will discuss some aspect of the music business. Of course, it's very hard to fake being an expert, so you won't find this happening very often. The seminar may also have panels with hit songwriters (who had a hit 30 years ago) or A&R people (who worked at a label a long, long time ago).

Of course, this doesn't mean you can't learn something from these people. Just make sure to check out who is going to be on the panel, verify their claims of success, and see what the syllabus of the conference will cover. You should be able to find a lot of information through the Internet or other resources. This way, you will know if the seminar is right for you. If the panelists have had some experience, you may get your money's worth. At the very least, you will learn not to go to the next one.

Pay-to-Play Clubs

There are some venues that actually make bands pay to play. These clubs are usually in bigger cities, but I've seen them pretty much all over. Some of these clubs even guarantee that there will be industry personnel in the audience, and claim that bands who have played there in the past have been signed by labels.

This practice is sometimes hard for bands to fathom, but you have to evaluate the pros and cons. If it's a very well-known club and your band is guaranteed to get some good exposure, it could be a good thing. You also have to consider what time you'll play and how many people will even be in the club when you go onstage. Sometimes, clubs will use pay-to-play to supplement their cash flow during downtimes. Some clubs are just so popular that they can charge for the exposure. It's a hard pill to swallow, but unfortunately, that's just the way it is sometimes.

Aren't These Practices Illegal?

I've often been asked whether song sharks, custom labels, and other scam artists can be criminally prosecuted. The answer depends on a number of issues. Many of these people are smart enough not to do anything outright illegal. What they do is unethical for sure, but not necessarily illegal. They may not help you out very much, but as long as they fulfill the terms of their agreement with you, they haven't broken the law.

However, you may have grounds for a civil action, and this brings us to the next question.

Can You Sue Them?

I was also asked, "Can I sue these unscrupulous people or companies that have taken advantage of me?" If they actually breach their agreement with my client, the answer is yes. However, most of the time these people don't breach their contracts at all. They're too smart for that. They may have made statements to induce a person to sign a contract, but those prior statements are not admissible in court under the parole evidence rule (see Chapter 12, "General Principles of Contracts"). In short, read your contracts. If the company makes a whole bunch of promises to get you to sign a contract, and those promises are not in the actual contract, don't sign it!

In some cases, these people may have engaged in actions that are unconscionable, so outrageous as to "shock the conscience" (see Chapter 12). This just means that they have charged an exorbitant price for something. In some of these cases they could be sued, especially is someone has paid thousands of dollars just to get one song recorded. However, it's extremely hard to prove that someone has ripped you off just because he didn't get you a recording deal. If you paid to get a CD made and you have the CD, even a bad CD, there's probably nothing you can do about it. It all depends on your particular circumstances.

In short, don't spend any money if you don't know exactly what you're paying for. Read your contracts and don't let yourself get taken. If you don't understand what's going on, hire someone who can represent your interests, like an entertainment lawyer.

It gets worse. Even if you sue these companies and get a judgment against them, you probably won't ever see any money. A lot of these companies will set up and run their business until enough people have filed complaints or lawsuits against them, and then they just close their doors and open up under a different company name. Remember, if you are dealing with a corporation or LLC, it can shield itself from any personal liability. (See the Chapter 2, "Choosing a Business Structure.") Of course, you could always try to pierce the corporate veil and go after these people individually, but more often than not, you'll be throwing good money after bad. And that just doesn't make any sense.

Unless you have spent a large sum of money and been ripped off, you're often better off chalking the whole thing up to experience. Experience costs money, and you may have just bought a whole bunch of it. The best advice is to avoid these situations altogether, and seek legitimate success through the normal channels that everyone else has to go through. Be wary of hollow promises of fame, and you won't get burned.

Consumer Protection Acts

Many states have enacted statutes called Consumer Protection Acts, designed to protect innocent consumers and exact stiff civil penalties on people or companies that prey on the uninformed. These include lemon laws, statutes to protect consumers from bait-and-switch schemes, and the like. In some cases, these statutes provide for treble damages (meaning you get three times the amount of your loss or damage) and in some cases attorney's fees. But you may not be able to find an attorney to take the case. The attorney may figure out pretty quickly that even if he gets a judgment against this defendant, neither of you will ever see any of the money. (See Chapter 16, "If All Else Fails, Sue.")

A lot of organizations have been set up to help the unsuspecting consumer. These organizations often keep lists of bad people and companies. Your first choice should be the Better Business Bureau. However, the Better Business Bureau cannot represent you in court or get damages for any wrongful conduct; they are merely a protective association that lists complaints and helps to resolve issues if it can. Companies that are members of the Better Business Association must follow certain guidelines and are required to answer any complaints that are filed. Other organizations include the Songwriters' Protective Association and the Music Publishers' Protective Association. You can also contact ASCAP, BMI, or SESAC. They may be able to tell you

about any of their publishers and whether they are
completely legitimate.

Summary

Many people have called my law office for simple advice
about song sharks, custom labels, talent agencies, or
other types of deals that bordered on scams. Sometimes
they were legitimate deals, but many of them were not.
Many of my clients had heard that they should *never* pay
anybody any money in regard to their careers. As a simple rule of thumb, you shouldn't just give your money to
people if they promise to make you a star.

However, if you're not prepared to spend a good deal
of money on your career, you can't expect to have much
success. Of course, good old-fashioned hard work, networking, diligence, persistence, intestinal fortitude, and
some degree of good luck are always going to be your
best allies.

CHAPTER 15

Collecting Your Money

"Where did it all go?"

....

The most important aspect of being in the music business is making sure that you get paid. After all, you can't really say that you're a professional songwriter artist, or musician unless you make money doing it. At some point in your career, you may realize that someone is not paying you, especially if you make your living from royalties you get from a third party.

I have had countless clients over the years who were trying to get paid for the work they had created years ago. Unfortunately, they had entered into agreements with some very unscrupulous businesspeople. Their managers had not paid them or misappropriated their funds, their record label didn't pay them royalties for record sales, their music publisher didn't pay them royalties for hit songs they had written, they weren't getting paid for international royalties because there were many people with their fingers in the pie before the money ever even reached the United States, and so on. In short, lots of people have paved the road for us, and many of them have been taken advantage of in one way or another. Don't let that happen to you.

I always had a long list of clients who were owed money in some way or another. Unfortunately, since these clients never got the money that they were due, they didn't have the money to hire an accountant to find out how much money was owed, much less hire an attorney to assist them in collecting their money. To make matters worse, in some instances they had waited too long to do anything about it. If the statute of limitations had run out, they couldn't file suit even if they wanted to. In other cases, they could file suit, but the money was already spent by the people who took it. In yet other cases, a client may have paid his accountant to find out how much money was owed, and hired an attorney to steer him through a long and tedious court case just to get a judgment, but he still couldn't collect any money because the culprit was judgment-proof and had no assets that could be converted into cash. This just adds insult to injury, but it happens. My clients had trusted the wrong people, and they kept themselves too far away from the money.

Too Far Away from the Money

Here is an anecdote that may shed some light on a simple principle of business and a hard lesson to learn.

I met a gentleman late one night in London. I was trying to hail a cab outside a hotel, where I had been meeting with some friends before we headed to the International Music Festival in Cannes, France, to secure some deals for our clients. This gentlemen offered me a ride in his limousine, and as we headed to my hotel across town, we had a pretty cool conversation. He asked me what I did, and I explained that I was an entertainment attorney in Nashville. He then asked if I represented a major record label, or just smaller companies and individuals. I explained that I didn't work for any major record labels, because if I did, I most likely wouldn't be over in Europe working. I further explained that most in-house counsel for record labels didn't really travel or have much to do with getting deals for their clients. The major record labels are the ones that *give* record deals, and not the ones who *look for* record deals. I further explained that I went to MIDEM to pitch deals for distribution, licensing, joint ventures for international exploitation of my clients' intellectual property, and other types of deals. He immediately told me that I was "too far away from the money."

He said it looked to him like I was paid by the songwriters, artists, musicians, and other smaller businesses, such as publishers and independent record labels. The smaller businesses were in turn trying to exploit the intellectual property of their songwriters, artists, and musicians through joint ventures or other types of business deals. He further explained that I didn't get paid until my clients had made their money. (This wasn't always the case, but it was true in certain cases. If my clients didn't make money, they couldn't pay their bills.) He further explained that by the time one of my clients was paid, the record store had gotten its money, as had the distributor, the record label, and the manager. If the artist had anything left over, *then* I got paid. That pretty much explained why my clients were always so broke.

I couldn't believe it. He had summed up my clients' entire careers in a matter of minutes. They were too far away from the money!

In short, you need to be standing at the cash register if you want to make sure you get paid every penny that you deserve. Unfortunately, this is nigh impossible if you're an artist or songwriter.

If you are involved in a money dispute over a one-night gig or a weekly stint on the club circuit, you should be able to ascertain quickly whether or not you've been paid. In fact, you should know immediately if you've been taken advantage of. If you are not paid, refer to Chapter 12, "General Principles of Contracts," and Chapter 16, "When All Else Fails, Sue."

However, if you are supposed to be paid by your manager, record label, or publisher, or you're relying on any type of royalty or percentage of sales, you may have more trouble getting closer to your money. Fortunately, you can take a number of steps to make sure you are getting paid the right amounts.

Exhausting All Possibilities

Before you start firing off demand letters, sending your accountant over to do an audit, or threatening to sue, you should make an honest effort to get information about your situation. Ask as many questions as you can, and try to ascertain the truth of the answers. As long as you are getting satisfactory answers, you may not have anything to worry about. You don't want to bite the hand that feeds you, so be very polite and patient. It's when people stop returning your calls or answering your correspondence that you have something to worry about.

Also beware of people who pat you on the back and tell you how great things are, while they're sticking it to you every way they can. Unfortunately, there's only one way to be absolutely sure you're getting the royalties you're supposed to be getting. You need to get an accounting.

Getting an Accounting

One of the first steps in finding out if you're owed money is to ask for an accounting. Of course, you probably receive a royalty statement already, but does that mean you're getting all that you're due? Sometimes it does, but not always. Pursuant to most contracts that call for payment of royalties, you should have a clause that allows you to inspect the company's books at a specified time, or at reasonable times. Either you or your CPA will have access to these books, and only at the company's place of business. However, before you can go barging in to see how much money you haven't been paid, you may be required to give notice that you will be auditing its books. I've had quite a few clients who have requested an accounting, only to get a nice fat check a few days before the accountant shows up to inspect the books. Amazingly enough, the books check out perfectly.

You may ask, "Why don't these companies pay out the money they owe, and on time?" You have to keep in mind that interest on a little money can add up from year to year. Interest on a *lot* of money adds up really quickly! It is usually in the best interests of companies that are holding very large amounts of cash to "slow pay" money to their writers or artists. If you take $10,000 and multiply by 100, you get $1,000,000.00. Ten percent interest on a million dollars a year is $100,000.00. Divide that by 12 and you get $8,333.33. That's one month's interest on $1,000,000.00. That's a lot of money. In other words, if a publisher owes 100 writers $10,000 each quarter and holds on to the money for an extra month, the publisher just made $8,333.33. If the publisher holds onto the money even longer, the money really starts to add up. Needless to say, that's a pretty strong incentive to be just a little late making payments.

Sometimes companies will keep two sets of books. I'm not saying there are a lot of companies that do this, but it can happen. There really isn't much you can do about it unless you can prove it. If you suspect that there are two sets of books, you can always go up the chain to see what has been paid to the company by Harry Fox, one of the big three performance licensors (ASCAP, BMI, and SESAC), or even by checking with SoundScan for actual record sales. With a careful and thorough audit, you can find out exactly what is due to you that should be on the books.

Of course, accountants don't come cheap, and a large audit can be quite expensive. But if you can show that you haven't been paid moneys that are due, you can take the company to court and ask for all of your expenses for the accounting back, as well as other damages.

Regardless, most likely you'll need to audit a company that collects money on your behalf and is therefore supposed to pay you a percentage of that money. But before you do, you will need to put someone at the company on notice. That means you will need a demand letter.

Writing a Demand Letter

The art of communication seems to have been lost over the years. Many of us read fewer books and watch more television. But being able to communicate is one of the most important skills you can possess. If you have ever read or heard someone read a letter that was written during the Civil War, you've noticed how articulate those people were. I have read letters by lowly privates that were so well-written and carefully constructed that I felt like the writer was truly communicating with me. I have also read letters from people who have college degrees, and I couldn't figure out what they were trying to say for the life of me. Remember, the written word can be taken the wrong way.

To make sure your letters are as professional as possible, always check your spelling and grammar. The more intelligent you sound in your letters, the more intelligent you will be perceived to be. Also remember that the written word doesn't come with emoticons (unless you are sending e-mail, and even then, emoticons are unprofessional). The way you write can be taken the wrong way, so be careful. Always try to start out as non-confrontational.

I'm not trying to be condescending by showing what a well-written letter looks like, but you would be surprised at how many people just can't seem to write a good letter. I'm going to assume that you may have not had much experience in this area. Therefore, here's an example of a request for an accounting:

Name of company
Address
City, state, & ZIP code

Dear Mr. Niceguy:

I am interested in seeing how my royalty account has been doing. To that end, I would very much appreciate the opportunity to inspect the books at your office as soon as we can agree upon a reasonable time. I look forward to your kind response.

Sincerely,
W. J. Artist
WJA/hds

This is a polite request, which is the best way to start out. It's simple and concise and anything but adversarial. Being audited by anyone is about as welcome as getting a tooth pulled, so don't get everyone's dander up by being demanding and rude right up front. If you say something like, "It has come to my attention that I have not been being paid all of the royalties that are due as per the terms of my contract," it may not go over very well. You are putting people on the defensive right from the start. Try to get what you are entitled to without putting the other side in such an adversarial posture that he tries to prevent you from getting the money he owes you. People can get so upset by the implication that they may be cheating that they might actually do so out of spite.

If you have a contact point at the company, address the letter to that person. If you don't know who should be receiving the letter, you can make a general address, such as "To whom it may concern." However, that's not the best way to get what you want. If you don't know who's responsible for your royalties, how do you know who's looking out for your interests? Having a contact point who you know and trust is key. If at all possible, you should develop a friendly relationship with your contact point. This way, if you have a problem such as a simple clerical error, a miscommunication, or a change of address, those types of simple human errors can be fixed quickly without need for any further action.

At the end of the letter, type your name. Below it, put the initials of the person who wrote the letter, and below that, put the initials of the person who typed the letter. In this example, I used WJA as the name of the writer, and hs as the acronym for the typist, his own self. Attorneys do that all the time, for a number of reasons. First, it makes them look like they are too busy to type a letter. Second, it tells them who typed the letter. If you know who typed the letter, you know which computer it can be found on. You also know who was responsible for making sure the letter was sent out, a copy was filed in the proper file, and courtesy copies were mailed to the appropriate parties. Courtesy copies are designated by cc:, which stands for carbon copy. If you are using e-mail, you could use bcc:, which stands for blind carbon copy. This prevents a recipient from seeing the e-mail addresses of the other people you sent copies to. This can be useful for maintaining his privacy.

Unfortunately, in some cases people will blow you off time and time again, and you will have no idea if you are being paid. Then it will be necessary to write a much stronger type of demand letter:

Name of company
Address
City, state, & ZIP code

Dear Mr. Deadbeat:

I have requested to inspect the books at your office on more than one occasion and have not met with any success. Based on information and belief, I have reason to believe that I am not receiving the full amounts due to me under the terms of my contract. Therefore, please be advised that pursuant to my contract, demand is made herein that I be allowed to inspect your company books on the _____ day of _____, 200_ at your business offices. As per the terms of my contract, I have retained John Q. Beancounter, CPA, as my accountant to inspect the books, and plan to retain Dewey, Cheatham, and Howe, Attorneys at Law, to represent me should any further action need to be taken.

Sincerely,
W. J. Artist
WJA/hds
cc: John Q. Beancounter, CPA
Dewey, Cheatham & Howe, Attorneys at Law

It is always a good idea to courtesy copy anyone who may be interested in your case, such as your accountant and your attorney. This does a couple of things. First, it keeps your accountant and your attorney updated on what you are up to. (But be careful, because they will bill you for reading your letter.) Second, it shows the addressee that you mean business. You are not just thinking about an action, but are ready to proceed with it. Once the company knows you are serious, it may decide to go ahead and cut you a check.

Whatever you do, don't sleep on your rights. Take immediate action. If you show the company that you are serious about getting paid, it may start taking care of its affairs more efficiently. Also, if you don't take action in the time allowed by law, you can be forever barred from any recovery pursuant to certain defenses to court actions.

Defenses to Court Actions

Always keep in mind that you can't wait forever to collect your money. A company can assert a number of defenses to prevent you from collecting. The most important of these are the statute of limitations, the doctrine of laches, and the statute of repose. If you have been paid all that you are owed, that payment constitutes an accord and satisfaction, and therefore you have no cause of action. Of course, there's always the possibility that you have just signed a bad contract. You may be able to set aside a contract if the terms are so completely unfair that the court will deem it void on its face, but this is very rare.

You may also be able to set aside a contract for failure to pay, or you can try to terminate any assignment of copyright (see Chapter 6, "Intellectual Property"). The courts are becoming more and more aware of the lack of bargaining power between large companies and individual songwriters and artists. But if you sign an agreement, you will have an uphill battle showing the court that the terms should not be upheld. It all depends upon your circumstances.

You would be wise to hire an attorney before signing any agreement that you don't understand. Never let someone tell you what a contract says. Read it yourself. If you don't understand it, don't sign it. Plain and simple.

STATUTE OF LIMITATIONS

The most obvious defense to any cause of action, and sometimes the most unfair, is the *statute of limitations*. Statutes of limitations are the rules of law governing the period of time during which a civil claim must be filed. This principle has been around for years and years, and was originally adopted to prevent people from bringing suit years after any court action should have been taken. It is intended to encourage people to bring their case while witnesses are still available and the facts are still fresh.

Statutes of limitations are different for each type of complaint or cause of action, such as breach of contract, negligence, fraud, etc. They also differ from one state to the next for state law claims, common law claims, criminal cases, and federal law claims. In some cases, the statue of limitations could be as short as one year. Therefore, you should check the law in your state or federal jurisdiction for any statute that could forever bar you from recovering for any action you want to bring.

Also, you should check your contract to see what law is controlling, or if there is a jurisdiction clause. The jurisdiction clause will usually state that you must file suit in a particular state, or even a particular county. This is very important: If you miss a date for filing, you will be out of luck and there's nothing that you can do about it.

Sometimes the statute of limitations can be *tolled*, depending on your state or the federal law that is controlling. This just means that the clock won't start to run until you have discovered (or reasonably should have discovered) the wrongdoing. As soon as you know that you are not getting paid, you need to take immediate action to find out what is going on. Otherwise, you will be left out in the cold. Many people have been forever barred from collecting any money whatsoever, just because they were one day late getting to the courthouse. Don't let that happen to you.

STATUTE OF REPOSE

The *statute of repose* is the final time limit after which an action cannot be filed. In other words, it's the ultimate and final time limit. More often than not, you will see this doctrine applied to construction contracts, but it could be used as a defense in a breach of contract case if you are trying to collect royalties long after they're due.

With construction contracts, if you buy or build a house and there is a defect in the construction, you have a certain number of years (whatever the statute of limitations is in that state) from the date of discovery of the defect to file suit. However, if the defect doesn't show up until 15 years after you move in, you may have a very short amount of time to file, much less than the original statute of limitations.

The statute of repose could apply if you left your copyrights to your estate, one of your beneficiaries didn't follow up on collecting the money, and later he found out that money was owed. If he did not take action quickly enough once he discovered the deficiency, the statute of repose could forever bar him from ever getting any of that money. In other words, the statute of limitations on contracts can sometimes be around 6 years, and if the beneficiary didn't discover that the money was owed until 10 years after you passed away, and then waited another 5 years to bring suit, he could be barred from recovery.

So make sure you take care of your business affairs, and that the people you leave behind know that money could be due.

LACHES

The *doctrine of laches* is a catchall way of getting around the statute of limitations to assert a defense to any cause of action. And it can work against you if the court finds that you didn't take action soon enough.

Basically, anyone who "sleeps on his rights" is forever barred from bringing any legal action. Unfortunately, this defense can be extremely unfair. The doctrine of laches could be used against you if you don't bring suit in a timely manner. This doctrine isn't used very much, and most courts aren't willing to impose such harsh and stringent penalties against someone who is owed money, but it can happen. Don't sit around and think about taking action; move as quickly as you can once you discover you are owed money.

Accord and Satisfaction

If you've been paid all of the money that you're owed, you really don't have any cause of action, unless maybe you were paid late. This is what is called *accord and satisfaction*. However, you may be able to collect interest on the amount that you should have been paid, especially if the interest adds up to a large amount. But you have to keep in mind the principle of diminishing returns. If you're trying to collect a small amount of interest, it may not be economically feasible. (See Chapter 16.) Sometimes it's better to chalk up some mistakes to experience, and forego spending a lot of money just to collect a little. As stated before, experience costs money. Sometimes you just have to buy more than you can afford.

In some cases, there is a chance that you can get your copyrights back for nonpayment. That sounds fair, doesn't it? Of course it does. But that doesn't mean it will happen. There is a principle in contract law stating that if there is no consideration or failure of consideration to support a contract, the contract is void or can be rescinded. Either the contract was never valid in the first place, or it can be set aside for nonpayment so that both parties are put back into the situation they were in before they entered into the contract.

But you won't find this happening very often. Again, don't forget that if you are in a really bad publishing deal, you can ask to terminate your assignment of copyright. (For more information, see Chapter 6.) But your best bet is to sign only agreements that you understand and that are completely fair to both parties.

Summary

If you don't keep up with all of your copyrights, contracts, royalties owed, and other matters where your money is involved, you could get the short end of the stick. If you aren't sure what you are owed and feel that you deserve more money, by all means, get an accounting and find out. Remember, if you are not timely in trying to find out what you are owed and whether you are receiving it, you could end up like so many others before you who don't have much money to show after years in the music business. Always keep in mind that what cannot be fixed must be endured.

CHAPTER 16

If All Else Fails, Sue

"Arm yourself... and prepare for war."

....

When you feel that you've been taken advantage of, and you can't set things right through negotiation or any other avenue, sometimes there is absolutely no other choice but to sue. But it's not something you should take lightly. In fact, people seem to take being sued very seriously for some reason. Be prepared, and you will stand a much better chance of success.

This chapter will discuss the principle of diminishing returns, what's involved in going to court, what types of courts there are, how much justice you can afford, whom you should sue, where you sue them, what to file and where, what to ask for, how to prepare for court, what to do when you get to court, how to make an opening argument, how to examine witnesses, how to make a closing argument, what to do if the case is going poorly, and how to collect your judgment if you win. But before you even think about whether you should file suit, you need to know about the principle of diminishing returns.

Diminishing Returns

There are many things you will have to consider before you file suit, and one of the most important is the principle of *diminishing returns.* This comes into play when you take on a case to right a wrong, collect money, or obtain an injunction to prevent someone from doing something you think he shouldn't be doing, but you end up spending more money than it's really worth.

Anytime you can avoid a lawsuit, it's best to do so. Although you may be dead set on getting even because a situation is not right and you don't want to let someone get away with it, fighting over principles is sometimes overrated when you stop to consider the costs. I once saw a picture of two people fighting over a cow. One person was pulling on the tail, the other was pulling on the horns, and a lawyer was sitting in the middle, milking the cow. Don't get stuck paying someone to milk the cow and having nothing left for yourself when it's all said and done.

Here's an example that I've often used to demonstrate the principle of diminishing returns: A duo act has played together for a long time, and scrimped and saved from gigs to buy a small PA system for about $2,500.00. After a number of gigs, a good deal of wear and tear, and normal depreciation, the PA is now worth about $1,000.00. Due to "creative differences," the duo is calling it quits. Of course, neither of them wants to part with the PA system, because they both plan to pursue solo careers and will need a PA. They have gotten very different opinions as to the value of the PA, and they cannot agree upon a price that either of them would have to pay the other to purchase it outright.

To make matters worse, each one of them feels that the PA should be his. One of them has booked all of the gigs, and the other has moved all of the equipment at all of their shows, and therefore they both feel that they are entitled to the whole PA system without any payment to the other party. They both have gigs coming up on the same date, and they need to get this issue resolved as quickly as possible.

If each one hires a lawyer for $500 to negotiate or sue to get the PA, the lawyers end up with the total value of the PA. The lawyers are the only ones who win. That is the principle of diminishing returns.

If both parties have the money to engage in legal warfare and neither one is willing to negotiate a reasonable solution, the only way they can resolve their differences legally is to go to mediation, arbitration, or court, and let the chips fall where they may. Even though there will be a winner based upon the decision of the judge, in reality, nobody truly wins. They just end up spending money that could have been spent more wisely elsewhere. In short, avoid litigation if at all possible.

Of course, in issues involving large sums of money, going to court is sometimes the only way to go. Before filing a lawsuit, you may want to consider a couple of options that could save you a lot of time and money.

Arbitration and Mediation

There are two alternatives to going to court that are becoming more and more popular and can save you a lot of time and money. They are known as *arbitration* and *mediation*.

Arbitration is when you choose a neutral third party to resolve a dispute. It can be binding or non-binding. *Binding arbitration* merely means that you are stuck with whatever decision the third party makes. You cannot appeal, and the matter is closed. However, if your arbitration is *non-binding*, you may have wasted all of these steps and you'll wind up in court anyway. So be very careful when you're deciding on this type of resolution.

Arbitration is similar to a legal proceeding, but it's much less formal. The normal rules of evidence don't apply, but they can still have an effect on how evidence is viewed. Hearsay, non-expert opinions, and poorly documented evidence will not carry much weight. However, there *are* rules, and they must be followed strictly. If you are going to be involved in this type of action, you should get a copy of these rules before you do. This could be a good choice for a lot of disputes, because lawyers are not required. In many cases they aren't even necessary, due to lax evidentiary rules and the like. But you can bring a lawyer, or consult with one to figure out how you should proceed.

Also, arbitration is usually much faster than legal proceedings and can cost a lot less. However, both parties must agree to submit to arbitration so neither one will be dragged into court to hear the issue. In some cases, you may have a contract that actually requires the parties to submit to arbitration in case of a dispute.

You have to pay the arbitrator a reasonable fee. Since that arbitrator is usually a retired judge or an attorney, this can be rather expensive. But keep in mind that it can be a whole lot cheaper than going to court. It just depends on the facts and circumstances of your case, and the amount of money that is involved.

Also, you probably won't find out who wins an arbitration for several days after your hearing. The arbitrator will want to take the matter under advisement, and won't want to make a decision in front of the parties to avoid any backlash.

Mediation is simply when you go in front a neutral third party who will help you come up with creative ways to resolve your disputes, but will not render a decision. This is a really good method of issue resolution, especially if the parties are in some type of ongoing relationship. If the mediation is not successful, the parties may then submit to arbitration or take up the matter with the courts.

Even if you go with arbitration, you will be encouraged to enter into mediation at all stages of the game. The whole point of arbitration and mediation is to get the two sides to resolve their differences. However, if neither party agrees to mediation or arbitration, there is nothing left to do but go to court.

What's Involved in Going to Court?

If you feel like you have no other choice but to go to court, you should at least know about the process.

I've had so many clients who really couldn't afford a lawyer, but had been seriously wronged in some way. The information that follows is invaluable if you decide to sue and you have to represent yourself for whatever reason. You should consult this chapter if you can't afford an attorney and the suit doesn't involve too much money. If you can't afford an attorney, you will have to be a *pro se* litigant (a person who represents himself). This chapter will come in handy even if you have hired a lawyer, because it will tell you what is going to happen when you're in court, and afterwards. However, this information is *not* to be considered legal advice. If you are not sure about what to do, you should seek competent legal assistance.

What Types of Courts Are There?

Before you even consider filing a lawsuit, you need to know what types of courts there are. The two main types of courts are civil and criminal courts. If someone has committed a crime against you, you will go see the police and end up in criminal court. However, if you want to sue someone for a civil wrong, such as breach of contract, you will need to go to a civil court.

I'm going to start at the top and work my way down, because you really only need to worry about the smallest courts. If you need to go to a higher court, you should hire an attorney. But small claims courts and justice courts were specifically set up for anyone who wants to file a good faith lawsuit over a small dispute that can't be resolved anywhere else. And you do not need to be a lawyer to represent yourself. However, if you are incorporated, an LLC, or any other business entity other than a partnership or sole proprietor, you may be required by law to have an attorney represent you.

Of course, you know about the Supreme Court of the United States. It is the final court in all the land, but it accepts only certain cases that have been appealed from lower courts. Under the Supreme Court are the federal courts of appeals in each of the federal districts, which are the next step after the federal courts in each state. Some states may have more than one federal court, depending on the size of the state. However, if you want to make a federal case out of some issue, or your case requires filing in federal court, such as a copyright infringement action, you're better off hiring a lawyer. Therefore, I am not even going to begin to cover filing, litigation, or any other issue in regard to federal lawsuits.

Next, each state has a final court that is the highest in the state, but each state doesn't necessarily call it the Supreme Court. Some states may call their highest court the Superior Court. Whatever it's called, it's the court that hears cases that have been appealed from the state court of appeals. The state court of appeals hears appeals from the circuit courts, also called superior courts. If you have a case involving a large enough amount of money, you need to bring your case to circuit court or whatever it may be called. However, I highly recommend that you hire a lawyer if there is enough money involved.

These courts are much more serious in nature, and the rules are difficult to grasp.

But what if you have a small case? Small claims court or justice court is where you need to go. This is the only time I suggest that you try to represent yourself, especially if you can't afford a lawyer or the amount of the dispute or lawsuit doesn't warrant the hiring of lawyers.

Each state's county seat will have a small claims court where you may bring your case. Usually, these small claims courts don't have a jury, but rather a judge who will decide your case. Don't worry too much about not having a lawyer, especially if your case is for a small amount that doesn't warrant hiring an attorney. If you feel that the judge doesn't give you the right decision, you can appeal your case to the next highest court. However, you will find that higher courts adhere more rigidly to rules and the law than small claims courts. Therefore, if either you or the defendant appeals your case for any reason, you will definitely want to consider hiring a lawyer.

How Much Justice Can You Afford?

Before you sue, you need to think about who you are suing, and for what. Do they have the money to pay if you win? Sometimes you spend a lot of time and money to sue someone, only to find out that you'll never get your money.

Furthermore, sometimes the people with the most money don't want to pay out any of it for any reason.

They will drag out your case for a very long time. Maybe that's how they have gotten so much money? Be that as it may, if you are going after someone with deep pockets, you have to consider what a defendant with lots of money can do. He can afford to fight you simply on principle. Or worse, he can afford to hire a big law firm and countersue you, just to keep from having to pay up.

In some cases, the defendant will just decide to pay you to avoid the cost of further litigation. If you have sued someone who wants to settle, make sure that he agrees to pay the court costs *and* the money he owes you, and then make him sign a release so that he can't sue you over the same facts and circumstances.

But again, remember the principle of diminishing returns. Sometimes it's better just to let sleeping dogs lie. Chalk it up to experience and move on.

On the other hand, you certainly don't want to get a reputation of allowing anyone and everyone to take advantage of you. If you must pursue a matter, you have to know exactly who you are suing so that you file suit against the proper entity.

If you are in the music business, the most prevalent type of case is breach of contract. Let's look at that.

Who Are You Suing?

Before you file a lawsuit, you have to decide exactly who you are suing. Are you suing a person, a partnership, an LLC, or a corporation? Make sure that you name the correct entity when you file any complaint, or your case could be dismissed. Then you'll have to start the whole process over and lose the money you spent trying to sue the wrong entity.

Next, you need to have service of process. Anytime you want to bring somebody before a court to have your case heard, you need to let that party know he is being sued. Therefore, you need to have him served with a copy of a complaint. (For more information, see "Service of Process" later in this chapter.) Most small claims courts will have a general form you can fill out, setting forth your cause of action. The *cause of action* is just the grievance set forth in writing, describing why you are suing. For example: "I'm suing to collect $1,000 that was not paid to me when I played a gig, as per the agreement with the club. The club only paid me $200.00."

Once the cause of action is filed with the court, you should ask how the entity you are suing should be served with process. In many cases, the court will have the sheriff serve the other party. However, if the party is from another state, you may need to serve him by certified mail, return receipt requested. (Again, see "Service of Process.") Also, if you're suing more than one party, you need to make sure that you sue *all* interested parties, or you may have to start over. Finally, you should also know that you must sue a party where the cause of action arose or in the state where it does business, so this brings us to the question of where to sue.

Where Do You Sue?

Before you file suit, you have to establish *jurisdiction*. Which court has authority to hear your case? Each state is different, but it isn't hard to find out which court you need to go to so you can file your suit.

If you are suing over a good deal of money, which cannot be handled in small claims court, your best bet is to hire a lawyer to guide you through the whole process. But every citizen has the right to represent himself in court, and sometimes it is not economically feasible to hire a lawyer to represent you. You can call the local courthouse and ask what the monetary jurisdictional limit is. You can also find out exactly what you will need to file, and where. Court clerks are not lawyers, and they cannot give you any legal advice. But if you are really polite to these people, they can be of great help. Remember, these court clerks have to deal with hundreds of litigants each week, and usually they're not very happy. So being rude and expecting good service is not going to work for you. Be patient and polite.

Now it's time to think about what you need to file.

What Do You File?

The first thing you need to file is the *complaint*, which is sometimes referred to as a *civil summons*. The complaint should explain why you are suing, such as breach of contract. Most courts will have a form that you have to fill out, and some will have boilerplate language so that you know which parts to fill out. Some courts require that you be very specific, while some don't. To be safe, make sure that you ask for everything that you are seeking in very plain English, and don't ramble on. If the case is about a breach of contract or failure to pay, just state on the complaint "breach of contract" or "failure to pay" and the amount of damages you are seeking. Read the summons carefully to make sure that you have filled in all of the information correctly. If you are nice to the court clerks, they will help you with any corrections you need to make. But remember, they can't give you legal advice.

What Do You Ask For?

All you need to ask for is the actual damages you are seeking and any other incidental damages you have incurred. You don't necessarily need to put down all of the facts of the case. Sometimes, if you are suing on a sworn account when someone owes you money, as per the terms of a contract, you may want to include an affidavit of the amount owed. This depends on your state, so check with the court clerks to see what is required. Again, they should have a template for you to use.

You may also ask the court for prejudgment and postjudgment interest, which is usually governed by state statute. *Prejudgment interest* is the amount of interest that has accrued from the date that the money was supposed to have been paid, up until the time you actually get your judgment in court. In other words, if you're owed $1,000, you don't get to court until one year later, and the interest rate is 10% per annum, you're owed $1,100.00. *Postjudgment interest* is the amount of interest from the date you get a judgment until the time that the balance has been paid in full. In other words, if it takes the defendant a very long time to pay you the total balance, you're entitled to the statutory interest rate in your state. This is intended to keep a defendant who has a judgment against him from taking forever to pay. However, be advised that some folks don't care if you tack on all the interest in the world, because they just won't pay what they owe until you take some action to make them. (See "Collecting your Judgment" later in this chapter.)

Also keep in mind that even if you get a judgment, you might have to get in line behind all of the other creditors trying to collect their money. Or worse, the person or entity you've sued may file bankruptcy to keep from paying its outstanding debts.

With that in mind, once you have filed suit, the other party must be served notice of the suit. Without this, you cannot have your day in court.

Service of Process

Before you can go to court, you have to pay some court costs up front. A good portion of those court costs are fees for service of process, which is how the defendant will be given notice that he is being sued. Usually, a copy of the complaint is given to the defendant in one way or another.

Valid service of process can be obtained in a number of ways. First, there is in-hand service of process. Either the sheriff or local agency puts a copy of the complaint in the hands of the defendant or his agent. Once the defendant has been served, the sheriff or local agency returns the service of process to the court. Then the court knows that the defendant has been served a copy of the complaint, and the defendant knows that a court date has been set. You may have to check back with the court to see if the other side has been served, or if service of process has been returned "not found." If that is the case, you will have to start the service of process over again.

Sometimes, the rules will allow for a person who's not a party to the lawsuit to obtain process. This is usually a company or individual who will go out and serve someone with process. These companies or private process servers may charge a fee. You could just enlist a friend or family member to serve someone with process, but it's not a good idea. It can be dangerous (people don't take being served lightly), and that friend or family member may have to come to court to testify that he personally handed a copy to the defendant or his agent. Please check with the court to see what type of service of process it will allow, and whether the type of service that you've obtained is valid before you get to court. Without valid service of process, your court date will be postponed. The whole process will have to be repeated until you can get valid service of process.

Service of process can also be had by certified mail. Usually, if the defendant or someone in the household who's over 18 has signed for certified mail with a return receipt requested, that's valid service of process. This is useful if the defendant doesn't reside in your county or state. However, the defendant must be shown to have done business in your jurisdiction. Your lawsuit can't take place where you live if the cause of action arose somewhere else. You may have to sue the party where he can be found, or where your cause of action arose.

In other words, if you weren't paid for a gig when you were out on the road, you may have to go to the state where the venue is and sue it there. However, if it contacted you for the gig where you work or reside, and signed a contract that states you can sue the venue in your home state if it breaches the agreement, you may be able to proceed. This just shows that it's a really good idea to have a contract for all your gigs.

If you have tried to obtain service of process by hand or certified mail and you can't find the defendant, you may be able to file for *publication process*. This is where a notice is posted in the local newspaper, at the courthouse, or in a business publication for a certain period of time, thereby giving the absentee defendant notice of the action. Not many people other than lawyers read these notices, so this is not the best way to go. But it may be the only way you can proceed with your suit.

Unfortunately, if you can't find the defendant to give him notice of your suit even after you publish service of process, you may not ever be able to collect your money from him. Furthermore, unless the defendant signs a certified letter or is served in person, there is always a chance that your service of process may be considered invalid. Any default judgment that you obtain could be set aside.

One thing is for sure: If the defendant doesn't have notice of the lawsuit based upon the rules of civil procedure for that county or state, no judge will hear the case. You can't just tell the defendant that you are suing him.

He needs to have actual legal notice. Then, if he doesn't show up, you can get a default judgment. (See "Default Judgment" later in this chapter.)

Pretrial Preparation

This step is just as important as trying your case. You need to get your materials and arguments together and rehearse what you are going to say. You also need to make at least three copies of all documents you plan to use as evidence, so that everyone in the court who needs a copy will have one. You will need a copy for the defendant, one for any of your witnesses, and one for you to keep so that you will know what the judge and the other side are looking at. Of course, the original document should be handed to the judge, unless there's a very good reason it's not available. The court may also wish to keep an extra copy for their files (especially if you didn't attach a copy to the complaint), but you should always keep the original after the trial is over.

Also, when you file your case with the clerk's office, ask for a copy of the court rules. Read them carefully! The rules will tell you what you are supposed to do and how to do it. The clerk will *not* tell you how to argue the law, but if you familiarize yourself with the rules, you will be much better prepared to present your case.

Finally, if there is even a remote chance that your case will be appealed (see "The Right to Appeal" later in this chapter), you may want to hire a court reporter to take a transcript of the case. Some courts will already have sound and video recording for your use, but this type of expense is usually reserved for courts of higher record. If you win your case and you have paid for a court reporter, you can always ask the court to make the other side pay for your court reporter fees. However, you will have to pay the court reporter out of your own pocket until you recover any fees awarded by the court, which sometimes means you will never see any of that money. This is just one more cost that you should consider when thinking about the principle of diminishing returns.

You may want to go to court a few days before your trial. Sit and watch as many trials as you can, especially the ones with lawyers, to get a feel for how that court works and how the lawyers handle themselves. Remember, a lot of judges don't like pro se litigants who fumble through their cases. The better prepared and more professional you are, the better your chances of succeeding.

Your Day in Court!

Where do you stand, what do you say, and how does this work?

First of all, remember always to show respect for the court, because everyone there tends to take things pretty seriously for some reason. Dress appropriately. If you are a man, this doesn't necessarily mean a suit, but it definitely means a nice pair of slacks, a clean and ironed shirt, a tie, and nice shoes. Never wear jeans, shorts, sandals, or any type of extremely casual wear. If your hair is long, consider a ponytail. If you don't have a beard or mustache, be clean-shaven. If you are a woman, you don't have to wear a dress. A nice outfit will suffice. Whatever your gender, you should dress like you're going to church or to a funeral, because court can be very much like either if you come dressed like a bum. The judge may make a decision against you just because he or she doesn't like the way you dress or act. Judges are human just like the rest of us, and a good first impression will get you started on the right foot.

Get there at least 30 minutes early. This will give you time to find the courtroom and familiarize yourself with your surroundings. If there is a court officer (who will most likely have on a badge), politely ask where you are supposed to sit before and after your case is called. You may also ask how cases are usually handled in that court, and if this judge has any preference for how a person should proceed. The court officer will usually be very helpful. Remember, these people are in the courtroom day in and day out for very little money, and they know what the judge likes and doesn't like. Furthermore, if you cause any problems or are rude to them or the judge, they can arrest you on the spot, ask the judge to hold you in contempt of court, and even put you in jail!

No matter what, speak only when it's your turn. Never interrupt anyone, especially the judge. If the other side is talking, let them. You'll have your turn to speak. If you are waiting for your case to be heard and you have to speak to someone next to you, leave the courtroom (unless the court has stated that you can't, in which case, sit there and be quiet). Keep in mind that it can be a distraction to have people going in and out of the courtroom, and the judge will definitely notice. Furthermore, if the judge has said there is to be no talking in the courtroom, you could be held in contempt, fined, or even put in jail. Also make sure that you turn off your cell phone or pager before you walk into the courtroom.

When court gets under way, the court clerks may call the case docket first. This is a list of the plaintiffs and defendants, and perhaps the case number that was assigned by the court clerk. Sometimes the court clerks will ask if all the parties are present, sometimes not. They may just decide to hear each case as the docket is called, so be prepared for either situation. If they are just calling the docket, make sure to speak up when your name is called so that the court will know you are present. If your case is going to be heard, the court will tell you that you may proceed. This is when you take your place where you are supposed to stand or sit.

If you're not sure when you are supposed to say something in front of the judge, keep your mouth shut. The judge will know that you aren't familiar with the proceedings, and he'll ask you when he wants something. If he's in a bad mood or he's not very helpful to pro se litigants, he may leave you to your own devices. If there's a long pause and the judge is looking at you, ask him, "May I proceed, your honor?" Once he says "yes," you can proceed.

Default Judgment

If you have obtained good service of process on the person who you are suing and he hasn't shown up, you can move the court for a default judgment. In some courts, you won't even have to say anything. The court will simply call the person's name who you are suing and if he doesn't answer, the court may automatically grant you a default judgment. Or the judge may wait for a while to see if the defendant shows up. If not, the situation is just like when a sports team doesn't have enough players or just doesn't show up, and the other team wins by default. So, if the court doesn't grant you the judgment automatically, just state the following very politely when the judge asks you to speak: "I would like to move for a default judgment."

The judge may fill out the default judgment by asking you what damages you are seeking. Just because the other side is not there to defend himself, don't try to get more than you deserve. That can come back to haunt you. If the court asks you to fill out any papers or sign anything, do so, and then the judge will sign it as long as the court approves what you are asking for.

If the other side does show up and you are ready to proceed, one of the first questions the judge may ask is whether or not you want "the rule."

"The Rule"

The court will sometimes invoke "the rule" without anyone asking for it. If you or the other side has witnesses and "the rule" is invoked, it just means that all of the witnesses must leave the courtroom. This prevents witnesses from hearing what the other witnesses say during the course of the trial and changing their testimony to fit what has already been said.

If the judge asks you about "the rule" and the other side has witnesses, just say "yes," unless you don't mind all of the witnesses hearing everything that is going on.

If the other side doesn't have witnesses, you don't want to invoke "the rule." Of course, the judge may just make your witnesses leave. If he doesn't, it will be up to you to ask for "the rule." You may want just the other side's witnesses to leave, but "the rule" doesn't work that way. It's both sides or none at all.

Once the court has decided who can stay or leave, it's time for you (the plaintiff) to make your opening statement. But before you say anything, always politely ask the judge if you can proceed.

Opening Statement

If you are the plaintiff (the person bringing the lawsuit), you will go first. Always stand when you address the court, unless the judge tells you to sit down. Begin by introducing yourself so that the judge and everyone else will know who you are. "Hello, your honor, I am John Q. Artist." Then begin with your opening statement. This is your chance to tell the judge why you are there. Start by stating the facts of the case. Don't embellish your story with emotional arguments about how it made you feel, or other things that really don't have any bearing on the case. Be concise, and be calm. Real court is never like you see on television, with people going off and raising their voice. In fact, if you get loud or belligerent, you will be asked to leave. Worse, you could end up in jail. Just tell the judge very simply what the case is about, and what you are seeking in damages.

For instance, if you are suing a club owner to get money that he didn't pay you, state that you had a contract with the club owner to play on such and such a date for however much money you had agreed upon. State that you played the gig as agreed. Then state what the club owner did, such as not paying you or paying less than the full amount, even though you demanded payment on numerous occasions. You may also state that you are asking for court costs and interest. Ask for what you are entitled to get, and that's it!

Be very direct and to the point. Don't go off on some longwinded treatise about how unfair it was, or how you've had to miss work to be in court, or anything else that has no bearing on why you're there. If you are seeking lost time for work or anything else, you had better have made claim for it in your complaint. (Many judges won't let you ask for anything that is not in the complaint.) Then you can talk about how much you should be compensated for missing work or whatever else. Once you have finished your opening statement, you may give the judge some sign that you are done, or just sit down and shut up.

It will now be the other side's turn to give his opening statement. You can bet that his story is going to be completely different than yours, and he may say some pretty ugly things about you. Whatever you do, keep your mouth shut and take it. Do *not* interrupt the proceedings for any reason. You'll have your turn to make any counterarguments.

Before we move on to presenting your case, it's important to know about rules of evidence. In most small claims courts, the judges are pretty lenient about the rules of evidence. Furthermore, their court rules may specifically say that the rules of civil procedure don't apply, which is a good thing. Otherwise, you would have to get a copy of the rules and learn them all. But even if the rules of civil procedure don't apply, the rules of evidence will, to some degree.

Rules of Evidence

The rules of evidence are extremely hard to learn and strictly adhered to by the courts. These rules govern what the court will allow as evidence. However, in most small claims courts, the rules of evidence are somewhat lax, because the court wants to hear each case and proceed to the next one quickly. Furthermore, in some small claims courts, some rules of evidence may not even apply. You should get a copy of all rules of evidence from the court clerk, so that you will be prepared to present your evidence according to how the court wishes you to.

Even if there are no written rules of evidence, there are a couple of rules that you should be aware of. The first is *hearsay*. You cannot say things like "so and so told me this," unless "so and so" is there to refute it. In short, try to avoid telling the court that someone who is not present told you this or that. This rule also applies to any of your witnesses. They cannot testify as to what someone else said, unless that person is available to refute it. In fact, if you or your witnesses start to testify about what someone else said, you will most likely hear an objection from the other side, which will be sustained by the judge.

The second rule of evidence you should concern yourself with is the *best evidence rule*. If you have any original documents, you should present them to the court. Copies won't do unless the originals are lost, damaged, or destroyed. Again, if you have the originals, produce them for the judge and give copies to everyone else.

There may be a host of other rules of evidence you may be faced with, but again, you should get copies of any court rules and learn them as best you can before the trial.

Let's move on to making your case.

Begin to Make Your Case

Now that both sides have told the judge their side of the story, it's your turn to begin the proof stage of the trial. This is your chance to present all of the proof that backs up your story. You may ask the judge if you can take the stand, or he may invite you to do so. You may be required to take an oath. Someone will ask you, "Do you solemnly swear or affirm to tell the truth, the whole truth, and nothing but the truth?" or something to that effect. Don't be cute and say, "I don't swear." Just say "I do," and be ready to move on.

Tell your side of the story in more detail. State all of the facts as clearly as you can. If you have the signed agreement or any other documents, pull them out, along with all of the copies. Hand the judge the original agreement and make a copy available to the other side, while keeping a copy of the original with you for reference. Don't read the contract to the judge unless asked to do so. He will read the document in his own time. If the judge is reading the contract, keep your mouth shut until he says to proceed. Then proceed to tell the judge how you played the gig at the agreed-upon date and for the agreed-upon amount of time. Explain how you were not paid the proper amount, and the reason the club owner gave you for not paying even though you asked several times. Then state how much money you're owed. You may also state any incidental damages you may be seeking, such as court costs, lost wages for bringing this suit, or whatever else you are seeking. Don't leave anything out, but don't ramble on.

Once you are done with your side of the story, it's time for the other side to ask you questions. This is known as *cross-exam*. But before we move on to that, let's discuss direct exam a little further.

Direct Exam

If you are the only person who will testify, your statements made in making your case will be your *direct exam*, and then you will be subjected to the other side's cross-exam. Then, you get to ask questions of your witnesses. You are not allowed to ask any leading questions. You are limited to questions whereby you can ask who, what, when, and where. In some cases you can ask why, but refrain from asking people for their opinions. Sometimes the court will allow certain opinions, but only if the person is qualified as an expert. And you must be able to show that he is an expert, so you need to ask him questions about his qualifications. If the court rules that he's an expert, you can ask for his opinion.

You are never allowed to ask questions like, "Isn't it true that you did this?" Those are leading questions and are strictly forbidden except on cross-examination. Of course, if you are the main witness to your case, which is likely, you have the absolute right to get up on the witness stand and tell your side of the story. Just make sure that you tell your *entire* story. If there are other witnesses that you need to call to back it up, make sure that you ask them every single question that is important, because you may not be allowed to get them up on the stand again.

While you or your other witnesses are on the stand, that's the time to introduce any evidence you may have, in the form of documents such as invoices, contracts, letters, tape recordings, pictures, etc. If you have a receipt, a contract, a letter, or something that was given or sent to you, tell the judge what the document is, how you got it, and the gist of what it says. Again, do not read the document without permission to do so from the judge. Make sure to have a copy to hand to the judge and a copy for the other side to read, and then ask for the judge to read it. Judges prefer to look at evidence themselves. The document that is the subject of your testimony or your witnesses' testimony is really what the judge is interested in, not necessarily what you have to say about it.

If you have pictures, sound recordings, or the like, make sure that you authenticate them by having the person who took the picture or made the sound recording testify that he did so, how and when, and of what. Without proper verification, the evidence may not be allowed. So if you weren't the one who took the pictures or made a recording of a conversation, you'd better produce the person who did.

Caveat: Don't get caught violating federal wiretap laws. If you are a party to a conversation, you can record it. But you cannot record a conversation that you were not a party to. However, you can bring in your answering machine if the other party left any messages on it.

Finally, make sure that you cover every issue, including who you are suing, why you are suing them, your relationship with them, and how the relationship came about, and the amount of damages you're seeking. The court will rule on all of your requests, so it doesn't hurt to ask for any relief you are seeking, especially if you have asked for it in your original complaint. If yours is a contract case, you also want to show the judge what you and the other side agreed to do, what you agreed not to do, or both. Immediately after you and your witnesses have testified, the other side gets to ask questions. This is what called cross-examination.

Cross-Examination

This is where the other side gets to ask questions of you or your other witnesses. Once you have testified, the other side has the absolute right to ask you any questions he wants, as long as they're relevant to the case at hand.

Furthermore, the other side may ask you or your witnesses leading questions. He can ask, "Isn't it true that you did this?" or "Isn't it true that you said that?" He can also ask questions that must be answered with a "yes" or "no." A good cross-examiner will ask questions like this so that the witnesses can't explain themselves before the next question is asked. This is a classic trick that is used to paint a witness into a corner. However, you may ask the judge for permission to explain the "yes or no" answer, especially if you or your witness is cut off by the cross-examiner. This way, the whole truth can come out, not just the part the other side wants the court to hear. Of course, this works both ways. When you get your chance to cross-examine the other side, you can ask leading questions and solicit "yes or no" answers. After you or your witnesses have been cross-examined, this is your chance to clarify any answers that may have caused confusion. It's also your chance to refute, soften, or clarify any statements that were made during cross-exam. This is called redirect.

Redirect

Redirect is where you get your witness to qualify some statement that was made previously. You may only ask him questions about what was asked in cross-exam. If the other side makes your witness look bad by trapping him in some logic trick or getting him to say something he didn't really want to say, you may ask him to qualify his statement so that he doesn't look so bad. You may have to ask your witness to qualify his answer to a "yes or no" question by asking what he meant by that yes/no answer and what other extenuating circumstances there may have been. This is your last chance to get the whole truth known, so make sure that you clarify any questions that may have come up.

Recross

This is where the other side can ask any questions that may clarify what was asked during the redirect exam. He may not ask any questions that fall outside of the scope of redirect. You cannot bring up some issue that you may have forgot to ask during cross-exam, so make sure that you produce all the evidence you can during your testimony and direct exam, or during your cross-exam of the other party or his witnesses.

Once all of this direct, cross, redirect, and recross exam is over, your part of proof in the case is over.

The Plaintiff Rests

Once all of your witnesses have testified and you have put in all of your proof, it's time to tell the judge that the plaintiff rests. In other words, you have nothing left to do but make your closing argument or to cross-exam if the other side calls any witnesses. More often than not, if there is a lawyer present on the other side, he will move to dismiss the case on the grounds that you have not proven it as a matter of law. If you feel that you have messed up your case or were not allowed to present all of your evidence, you can always ask the court for a voluntary non-suit before the defendant makes a motion to dismiss.

Voluntary Non-Suit

At any time before the judge or jury renders a verdict, you may take a voluntary non-suit without prejudice. In other words, if it looks like you are not presenting your case well, one of your witnesses doesn't show up, there is some problem with your evidence, the judge rules against an issue of evidence that is crucial to your case, or it just feels like you are going lose your case, you can dismiss it. But you must remember to dismiss *without prejudice*. This just means that you will have the opportunity to try your case again, and the first trial is treated like it never happened. You get to start over without jeopardizing any of your rights. However, if your case is dismissed *with* prejudice, you cannot file it again, and you are forever barred from asserting the rights that arose out of that cause of action.

Once you have rested your case and you have won any motion to dismiss, it's the other side's turn to present his case, call his witnesses, and give his evidence.

Defendant's Case

Unfortunately, now comes the time where the defendant gets to call witnesses and provide direct proof. But the good news is that you get to cross-examine the other side and his witnesses. He can also redirect his witnesses and you can recross his witnesses, just like he did with your case.

If the party you are suing or his witnesses say something that you don't agree with during his testimony, don't argue with him. Be patient and keep your mouth shut. Never try to argue with the other side, because you *cannot* make any more statements about the case. Your turn to testify is up, and you may only ask questions until you get to make your closing argument.

After the defense rests, you may ask the judge if you can recall another witness or take the stand, but only to clarify something that was brought into evidence by the other side. You cannot reopen your case and bring up any other witnesses, or even try to argue any other issues. If you didn't get it right the first time around, you may be out of luck. But remember, if the other side's motion to dismiss was overruled, and you still feel like you could lose based upon the way the court proceedings are going, you can always take a voluntary non-suit and start the whole process over.

If you've made your case and you stand a good chance of winning based upon all of the evidence that was presented, now you get to make your summation of the facts and evidence in the form of a closing argument.

Closing Argument

Once all of the witnesses have testified for the other side, it is your turn to make your *closing argument*. Try to keep it very brief. The judge has already seen all of the evidence and heard all the testimony, so just restating it won't help much. Instead, you really want to get across what the judge should glean from that evidence and testimony.

For instance, in a breach of contract case for non-payment of a gig by a club, you would want to say something like this:

"Your honor, the evidence has shown that the parties had entered into a contract, as evidenced by the contract that was submitted into evidence [or by the statements of the parties and their witnesses]. The evidence further shows that the defendant failed to pay me the amount of [x] dollars. Therefore, I am seeking [x] dollars, plus court costs."

Of course, if you are seeking lost wages or any other damages that stem from the club's breach of contract, you should ask for them. Also, if you have suffered any ancillary damages, such as if you played that gig for that club even though you were offered a much bigger gig for more money somewhere else, you could have a claim for more money. (For more information, see Chapter 12, "General Principles of Contracts.")

After you make your closing argument, the other side makes his closing argument and then the judge will rule. He may take the matter under advisement and come back to your case at a later date. You can always take a non-suit before the judge rules. However, once the judge rules, you have to live with the decision or exercise your right to appeal. But before I discuss appeals, take a look at Rule 11 sanctions.

Rule 11 Sanctions

There is a very important rule of civil procedure that you must always take into consideration. You hear about frivolous lawsuits all the time, and people often think that a lawsuit should have never been brought in the first place. But there is actually a rule in the civil rules of procedure that is designed to prevent such lawsuits. Someone who has been the victim of a frivolous lawsuit can ask the court to make the plaintiff pay extra damages for bringing the suit. Under the Federal Rules of Procedure, this is known as Rule 11, and it's also included in most state rules of procedure. But as long as there's even a small chance that the plaintiff can win or the suit can change the law in some way, the court will be reluctant to impose any penalties. It's up to the judge to decide what you are entitled to.

But what can you do if you lose your case? What can the other side do if he loses? Each side has the right to appeal.

The Right to Appeal

If you lose your case, do *not* argue or say anything else about it once the judge makes a decision. Even if you win but don't get exactly what you were asking for, don't make any further statements to the court. It's neither the time nor the place to express your feelings. Arguing with the judge after the case is over is very disrespectful, and you could be held in contempt of court. The last thing the judge wants to hear is that he has made the wrong decision. Just collect your stuff and leave quietly without causing a scene. You will get your chance to fix the situation, if it can be fixed.

Each side has the right to appeal any case. Furthermore, in many states, if you appeal a case in small claims court to a higher court, it will treat the case as if it were never tried in the first place. Basically, you will have to start the case all over again, but this time in a higher court. You will definitely want to hire a lawyer at this level, because the rules of evidence and rules of procedure will be strictly adhered to. Trying to represent yourself at this level can be very difficult, if not outright foolish. Remember the old adage: "He who represents himself in court has a fool for a client."

Unfortunately, if you win (even by default) and the other side appeals, you are going to quickly run into the principle of diminishing returns. Trials at a higher level take longer, are much more involved, and thus are much more expensive. Furthermore, since these courts are often extremely busy and can hear only a couple of trials a day at most, it can be a very long time before you get your day in court just to retry your case.

Collecting Your Judgment

Let's assume that you've won your case and are awarded the full amount of damages. Unfortunately, all the court has given you is an empty bag, and it's your responsibility to fill it up.

You have a number of ways to get your money. But before you do, you have to wait until the time to appeal has passed. In some cases, this could be 10 days, 14 days, or up to a month. Check with the court clerk or read the rules of the court to ascertain this time period. Once the time to appeal is up, you can try to collect your money. Of course, you can always take your judgment to an outside collection agent. For a fee, he will try to collect your judgment. But you may not end up with much. You can try to collect the money yourself, but this is not as easy as you might think. There are a lot of steps you need to take that will cost you more time and money.

The main ways to collect your money are to file a garnishment or an attachment, or to levy the assets of the defendant.

If you have the bank account number of the person or company you have a judgment against, you can file an *attachment*. The sheriff or some other agency of the court will send a notice to the bank, and he will take the money out of that account and send it to the court. The court will hold it for a time and then release it to you.

You can also send the sheriff or other agent of the court to go out and literally take the personal property of the defendant. He'll actually go to the defendant's residence or place of business and take his property to be sold at auction. After it's been sold and the required time has passed, you will get your money.

If you are suing a club and you know that it is taking money at the door, you can ask the sheriff to go garnish that money when the owner has it in his hands. The sheriff will show up and take the money, and you will get paid. However, if the door money is for the band that is playing that night, you can't have it. But you can ask the sheriff to take any money from the cash registers and then deposit that with the court for you to collect later.

Unfortunately, some defendants are pretty crafty, and they know that all they have to do is file an affidavit that they are indigent, or claim an exemption for their personal property. If they do that, the sheriff or court agent can't take any personal property over a certain amount that's exempt from levy or attachment.

If that happens, you can file a garnishment on the wages of a defendant if he has a job working for someone else. The employer of the defendant is required to take out the money that you are owed from his paycheck each payday. This may take a while because you're limited to a certain percentage of his income until the debt is paid in full. If you take this avenue, make sure to keep up with it, because in many cases the employee will just quit and go work somewhere else to avoid having to pay you any money.

If you want to know how a defendant is going to pay a judgment, or if you want to find out what assets a person has, you can file *postjudgment discovery*. This will allow you to ask the defendant written questions (or in some cases oral questions) about where his money is and what property he owns, so that you will know what you can attach or levy upon. If the defendant refuses to comply with your discovery, you can file a motion to compel, which will force that defendant to comply. If he fails to do so, the court can issue an attachment that will order the court agency, such as the sheriff's office, to bring the defendant to court to answer your questions so that you can get your money. If the defendant refuses to answer your questions, he can be jailed for contempt of court until he complies.

But again, the defendant may know all about this process, and may file a *motion to slow pay*. If this motion is granted, the defendant will be allowed to make payments on the debt until it is paid in full. Since we don't have debtors' prison in this country, the courts are pretty lenient and will let debtors make payments in a reasonable manner. But it's up to you to keep up with this whole process. You can spend a whole lot of your precious time trying to collect very little money, and this brings us to the next point.

Just Because You Go to Court, Don't Expect Justice

Our legal system is far from perfect, and I would be doing any potential litigants a disservice if I didn't tell them how arbitrary a court hearing can be. There are many issues involved in a court's final decision. Sometimes the court may decide an issue purely based on the facts and the law. However, sometimes matters are decided on pure politics, or whether the judge likes you better than the other side. I've seen many things that make no sense, such as a judge falling asleep on the bench during testimony, and a judge deciding for a party just because he used to be in private practice with its attorney. So be ready for anything.

But if you've been polite and made your case clearly, you should prevail. If you don't win at the lower level, you can appeal. Just remember the old adage: "How much justice can you afford?"

What to Do If You Are Being Sued

If you are being sued, all of the same rules apply. However, you're the one who will be served with the complaint or the summons. You will have to appear in court, or you will get a default judgment against you. Furthermore, if you actually owe the money or are found liable, you will have to pay the judgment. But you can file a motion to pay slowly, or file an affidavit that you are indigent and can't pay. There are a number of defenses at your disposal, but the best defense is to pay your bills in the first place and don't do anything that would make you a party to a lawsuit.

What to Do If You Just Can't Pay Your Bills

You may get so far behind on your bills that you can never pay off all of your debt. You should hire a credit counseling company that will negotiate on your behalf, so that you can forego a lot of interest payments that could keep you paying for many, many years to come. But be very careful. There are a lot of disreputable companies playing this game. Check with the Better Business Bureau to make sure you are dealing with a solid company that can really save you a lot of money in the long run.

The only other option if you can't pay your bills is to file bankruptcy. Of course, this option is available to anyone you have a judgment against, so it works both ways. If you file bankruptcy, your creditors will never get their money, so most creditors would rather work with you than simply lose all of their money. Even if you can renegotiate your debt and your payments, sometimes you still may not be able to keep up and will be forced to file bankruptcy. You will have to rebuild your life and your credit, so consider this your last resort.

Since bankruptcy is such a complicated area of the law, don't try to do this by yourself. Find an attorney who does this all the time, and he will tell you exactly what you have to do.

Summary

As you can see, going to court is a huge hassle. You can spend a lot of time trying to collect a little money. Of course, if you are looking for a large amount of money, you should get an attorney. Unfortunately, your attorney will get quite a bit of the money you are owed. However, if you have a contract that states that you get reasonable attorney's fees if the other party breaches, you definitely will come out ahead. (See Chapter 12.)

More often than not, nobody really wins when they go to court. If you go the arbitration or mediation route, you may still incur costs or find yourself with some unsatisfactory solution. So, sometimes you'll just have to chalk up your losses to experience. You now know that experience costs money, so try not to buy too much of it.

CHAPTER 17

Organizations

"Strength in numbers...."

There are a number of organizations you may want to consider joining. Most of these organizations offer a wealth of benefits, including health insurance, pension plans, money collection, and a number of other vital functions. They also offer seminars, workshops, and events where you can network, catch up on changes in the industry, and a whole lot more. These organizations are specifically designed for the benefit of their members, and strength in numbers helps them accomplish their goals. When you join a large group of like-minded people with the same interests, you have a much louder voice in today's ever-evolving music business.

These organizations are an excellent place to meet people, network, gather invaluable information, look for work, etc. Use as many of an organization's resources as you can. Attend its functions and get to know the members, because they're a great source of information, networking contacts, and much more.

There are so many organizations that I couldn't possibly name them all in this book. Your city, region, or state may have several organizations that will be of interest to you. To that end, I will cover only the major organizations, what they do, how to join, and how much membership costs.

Before you decide to join an organization, feel free to contact it and perhaps even schedule a meeting. Meet with as many people as you can in these organizations, and ask as many questions as you need. Remember that the more information you have, the better your chances of joining the right organization and getting the most out of your membership.

American Federation of Musicians (AFM)

The American Federation of Musicians was founded in 1986, in conjunction with the American Federation of Labor Unions, to protect the rights of its members. It is involved with lobbying for legislation to benefit musicians all over the United States and Canada.

The AFM offers a host of services and benefits. It has formed Mutual Aid Societies to provide members with loans, financial assistance during illness or extended unemployment, and death benefits. It assists in negotiating fair agreements, and in securing benefits such as health care insurance and pensions. It also protects the owners of musical compositions.

AFM
New York Headquarters
1501 Broadway
Suite 600
New York, NY 10036
Phone: (212) 869-1330
Fax: (212) 764-6134

Legislative Office
1717 K Street NW
Suite 500
Washington, DC 20036
Phone: (202) 463-0772
Fax: (202) 466-9009

West Coast Office
3550 Wilshire Boulevard
Suite 1900
Los Angeles, CA 90010
Phone: (213) 251-4510
Fax: (213) 251-4520

American Federation of Radio and Television Artists (AFTRA)

AFTRA represents actors, other professional performers, and broadcasters in television, radio, sound recordings, and non-broadcast/industrial programming. It also represents newer technologies, such as gaming voiceovers, interactive programming, and CD-ROMs. Its members are seen or heard on television, radio, and sound recordings, and include actors, announcers, news broadcasters, singers (including royalty artists and background singers), dancers, sportscasters, disc jockeys, talk show hosts, and others. AFTRA also enforces and negotiates collective bargaining agreements, which are drawn to establish fair levels of compensation for its members.

To join, you must have performed or intend to perform within AFTRA's jurisdiction. New members must pay a one-time initiation fee, plus dues that cover the first dues period. The current standard initiation fee is $1,200.00. The minimum dues for the first dues period are $58. After joining, a member's dues are based on his earnings within AFTRA's jurisdiction during the prior year.

AFTRA National Headquarters
260 Madison Avenue
7th Floor
New York, NY 10016-2402
Phone: (212) 532-0800
Fax: (212) 532-2242
info@aftra.com

Los Angeles Local
5757 Wilshire Boulevard
9th Floor
Los Angeles, CA 90036-3689
Phone: (323) 634-8100
Fax: (323) 634-8194
info@aftra.com

Screen Actors Guild (SAG)

The Screen Actors Guild (SAG) is a labor union that was founded in 1933 to protect performers. It is affiliated with a very powerful union organization, the

American Federation of Labor–Congress of Industrial Organizations (AFL-CIO), through the Associated Actors and Artists of America.

SAG, like many other unions, deals with working conditions and wages for member performers, as well as benefits such as health insurance and retirement. It offers workshops and seminars on different issues of concern to screen actors. It also enforces and negotiates collective bargaining agreements, which are drawn to establish fair levels of compensation for its members.

To join SAG, you must have worked at least one day as a principal performer on any SAG-authorized project produced by a company affiliated with SAG. You should have been engaged in a weekly, three-day, or daily contract with the production company, and should have been paid the appropriate union wage. You can also join if you were a background performer who worked on a project with an affiliated production company for a minimum of three days, consecutive or not.

Finally, you may join if you're already a member of the American Federation of Television and Radio Artists (AFTRA), the Alliance of Canadian Television and Radio Artists (ACTRA), the Actors Equity, the American Guild of Musical Artists (AGMA), or the American Guild of Variety Artists (AGVA) for at least one year, and you've worked as a principal performer under the jurisdiction of one of these unions.

The fees for joining are $1,360.00.

Hollywood SAG
5757 Wilshire Boulevard
Los Angeles, CA 90036-3600
Main switchboard: (323) 954-1600
saginfo@sag.org

New York SAG
360 Madison Avenue, 12th Floor
New York, New York 10017
(212) 944-1030
saginfo@sag.org

Academy of Country Music (ACM)

The Academy of Country Music is dedicated to the promotion and advancement of country music throughout the entire world. It has been very active in lobbying for the protection of artists and songwriters, and their work. It is an excellent source for information about the country music industry, including but not limited to country music artists, music publishers, record labels, booking agents, radio stations, venues, and nightclubs that are affiliated with the country music industry. As a member, you receive a subscription to a bimonthly newsletter that gives updated information on personnel changes in the industry, which is very valuable considering the turnover in this difficult business. The newsletter also covers new artists, new music, and related events or activities.

To join as a professional member, you must derive a significant amount of your income directly from country music. You must have two references from current ACM members, and you will be classified as one of the following: Affiliated Artist/Entertainer, Composer,

Club Operator/Employee, On-Air Personality, **Manager**, TV/Motion Pictures, Music Publisher, Publicity/Public Relations, Record Company, Musician, Band Leader/ Instrumentalist, or Publications Person.

Annual membership is $60.00.

Academy of Country Music
4100 West Alameda Avenue
Suite 208
Burbank, CA 91505-4151
Phone: (818) 842-8400
Fax: (818) 842-8535
membership@acmcountry.com
www.acmcountry.com

American Guild of Musical Artists

The American Guild of Music Artists is the labor organization that represents creators and performers of operatic music, choral music, and dance. It is affiliated with the AFL-CIO and represents its members in collective bargaining agreements to protect their rights. It has a number of benefits, including notice of auditions.

For costs to join, go to www.musicalartists.org.

American Guild of Musical Arts
14300 Broadway
14th Floor
New York, NY 10018

American Society of Composers, Authors, and Publishers (ASCAP)

Composers, writers, and publishers of music founded ASCAP in 1914, and to this day, it is the only U.S. performing rights organization with a board of directors elected by and derived from its membership. When you are a member of ASCAP, you are a part owner of the organization and have an voice equal to all of the other members.

ASCAP spends a great deal of time lobbying for the rights of its members throughout the world, and licenses and distributes royalties for the non-dramatic public performances of its members' copyrighted works. It can be a great ally when you're trying to get paid for your work. ASCAP also allows for your writer's membership to pass on to your heirs, so that you know they'll be paid long after you are gone.

ASCAP offers a wealth of benefits, including affordable group rates on health and instrument insurance, a credit union, discounts on many tools of the trade such as musical equipment, travel discounts, and a whole lot more. It also offers a number of workshops, showcases, events, etc.

You may join as a writer, publisher, or both. To join as a writer, any of the following must be true: You have written or co-written a song or musical composition that has been published and is available for sale or rental; your work must have been performed in any electronic or audiovisual medium, such as radio, television, film, cable (including cable access), the Internet, etc.; your work must have been performed publicly in any venue that's licensed by ASCAP, such as live concerts, colleges or universities, or clubs (this could even be your local bar, if its paying ASCAP licensing fees); or your work is on a commercially recorded CD, album, tape, etc.

To join as a publisher, you must have a publishing company with a unique name. You will submit a list of five names for approval. You must also have published any of the things mentioned in the previous paragraph.

Please contact ASCAP for more information on application costs. However, don't expect it to get you a writer's deal, because that's not what the organization is about.

ASCAP New York
One Lincoln Plaza
New York, NY 10023
Phone: (212) 621-6000
Fax: (212) 724-9064

ASCAP Los Angeles
7920 W. Sunset Boulevard, Third Floor
Los Angeles, CA 90046
Phone: (323) 883-1000
Fax: (323) 883-1049

ASCAP London
8 Cork Street
London W1X1PB
Phone: 011-44-207-439-0909
Fax: 011-44-207-434-0073

ASCAP Nashville
Two Music Square West
Nashville, TN 37203
Phone: (615) 742-5000
Fax: (615) 742-5020

ASCAP Miami
420 Lincoln Road/Suite 385
Miami Beach, FL 33139
Phone: (305) 673-3446
Fax: (305) 673-2446

ASCAP Chicago
1608 N. Milwaukee Avenue
Suite 1007
Chicago, IL 60647
Phone: (773) 394-4286
Fax: (773) 394-5639

ASCAP Atlanta
PMB 400
541 Tenth Street NW
Atlanta, GA 30318
Phone: (404) 351-1224
Fax: (404) 351-1252

Broadcast Music International (BMI)

BMI, founded in 1940, is a nonprofit organization dedicated to collecting license fees on behalf of the American creators it represents, as well as creators of musical works from around the world who have chosen BMI for representation in the United States. BMI collects license fees for the public performances of the works in its catalogue on radio, broadcast and cable television, the Internet, and live and recorded performances by all other users of music. BMI then distributes royalties to the writers, composers, and copyright holders it represents.

BMI also does a great deal of lobbying to protect the rights of its members, as well as offering a number of benefits such as workshops, events, and activities. It also offers a number of other benefits you will find useful in your music career.

The BMI Foundation (www.bmifoundation.org) was set up to promote the interests of up-and-coming composers. It's dedicated to encouraging the creation, performance, and study of music through awards, scholarships, internships, grants, and commissions.

You may join BMI as a writer or publisher if you have a commercially recorded CD, your music has been played on radio or television, etc. For costs of membership and other information, please check with BMI at www.bmi.com. Just don't expect it to get you a writer's deal.

New York
320 West 57th Street
New York, NY 10019-3790
(212) 586-2000

Nashville
10 Music Square East
Nashville, TN 37203-4399
(615) 401-2000

Los Angeles
8730 Sunset Boulevard
3rd Floor West
West Hollywood, CA 90069-2211
(310) 659-9109

London
84 Harley House
Marylebone Road
London NW1 5HN, England
011-0044 207486 2036

Miami
5201 Blue Lagoon Drive
Suite 310
Miami, FL 33126
(305) 266-3636

Atlanta
P.O. Box 19199
Atlanta, GA 31126
(404) 261-5151

Country Music Association (CMA)

Founded in 1958, the CMA was the first association that focused on a particular type of music. Membership is available to any person or company that works in the country music industry. It has memberships for performers, publishers, record labels, managers, etc. CMA also publishes a directory with contact information for artist managers, publicists, record labels, talent agents, country radio stations, and much more.

The CMA hosts the CMA Awards and also presents Fan Fair, one of the most popular events among country music fans. They can come to Nashville and actually meet the artists who are such a big part of their lives. It's a great promotional tool for the record companies and artists alike.

The annual dues for an individual are $50.00. Organization memberships are offered in a range of costs and benefits, depending on how much your organization would like to spend. For more information on membership, write to membership@CMAworld.com.

CMA Headquarters
One Music Circle South
Nashville, Tennessee 37203
Phone: (615) 244 2840
Fax: (615) 726-0314

Dramatists Guild of America

The Dramatists Guild of America is the only professional association in the country for playwrights, composers, and lyricists. Membership is open to all dramatic writers, regardless of their production history. The organization offers a host of services, such as a Dramatists Guild credit card, free or discounted theater tickets to certain New York productions, national hotel and travel discounts, and much more.

One of the best services it offers is having its business and legal affairs department review your contracts and give you detailed information on contract issues and how to negotiate them. It can also provide you with standard contracts for that industry to use as a boilerplate. Also, members may receive advice on many theater-related matters, such as options, commissions, copyright, producers, publishers, agents, and attorney referrals.

Your membership includes a subscription to its bimonthly journal *The Dramatist*, a newsletter, and most importantly, a resource directory with information about conferences and festivals, contests, producers, publishers, and theaters, as well as agents, attorneys, colonies and residences, emergency funds, fellowships and grants, membership and service organizations, and workshops.

The cost of membership depends on the level for which you want to apply. For more information, contact the Dramatists Guild.

Dramatists Guild of America, Inc.
1501 Broadway, Suite 701
New York, NY 10036
Phone: 212-398-9366
Fax: 212-944-0240
Igor@Dramaguild.com

Gospel Music Association (GMA)

The Gospel Music Association was founded in 1964 to support, encourage, and promote the development of all forms of gospel music. It's a place where artists, industry leaders, retail stores, radio stations, concert promoters, and local churches can coordinate their efforts to benefit the industry as a whole.

The GMA is in charge of the Gospel Music Hall of Fame, which is the only place completely dedicated to recognizing the contributions of its members and other people in all forms of gospel music. The Research Library and Archives is the largest collection of gospel music recordings, periodicals, research materials, and memorabilia in existence today. The GMA also hosts the Dove Awards, which honors outstanding achievement and excellence in contemporary Christian and gospel music. The awards honor a wide variety of musical styles within the genre of Christian music.

It also offers Gospel Music Week every year, which provides educational seminars and concert showcases for music professionals in various areas of the Christian music industry. It also provides a number of other seminars, activities, and publications for the benefit of its members.

The GMA offers three types of memberships: Professional membership, which costs $85.00, is for those who make a portion of their living from gospel music; Associate membership, which costs $60.00, is for supporters of gospel music and those whose involvement in the industry does not provide them with a source of income; and College Student membership, which costs $25.00, is for full-time college students who do not make any income from gospel music.

Gospel Music Association
1205 Division Street
Nashville, TN 37203
Phone: 615-242-0303
Fax: 615-254-9755
info@gospelmusic.org
www.gospelmusic.org

Harry Fox Agency

The Harry Fox Agency was founded in 1927 as a musical copyright information and licensing agency focusing on mechanical use of copyrighted music. It licenses, collects, and distributes mechanical royalties on behalf of musical copyright owners. Mechanical licensing is the licensing and administration of copyrighted musical works for use on CDs, tapes, records, and other mechanical or digital means of reproducing sound recordings, including downloads and streaming audio. In other words, if you want to use a cover song on one of your records, you must pay a mechanical license to the owner of the copyright.

Joining Harry Fox is also a very cost-efficient way to monitor international mechanical royalties through its many affiliates around the world.

www.harryfox.com

International Association of Fairs and Expositions (IAFE)

The International Association of Fairs and Expositions (IAFE) was formed in 1885 from a consortium of six different fairs. Now it's a voluntary, nonprofit corporation that organizes state, district, and county agricultural fairs. It also deals with state and provincial associations of fairs, expositions, related associations or corporations, and individuals who are interested in the improvement of fairs and related fields.

This can be a great place to find information about fairs and expositions so that you can obtain gigs and gain exposure for your act.

IAFE
3043 E. Cairo
Springfield, MO 65802
Phone: 417-862-5771
Toll-free: 1-800-516-0313
iafe@fairsandexpos.com
www.fairsandexpos.com

Information Entertainment Buyers Association (IEBA)

The International Entertainment Buyers Association is a nonprofit organization made up of professionals in the entertainment industry who represent all types of music. It conducts a yearly seminar that focuses on current issues in the music business. Membership is open to entertainers, talent buyers and sellers, artists, managers, agents, and venue managers, and also to related services, such as print and television media personnel, advertising, publicity/PR, equipment, lighting and sound, and staging or production companies. A number of membership levels are available.

International Association of Entertainment Buyers
P.O. Box 128376
Nashville, TN 37212
Info@ieba.org
www.ieba.org

International Fan Club Organization (IFCO)

The International Fan Club Organization was founded in 1967 as a regulatory body, a clearinghouse for fan clubs, and a consumer advocate for fans. It started out in country music but has now expanded to all genres of music, as well as athletes, actors, etc.

IFCO can provide contact information on artists' fan clubs. You may want to check out how it can help you with your own fan club.

IFCO
www.ifco.org

Nashville Songwriters Association (NSAI)

The Nashville Songwriters Association is a not-for-profit company that was formed in 1967 to serve the needs and protect the rights of amateur and professional songwriters in all types of music. It does a great deal of lobbying on behalf of its members and other songwriters throughout the world. It also offers a number of benefits, including discounts with different vendors, writers' rooms, song evaluation services, workshops, songwriter showcases, on line workshops, and much more. It hosts the Annual Tin Pan South songwriters' festival, the Song Cruise, song camps, and many other festivals. It's there to help you learn about the art and business of songwriting. You can network with a vast array of songwriters and other music industry professionals.

To become an active member, you must have at least one song assigned to a music publisher and $100.00 to spare. To become an associate member, you must be a songwriter or anyone who wants to support songwriters, and the cost of membership is also $100.00. If you are a full-time college student carrying at least 12 hours a week, or a student attending an accredited high school, you may join for $80.00.

NSAI
1701 West End Avenue
Third Floor
Nashville, TN 37203
Phone: (615)-256-3354
Toll free: (800)-321-6008
Fax: (615)-256-0034
nsai@nashvillesongwriters.com
www.nashvillesongwriters.com

National Academy of Recording Arts and Sciences (NARAS)

NARAS is composed of industry professionals, and is the only peer-based organization that was formed to celebrate the artistic achievement of not only talented musicians and singers, but also the all-important behind-the-scenes contributors such as producers and engineers. It brings us the Grammy Awards, which recognizes achievements, technical proficiency, and excellence in the recording industry without regard to chart positions or album sales.

NARAS has three levels of membership. Voting membership is for professionals with a certain number of credits on commercially released tracks. Associate membership is for those who work in the related industry positions but do not have enough credits. Affiliate membership is for educators, students, record merchants, or anyone else who wishes to support the academy.

The Recording Academy
3402 Pico Boulevard
Santa Monica, CA 90405
Phone: (310) 392-3777
Fax: (310) 399-3090

Atlanta Chapter
3290 Northside Parkway, Suite 280
Atlanta, GA 30327
Phone: (404) 816-1380
Fax: (404) 816-1390
atlanta@grammy.com

Chicago Chapter
224 S. Michigan Avenue, Suite 250
Chicago, IL 60604
Phone: (312) 786-1121
Fax: (312) 786-1934
chicago@grammy.com

Florida Chapter
311 Lincoln Road, Suite 301
Miami Beach, FL 33139
Phone: (305) 672-4060
Fax: (305) 672-2076
florida@grammy.com

Los Angeles Chapter
3402 Pico Boulevard
Santa Monica, CA 90405
Phone: (310) 392-3777
Fax: (310) 392-2306
losangeles@grammy.com

National Association for Campus Activities (NACA)

The National Association for Campus Activities is a
not-for-profit association composed of colleges and
universities, talent firms and artist/performers, student
programmers, and professional campus activities staff.
NACA is a center for informational services and promotes a variety of college and university activities, from
leadership development to student programming.

NACA
13 Harbison Way
Columbia, SC 29212-3401
www.naca.org

Recording Industry Association of America (RIAA)

The RIAA is the trade organization for the recording industry in the United States. It protects the intellectual property rights of its members throughout the world, as well as the First Amendment right to free speech and press for artists. It also researches technical issues related to the music industry, and it monitors the consumer industry, state and federal laws, and legislation regarding the recording industry.

The RIAA is the body that certifies the Gold, Platinum, Multi-Platinum, and Diamond sales awards. Its members create, manufacture, or distribute about 90% of the sound recordings produced and sold in the United States. It's also extremely active in fighting the widespread music piracy in today's digital world.

www.riaa.org

Society of Composers and Lyricists (SCL)

The SCL provides information for those interested in writing music for film or television. It can help writers with issues such as the financial, technical, and contract matters they may encounter when trying to obtain deals for film and television. It offers a variety of forums and an annual conference to educate its members, and it strives to improve working conditions by actively working with filmmakers and television producers.

It has several membership opportunities for film composers, television composers, songwriters/lyricists, and composers of music for computer games. It also offers associate memberships if you do not qualify for full membership, you are a student, or you are an agent, manager, music executive, or industry professional. An associate membership allows you to join without any voting rights. For more information on prices for membership, go to www.filmscore.com.

The Society of Composers and Lyrics
400 S. Beverly Drive,
Suite 213
Beverly Hills, CA 90212
Phone: (310)-281-2812
Fax: (310)-284-4861
administrator@filmscore.org

Society of European Stage Authors and Composers (SESAC)

SESAC was founded in 1930, making it the second-oldest performing rights organization in the United States. SESAC's catalogue was once limited to European and gospel music, but has since diversified to include some of today's most popular music, including dance hits, rock classics, Latino music, jazz, country, and contemporary Christian music. It offers many of the same services as ASCAP and BMI, but takes pride in the fact that it's interested in quality rather than quantity.

SESAC is considered to be the smallest of the big three licensing organizations, but that means you may get more personal attention. You can join as a writer, publisher, or both. For more information, contact SESAC.

SESAC Headquarters
55 Music Square East
Nashville, TN 37203
Phone: (615) 320-0055
Fax: (615) 329-9627

SESAC
152 West 57th Street
57th Floor
New York, NY 10019
Phone: (212) 586-3450
Fax: (212) 489-5699

SESAC
501 Santa Monica Boulevard
Suite 450
Santa Monica, CA 90401-2430
Phone: (310) 393-9671
Fax: (310) 393-6497

SESAC International
6 Kendrick Place
London W1H 7Qx
England
www.sesac.com

Songwriters Guild of America (SGA)

Organized in 1931, the SGA is the nation's oldest and
largest songwriters' organization, giving its members
vital information and programs to further their careers
and understanding of the music industry.

Administrative/Executive Office
(201) 867-7603
SongwritersNJ@aol.com

Los Angeles Office
(323) 462-1108
LASGA@aol.com

Nashville Office
(605) 329-2623
SGAN@aol.com

New York Office
(212) 768-7902
SongNews@aol.com

Performing Rights Societies

I have often been asked, "Which licensing organization is the best to join: ASCAP, BMI, or SESAC?" That depends on a number of factors. In the past, each organization paid its members different amounts for their performances. This was made evident when a song was co-written by members of different licensing organizations, and each writer/publisher was paid a different amount. Sometimes one organization paid more than the other, and sometimes it was the other way around. However, in many cases there is a check-matching strategy. For instance, if two writers have a hit song, but one is with ASCAP and the other is with BMI, they may get the same pay for the work.

Also, you should consider your personal contacts at one organization or another. If you are not affiliated, your best bet is to read as much as you can about each organization, get to know people at each organization, and then base your decision on what you feel is going to be best for you. It is an entirely subjective decision, but keep in mind that you can always apply for a change of membership if you are unhappy with the organization you've joined.

Summary

There are many, many more organizations that could be of benefit to you. Do your homework and find as many as you can. You never know where you might meet the person who will steer your career in the right direction. Once you've joined, be proactive and use the organizations benefits and services to their fullest. Get involved and see what you can bring to these organizations. Meet people and continue to build your network of friends and associates. Always remember that there is strength in numbers, and it takes whole lot of help to make it on your own.

CHAPTER 18

Music Conferences, Festivals, Trade Shows, and Seminars

"Go to where the action is."

There are a number of trade shows, seminars, music conferences, and festivals that you can attend. You can showcase your talent, network with a number of like-minded people, see and be seen, and most importantly, learn. I have provided a very short list of these events in this chapter, but there are just so many that it's impossible to list them all. You can also search the Internet for more events in your area that may suit your needs.

Many of these events will come and go, depending on their success. The good news is that finding one in your area is not difficult. If you do your homework, you should be able to find a very good conference or festival in your area that suits your needs and can expose you or your band to whole new market and networking opportunities.

But just attending these events is not the best way to take advantage of all that they have to offer. Don't just go to a music conference or festival and hope for the best. Get involved! See what you can do to make the conference more valuable to you and everyone else. Ask the people who are sponsoring it if you can do anything to help them. The more you get involved, the more you will get out of it.

Do your homework at least a year before attending. Get as completely prepared as you possibly can before you go. Save your money, plan way ahead, and think about how you can dovetail your trip with taking care of other things, such as getting a gig in each city on the way to the conference and on the way back. You may also consider taking different routes on the way to and from the conference, assuming that it's out of town.

If you can't get any gigs on the way to or from the conference, go to each town on the way there and back, and meet with some club owners to leave a CD or demo and try to get a gig. Stop by the local radio stations and college stations to leave a CD. Some stations may even allow you to do an on-air interview. You never know unless you ask.

See if the local newspaper or college paper does music reviews. If it does, drop off a CD and meet the reviewers, invite them to your shows, and ask questions about who and what they know in the local music scene. Newspaper folks can be a great source of information. You never know, they might give you some good press. That's always a good thing.

If you visit a college campus, stop off at the student union and ask for the music activities director to see if you can get a gig. Or check out the local frats and

sororities to see if they want to hire you or your band.
Also, go to the local music stores and leave your CDs
on consignment. Use every chance you can take to
continually expand your market and develop your
brand. Plus, you can learn about towns and cities that
may be new places to showcase your talent.

Be ready to meet as many people as you can at these
conferences, and continue to network with the people
you know. You may hear something like this: "I know
a guy who's going to be at this conference whose sister
dates this guy who is the brother of a guy at a record
label who said he'd like to meet with you because he's
heard so many good things about you...." You never
know, it could happen! If not, the worst that can happen
is you'll meet a lot of new people and learn a whole
bunch of good information. You may even learn what
not to do, which can sometimes be better than learning
what you *should* do. But again, don't just show up and
expect something to happen. Get involved and make
the most of your time and money. Although you are not
very likely to come away from a conference with a record
deal, you should be glad that you attended. You have a
better shot at getting noticed by someone who can help
your career than if you just stay at home and play your
local club scene.

Check on deadlines for registration and get yours
in as soon as you can. Ask about the registration
procedures and whether you can get advance notice of
who will be in attendance. Then set up some meetings
with as many key people as possible. This will save you
a lot of grief trying to track down busy folks once the
conference has started. Be prepared for the meetings.
Ask as many questions as you can, and make sure that

you get across what you can do for them, not just what they can do for you.

Give some serious thought to having flyers and posters made. Put them all over the place. What better way to get the attention of the attendees than to have you or your band's name plastered everywhere you look? Since there should be a lot of music industry people wandering around, you can reach a very direct market and get more bang for your advertising buck. If you plan to put up a whole lot of flyers and posters, you may want to check with the local government offices to see if you need a permit. Getting hit with a fine or having a brush with the law should be a serious concern.

If you live near the conference or know much about the city where it's being held, get in touch with a restaurant, music store, or any other business that may be able to sponsor you. This might be a hard sell, but you may be able to convince a business to help pay for your posters, fliers, handouts, or other advertising if you give it a plug.

There are many different ideas like this that can help you out. So be creative, and don't ever be afraid to ask. Try to think outside of the box. If you can come up with some gimmick that makes you or your band stand out in the crowd, that will be helpful too!

Be prepared to whip out your business card at any given time. Make sure you put all of your contact information on it, including your Web site address. When you give out your card, make sure to ask for one in return. That way, you can follow up with everyone you meet. If you have someone's business card, you're one step closer to having that person as an ally. Make the best of the contacts that you meet. You may even consider sending them a small note after the conference, expressing your appreciation for them meeting with you.

Have your CD or demo tape ready to hand out to anyone who may be a good lead, but don't just give it away to anyone on the street unless you can afford some less expensive promotional CDs. Another thing to consider is getting someone's business card and then sending him a CD later. Many people won't want to lug around a bunch of CDs. At MIDEM in Cannes, France, I actually had to ship home all of the CDs I got from various people. There just wasn't any way to bring them all with me. Another thing to consider is that since making CDs is now so affordable and easy to do with computers, you may want to forego cassette tapes altogether.

Put your best stuff on the CDs or tapes that you hand out, to make sure that you make a good first impression. You may even want to bring a boom box or CD player with extra headphones so that people can listen to your stuff wherever you are. This way, you don't have to wait for weeks to hear back from people, assuming they ever get back to you at all. However, don't try to force the issue and make anyone listen on the spot. I never liked listening to people's CDs right in front of them, as they eyed my every reaction like a hawk. It made me feel like I was being put on the spot, especially if I didn't really care for what I was hearing. I much preferred listening to a prospective client's music on my own time and in my own preferred listening environment. Then I could compare what I was listening to against what I was used to hearing. I could immediately tell how well something was recorded, and how the songwriting or overall music stacked up to what I viewed as commercially exploitable.

If you have a list of attendees but you can't schedule a meeting with the key people you'd like to see, at least call or write them and invite them to your show. You find some of these people during the day at their booths. Do *not* send promotional packages to record labels, major publishers, or established managers unless you have been asked to do so. However, you can send them to attorneys, managers, etc. Whether or not you can get an early list of attendees, arrive at the conference as early as you possibly can. Usually you'll get a goody bag with a handout listing all the scheduled events and activities. It will take a while to read through all of it so that you can plan out your time and make the most of the opportunities offered.

If your band is going to play a showcase, make sure you get to the venue early. Do an inventory of all your gear and make sure you have everything you will need. This is the time for last-minute trips to the music store for guitar strings, fuses, or whatever. Make sure that you introduce yourself to the people who are handling your showcase. Be polite and professional, and try to stay away from any outrageous requests. Remember, these guys are going to be pretty stressed out trying to make sure that everyone is on time and the show goes off without a hitch, so do your part to make that happen. Familiarize yourself with the equipment, and get to know the soundman. Try to make his job as easy as possible. He won't have time to learn about your sound, so give him the easiest instructions you can, such as how much reverb or delay you like on your voice.

You may also want to give CDs or t-shirts to the people from the conference who help you out. You'll at least get some free advertising when they wear it. Plus, it will ingratiate you with those people. The more allies you have, the better, so remember the people who help you out in any way.

Make sure that you hit the exhibit floor and meet as many people as you can. Ask questions and keep notes, and you will learn a great deal. Also plan on attending the most important panels. These panels are a great way to learn about the most recent trends in the business. When a panel is over, don't just leave. Stick around and meet the panelists. Also, on nights when your band isn't playing, hit all the local venues, drop off your CD if a place looks promising, and get their contact information to see if you can get any gigs there.

After the conference is over, you need to follow up with the people you've met. Enter everybody who gave you a card into your database and put them on your mailing list. Send CDs to people who requested them and seemed interested enough to help you out. (Sending out CDs to everyone may be cost-prohibitive.) Send personal thank you notes to people who you had scheduled meetings with, and those you met along the way who seemed to be interested in what you're doing. Thank them for their time and information.. Again, a personal note can go a long way toward making your band more memorable.

Finally, begin planning to make the conference the next year. You'll know more people and be even better prepared. You never know… that may just be your year!

Music Conferences

The following is a short list of the major music conferences. There are too many to list them all here, and new ones are popping up all the time. Be that as it may, you need to keep up with what's going on. Attending these events could be extremely crucial to your advancement in the industry.

WORLDWIDE MARKETS: THE INTERNATIONAL MUSIC CONFERENCE AND FESTIVAL (MIDEM) IN CANNES, FRANCE

This is the premier music festival in the world. It's held near the end of January every year, at the very same place as the International Film Festival, and it can expose you to markets throughout the entire world—and I do mean the *entire* world. The biggest players in the music industry attend this festival, and you will not find a better place to make deals.

I cannot stress how incredible this festival is. There are more people there (with more money!) than you can imagine. They all have their beginning-of-the-year budgets, and they're all looking to buy, license, distribute, set up joint ventures, and make just about any type of deal you can imagine.

Reed Midem Paris Headquarters
BP572
11 Rue du Colonel Pierre Avia 75726
Paris Cedex 15 France

Paris Office
Ana Vogric-Martinez
Director of Sale Worldwide
Phone: 33 (0) 1 41 90 44 51
Fax: 33 (0) 1 41 90 44 50

New York Office
Bill Craig
Vice President of Sales
Phone: (212) 284-5130
Fax: (212) 284-5148
www.midem.com

REGIONAL MARKETS: SOUTH BY SOUTHWEST (SXSW) IN AUSTIN, TX

One of the most popular music conferences is the Music and Media Conference and Festival, also known as SXSW. It began in 1987 and is held in March each year in Austin, Texas. In 1993, the organizers added conferences and festivals for the film industry (SXSW Film) and interactive media (SXSW Interactive Festival).

The Music and Media conference offers a trade show by day. You'll find a host of seminars, with a vast array of music professionals discussing a wide range of topics about the music industry. Each night, a number of stages feature several genres of music, so just about any type of act can get a chance to be heard by record labels and other music professionals. However, there are so many bands playing in so many places that it's impossible for someone to attend all the performances.

It is important to get your slot booked as early as possible to ensure that your act will be able to play.

SXSW Headquarters
Box 4999
Austin, TX 78765
Phone: (512) 467-7979
General fax: (512) 451-0754
General e-mail: sxsw@sxsw.com

SXSW also organizes NXNE and NXNW, which are basically the same, but held in other regions. If you are interested in these areas, contact SXSW for more information.

Again, there are of plenty of cities that host regional or even statewide events. New York, Boston, Nashville, Memphis, Chicago, Atlanta, Miami, Los Angeles, and many more cities have at least one of these events, and sometimes more. There are also events all over Canada. Again, check the Internet for more information on any events near you. Remember, if you are going to showcase your act, make the most of your time and money spent there through careful planning and willingness to network as much as you possibly can.

Fairs and Festivals

Music conferences are usually geared toward all genres of music and include seminars, panels, exhibition floors, etc. However, a number of music festivals and fairs are geared more toward helping out bands, artists, songwriters, and the like. Many of these festivals are geared more toward promoting genres of music, and they're not set up to educate attendees through workshops and panels.

You may find that some conferences are much like festivals, and vice versa. It all depends on the event. With a little research and some hard work, you can find the conference or festival that's best suited to your needs. Of course, you should also try to attend many of these other types of events and get booked for these shows. More shows equals more exposure, and getting your music out there is what it's all about. Many of these festivals are custom-tailored for songwriters and individual musicians.

I highly recommend that you use the Internet to find the festivals that are best for you or your band. To that end, I have included a few links that may be of some help:

http://directory.google.com/Top/Arts/Music/Concerts_
   and_Events/Festivals/Rock/
http://www.expocentral.com/arts_and_entertainment/
   industry_arts_and_entertainment_music.html
http://dir.yahoo.com/Entertainment/Music/Events/
   Concerts/Festivals/
www.festivalfinder.com

Trade Shows

Depending on the nature of your business, you may consider attending certain trade shows that cater to your branch of the music industry. Most of these shows aren't intended to break new bands, though. They are designed to show the latest and greatest equipment, new technologies and processes, etc.

Don't try to do too many things at the last minute. Book your hotel and car rental reservations early, and get a hotel as close to the venue as you can afford. Pre-register to save time when you get there. Use any materials you're given, such as the trade show plan, to find the hot spots that you need to see. Find out about important seminars and make time to attend, because you will learn some very valuable information about new developments in the industry.

Some of these shows are massive, and the atmosphere can be like a shark feeding frenzy. Finding the time to see everyone and everything on your list can be a daunting task. However, if you do some careful planning before you go, your experience will go a lot smoother and you can maximize your time.

www.expocentral.com/arts_and_entertainment

Seminars

Seminars may be a part of any festival or other event that you attend. They're usually chock-full of information on recent developments or trends in the music industry. If they're part of a bigger event, you should carefully plan out your time so that you can attend.

However, some seminars are held outside of any other event. Some are designed to focus on certain issues, and others provide broad coverage of many issues. For instance, songwriting seminars and camps are offered by a number of licensing and songwriting organizations. There are seminars about publishing, legal issues, getting a deal, etc. Just make sure that you focus on the seminars that best suit your needs and fit within your budget. The more you can afford to attend, the more you will learn. Remember that attending these seminars is an investment in your career and could be tax-deductible.

Make sure that you have business cards with your Web site address, and always keep press kits available just in case. Even though you may be attending the seminar just to learn, you never know who you might meet. You may also want to e-mail yourself any important documents, just in case you're asked for any extra materials. However, don't go to the seminar with the sole intent of handing out press packets. The professionals on the panel are there to pass along information, so they won't be very interested in taking your package. Of course, it never hurts to stay after the seminar and meet the panel members, and ask for a card if appropriate. You just might meet the person who's going to launch your entire career.

Attending seminars is an excellent way to learn more about your field, and they don't require much preparation. You should take notes and make sure to keep up with any handout materials. After the seminar, make sure to reread all of the information you're given so that you don't miss out on good information that may have come at you too fast.

Summary

Although you can attend a number of trade shows, music conferences, festivals, and seminars, you should make the most of your yearly budget and pick the ones that best suit your needs. Networking is one of the keys to success, so be prepared and extremely professional. Showcase your talent, see and be seen, but most importantly, learn. The more you learn, the better prepared you are for the next step. You never know, you may just get signed if all the right pieces fall into place. Stranger things have happened.

CHAPTER 19

Insurance

"The necessary evil...."

....

You just can't escape the need for insurance these days. It's a cost of living and a part of our everyday lives. Many people are very tired of paying large premiums just to be insured for some unknown or unforeseen event, especially if they never even have to file a claim. It seems like money down the drain. Also, some people don't agree with many of the government's policies in regard to forced insurance, which is insurance required by legislation such as car insurance, without which you can have your driver's license revoked.

In short, a lot of people in this country aren't huge fans of the insurance industry as a whole. Of course, you don't hear many insurance agent jokes the way you hear lawyer jokes.... Be that as it may, insurance is a necessary evil, and you will have to learn to deal with it. Unless you have some type of insurance to cover major problems, you could lose everything.

If you visit your state legislature or the U.S. Congress and Senate, you'll see a number of lobbyists pushing legislation for the insurance industry. Insurance lobbyists far outnumber consumer advocates. The consumer hardly stands a chance. It's very much like the difference between an unsigned artist and the record companies, in that the consumer doesn't have much negotiating power with the insurance companies.

To make matters worse for the consumer, more and more legislation is being passed that will benefit the insurance companies, such as more forced insurance and possibly even tort reform, which will put limits on the amount of recovery you can get if you're seriously hurt by someone else's negligence. You will be able to recover only a fixed amount of damages, instead of having a jury of your peers decide what you should get. If you lose a hand in an accident and can never play guitar or piano again, you will be able to get only a set amount. How can anyone possibly put a fixed value on your ability to play music and make a living in the music business?

Unfortunately, there isn't much you can do about it, unless more people are willing to step up to assert their rights and tip the scales in favor of the consumer. Needless to say, the insurance industry is a very powerful entity, and it's here to stay. You should learn as much as possible about insurance so that you can get the best protection for the best price.

Throughout your life, you will have to pay for several types of insurance policies. You should maintain the most important types of insurance, such as health, car, homeowners, and personal property insurance, to shield yourself from a number of bad scenarios that may occur. If you don't have insurance for major problems, you could lose everything you have, or perhaps end up in bankruptcy court. To that end, I will describe some of the main players that could be involved, the most important types of insurance that you may need, and what to do if you need to file a claim or you have any problems filing one.

First, let's look at some of the players in the game.

Agents

Most towns in America have a large number of insurance agents. You won't have much trouble finding someone to sell you an insurance policy. You may have had an insurance agent call on *you*. The more aggressive agents are proactive and actively seek out clients, especially if they know that you're making money! The most important question is, "Can I find an insurance agent who will sell me the right type of insurance to suit my needs, and at the best price?"

You should definitely shop around and make sure your agent has your particular needs in mind. Some agents will offer that little bit of extra personal service to make your entire experience much easier. They may also help you deal with the company in obtaining the right policy for your needs and for the right price. A good agent should also assist you if you need to file a claim.

Some agents are just about selling and have no intention of assisting you with any problems or explaining something you don't understand. They are playing the numbers game, and the more time they spend on actual selling, the more money they make. Stay away from these types of agents, and try to find one who has your best interests in mind. If you can find a good agent, he or she may be able to handle most if not all of your insurance needs.

Also, your agent should explain every single aspect of any insurance contract to your satisfaction. If he can't, you may not be getting what he says he's offering. You should also read the entire policy so that you completely understand exactly what you are paying for, what occurrences are covered, how much your deductibles are, and how much actual coverage you have. Don't be afraid to ask questions, ask for clarifications, or even pose some hypothetical situations. If you're not getting the right explanations or you're being treated like a number, get another agent. You have the absolute right to know exactly what you are paying for and exactly what your coverages are.

Finally, remember that agents work on a commission that is paid upon your initial payment, and in most cases, every time you re-up your policy or make any additional payments. If you don't feel that your agent or insurance company is giving you the products or services you need, feel free to discuss that with your agent. If he doesn't want to lose your business, he should meet your needs with a creative approach. If your agent isn't willing to assist you with these decisions or explain all of the ins and outs of each type of policy you're purchasing, find another agent. You don't want to just write a check every month, or however often the policy calls for payment, without knowing exactly what you're getting in return.

Underwriters

These are the folks who decide which policies will be issued to which individuals or companies, and why. You rarely see these people, and yet they have the power to deny the issuance of your policy if they feel that the insurance company is taking too much risk.

Underwriters use a wide variety of manuals, charts, tables, graphs, and of course computers to calculate the risk to the company versus the gain from your premiums if a policy is issued. But there are ways to get around the cold, hard facts of calculated risks, especially if you negotiate. If you have a really good agent, he can influence these underwriters to help you get the right policy for your needs and for the best price available. Remember, if you are denied coverage for something that you really need to insure, continue to shop around. This is especially true if you're insuring your special guitar or some other expensive equipment that could be stolen, damaged, or lost. The policy you need may cost a good bit, but that's a whole lot better than losing your entire investment in something that you need to make money.

Claims Adjusters

These are the folks who are called when there is a claim by you or your company. They are the ones who decide what the insurance company will pay, or if it will even pay at all.

Dealing with adjusters can be a pleasant experience, if you are lucky enough to get what you think you deserve. However, in some cases they can be very adversarial.

They are not looking out for your interests, but rather the interests of the insurance company. The less money the adjusters pay out, the more money the insurance company keeps. So don't expect them to just cut you a check immediately, unless they think they can get you to accept a lesser amount than you deserve. Never just accept an initial offer, unless you are certain that you will be made whole by the amount offered. Feel free to get your own estimates, and always demand that you get the best people to repair your property. Don't settle for some inferior service or product from the list of people that the insurance company recommends. Remember, you pay your insurance company good money to be covered, so don't get less than what you've paid for.

How to Shop for Insurance

First, determine the types of insurance you need, and the types of insurance you already have. You can sometimes get discounts for having multiple policies with the same company, such as both homeowners and auto insurance. Get as many quotes from as many companies as you can, and find out about every option that is available to you. Most companies offer a wide variety of coverage, with different deductibles, premiums, etc. Remember that the higher your deductible is, the lower the cost of the insurance will be. But a high deductible could force you to pay more than you can afford just to get a problem fixed. You will need to figure out what you can afford to pay if you're hit with a large deductible, and weigh that against what you can afford to pay for a policy on a monthly, quarterly, or yearly basis.

Also try to eliminate double or duplicate coverage if possible, so that you don't have too much insurance. However, in some cases, double or duplicate coverage is a good idea. Let's say you have a decent health coverage plan, and also medical coverage for car accidents. This way, if you are not covered by one policy for major medical, the other policy may cover it. In some cases of double coverage, you would not have to pay as much of a deductible.

Make sure that you ask about discounts, and negotiate with your agent to get the best deal that you can possibly get. Just because an agent makes an offer doesn't necessarily mean it's a "take it or leave" proposition.

Also, make sure the insurance company has been in business for a long time, and that it will be able to pay your claim when it's time to make one. If you buy from a company that ends up filing bankruptcy, you could be out a large sum of money. There won't be anything you can do about it, except wait in line at bankruptcy court with all the other claimants.

If you have any questions about insurance companies, requirements, or laws, contact the National Insurance Consumer Help Line at (800) 942-4242, or contact your state commissioner of insurance.

You should also find out which types of insurance are tax-deductible. If you are incorporated or have an LLC, a great deal of the money you spend on insurance will be tax-deductible. If you are paying for lots of coverage, you could be getting a lot of deductions. Make sure to check with the IRS and your state tax commission for more information.

Finally, make sure that you ask whether your contract covers replacement value or the fair market value of the item that is insured.

Replacement Value versus FMV

Replacement value is the cost that will be incurred to replace an item of property if it is lost, stolen, or damaged. Sometimes you may get insurance coverage on an item, and then when it's time to make a claim on it, you'll find that it costs more to replace the item than what you paid for it in the first place. If you're in love with your Les Paul and it's stolen, you won't want to have to buy a cheaper model or cheaper brand to replace it. So get insurance that covers the replacement value. Also, many insurance policies allow for depreciation of certain items that are lost or stolen. Keep in mind that your Les Paul may be appreciating in value, and you want to make sure your policy will cover that.

On the other side of the coin is insurance that covers only the fair market value (FMV) of an item. *Fair market value* is the actual market value of the item at the time of the loss, including the depreciation of the item. Let's say that you buy a really awesome PA system, and after a few years of use, the whole thing is stolen from your rehearsal space. If your insurance pays only the fair market value of stolen items, you may not be able to replace the PA with similar equipment for a similar price, because the price of equipment will have gone up. You may have to pay more for replacement insurance versus fair market value coverage, so think about that before you sign any contract with your insurance company.

Of course, not all insurance covers the loss of property. If you are permanently injured or disabled and you have insurance for that, there is really no way to give you back an arm or replace a leg. However, you *can* be compensated based upon your loss of ability to earn money at a particular job or in a particular field. In other words, if you're a surgeon who loses an arm, you will be compensated well, because now you can't do what you've trained for half your life. However, if your injury doesn't prevent you from working, such as if you're a lawyer who ends up in a wheelchair, you'll be compensated for your medical bills, costs of rehabilitation, and in some cases your pain and suffering.

Pain and suffering are also recoverable under many types of insurance. This is a monetary sum that's intended to compensate you for all the pain and suffering that you've experienced due to an accident. Of course, there are other types of recovery, such as loss of consortium (being unable to have sex with your spouse) and many others, so you should ask your agent exactly what you could recover for after an accident or permanent injury. Again, if you can't get the policy that you think you need, look for another agent or company that will offer what you need.

Finally, there is another measure of value that just isn't recoverable: sentimental value. Unfortunately, this is neither measurable nor insurable. If you lose something through theft or accident that has tremendous sentimental value, you may only be able to recover the fair market value or replacement value.

Changes to Your Contract

A number of different changes can take place once you have signed an insurance contract, so be very wary of any changes and don't just accept them unless you think they are fair.

EXCLUSIONS

Basic contract law states that a contract cannot be changed unilaterally (see Chapter 12, "General Principles of Contracts") without some type of consideration. A *unilateral* change to a contract means that the terms will be changed without your approval. It has always struck me as unfair that even if you have never made a claim on an insurance policy, the insurance company can decide that it cannot cover you for certain types of occurrences. All of a sudden, you get a notice in the mail stating the occurrences for which you are no longer covered. I certainly understand that prices go up, but insurance companies just think that you will blindly accept any and all changes that they decide to make. Before you acquiesce to any of these unilateral changes, be sure to read your policy carefully to determine what the insurance company can and cannot change without your approval. If you have concerns about any changes, contact your insurance agent or insurance company. If you cannot come to terms with that company over any changes, find another company that offers the insurance that is right for your needs.

RATE HIKES

I have had to make a few claims for damage to my car, and I found it kind of strange that my insurance premiums seemed to increase even though I was not at fault. Obviously, the insurance company was trying to recoup its losses. You may also see rate hikes when it is time to pay for your next year's insurance. Of course, the cost of insurance will continue to go up along with inflation and the general cost of living, but don't be complacent. If your contact period is up, you can renegotiate with your insurance company, or you are free to go to another company. But find out why prices are going up before you blindly write a check for more money.

Exclusions and rate hikes usually come to you in the mail from your insurance company. They will advise you that you're no longer covered for this or that, or that your premium has increased. Be mindful of these exclusions, because they can affect your ability to get recovery for certain occurrences. Also, don't just agree to a cost increase unless you know that you can't get better coverage elsewhere. This is where the insurance companies don't have to get one up on you. If you're facing a rate hike or exclusion, you don't have to continue doing business with that insurance carrier. Feel free to shop around and find a policy that suits your specific needs.

Types of Insurance

There are a number of different types of insurance that you may need throughout your life, such as car insurance, homeowner's or renter's insurance, premises liability, inland marine or personal property floaters, specialty insurance, as well as errors and omissions, inventory, health, dental, disability, life, and burial insurance. There are also workman's compensation and bonded workers, which you may need if you are an employer or employee or if someone is working on your home. In some cases you are required by law to have insurance such as for your car or if you have a certain number of employees, which is sometimes referred to as "forced insurance," as mentioned previously.

AUTO INSURANCE

In many states some type of auto insurance is now mandatory, so you really don't have any choice. Auto insurance is made up of several types of coverage:

Collision: This is the part of your policy that pays for repairs after a collision, and in some cases it doesn't matter how the damage was caused or who did it. If the collision was not your fault, your insurance company will hire a lawyer to go after the party who was at fault, or his insurance company. You may have a deductible, which is the amount that you are required to pay before the insurance company pays the rest.

Liability: If you are at fault in an accident, this covers the injuries and damage you cause to other drivers and their cars. If you are taken to court, this part of your insurance will apply to your legal costs. Most states require this one, but the amount required varies from state to state.

Comprehensive: This type of coverage takes care of any damages to your car caused by something other than a crash, such as vandalism, hail damage, water damage caused by flood, etc. Depending on the deductibles and the cost, you should give some serious thought to this type of coverage.

Uninsured or underinsured coverage: Uninsured coverage takes care of any damages caused by another vehicle that's not covered by insurance, while underinsured coverage takes care of damages that cost more than the other driver's insurance can pay, if the other driver was at fault. Some states require either or both, so check with your state laws to see what you are required to carry.

Leasing or financing: When you lease or finance a car, you may have to take out an insurance policy with terms that are dictated by the leasing or financing company. You may find that the required coverage is more expensive than the minimum state requirements for liability coverage, and therefore more than what you would have paid for car insurance if you were allowed to choose. A similarly high level of collision and comprehensive insurance may also be required. To make matters worse, the leasing or financing company may demand that you set your deductibles at a fairly low rate, which equals a higher premium.

No-fault insurance: This has been adopted by some states to cut back on large insurance claims or judgments, and to help curb the cost of insurance. This type of insurance pays you for your injuries regardless of fault in an accident, and in some states you can still go after the party at fault.

Rental insurance: When you rent a car, van, truck, or trailer and your personal insurance does not cover you, you are much better off getting any insurance that is offered with your rental agreement. Even if your existing insurance does cover you, it can sometimes be a good idea to get the extra insurance that comes with the rental. This way you have two policies that will cover you in case of any serious accident or loss. You should take into account that a rental car, van, or truck will drive differently than your regular means of transportation, so there's more chance of an accident. Even if you just rent a trailer, your car, truck, or van will drive differently, so extra insurance may be a good idea. You should also make sure that the insurance covers the contents of your car, truck, van, or trailer. If you're in a band that's hauling all of your equipment, which has taken you years to buy, and it's destroyed in an accident, you would at least be able to replace it. After all, isn't that the reason to have insurance in the first place?

You can also get policies to help pay medical bills from an accident, which can also include injuries to people in your own car if you were at fault. Sometimes gap insurance is required with a leasing or finance deal. This type of insurance will pay the difference between what other policies have paid out and the amount you owe on the vehicle if it's wrecked or stolen.

HOMEOWNER'S INSURANCE

This type of coverage pays for any damages to your home, or for any injuries or damages due to some accident on your property. If you have a mortgage on your home, most likely you will be required to have some type of homeowner's policy. Basic homeowner's insurance will cover you if an aircraft lands on your home, a car or truck hits it, wind or hail damages it, or an explosion damages it, a fire burns it, or lightning strikes it. Likewise your home is covered if there is some sort of smoke damage, a volcanic eruption, or a riot or some sort of civil unrest, or if you are a victim of vandalism or theft, part of your home collapses, or other structural damage occurs.

There are some types of coverage that may not be included in your homeowner's policy, for which you will have to purchase supplemental insurance. These can include excessive snow that causes damage, falling objects, water damage, electrical damage, floods, earthquakes, war, and nuclear blasts.

You can also get mortgage insurance that will pay off your house note if you meet an untimely death, which is a very good idea if you are married and/or have children. This way, if you pass away unexpectedly, your surviving beneficiaries won't be saddled with a house note that they may not be able to afford after losing your income.

RENTER'S INSURANCE

There are a number of insurance companies that will issue you a policy for renter's insurance if you are renting a house or apartment. Landlord insurance will often cover the dwelling but not any personal property in the dwelling, while renter's insurance will cover the personal property but not the actual dwelling. Renter's insurance is an especially good idea if you have a lot of expensive belongings. The landlord should usually have insurance that will cover your personal property for any loss due to theft, flood, fire, or severe weather. But you may need extra protection for occurrences that are not covered by the landlord's insurance, or for claims that exceed the amount that the landlord's insurance will cover.

Also, make sure that your landlord has insurance that covers physical injury to any of your guests, in the form of premises liability. If your landlord doesn't have coverage, you could be on the hook if someone is injured by any accident while visiting you. Also, if you are running a business out of your apartment, you should make sure that your business invitees will be covered if they're injured while visiting you, especially if you are not supposed to be running a business out of your rental property. The landlord's premises liability coverage would not have to pay. (See "Premises Liability" below.)

PREMISES LIABILITY

This the type of insurance protects a renter, business operator, and the like from accidents when someone visits for personal or business reasons. If you own a home, your homeowner's insurance may cover this, but you should always make sure.

One cause of action that is often filed is the slip-and-fall claim. This is where someone comes on your property and somehow manages to slip and fall down. Just ask any fast food place or grocery store about this type of claim. They see more than their fair share, including a lot of fraudulent claims.

Just remember that you have a duty to warn all business or personal invitees who visit your place of business, residence, or rental unit of any dangerous conditions, such as a hole in the yard, a broken step, a freshly mopped floor, or any other conditions that could cause someone to get hurt. You should always fix any dangerous condition as quickly as possible. In the meantime, as long as you have told someone about a dangerous condition, you have a defense that they assumed that risk yet still managed to get hurt. There is just no way to predict how stupid some people can be, or whether they will sue you in a heartbeat just to see how much money they can get from your insurance company.

INLAND MARINE/PERSONAL PROPERTY FLOATER

Inland marine insurance covers boats and other types of property, such as a trailer that you haul behind your car, truck, or van.

If inland marine is not available, sometimes you can obtain a personal property floater policy that will cover your property that goes out on the road with you. It covers property that is not covered by your homeowner's insurance or renter's insurance on your personal property. This type of insurance is very handy. You don't want to lose any of your musical instruments or other equipment that has taken you a long time and a lot of money to acquire.

SPECIALTY INSURANCE

You may have heard about certain film stars insuring their legs for millions of dollars. It may sound outrageous, but if they rely on their legs to make a living, it makes perfect sense. In fact, if you are willing to pay enough, you can purchase insurance for just about anything you want. Just be advised that if you decide to insure your hands in case you won't ever be able to play guitar again, you will need to pay a whole lot for the insurance company to take that risk.

The only way to find specialty insurance is to shop around. Eventually you should be able to find an insurance company that will take a chance, as long as you can pay.

ERRORS AND OMISSIONS INSURANCE

This type of insurance covers you if you make a mistake, forget to do something that you should have done, or make a similar type of faux pas in the course of your business. Sometimes this is also known as *malpractice insurance*. The type of work you do dictates whether you need this type of insurance. If you own a studio, it may be a good idea to get some type of coverage in case someone's masters get erased or your hard drive crashes due to some mistake.

INVENTORY INSURANCE

This type of insurance covers your inventory if there's a loss from theft or fire. If you own a music store, record store, or a similar business that maintains a stock of inventory, you should definitely consider this type of insurance. If you own a recording studio, you may want to get extra insurance to cover the loss of your master recordings or hard drives in a fire or other occurrence. The last thing you want is to lose all of your work and only be able to recover the costs of the master tapes or the hard drives, and not all of the money that it would take to remake your masters.

HEALTH INSURANCE

Health insurance is an absolute must-have in today's world. Currently there's an epidemic of uninsured Americans. If you need any type of health care, especially for a major surgery or treatment for a life-threatening accident or disease, you probably can't afford the kind of treatment you need without insurance. In fact, you may be turned away at the emergency room door if you don't have insurance.

You can structure health insurance in a number of ways, including having higher copays, which are payments you make to your health care provider out of your own pocket. The higher the copay is, the less your premium. You can also get some type of supplemental insurance that will cover costs not paid by any primary insurance provider. In some cases, you may even have double coverage. For instance, if your employer and your wife's employer both offer family coverage, you will be covered by either your own health insurance or your wife's policy. If you have two policies, the secondary insurance will pick up where the first left off.

Regardless, find out what coverage you do have so that you will get the most of your health insurance. Make sure that it covers regular visits to the doctor, prescriptions, and other expenses. Otherwise, you will be stuck with these costs, and you may not be able to afford the care you need. Never take your health for granted.

DENTAL INSURANCE

Some health insurance policies may have a dental plan, but most do not. You have to take into consideration how important your teeth are, because you can't replace them once they are gone—unless you don't mind wearing dentures, of course. If you can afford it, you should try to carry some type of dental insurance, because the cost of dental care continues to go up.

DISABILITY INSURANCE

This type of insurance covers you if you're injured, on the job or not, and can't work for a certain period of time. Your disability insurance can help pay your salary, overhead, payroll, or other expenses if you're unable to work for a month or two. It can even pay you for life if you are permanently disabled. If you own a business, doing without this type of insurance could come back to haunt you if you suffer an accident and can't work.

This type of insurance is not cheap, so look at your options. The more months you need to be off work before you can recover, the cheaper the premiums. Also, the more money you make at your job, the more the premium is going to cost.

If you own a company, this type of coverage could be tax-deductible.

LIFE INSURANCE

There are two main types of insurance, whole life and term life.

Whole life is where you pay premiums, but the money goes into an account that accumulates over time. If needed, you can even withdraw money from your account. Once you have paid enough premiums, your policy will begin to pay for itself and gain more equity. Before you die, you can withdraw all of the money in that account, or upon your death, that policy can be paid out to anyone you name as a beneficiary.

Term life insurance pays a fixed amount to the beneficiary of your choice upon your death. This type of insurance is much cheaper than whole life, but the money is frozen until you die. You can also get a double indemnity policy, which will pay double the policy amount if you die in an accident and not of natural causes.

If you have a spouse or family, you should get life insurance to make sure that your loved ones are cared for financially.

BURIAL INSURANCE

A number of burial insurance policies are available. If you don't have a lot of assets or money in the bank that can cover these expenses, this type of insurance policy could be an extremely wise choice. Burial can be extremely expensive, and you don't want to leave your loved ones stuck with the bill. There are also a number of prepaid burial plans. You should definitely shop around and consider including this in your will. (For more information, see Chapter 20, "Wills Trusts and Estates.")

WORKMAN'S COMPENSATION INSURANCE

This type of insurance covers workers who are hurt on the job. Some injuries you might see in workman's compensation cases are broken arms, lacerations, electric shock, carpal tunnel syndrome, lost fingers, and a whole host of others. In most states, companies with a certain number of employees are required by law to maintain workman's compensation insurance. Check with your state's insurance offices to see how many employees you need to have before you are required by law to maintain workman's comp.

Even if you don't have enough employees to require this insurance, you definitely need to think about getting it in case someone is hurt on the job. Check with your employees, partners, or associates to see what type of health insurance they have, and then you will know whether you need the extra coverage.

If someone is hurt on the job, you could get sued by his health care insurance provider so that it can *subrogate* the amounts paid to you. If the insurer wins and you don't have the right insurance, you could end up paying out of your own pocket for all the damages.

LICENSED AND BONDED WORKERS

If you have some major work done on your house and someone gets hurt in the process, you could end up having to pay for his accident from your homeowner's policy. Therefore, before you ever put someone else in a possibly dangerous situation, like removing trees from your yard, sweeping your roof, or any number of situations where someone could get hurt, make sure that you only hire workers who are licensed and bonded. That way, the contractor's or worker's insurance will pay first if anyone is injured, or even if your property is damaged due to some unforeseen accident. If the contractor's or worker's insurance is insufficient to pay the claim, your homeowner's insurance will have to pay the difference before you're required to pay any money out of your own pocket.

In the music business, you want to check if the sound company doing light and sound for your shows is bonded, just in case one of its roadies is hurt doing his job. Some companies may have workman's compensation to cover anyone who's hurt doing the job, but you should ask what happens if the PA system falls on your fans. Who will be responsible? Make sure that you don't end up footing the bill for someone else's negligence.

What to Do If You Have a Claim

If anything happens that requires you to make a claim, you should take several steps to preserve the record of events, and to make sure that you get fairly compensated for your damages. Remember that the more information you document, the more likely you'll be fairly compensated. If you have to go to court, you don't want to get into a "he said, she said" type of argument. To prove your case in court, you need to have documentation in the form of written estimates, pictures, etc. It doesn't matter what you think or how you feel, only what you can prove. So why not gather the best proof you can?

If you get into a car wreck, do *not* leave the scene of the accident unless you are carried away in an ambulance or have to seek immediate medical attention. That is a crime in most (if not all) states, for which you will be charged and most likely convicted. You really don't need that type of problem. Make sure that you call the police and exchange all relevant information with the other driver. Get the driver's name, address, work and home telephone numbers, place of employment, and insurance information (insurance provider, policy number, and so on). Also make sure to get his driver's license number. If you are not at fault and the driver does not pay for the damages, in many states that person's driver's license can be revoked. The threat of losing his license can be a strong incentive at least to make payment arrangements with you. This can be crucial if you don't carry underinsured or uninsured motorist coverage.

No matter what type of claim you have, make sure that you take photographs and document everything you possibly can about the loss. It's a good idea to get as many witnesses as possible, so that they can be called to testify on your behalf if you have to go to court. They can testify to what they saw about the accident, and if they are friends or family members, they can testify to how the accident has affected you, so you can recover for pain and suffering.

Get estimates from someone who's in the business of fixing your particular problem, even if you have to get a doctor to estimate the amount of health care costs you could incur in the future. Just make sure that he knows your insurance company will be paying him if he cures or treats any damage.

If you have damage to property, there may be problems with letting estimators know that insurance is involved. They will know that they may be subpoenaed to appear in court and testify on your behalf, and most people try to avoid that at all costs. Doctors are exempt from subpoenas to court in most cases. They only have to do a deposition to allow their expert testimony to be heard in court. But auto mechanics or other repairmen may be subject to subpoena, and they don't like getting involved in court actions.

Statute of Limitations

Each state has different statutes of limitations, which are the legal time limits within which you must file a lawsuit to protect a claim. If your state has a one-year statute of limitations, you must file a lawsuit before one year has passed or you can be forever barred from recovery. You don't want to sleep on your rights and then fail to recover the damages you were entitled to.

Is There a Standard Procedure of Denial?

I can't say whether insurance companies have a policy of denying most if not all claims. However, I do know that the more claims an insurance company pays, the less money the company makes. So it's not too much of a stretch to say that paying out claims is not in the best interests of an insurance company, even if the claims are valid.

Let's put it this way: If an insurance company has 10,000 claims during a one-year period that are worth $10,000.00 each, the insurance company could pay out $100,000,000.00. If the company denies all of those claims, it will have an extra $100,000,000.00 in its coffers. Some of the folks whose claims are denied won't be able to afford to sue, some will let the statute of limitations to file a claim go by, and some won't even want to deal with the hassle of suing. Even if only 10% of the claimants just let the matter go, the insurance company has just pocketed $10,000,000.00. That's not a bad profit just for denying some claims.

Now, let's assume that the insurance company has the full $100,000,000.00 invested and is getting about a 10% return annually, which I'm sure is low for companies with so much money. That's $10,000,000.00 per year in interest alone! Let's further assume that the vast majority of these claimants will need to hire a plaintiff's lawyer to get the money that the insurance company should have paid them in the first place. Even assuming that the suit is filed in time, the legal process can be very slow, to say the least. The defense teams hired by the insurance companies are going to dig in their heels and stall the case as long as they possibly can and to engage in protracted discovery before deciding to settle. And why not? They need to make sure the case can't be won in court before they advise the insurance company to pay the claim. The more hours the defense teams put into the case, the more money they make.

Furthermore, the longer the case is drawn out, the more interest the insurance company collects, which gives it even more money to pay its defense teams. This is a vicious cycle. You can rest assured that your claim won't be that important to the insurance company when you are just one of 10,000 potential claims.

The bottom line is that the insurance company will pay if it knows it will lose the case in court or if it means staying out of trouble by denying a valid claim. But it is going to hold onto its money as long as it can.

Of course, insurance companies blame their high premiums on fraudulent claims, and that's a very real problem. However, a lot of hard-working people have faithfully paid their premiums, and yet they can't get their insurance companies to pay their claims in a timely manner such that they're made whole.

But then, that's why there are plaintiff's lawyers. If you don't know how to file a suit to protect your rights, you will have to hire an attorney. I'm sure you've seen tons of TV ads for attorneys who handle car wrecks, personal injuries, or workman's compensation. These lawyers give free consultations because they usually work for a percentage. Just remember that these attorneys have to make a living too. Most people can't afford to shell out thousands of dollars for legal help, so these attorneys charge a percentage of any recovery you get, as much as

50%. In addition to that, you'll need to reimburse the attorney for all his costs just to try the case in the first place. It's expensive, but you may have no choice if you have a claim and can't get the insurance company to pay.

Bad Faith

What if the insurance company just won't pay for any reason? Some states have adopted *bad faith* or *failure to pay* statutes, which give the consumer a way to get some redress if an insurance company refuses to pay a claim. Sometimes these statutes make the insurance company pay your total damages plus a certain percentage, and sometimes you can recover all of your attorney's fees if you prove that the insurance company's failure to pay was based upon bad faith. Keep this in mind when you're dealing with an adjuster who doesn't want to pay you; you can always use it as a negotiating tool.

I once made a phone call from my law office to an adjuster who was refusing to pay a claim. I threatened him with a bad faith lawsuit and said I would be seeking all of my attorney's fees, as well as a percentage to be paid on top of the total damages. You guessed it: The adjuster asked where he could send the check for the full amount!

Hiring a Lawyer

Lawyers can be very expensive. Since most lawyers will work for a percentage in a case involving personal injury, workman's compensation, or some other accident-related injury, you won't have to pay unless you recover damages. But you can bet that the attorney is taking the case in the hopes that he will make more money from it than he would taking a case where he bills by the hour.

When it comes to property damage, though, hiring a lawyer automatically brings about the principle of diminishing returns. The more you pay your lawyer, the less money you will have to fix your property when and if you recover damages. Also, if you're seeking damages only for loss or damage to property, you may have a hard time finding a lawyer unless the property is worth a lot of money. But if you can't handle the matter yourself, you should seek the advice of the best attorney you can afford.

Summary

Insurance is a part of life in today's world, unless you can afford to live without it. Not having insurance can be too big of a risk, especially when it comes to major medical problems, loss of your home, or loss or destruction of your equipment. When you're deciding what your insurance needs are, keep in mind that it's better to be safe than sorry. Get the most protection you can afford, so that you won't be stuck paying off a major debt that could have been prevented with the right amount of insurance.

CHAPTER 20

Wills, Trusts, and Estates

"Planning for the end...."

The end of this book is as good a place as any to discuss planning for the ultimate end. Nobody wants to think about dying, but it's going to happen to everyone someday. You might as well start to plan for it.

Estate planning is all of the legal preparations that one does before his death. Careful planning will ensure that the least amount of taxes and probate fees will be incurred. Furthermore, good estate planning will ensure that one's property can be passed to one's beneficiaries for the least amount of money, time, and frustration.

Doing a will, especially if you are in the music business, is a really good idea. If you own your own business, you can provide for what will happen to your interest in it, unless you are a sole proprietor and you have to close the business. Also, since copyrights are vested to the author for life plus 70 years, it's extremely important to make a will to provide for the rights to these copyrights.

Since many of us in the music industry are the owners of copyrights or have an interest in some kind in copyrights, making a will can instruct those we leave behind as to who will receive the copyrights by assignment, or the proceeds of those copyrights by direction.

Furthermore, many of us have acquired a good deal of stuff during our stay here on Earth, and it's good to leave specific instructions about who is going to be getting that stuff when we shuffle loose this mortal coil.

Finally, as you're preparing a will, you can give some thought as to what will happen to your remains, such as burial or cremation. You can also specify how you'll provide for those you leave behind, such as your spouse, children, family, or other loved ones.

If you don't make a will, or you use some other legal method such as a trust to transfer your property before you die, state law will determine what happens to your property and even your *intellectual property*. The laws of *intestacy* will be controlling. This means you or your loved ones will have no say in what happens, which is definitely not a good thing. Your assets will be distributed *per stirpes*, which is a legal term meaning by right of representation. The inheritance will pass to your heirs in equal shares, but only after a good deal of taxes, fees, and other expenses have been paid. In other words, your property will go to your spouse and children, or if you have neither, to other relatives such as sisters, brothers, cousins, etc., according to a statutory formula that differs from state to state. But this happens only *after* the government gets its fair share. In some instances, the government will get as much as half. Most if not all of your assets may be sold to pay the estate taxes, as well as all of the other debts you incurred during your life. If no relatives can be found to inherit your property, all of it will go to the government (more than likely your state government), and it will use it as it sees fit.

Also, in the absence of a will, a court will determine who will care for your young children if the other parent is unavailable or deemed unfit. This is not a very good thing either. The state usually is not the best entity to be making decisions about your children. Social services are supposed to have the best interests of minor children in mind, but whoever's placed in charge of the case will have to make decisions that you may or may not have approved of if you were around.

Who Can Write a Will?

You don't necessarily need to be a lawyer to write a will. In fact, you can get do-it-yourself kits at office supply stores, other retail outlets, or even the Internet. You can do your will yourself if you want to save money, but it is wise to see a lawyer to make sure that it's done right and complies with all applicable laws in your state.

You don't have to let your lawyer write your will from scratch. You can prepare it yourself and then ask your lawyer for advice to make sure that you have covered all your bases. Then you can finish making your will based upon that advice. Once you have done the final draft of your will, it is a good idea to have your lawyer approve it. He should also write a letter approving the will based upon his legal advice, and you should keep that letter along with your will in a safe place that will be easy to find. This way, if the lawyer makes a big mistake, your heirs may be able to rectify the problem, or at least sue the attorney for malpractice.

Any adult who is of sound mind and body can make a will. The document must expressly say outright that it is your "last will and testament." You must date and sign the will, and usually it must be signed by two or more witnesses, depending on your state laws. The witnesses usually don't need to read your will, but they must see you sign it. And usually they can't be receiving anything from the will.

You don't necessarily need to get your will notarized, but it's a good idea. If you and your witnesses sign an affidavit that is notarized, most states will not require anyone to prove in court the validity of your will. Therefore, the court proceedings will go a lot faster and smoother for those you have left behind.

Types of Wills and Trusts

There are several types of wills, each with its own advantages and disadvantages. You can also set up a number of different types of trusts, which will allow your wishes about the financial aspects of your estate to be carried out. A *trust* is a legal arrangement whereby a certain person, or persons, company, or other institution is given control of property that has been given by another person for the benefit of any third party or parties. These third parties are known as *beneficiaries*. The *trustee* is the person, company, or institution that manages the trust and the money or property incorporated into it, according to the wishes of the trust's creator.

Simple Wills

A simple will is a legal document that lets you decide how your property will be distributed once you are gone, as well as nominate a guardian who will care for your minor children. A guardian's legal responsibility is to provide for your children's physical welfare until they become legal adults. Ultimately, a court makes the final decision when appointing a guardian for your children, but the court will usually accept your nomination.

You will find that making a nomination is a whole lot better than a court making a decision without a nomination. In the court's opinion, sometimes relatives are not always the best choice to be the guardian. This means that the court could place your children in foster care, which could be a bad thing, depending on the circumstances. The court will take into consideration the age, health, financial situation, willingness, and ability of any potential guardian before making a final decision.

Finally, a simple will allows you to choose the beneficiaries of your estate—in other words, who is to receive specific items from your estate, and which other beneficiaries are to receive everything else. While making a simple will or any other will, you will want to consider specific devises, as well as who is going to be the executor of your will.

SPECIFIC DEVISES

If you have certain personal items that you absolutely don't want to be sold for cash, and you want to make sure that a certain person receives these items, you must make a statement in your will providing for these *specific devises*.

In other words, if you want to leave your favorite guitar or any other item to a special person, even an intellectual property right, you must make it clear who is supposed to receive it. If you don't do this, all of your assets will be lumped together, and you run the risk that someone will get that favorite guitar or intellectual property rights (such as the ownership of the copyrights to your songs that you spent years writing), even though that was not your intention at all. At that point, there is nothing that you can do about it.

If you have built a good brand with your name and likeness, make sure to leave it in the hands of someone who knows what he is doing and can manage the financial aspects of your publicity rights after your death. Take a look at what is happening with the Elvis estate.

NAMING AN EXECUTOR

The *executor* is in charge of handling all matters in relation to your estate. (If the executor is a female, she is called the *executrix*.) The executor can be anyone who is not a minor, but be careful about who you choose. He will be charged with paying off your debts, paying your death taxes, selling your property, distributing your specific devises, and many more tasks. Some people choose their wives, but that can be a real burden on a surviving spouse. There are a lot of time demands, and being an executor can be very stressful and frustrating, especially when you have just lost a spouse.

The executor is entitled to a reasonable fee for his services, but it is usually a thankless and demanding task. In some cases, you may want to consider a trust company to handle these services.

HANDWRITTEN WILLS

In this age of computer printouts, typewritten manuscripts, and copy machines, you will not find many holographic wills in circulation. *Holographic wills* are written entirely in the handwriting of the will maker and signed by the will maker, but not always with verifying witnesses. You should definitely make sure a handwritten will is valid in your state, and determine whether it must be witnessed. If the will doesn't need to be witnessed, let someone know where the will is located, and have some way to prove that it was written in your handwriting. You can leave a sample of your handwriting with someone who is not a beneficiary, but the best way to make sure that nobody can contest the will is to have it witnessed by two or more people and have each signature notarized. The notary public will be insured or bonded for any mistakes he may make, such as not checking if the persons signing as witnesses are who they say they are.

Oral Wills (Dying Declarations)

You may think all wills must be written or filed somewhere for documentation, but *oral wills* are legally binding in some states. The legal term for this type of will is a *non-cupative will*. It can be taken at any time, in some cases on the testator's death bed, as long as the testator is of sound mind.

In court, dying declarations are allowed as evidence, despite the hearsay rule. The general idea is that the court feels that most people will tell the truth when they are about to die. Whether or not that is a sound reason doesn't really matter. The real problem with an oral will is that there is absolutely no writing. Therefore, there's no evidence other than a statement from the witness or witnesses, or perhaps a tape recording, that allows the court to determine if the oral will is valid. Unless there is a tape recording, you get into the classic "he-said, she-said" argument. You have to rely on the memory of the witness or witnesses, which can be less than accurate.

You are better off preparing a written will with witnesses and a notary. And you should do it now, because you never know. Life is unpredictable, and death is certain.

Joint Wills

Sometimes a husband and wife will draft a *joint will* to cover their joint assets in one document. Usually a joint will provides that the surviving spouse shall inherit the entire estate. This can be good thing if the surviving spouse remarries and then tries to leave the first spouse's assets to the new spouse.

This type of will is not always the best idea because problems can occur, such as a divorce or the separation of the parties. One of the survivors could violate the provisions of the joint will or perhaps sign a new will, thus invalidating the first joint will. Also, joint wills can be tied up in probate for years until the surviving spouse dies.

However, if you insist on having a joint will, it is best to see an attorney who specializes in wills and estates to advise you on the pros and cons, such as what could happen upon the death of both parties, or if one spouse survives the other. There are very rare exceptions when a joint will can be broken so that the surviving spouse can distribute the proceeds of the estate. You may be able to distribute the proceeds based upon any changed circumstances from the date of the death of the initial spouse who was a party to the original joint will.

Living Wills

While most wills become effective upon your death, a *living will* is intended to carry out your wishes while you are still alive. In reality, a living will is not a will at all, because it won't distribute property or assets. It is a signed document that expresses your desires about medical treatment, such as termination of life support, in case you become incapacitated and cannot communicate with your family, doctors, or other interested parties.

As a matter of convenience, living wills are often signed at the same time that testamentary wills are signed, but they involve decisions about life support during periods of unconsciousness and terminal illness. Many living wills are combined with a *durable power of attorney*, which gives someone else the authority to make these decisions if you can't. You should be aware that some states do not allow these two instruments to be combined into a single document.

Power of Attorney

A *power of attorney* is a document that a person signs to allow another person or entity to take control over certain aspects or issues that the person cannot or does not want to deal with himself. A power of attorney can be drawn up to allow someone to do just one specific task, or a host of tasks. In some cases, you may be asked to sign a power of attorney to allow your manager or publisher to conduct business on your behalf, transfer copyrights, file copyrights, or any number of different things. But be very wary of these documents. They take away your control over some or even all of your affairs, which is hardly ever a good thing.

DURABLE POWER OF ATTORNEY

This is a power of attorney that will continue to be valid after its maker becomes incapacitated or incompetent.

DURABLE HEALTH CARE POWER OF ATTORNEY

This is a special power of attorney in which the maker gives another person authority to make health care decisions when the maker is unable to do so, due to injury or sickness.

ATTORNEY-IN-FACT

This is just another term for the person who holds the power of attorney, and thus has been designated to transact business and execute documents on behalf of another person.

Caveat: Be very careful who you give the power of attorney to. You may end up regretting it, because he may not do what you feel is in your best interests. At that point, there isn't much you can do about it.

Testamentary Trust Will

This type of will allows for a trust to be created at the time of your death that is funded by assets from your estate. A trust can be created for your minor children so that they receive the benefits when they reach a certain age, such as 18, 21, or any other age. A trust can be created to fund education for your children, your nieces and nephews, or even your grandchildren.

You may also create a credit shelter trust to avoid federal estate taxes, or a charitable trust that pays out money for education or any other charitable contribution. However, these trusts will not come into existence until after your death.

Living Trust

A *living trust* is designed mainly to avoid probate, but can also be used to manage assets for beneficiaries, such as young children who are not ready to handle the financial responsibility of inheriting money or assets. The living trust specifies that certain assets or money will be transferred to the beneficiaries when they are able to handle the responsibility. Sometimes this can be in a lump sum, or you can set it up as a spendthrift trust so that money will be paid out at certain times of the year, yearly, every certain number of years, or however you want. A spendthrift trust is a good idea, because it allows your money and/or assets to be doled out a little at a time.

Tax-Saving Will

Your will can be used to create a *testamentary credit shelter trust*, which provides for lifetime benefits to the surviving spouse without having those assets included in the survivor's estate. This type of will or trust permits a married couple to pass a substantial amount of money to their beneficiaries without any federal or even state estate taxes. Obviously, the less money that is paid out in taxes, the more money there is to go to the beneficiaries. Therefore, this is a very good idea.

Pour-Over Will

A *Pour-Over Will* is used in conjunction with a living trust. Even if you have set up and funded a living trust, some assets may have been left out. At the time of death, the pour-over will is used to transfer those remaining assets into your trust, from which they are distributed to your beneficiaries. However, if you intend to avoid probate of the pour-over will, you should transfer most, if not all, of your assets into the trust during your lifetime.

Codicils

A *codicil* is an amendment to a will, a separate legal document drawn up after your initial will has been finalized. You can change certain parts of your will or add new provisions without having to redo the will completely.

A codicil can be like an amendment or supplement to your will, but it must be properly executed and witnessed. This is a great way to make changes as needed without the cost and time required to do a separate and distinct new will, which must revoke all other previous wills. This is one of the reasons that most wills state "This is my *last* will and testament."

Probate

Probate is simply the legal process whereby you wrap up a person's affairs, paying any outstanding bills and distributing any and all assets. Usually, notices must be posted in newspapers and other places to give creditors and others notice of death and pending probate proceedings. If there is no will, the probate court will usually require a fiduciary bond to be posted by the administrator or executor of the estate, to guarantee the replacement of any funds that may be diverted by the administrator or executor. The estate usually pays for this cost, so if you have a will, you may want to specifically waive the bond requirement.

You can avoid additional costs to the estate if you allow the sale of assets without requiring the executor to publish a notice of sale, but the sale of assets may have to be done just to pay death taxes and the actual expenses of probate. Also, if the will doesn't authorize the continuation of a business, the executor must operate the business at his own risk. Often, the executor will choose not to administer the estate unless that risk is borne by the estate.

There are a number of other types of trusts and other tax-saving devices that you can employ, but they're very difficult to understand, much less draft. Therefore, they should be done by a qualified tax attorney, estate attorney, or accountant. These include the living credit shelter trust, QTIP trust, qualified domestic trust, irrevocable life insurance trust, dynasty trust, wealth trust, and many others. Again, I can't express how important it is to seek a qualified professional to assist you with these types of trusts and other estate planning. If you have enough assets or money to worry about these types of trusts, you can afford the rather stiff fees associated with this type of work.

Life Insurance and Funeral Prepayment Plans

If you have any dependents, it is always a good idea to have some type of life insurance. That way, you can make sure your surviving dependents will receive a certain sum upon your death, and in some cases double indemnity for accidental death. (For more information, see Chapter 19, "Insurance.")

Furthermore, a number of companies will sell you insurance and/or funeral prepayment plans so that all of your burial expenses will be paid out immediately upon your death. This means your estate or family will not have to pay these expenses until the estate has been settled. Since it can be a long time between your burial and the settlement of your estate, you should consider this. The plans are usually quite reasonable.

You may find that burial expenses can be extremely costly, so it's a very good idea to cover these costs.

Summary

Nobody really likes to think about the end. But you know it's going to happen someday, so being prepared is worth the time, effort, and expense. A will allows you to rest easy at night, knowing that your family is taken care of and your wishes will be carried out. Letting the state decide what happens to your property and leaving your family to decide what happens to your body is unfair to everyone. So give this a good deal of thought. You will find that writing a will won't take too much time, and your family and friends will be glad you did.

Conclusion

Writing this book was an enjoyable exercise that brought back some good memories and made me think about a lot of things that I've done over the years. I hope that this information will bring you much success, and that you will get it right... the first time.

All the best... as always,
Steve Moore

Index